Geogra
and Politics
in a World
divided

Saul B. Cohen
nd Edition

Geography and Politics in a World Divided

GEOGRAPHY
and POLITICS
in a WORLD
DIVIDED

SECOND EDITION

SAUL BERNARD COHEN

New York
OXFORD UNIVERSITY PRESS
London Toronto 1973

Preface to the Second Edition

Ten years have passed since publication of the first edition of *Geography and Politics in a World Divided*. During this period, and especially over the last five years, many have judged that "America has come unglued." Characteristics of this period have been internal discord, assassination, violence in the streets, anguished and bloody withdrawal from Vietnam, and repudiation of an administration followed by the revelation of war crimes and the deception of a nation. All have contributed to an air of national confusion and anxiety that is unprecedented in American history. The urban crisis and the bitter opposition to the war in Southeast Asia, an unfavorable balance of payments and tension in relations with Maritime Europe over NATO, hesitation over nuclear disarmament treaties and the frustration over the Soviet's continued use of naked force in Eastern Europe and intervention in the Middle East—these are testimony to the interconnection of major internal and external events in the life of the nation.

The America whose cohesiveness has been shaken by Black militancy and student unrest is also the America whose faith in the wisdom of its post-World War Two international posture is being put to severe test. Some voices are urging a turn to a global "reality" position that verges on neo-isolationism. These would question not merely the maturity and good judgment of recent American policy, but perhaps more importantly, our very ability to confront rationally the complex forces of global interdependence that characterize this age of flight to the moon, disease and starvation in Biafra and Bangladesh, the dollar drain, environmental deterioration, the stress of modernization, and polycentric Communism. Others regard our present national drift as a mere momentary aberration, a time for rethinking.

If neo-isolationism is not the danger, then something else is. Loss of international purpose, lack of confidence in America's ability to chart its international affairs, and reluctance to adopt positive policies may well be the heritage of the bankruptcy of the containment strategy of the 1950's and the domino theories of the 1960's. This bankruptcy could leave its imprint in many subtle ways, not the least of which would be hesitancy to take stands, to delay responses, or to make hasty, ad hoc decisions—all stemming from the absence of a clearly articulated foreign policy strategy. It is such a course, not neo-isolationism, which is the real danger.

Geography and Politics in a World Divided was first published in 1963. It offered a rationale for global geopolitical equilibrium as seen from an American perspective in particular, and from a Maritime World view in general. The major premise of the work is that the dynamic balance that characterizes relations among states and larger regions is inherent in the ecology of the global political system. This world is organized politically in rational, not random fashion. It can therefore be likened to a diamond, not a pane of glass, in the sense that its cleavages can be anticipated along specific lines, rather than haphazardly. This world is hierarchical in its polycentric nature and is becoming progressively more differentiated and integrated.

Publication of this revised second edition warrants some commentary. The 1963 edition warned against the political-cultural iron curtain in the making in the United States between the Black central city and the white suburbs. This danger is ever more apparent, and real desegregation of the suburbs is urgently needed in order to head off the catastrophic effects of an American apartheid.

The 1963 volume, in analyzing French-North African relationships, called for positive action by France to maintain the geopolitical unity of Maritime Europe and the Maghreb, (Northwest Africa). In adopting positive positions that had to contend with the post-war bitterness of French-Algerian relations and the strong drives for neutralism that operate in Algeria, French and Algerian leadership have taken giant strides forward in forging a new accommodation. Indeed, France's steps to find a modus vivendi with the Arab world are entirely rational from her perspective, and help to explain the *volte face* in Franco-Israeli relations. To the French, Israel is pawn in France's drive to secure its Maghrebian flanks.

Still again in 1963, it was pointed out that complete control of the world's two Shatterbelts—Southeast Asia and the Middle East—was neither possible nor theoretically desirable for the four great power nodes of the world, the United States, Maritime Europe, the U.S.S.R., and Mainland China. South Vietnam was described as an important foothold and justifiable battleground, but the falling domino theory was rejected and the strategic value of South Vietnam to offshore Asia was questioned. It was posited that a distinction has to be made between battles and wars—that we could lose the battle for South Vietnam (and even Thailand) without losing our legitimate interests in Southeast Asia. It is incredible to the author that long after it became clear that the battle could not be won, and the reality of South Vietnamese leadership was exposed, we in the United States continued to persist in our efforts to intervene. The suggestion that SEATO needs replacement with a Maritime Asian Treaty Organization (MATO) as a global complement to NATO continues to have validity to this author. In the Middle East Shatterbelt, the illusory policy of attempting to maintain or create Western footholds in the Arab World at the expense of Turkey, Iran, or Israel was condemned. Events of the past ten years appear to have justified this outlook.

Finally, in 1963, attention was turned to Offshore Asia, the region that extends from Japan and South Korea through Australia and New Zealand and which was viewed as possessing favorable opportunities for geopolitical unity. Certainly Offshore Asia has emerged as a powerful economic and ideological component of the Maritime World in a remarkably brief period. In the search for a new American position in the Western Pacific in the wake of a changing Vietnamese situation, it is clear that it is Offshore Asia above all whose independence and integrity is vital to the maintenance of global equilibrium.

Two interrelated themes, the deterioration in Sino-Soviet relations and the polycentric nature of power in both the Trade-Dependent Maritime and the Eurasian Continental Geostrategic Regions, were discussed in the volume. A new chapter on Mainland China is now included to explore more fully the geopolitical nature of the Chinese role in world affairs. The search for detente with the Soviet Union and China by President Nixon reflects a growing awareness by the American public of the polycentric nature of global power.

To take stock of this world divided in 1973 is a difficult task, given the welter of tensions and upheavals that prevails. The violent power struggle within the People's Republic of China and the ideological schisms within the international Communist fold; the iron-fisted reimposition of the Soviet-organized "Commonwealth" of Eastern Europe concurrent with attempts by the U.S.S.R. to achieve a detente with the United States; Arab-Israeli and Soviet Union-United States confrontations in the Eastern Mediterranean and the Middle East; French economic and military policies in the North Atlantic; and Vietnam—the rifts that exist are to be found within as well as across geostrategic and geopolitical regions. But the distinction must be made between matters of a strategic and of a tactical nature. Sino-Soviet differences continue to be tactical within the Eurasian Continental World (although strategic within the international communist camp), as are Franco-American differences within the Maritime realm.

We reject the proposition that interest spheres do not, or should not, exist. For spheres of influence are essential to the preservation of national and regional expression. Indeed, without them, the alternative is either a monolithic world system or utter chaos. The real issue lies in recognition of the hierarchical differential and integrative nature of political regional spheres. With such recognition can come both Great Power accommodation and respect for the role of all nations within the context of the world political system in which we live.

S.B.C.

Clark University
Worcester, Massachusetts
1973

Contents

Maps and Charts

Tables

INTRODUCTION

Ours is a politically divided world. It is divided because man wills it and because nature reinforces this will. Aspiring to be unique, groups of people organize themselves within politically ordered societies and associations thereof. These societies are territorially framed. The edges of the frame are political boundaries. A geographical approach to international affairs requires appreciation of the reciprocal relations between these political groups and their physical and cultural setting.

From the reign of Henry IV of France at the close of the sixteenth century until the First World War, the national state was the unchallenged cornerstone of the politically divided world. There were other political components—internal, such as provinces or cities, and external, such as colonies or trusts. However, such components had relatively limited functions to perform—generally, the functions were subordinate to those of the state. While pressures of arms and economics at times compromised national sovereignty, the important elements of this sovereignty were never transferred.

Following the close of the First World War, two new forms of political unit emerged: the (British) Commonwealth of Nations and the Union of Soviet Socialist Republics. Although they differed in structure and objectives, they shared a political format that embraced more extensive and more varied territories than those occupied by the traditional national state.

The Second World War and its aftermath have witnessed the creation of additional multinational units. The North Atlantic Treaty Organization, the Warsaw Pact, the European Economic Community, the Organization of American States, the Organization of the

Petroleum Exporting Countries, the Federation of Arab Republics—all are vehicles for grouping larger areas than those embraced by national states. The purposes of such units range from the strategic to the economic to the ideological. Most are regionally oriented, some embrace continents, still others are extracontinental. All have in common the desire to exploit the specific advantages that larger territorial frameworks have to offer. Because of their varied objectives, these new territorial units differ in features and in size. Some lack cores, others have a multiplicity of cores. Moreover, they fluctuate in area and significance, as strategic, economic, or ideological conditions change. Finally, some lack land contiguity vital to their integration (e.g., Israel stands as a geopolitical barrier to Egyptian-Syrian links).

While supranational units are appearing in increasing numbers, the national state-formation process is by no means slowing down. On the contrary, over eighty new states have joined the United Nations since 1945. Many of these states have been carved out of relatively homogeneous economic or political regional organizations. This disruption of regional lines appears superficially to be turning the clock back. More probably, however, the establishment of these new national states is the first step in the creation of additional supranational units.

The reshaping of the world's political map is a result both of technological innovation and ideological ferment. Technological innovation has made it possible and even necessary for states to take a global or regional approach to their problems of military and economic security. It has emphasized the military and economic power disparity among states, causing an increase in the number of political satellites that revolve around Great Powers.

Ideological ferment expresses itself in two ways. First, in terms of the spread of nationalism, it shatters formerly unified colonial empires into a plethora of independent political entities. Colonial empires were a means of dividing the world into broad strategic units that represented a balance of Great Power interests. The rise of today's newly independent states has upset this balance. Long-established intra- and extra-regional economic and military ties have been swept aside without advance notice. The events of the past few years have proved that political, economic, and cultural commitments are a poor match for the fervent idealism or even the whims of small groups of men who are bent upon upsetting the status quo.

Second, international doctrines easily leapfrog space, thanks to modern communications and transportation. We need no longer assume that only areas that are contiguous to ideological centers are areas into which this ideology can spread. True, contiguity makes the spreading of doctrines easier. Thus Communism has been extended from North Vietnam into South Vietnam, Laos, and northern Thailand; anti-Westernism from the Arab Republic of Egypt into Libya and the Sudan, and Western-style cultural and foreign affairs orientation from Europe into Turkey. But the absence of contiguity is no assurance against the spread of Communism into the Caribbean, Africa, or South Asia, or against the re-establishment of Western influence in Indonesia or its maintenance in Iran.

Changing Geopolitical Patterns

The regrouping of political units on a regional or a national basis does not seem to be occurring in random fashion. The regional processes are strongest within the geopolitically more mature parts of the world. The national processes are strongest in the underdeveloped reaches. Older, mature states seek in regional activities a means of providing broader scope to their highly developed, specialized societies. Newer, underdeveloped states, which have yet to harness their internal forces, seek not so much to specialize as to broaden and to diversify their economies. Frequently this can only be achieved by a self-imposed form of national economic and political isolation.

How are these political regroupings affecting our ideas about the divided world? Certainly, they have altered the pattern of geopolitical relations across the various parts of the earth's surface. The clearcut division that existed after the Second World War between the "Free" and the "Iron Curtain" worlds no longer exists. Generally speaking, there now is a threefold division—"Western," "Communist," and "Neutral." Each of these divisions has subdivisions which are quite distinctive and which occasionally are in contention with one another. This division is in a state of flux. The boundaries of the three groups are constantly changing and vast areas are shifting from one camp into another. The contending forces are polycentric rather than monolithic. The "Western" or Maritime has ideological ranges from democratic to totalitarian; the Communist from revolutionary to revisionist; the Neutral from passive to active, and from neutralist at the global scale to interventionist at the regional scale.

This new division reflects the most significant geopolitical event of our times—the post-1945 retreat of the West from positions that tightly encircled the Eurasian interior. Today, we can liken the political world to a series of concentric rings, with the Communist bloc in the Eurasian center, the West partly surrounding this region, and the Neutral grouping taking up intervening positions between the two. The two inner rings have, since the Second World War, extended their areas; the Communist ring at the expense of both the Neutral and the Western-controlled world, and the Neutral ring at the expense of the Western world. These rings are not unbroken: witness Castroite Cuba and Neutralist Chile in the Western Hemisphere, and Neutralist to anti-Western Guinea in West Africa, and Tanzania and Uganda in East Africa.

Following World War Two, the prime objective of the Western alliance was to contain the Soviet landpower within continental Eurasia by keeping the littoral portions of Eurasia within the Western political fold. With the loss of China, containment became the major motif of American foreign policy. Despite our efforts, however, more of this littoral has fallen under the sway of the Communist or the Neutralist blocs. Strict containment of the Eurasian Heartland has not been possible, whether accompanied by the strategic doctrine of massive retaliation or not. This fact must be forthrightly faced by America's leadership if a new power balance on a global scale is to be achieved. Because realistic global strategic frameworks have not been proposed to the public, many in the Western world have not been able to face up to the fact that the containment policy can no longer be the cornerstone of our foreign relations with the Soviet Union and China. Indeed, the turn of recent events has made a complete jumble of our past ideas on global strategic frameworks, leaving us adrift in a sea of confusing and frequently contradictory international policy statements and actions. Immediately after World War Two, areas that many American and Western European strategy-makers considered essential to the security of their peoples, such as China and Eastern Europe, were pulled into the Soviet orbit. Since 1948-49, North Korea and North Vietnam have been lost, and the battle for the southern halves of these countries is by no means resolved. Elsewhere along the Eurasian periphery, other losses are imminent. Pro-Western governments have been displaced by Neutral or pro-Soviet governments in such countries as Egypt, Iraq, Burma, and Yemen; and Lebanon, Saudi Arabia, Jordan, and Kuwait could follow suit. Pakistan has taken an ambivalent position, as has Malta. Within states like Iran, Thailand, Taiwan, and Greece, alliances with the Maritime World depend upon narrowly based governments whose long-term stability is questionable. Of course, the impermanence of alliances plagues Communist states in the Eurasian periphery as well—witness the anti-Communist upheaval in Cambodia, the anti-Chinese stand in Indonesia, the cooling of relations between Burma and China, and the Neutralist stance of Yugoslavia.

Thus, in looking at Eurasia, we find that Soviet influence has pushed outward from its core so that the Elbe has been reached, the northern Middle East leapfrogged, and Monsoonal Asia deeply penetrated. Waters formerly denied to the Czars, like the Western Baltic, Eastern Mediterranean, Red, South China, and East China Seas, are now open to the Commissars both for peacetime commerce and preparations for war.

But the Eurasian periphery is not the only part of the world where age-old links with the West have been broken. While Cuba is the most noteworthy example, many parts of Africa south of the Sahara, and Latin America are subject to violent political currents that can lead to Soviet Union or Chinese People's Republic alliances, or strongly Neutralist stands. Libya, the Sudan, Tanzania, and Chile have moved out of the Maritime orbit, although the first two, because they resist Communization, have difficulty in accepting a full alliance with the U.S.S.R. Guayana, Guatemala, Chad, or Niger could follow suit. Even Antarctica is the laboratory for Soviet scientific activities as much as it is for Western ones. Here, too, however, the picture is not one-sided, as illustrated by the swing out of the Communist or Neutralist orbits by Ghana, Indonesia, and the Congo (Kinsaha). The Chinese, too, no longer content to try to exercise their sovereignty over East and South Asia alone, are making probes in Africa and Latin America, with particular emphasis upon the western reaches of the Indian Ocean.

It may be asked whether Soviet and Chinese influence throughout the world is being extended according to a broad design or strategy, or whether the extension is an opportunistic one that probes all areas of possible discontent and seizes upon any opportunity that presents itself. Communist ideologists discredit ideas of environmental determinism, and they discount various schools of national geopolitics. This anti-environmental determinism and belief in the inevitability of Communist victory seems to contradict any suggestions that Soviet or Chinese strategists hold doctrines that give priority to penetration of specific areas. However, there is little doubt that both continue to show very special concern over those areas that adjoin key population and industrial centers. These are areas from which invasions of Czarist Russia and the U.S.S.R., or of China have been launched, and which the U.S.S.R. has attempted to secure with a great measure of success during the past three decades. Thus it was that Stalin insisted upon control of eastern Poland, Estonia, Latvia, southern Finland, and Bessarabia in his pact with Hitler in 1939, and subsequently moved into Lithuania and Bucovina. These advance positions did not stem the onslaught of the Nazi invasion in June 1941. From prepared positions in northern and southwestern Finland, East Prussia, central Poland, Silesia, and Romania, the Wehrmacht simultaneously launched its attack against Leningrad, Moscow, and the Ukraine. After the defeat of Nazi Germany, considerable territorial reshuffling took place in Eastern Europe. It is significant that as a result of these boundary changes every one of the positions from which the Nazi attack was launched, with the exception of Silesia and part of Romania, is now Soviet territory. In the east, Outer Mongolia and Manchuria, which presented serious threats to the survival of the Bolshevik regime in 1919-21, have also been brought into the Soviet orbit or neutralized (although these frontier areas are by no means free of the threat of long-range Sino-Soviet differences). Two other areas of extraordinary Soviet concern are Turkey and Iran, opening as they do onto the Ukraine and Central Asia.

Beyond this specific concern for strategic frontier reaches, however, there seem to be no area priorities for Soviet pressures, unless we include the former colonial world as one great target for Communist ambitions. The same might be said for the People's Republic of China. Concern for frontier reaches brought the Chinese Communists into contact with the Soviet Union over the question of territorial integrity, first through co-operation and more recently through contention. The zone of conflict with the United States in Korea, the Chinese offshore islands, and Vietnam, reaches out from China's heavily populated and industrialized east coast, and pressures for border adjustments with India, Pakistan, and Burma have erupted into war as well as taken peaceful negotiation. But elsewhere, in Asia, Africa, and Latin America, Maoist probes seem random.

The colonial world is, in Communist eyes, on the threshold of the second, and socialist, revolt against the "Capitalist-Imperialist" world. The nationalist revolt has succeeded for the most part without Communist intervention. It is not likely that the socialist revolt will be conducted against a background of similar Soviet, or at least Chinese Communist, restraint.

In 1923 Lenin said, "The outline of the struggle in the last analysis depends upon the fact that Russia, India, China and so on, constitute a gigantic majority of the population of the globe . . . and it is precisely this majority which is being drawn with extraordinary rapidity in recent years into a struggle for its own liberation."[1] Lenin's hopes for the world Communist victory were, to a great extent, based upon the sheer numbers of people who had been under colonial rule; they were not based upon the presumed strategic significance of the U.S.S.R. in a global location sense. From what has happened since Lenin, it appears that most Soviet probings into the former colonial world are based upon moments of opportunity. Therefore there is little reason to suspect that Soviet pressures against Thailand or Algeria would have a higher priority than those against Indonesia, Guinea, or Cuba. In the face of American pressure, initial Soviet agreement to dismantle missile bases built in Cuba during the fall of 1962 is evidence of the secondary strategic value assigned Cuba by the U.S.S.R.

During the Containment-Massive Retaliation era, the policy of the Western alliance was to try to maintain the status quo in a spatial sense, without apparently attempting to ascribe priorities to different parts of the world. This status quo has been broken. What is now called for is the recognition that new global geopolitical divisions exist. They are based upon the strategic needs and capabilities of both the U.S.S.R. and the United States. We are not suggesting that static global equilibrium or balance of forces exists or is attainable. Static equilibrium is contrary to the essence of geopolitical life, which seems to be change. We are suggesting, however, that the world is divisible into broad groupings, and that within these groupings, today's two great powers and the major powers of Maritime Europe, China, and Japan can find economic, political, military, and psychological security. We speak, then, of a world divided, not referring to a twofold division of isolated, self-contained parts. We seek to describe, rather, a framework of partition across which various forms of interaction, competition, and contention will continue to flow, in keeping with the dynamic changes and needs of the major power cores.

[1] Quoted by Bertram Wolfe, *Khrushchev and Stalin's Ghost* (New York: Praeger, 1957), p. 50.

The Strategic Value of Space

Political relations among states are influenced by an area's strategic value. These relations in turn affect this value. We can view the strategic importance of parts of the earth's surface in terms of three dimensions: space, time, and national vantage points. The term *space* includes natural resources or location with respect to the lines of movement that carry these resources. But the endowments of areas change, in time, with technological innovation. Moreover, what is considered strategically important to one state may be unimportant to another. The Suez Canal was of crucial importance to Maritime Europe, of secondary importance to the United States, and of almost no importance to the U.S.S.R. until about a decade ago. Emergence of the Maghreb (Northwest Africa) as a source of petroleum supply, as well as the development of the supertanker, has kept the closing of the Canal in the wake of the 1967 Arab-Israeli War within tolerable limits for the West. To the Soviet Union, on the other hand, with its dual navy needs in the Eastern Mediterranean and Indian Ocean, and with its commitments to India and North Vietnam, the Canal has become of potentially major importance.

Finally, an area's strategic significance cannot be assessed in terms of the needs of a single power core. Two parties, and frequently more, will be involved. Thus, Mainland China, the United States, the U.S.S.R., Japan, and Australia are all directly concerned with Korea and Southeast Asia. While Eastern Europe is of primary concern to the U.S.S.R. and to Maritime Europe, as is North Africa to Maritime Europe, the fate of these regions is of secondary importance to other power cores of varying sizes and strength.

In the following chapters, the salient political geographical characteristics of the major power cores of the earth—Anglo-America, the U.S.S.R., China, and Maritime Europe—will be discussed. Background for the discussion will be global strategic frameworks within which these power cores can function and interact in relative stability. Stability by no means implies harmony. It does suggest a dynamic equilibrium in the political and economic relations that each of these cores may be expected to seek with one another and with other parts of the world.

While the world is constantly shrinking in a time-communication sense, some of its components are maturing economically and politically at a rapid rate. Such a maturation process enhances the prospects for the striking of a global strategic balance built upon a multiple-core base. Unlike those who believe in the inevitability of one-power world domination—a belief best articulated by nineteenth-century German philosophers—the author holds that coexistence is geopolitically possible. A global geopolitical balance is a practical goal for the statesmen of our time. One basis for such a goal can be found in the distribution patterns of the earth's physical and cultural environment.

This book is in three sections. Part One discusses the earth's geopolitical foundations and provides a contemporary view of the global geographic setting from which a framework for dynamic geopolitical equilibrium is formulated. The essence of this framework is a division of the world into geostrategic regions. As background to this contemporary discussion, the nature of political geography and a short history of geographical thought along geopolitical lines are examined.

Part Two deals with the major power cores. Emphasis is upon the four strongest powers of the earth (the United States, the Soviet Union, Mainland China, and Maritime Europe) and the changing geopolitical environments within which they function.

Part Three treats the Middle East and Southeast Asian Shatterbelts, and the African, South American, and Offshore Asian portions of the Maritime World, focusing upon zones of contact and influence from the standpoint of Western interests.

Part One

GEOPOLITICAL FOUNDATIONS OF A WORLD DIVIDED

1 POLITICAL GEOGRAPHY

Concept and Application

The Nature of Geography

This volume is a study in political geography. As such, its themes rest on a spatial approach to international affairs. Thus, while political geography has much in common with international politics in terms of its concern with the relations among states and other political entities, it differs in its method. Political geography belongs to the field of geography. Its manner of inquiry, spirit, and purpose is geographical. Geography can be defined as the *science of area differentiation*.[1] Alternately, geography may be defined as the *science of spatial relations and interaction,* or as the *science of distributions*. In all three definitions, physical and social processes are implicitly or explicitly assumed, and in this sense geography may be defined as dealing with the spatial consequences of processes, be this in an areal, correlational, or movement framework. Its essence is to observe, inventorize, map, classify, analyze, and interpret patterns of earth-man relationships over different parts of the earth's surface. We may wish to emphasize contrasts from place to place—or we may wish to point out similarities from place to place. In so doing, geographers are concerned with the uniqueness of given areas. Geographers seek out subdivisions within the physical environment (climate, soils, vegetation, and landform) and subdivisions in the cultural or man-made environment. Finally, they search for correlations between and within the two sets of environmental patterns.

Thus, the geographer relates densely populated areas with soil,

---

[1] Introduced into American geographic literature by Carl Sauer, this definition was adapted from Alfred Hettner's concept of geography. It is quoted in Richard Hartshorne, *Perspective on the Nature of Geography* (Chicago: Rand McNally, 1959), p. 12.

mineral, or water supply distribution patterns, or with favored focal points of transportation. He measures the distribution of housing
types against the background of climate, building material sources, or
place of origin of the builders of such houses. He observes how cities
have grown, noting the relation of residential areas to prevailing
wind patterns or agricultural land use; and manufacturing areas to
rivers, highways, and less desirable soil areas. If no valid case can be
made for the interrelationship of patterns of the physical and human
environment, then the geographer has at least fulfilled one valid
function in pointing out the distribution and movement patterns of
single-featured elements, regardless of the causes for this distribution.
But it is the search for correlations that tests the geographer's mettle.
During the Middle East's Khamsin periods (the hot, dusty, desert-
born winds), human energy and productivity decrease. Knowing
that humid coastal areas are even more adversely affected by such
winds than higher plateaus helps us to understand people's actions
during that period. Or the geographer may point out that in as volatile a region as the Middle East it is noteworthy that no revolts have
broken out in recent years during the month of Ramadan, while revolts have broken out in non-Muslim lands elsewhere in the world
during this period.

Differences among peoples within a country may have developed
or become accentuated because of isolation imposed by the terrain.
The Basques did not accept the language and way of life of the people of the Spanish Meseta, because of the isolating effects of the Pyrenees. The Kurds, in northern Iraq, are a mountaineering, grazing
people, who differ racially, linguistically, and culturally from the
Arabs of Mesopotamia. They constitute a separatist element in modern Iraq. Often such differences make it difficult for a state to achieve
strong, centralized control.

These and other examples can be cited, but the essence can be
summed up thus: people and their activities differ or are similar
from place to place. Often, although certainly not always, these differences or similarities can be explained in cause-effect terms that
stem from the study of geographic relationships. However, in examining the cause-effect relationships between the earth and man,
many have been tempted to overinflate the influences of the environment. A popular example that is cited to point up man's relative insignificance in relation to nature is to note that were it possible to
pack all mankind into a box, like sardines, such a box would be small
enough to fit into the Grand Canyon. And the story attempts to

heighten man's insignificance by suggesting that if the box could teeter on a knife's edge at the lip of the canyon, the wagging of a dog's tail could push the box and all mankind with it into oblivion.[2]

While such an example emphasizes the grandeur and scale of the physical environment in relation to man, it is not especially appropriate because it tends to cast a shadow over the role of man as an active agent in molding the environment. Thus, to use the size of the Grand Canyon to express nature's dwarfing of man is not particularly apt. Man can dam the Colorado and fill the Canyon with water if he is so disposed. He can, with nuclear energy, blast new holes of equal magnitude or fill present ones. He can bridge the Canyon or fly over it. If he desires and is willing to pay the price, man *can* move mountains. This is stressed not because man is likely to move many mountains, but to point out that nature only overpowers us with its immensity when we don't want to go through or over it. Obviously man's sights, desires, and capabilities differ from place to place over the earth's surface. What we can think of and are capable of carrying out in the United States is far different from human aspirations and capabilities in Mozambique, and part of what we are is a product of our physical environment. When, therefore, we consider man and his activities in relation to his environment, we have to take into account his specific framework of thought and activities. Let us not make the mistake, however, of underestimating man as an active agent in relation to nature.

The Nature of Political Geography

Hartshorne has defined political geography as "the study of the variation of political phenomena from place to place in interconnection with variations in other features of the earth as the home of man."[3] Whittlesey said that "the kernel of political geography is the political area . . . the political significance of any area bears a well-defined relation to its climate, landforms and natural resources."[4] Jones, for whom the political area becomes a "field of interaction" of forces, has pointed out that man's political ideas generate political

<hr />

[2] Hendrik Willem van Loon, *Van Loon's Geography* (New York: Garden City Publishing Company, 1940), p. 3.

[3] Richard Hartshorne, "Political Geography in the Modern World," *Journal of Conflict,* IV, No. 1 (March 1960), p. 52.

[4] Derwent Whittlesey, *The Earth and the State* (New York: Henry Holt, 1944), p. 585.

forces within specific areas, the area first being an inactive recipient of these ideas. As the areas become political in character, they in turn begin to shape political ideas and processes.[5]

These definitions have in common the thesis that the essence of geographical thought is area differentiation. As such, the differentiation of political phenomena from place to place is the essence of political geography.

Political area, or space, is multidimensional. Space is *horizontal* as viewed from the standpoint of the shape, size, location, and natural resources of one political unit. Space is *vertical* as viewed from the interplay of man's objectives, laws, and economic and cultural tools upon the horizontal plane. Space has a third dimension, *time*, which considers the interaction of horizontal and vertical space at any given period. Thus, time can be thought of as a series of points that constitute a curve along the horizontal and vertical space axes. These three dimensions are not absolutes because the selection of the criteria for their measurement and their interpretation is subjective. Space dimensions vary according to the point of projection, or point of view, that is applied to them, just as maps vary in size, shape, and data with their cartographic projection and timing. Distortions occur in maps that reproduce space frameworks; distortions also occur in the analysis of spatial relations. For political geographers, this point of projection varies with national or regional outlooks. To a lesser extent, it varies with a number of other subjective elements, which are bound to temper any process of inventory and analysis.[6]

While accepting the general utility of these definitions, I am concerned with the need to focus more clearly upon political process. Therefore my definition of political geography is as the *spatial consequences of political process*. Consequences, or attributes, are offered as multi-meaning words. Political processes occur in space and therefore have distributional patterns. They also have spatial relational implications as they affect or are affected by other processes. Finally, the occurrence of political processes in space creates unique fields of

---

[5] Stephen Jones, "A Unified Field Theory of Political Geography," *Annals of the Association of American Geographers*, XLIV (1954), pp. 111-23. This, in a sense, is an extension of Jean Gottmann's recognition of ideas and circulation as the two main and contradictory factors that shape and reshape the political map.

[6] Harold and Margaret Sprout, *Man-Milieu Relationship Hypothesis in the Context of International Politics* (Princeton: Princeton University Press, 1956), p. 16.

activity, some of which eventually emerge as unique areas known as political areas.

Six Approaches to the Study of Political Geography

Geographical study of the political environment rests upon survey and analysis within a cartographic framework. Various approaches can be employed in such studies. Hartshorne recognizes four distinct ones within the field of political geography: 1) power analysis; 2) historical; 3) morphologic; 4) functional.[7] To these approaches, we should add two more, the behavioral and the systemic. Power analysis refers to "an analysis of political units of power and the relations among them."[8] These are units that are defined in space, whose internal character is influenced by space, and whose relationship with other units is conditioned by space. Historical political geography has, as its focus, the political landscapes of the past. The morphologic approach examines political areas according to form and features. Functional political geography is concerned with the functioning or operation of political areas. Behavioral political geography is concerned with the spatial character of attitudes and perceptions that underlie specific political actions, such as voting or legislation. Systemic political geography deals with the spatial consequences of political systems.

I   THE POWER ANALYSIS APPROACH

The power analysis approach is very commonly used by non-geographers, some of whom like to define geography as one of the several power resources in international relations. One such study, for example, divides national power into five components: geographic, economic, political, sociological, and military.[9] The geographic element is defined as "including the location, size and shape of the area which comprises the nation . . . the extent to which it provides access from, and egress to, the world community . . . the degree to which the land is arable or barren . . . the effect of climate, not only on the fertility of the land, but also upon the hardi-

---

[7] Preston James and Clarence Jones, editors, *American Geography Inventory & Prospect,* Association of American Geographers, Syracuse University Press, 1954. Chapter by Richard Hartshorne, "Political Geography," pp. 167-226.

[8] *Ibid.,* p. 174.

[9] U.S. Army War College, *Power Analysis of the Nation-State,* Discussion Topic 2-B, Carlisle Barracks, Pa., 1960, p. 2.

ness and energy of the people, [and] the reservoir of natural resources with which the land is endowed."

This, however, represents a limited geographical approach, for geographers do not isolate geography as a determinant of national power. A fully geographic approach would make an inventory of pertinent categories and relate this inventory to politically significant phenomena. Let us enumerate the inventory categories, and then cite examples of their political applicability. The categories include:

1) *The physical environment* (landforms, climate, soils, vegetation, waterbodies, etc.);
2) *Movement* (the directional flow of the transportation and communication of goods, men, and ideas);
3) *Raw materials, semi-finished and finished goods* (employed and potential, in both time and space terms);
4) *Population* (in its various characteristics, particularly qualitative and ideological);
5) *The body politic* (its various administrative forms, ideals, and goals in their areal expression, such as county, state, national and international bloc frameworks).

Physical Environment. An example of this first approach would be to measure the Norwegian coastline and to indicate how the high ratio of useful coastline in combination with fertile fishing grounds and poverty of land base has influenced Norway's development as a commercial, fishing, and NATO-oriented state.

Movement. An example would be to measure the reach and diffusion rate of Radio Cairo within Africa, with reference to its impact upon emergent nationalism.

Raw Materials and Goods. An example would be to measure the distribution of Maritime Europe's coal, iron ore, and limestone resources in terms of the economic and political impact of the interchangeable use of these resources by various national steel industries. Thus, Saar coal is more rationally used by French steel makers in Lorraine than by German steel makers in the Ruhr.

Population. An example would be to map population by ethnic characteristics in Iran. Such a map would show the majority of the population of Khuzistan to be Arab. This would help explain why the oil-rich province that borders Arab Iraq has been a tension area in Iraqi-Iranian relations, with the unresolved Shat-al-Arab border dispute as the major irritant.

Body Politic. An example would be to analyze the effects of the internal political organization of national states upon land use-patterns. The division of England into electoral constituencies enables the relatively small rural population (less than 10 per cent of the total) to exercise a disproportionate political influence on the national level. As a result, grazing obtains tax benefits and rough land areas that might otherwise be lost as a utilizable resource continue to have economic and recreational value.[10]

While these five categories are all viewed from within a spatial framework, geographers also work with space as a sixth and distinct category. In this sense the location, shape, and boundaries of political entities are analyzed, as well as the impact of space upon the internal character and external relations of such political entities. An example can be drawn from an examination of Israel's boundaries, prior to the June 1967 war.

The length of Israel's land borders relative to its total land area of 7,845 square miles was in a ratio of one mile of border for every 13 square miles of land area. As a result, an inordinately high expenditure of national energies is needed to secure this border. One way to secure a border is through fixed military garrisons. An alternative to garrisons are farm settlements. The path that Israel has chosen has been to encourage border farm settlements in poor, as well as fertile, agricultural areas, thus draining off capital that might be invested elsewhere in manufacturing pursuits. Since the 1967 war, Israel has become much more viable defensively, the increment of the occupied territories including Sinai, the Gaza Strip, Jerusalem, the West Bank, and the Golan Heights having increased the total territory by 26,648 square miles, but having changed the ratio to one mile of border for every 65 square miles of land area. The total linear miles of land border is now 533, compared with 613 miles prior to June of 1967.

It is not difficult to collect data for the power inventory. The difficulty lies in the sifting and weighing of the data. The fact of the matter is that not all available data need be taken into account in comparing specific political areas in terms of geography-strategy interrelations. Indeed, much comparative analysis suffers from including all features of the physical and cultural environment, regardless of their pertinence or their comparability. The crux of the problem

---

[10] L. D. Stamp, *Applied Geography* (Baltimore: Penguin Books, 1960), pp. 151-60.

is to search out the elements that are germane and can be fruitfully applied.

For example, we have become increasingly concerned with space and numbers in assessing the relative strength of nations and blocs. China and India especially loom important on the power scene to those analysts who feel that the weight of their populations may tip the balance of world power. The geographer has to concern himself with space and numbers—but not as the statistician does. Instead he searches out meaningful relationships. Sheer numbers are translated into population densities. These densities are expressed in terms of arable land (which in turn reflects climate, soil, slope, etc.). The numbers are expressed in terms of persons employed in manufacturing and proportion of urbanized population—a good index for reflecting technology. The raw material base can be expressed by such a factor as steel production or electrical energy. Educational level reflects manpower quality.

While the power inventory is generally a method of comparative analysis that has been reserved for the national state, it is becoming increasingly important to examine its applicability to various levels of regionalization, and to include indices of growth or development rate to insure a reflection of areal dynamics in any study that is undertaken.

Tables 1 and 2 suggest how the power inventory might be made in simplified terms. Table 1 draws together the basic data and the index.

Table 2 shows that there is no single answer to the power base, but rather a series of answers that depend for their selection upon the intelligence and experience of the analyst (for which no electronic computer can substitute). Using two groupings, Maritime Europe is the leader; using another set, the United States leads; and a third points to the Soviet Union. By comparing data over different periods, an appreciation of trend can be obtained.

But this method cannot quantify the ideological strength, motivation, policies, and goals of the political units. It can only give the framework in which to study these aspects. And even quantifying certain elements presents pitfalls. For example, steel, aluminum, and petroleum might be selected as indices for evaluating national strength. However, shall these industries be measured in terms of output, or in terms of capacity? If capacity is selected because it best measures potential and can be regarded as a stored resource, do we have common yardsticks for measuring capacity from state to state?

TABLE 1

An Inventory of National Power*

	Total Area in sq. miles	Total Population	Population Density of Arable Land per sq. mile	Percentage of Urban to Total Population	Persons Engaged in Manufacturing	Steel Production in Tons	Electrical Energy Production in mil. kw. hours	Armed Forces Personnel	Students Enrolled in Secondary Schools
United States	3,615,123	204 mil.	270	70%	20 mil.	131	1.43	3.5 mil.	18 mil.
Maritime Europe	1,219,300	325 "	1,050	65%	37 "	154	.74	3.9 "	21 "
U.S.S.R.	8,649,489	238 "	345	56%	25 "	117	.64	3.3 "	N.A.
Chinese People's Republic	3,691,502	730 "	1,740	21%	N.A.	16	N.A.	2.8 "	10 "
India	1,261,810	524 "	845	18%	4 "	7	.05	.9 "	7 "
Canada	3,851,787	22 "	138	73%	2 "	11	.18	.1 "	1.5 "
Brazil	3,286,470	88 "	1,100	45%	2 "	5	.04	N.A.	2.5 "
Japan	142,811	101 "	4,000	68%	10 "	74	.27	.2 "	10 "

Most data are for 1968.

*Same Data Translated into Index Terms**

United States	112	71	260	135	143	200	300	167	180
Maritime Europe	38	116	67	125	266	237	154	186	210
U.S.S.R.	270	85	200	108	179	180	133	157	N.A.
Chinese People's Republic	112	225	41	40	N.A.	25	N.A.	133	100
India	39	187	83	35	29	11	10	43	70
Canada	122	8	500	140	14	17	38	5	15
Brazil	100	31	64	87	14	8	9	N.A.	25
Japan	4	36	17	130	71	114	56	10	100

* Index of 100 is the mean of each column.

TABLE 2
Index Base for National Power Inventory

	Average Composite Index	Average Index Excluding Population Density of Arable Land, and % of Urban to Total Population	Average Index for Persons in Manufacturing Steel, Electrical Energy, and Secondary School Studies	Average Index for Total Area, Total Population, and Armed Forces Personnel
United States	174	168	206	117
Maritime Europe	155	173	217	113
U.S.S.R.	164	167	164	171
Chinese People's Republic	97	129	62	157
India	56	56	30	90
Canada	96	31	21	45
Brazil	42	31	14	65
Japan	60	56	85	17

Also, we accept urbanization as a measure of national strength. And so it is, because urbanization usually reflects greater national cohesiveness, more effectively centralized authority, and higher productivity-per-man effort. Highly urbanized societies are now more stable politically, showing a lower proportion of revolutions, for example.[11] Nevertheless, there are exceptions, such as situations in developing countries or areas where larger numbers of urbanized people mean greater instability rather than stability. The size of Naples, as a measure of urbanization, bears little relationship to manufacturing strength and political stability. This is because the economic base of the city is so narrow. Consequently, hundreds of thousands of persons are affected by unemployment or underemployment, and society is far from stable. And in the restless, underdeveloped, rural countries, revolutions are generally fomented and led by urbanites or by military juntas that exploit the presence of urban mobs to gain and maintain power.

These qualifications do not mean that power indices cannot be used. They simply mean that indices must be weighted and then employed with judgment and skill. The final results can be no more than useful guides for comparative analysis.

[11] Hans Weigert *et al.*, *Principles of Political Geography* (New York: Appleton-Century-Crofts, 1957), p. 307.

2   THE HISTORICAL APPROACH

Historical political geography has as its focus the past, both for the sake of understanding the past better and for analyzing current problems. Whittlesey's discussion of the evolution of the French national state in *The Earth and State*[12] is an outstanding exposition of the historical approach. He traces the growth of France from its seat of political origin in the Île de France to the attainment of its current territorial form. The sequence of state growth in relation to the physical and cultural environment is carefully sketched out. This discussion covers a range of varied elements in earth-state relations. One is the defensive significance of a series of outward-facing limestone cuestas to the security of Paris. Another is the focal significance of Paris in an over-all physiographic and transportation sense. The location of Paris helps to explain both the step-by-step growth of the French national state and France's high degree of political and economic centralization.

While much that now exists can only be understood in terms of what existed in the past, most studies in historical political geography have their greatest value in explaining the past. To rely upon them as guides to projecting the political roles and activities of states today can prove fruitless and even misleading.

3   THE MORPHOLOGIC APPROACH

The morphologic approach studies political areas according to their form—that is, their patterns and structural features. *Pattern* refers to the arrangements formed by the association of political units, whether national states, regional blocs, global alliances, or internal administrative divisions, as expressed by location, size, and shape. *Structure* refers to the spatial features that political units have in common—i.e., population and economic cores, capitals, components, boundaries, and underdeveloped or otherwise problem units.

Italy's pattern, for example, can be understood within the context of the country's location within the broader European economic union. As a component of E.E.C., Italy has gained steel manufacturing advantages through the introduction of international rail through-rates on scrap shipments from Lyon to Turin.

Its geopolitical pattern can also be viewed from the standpoint of its location and shape within the Mediterranean. Italy is especially

[12] Whittlesey, *op. cit.*, pp. 129-65.

concerned with the co-ordination of NATO naval activities in the Mediterranean. While France's withdrawal of its naval units from the co-ordinated command affects all NATO countries, it particularly affects Italy. On the one hand, Italy is more vulnerable to Soviet submarine activities; on the other hand, Italy becomes NATO's Mediterranean mainstay and its navy the recipient of a greater share of allied material and training support, precisely because of the increased Soviet Mediterranean presence, and the dubious nature of the long-term NATO position in Malta and in Greece, given political change there.

Among Italy's geopolitical structural features are:

Population and economic core area. The Po plain concentrates within it not only the bulk of Italy's manufacturing but also its most productive farm areas. Proximity of this core to the Alps means readily available hydroelectric power for industry, in a country poor in fossil fuels. Such a location also favors trade exchange with Northern Europe.

Capital. Rome, a very large city, is removed from the economic core area. Absence of a broad Roman manufacturing base, as well as the presence of the Vatican, helps to explain why Rome is relatively immune from Communist mob pressures. Rome lives from such industries as tourism, government, and movie-making. Its workers are not strongly organized within the framework of Communist- or Socialist-controlled trade unions. Much of the local Communist strength is derived from clerks, shopkeepers and intellectuals, whose challenge to the Church and government comes in nonviolent forms. As a result, the central Italian government has been able to operate within a general atmosphere of stability and security.

Boundaries. Italy's northern boundaries are a traditional source of instability. In modern times, the boundary line has fluctuated in all directions, northeast, north, and northwest. The Yugoslav border dispute over Trieste was settled less than twenty years ago. Following the end of the Second World War, France annexed minor territories, providing it with strategic control over those areas from which Italy had invaded France in 1940.[13] Alte Adigo has been Italian since

---

[13] Some of these changes were essentially defensive, giving France the Little St. Bernard Pass and command of the heights that overlook Briançon and the Briançon-Modane Road. Others are potentially of offensive significance, such as the Mont Cenis Plateau that overlooks Turin and furnishes it with water power; and Tenda-Briga, whose hydroelectric plants supply the Italian railways in Liguria and South Piedmont.

World War One. It remains, however, a major irritant to Italo-Austrian relations.

By and large, modern Italy is strategically exposed to threat of attack from Alpine-based neighboring states. After the *Anschluss* in Austria, for example, Nazi Germany was in a far better position to dictate to Mussolini than was the case prior to 1938.

Underdeveloped unit. Italy can also be analyzed according to its north-south internal regional units. The underdeveloped South, plagued by soil poverty, lack of water, and tenancy, is rurally over-populated. Unable to support its population, the South has had to export people to such areas as northern Italy, France, the United States, and Germany. Many people of the South consider themselves to be unfairly exploited by the industrial North, which receives the bulk of Italian national investment, and have turned to political extremism, both Communistic and Monarchical-Fascistic. This turn to extremism applies in particular to Southerners who migrate northward. Thus, Italian political stability suffers from the vast disparity in the resource base and economic levels of the north and south.

4   THE FUNCTIONAL APPROACH

The functional approach, as conceived by Hartshorne,[14] is concerned with the functioning of an area as a political unit. Every political area is subdivided into subordinate areas of organization, each with its own governmental functions. These subordinate areas must have stronger political associations with the state than with one another or with outside states. For the state to function properly, it must have unity. Homogeneity, coherence, and viability are basic requirements for such unity. Viability of the state is related, not only to domestic economic considerations, but to economic, strategic, and political relations with other states.

Thus, the functional approach would study state-strengthening or centralizing forces, and state-weakening forces as they are related to space. Within the United States, one of the functions of the state is to guarantee freedom of passage across interstate lines. In theory, therefore, none of the fifty subunits, or states can interfere with such passage. In practice several do. It is a fact of distribution that such interference occurs in Southern states because of discriminatory edu-

[14] Richard Hartshorne, "The Functional Approach in Political Geography," *Annals of the Association of American Geographers*, XL, No. 2 (June, 1950), pp. 95-130.

cational practices and in Northern states because of residence requirements for welfare recipients. That these states have a set of
White-Black race relations that are reciprocally related to the physical and cultural environment is also geographical in nature.

Another example of the functional approach can be drawn from
a state's external economic relations. The function of the state is to
create or to maintain economic viability for its citizens. Laws on foreign trade, including subsidies, tariffs, and embargoes, are tools used
by the state to promote this particular function. For example, the
desire of the United Kingdom to increase its sales in automobiles and
chemicals to Maritime Europe has spurred the United Kingdom to
join the Common Market to the possible detriment of trade with
the United States. In most cases, laws that relate to foreign trade
cannot help but have internal ramifications. For example United
States tariffs upon men's shirts from Japan protect eastern seaboard
manufacturers. Higher shirt prices in the East will be offset by the
jobs provided directly and indirectly by the shirt-making industry.
This will not be the case in the Pacific Northwest, however, where
domestic shirt manufacturing is unimportant. A counterpressure
might be exercised by the Pacific Northwest to raise imposts on Japanese tuna and salmon. As a result, the Northwest and the eastern
regions would have worked out a *quid pro quo*. At the same time,
both regions might look dimly at continued U.S. trade with Japan.
The Middle West, on the other hand, might find its interests better
served if there were no tariff on Japanese shirts and tuna. Moreover,
it might regard continued United States exports to Japan as being
of particular benefit in stimulating United States-Japanese trade in
machine tools.

5   THE BEHAVIORAL APPROACH

Behavioral political geography is concerned with those cases where
space can be identified as an independent variable. Kasperson and
Minghi distinguish between behavior in space that refers to analysis
of the spatial patterns that behavior takes, and another form of behavior—territoriality, which refers to the innate feelings that have to
do with occupying and defending space.[15] Behavioral methodology
involves empirical testing of situations, with appropriate controls—

[15] For an excellent review of the topic of behavioralism in political geography
see Roger Kasperson and Julian Minghi, eds., *The Structure of Political Geography* (Chicago: Aldine, 1969), pp. 299-318.

no mean feat in dealing with aggregate behavior. What we know, feel, and value about space is important to explanation, which is the central focus of behavioral research.

The behavioral approach in political geography could, for example, deal with the spatial behavior and perceptions inherent in the voting process of legislative bodies. The specific location of each potential voter in terms of personal ambience; his locational relations to other colleagues, to the chairman and to the votekeeper; the time lag involved in seeing or hearing how others have voted—all are elements to be analyzed. Legislative bodies that have switched from the traditional hand tally to push button electronic voting, or from compact, circular seating arrangements to very large chambers in which seating is spread out and line-of-sight restricted are likely to exhibit different patterns of voting behavior. For example, when electronic tallying is introduced, the influence formerly held by strategically located leaders is reduced. Their followers or the undecided are unable to see how the leaders vote, and political behavior of the body as a whole is affected.

6 THE SYSTEMIC APPROACH

The systemic approach is derived from general systems theory. The essence of general systems theory is that its focus is a system of interrelated objects (persons or things), which enter the system or framework as inputs, exit it as outputs, and interact within it as elements that feed or flow internally. The emphasis is on the unity or the wholeness of the framework. Systems into which new elements enter and from which elements leave are open systems, in contrast to the closed ones which function through the internal generating of energy.

In a study by the author and a colleague,[16] the geopolitical system was advanced as the unit within which the political process interacts with geographical space. Political transactions, structures and societal forces are the components of the process; place, area and landscape are the components of geographical space. Process and space interact through the formation of political action areas, and various ideological attachments, organizations, and perceptions characterize these action areas. The case of Venezuela and petroleum was

[16] Saul B. Cohen and Lewis D. Rosenthal, "A Geographical Model for Political Systems Analysis," *The Geographical Review,* LXI, No. 1 (January 1971), pp. 5-31.

cited in the study. Overriding societal forces—such as nationalism and statism—affect governmental institutions—such as the Corporación Venezolano de Petroleo (CVP)—that in turn shape and carry out the enacted petroleum legislation. This legislation gives the monopoly on oil exploitation to the state enterprise, which in turn operates through service contracts to foreign companies. No direct concessions are therefore permitted to foreign oil companies. Legislation also covers the desulfurization of hydrocarbons, pressing foreign companies to build plants in Venezuela to reduce the sulfur content of the heavy fuel that is exported. The net result of petroleum legislation is to provide Venezuela with a higher percentage of the income generated by oil, to expand the petrochemical industry, but to slow down new drilling and the expansion of recently discovered fields.

The impact upon geographical space is seen in the development of new places of intense activity (e.g., the coastal area at Morón where the national petrochemical industry has been established). The action area has been expanded to include areas outside of the national boundaries where desulfurization plants have been built (Curaçao and Aruba). Finally, the landscape is undergoing change as new natural gas pipelines are constructed, oil revenue-supported highways are built, the national company begins to supplant foreign-owned chains of service stations with its own, and the petrochemical industry expands.

Further analysis could take one into a discussion of regional development institutions established by oil-generated revenues or the impact of the Petroleum Workers Union on trade union economics and politics in general. The case for employing systems analysis in political geography is especially compelling, given the application of systems thinking to political process, as exemplified in the works of David Easton and E. R. Leach. It is in keeping with the call of the Ad Hoc Committee on Geography of the National Academy of Sciences–National Research Council for dedication of geographers' efforts to the study of the Man-Environment System.[17]

In all of these approaches, we face the problem of measuring and describing the distribution of political phenomena as they *exist in space*. This presents dangers of relying upon static elements to describe inherently dynamic situations.

[17] Edward A. Ackerman, editor, *The Science of Geography* (Washington: NAS–NRC Publication 1277, 1965), pp. 1-2.

Change Through Movement

Space and man's use of it are dynamic. The constant process of change vitally affects international politics. One way of indicating change is through mapping political processes and phenomena *in time*. Such a sequential approach has long-term usefulness. Thus, as we view the shifting of the energy sources of the United States from Appalachian coal to Texas petroleum to Venezuelan, Canadian, Maghrebian, and Middle Eastern oil, we gain an appreciation of change that has political implications. Similarly, the move of a country's capital, such as Brazil's from Rio de Janeiro to Brasilia, or the greater weight recently assigned to non-European states within United Nations councils, reflects this process.

But examination of change through time is a slow process. It is much faster to seek such an appreciation through analysis of the movement factor.

Halford Mackinder recognized movement when he spoke of the "man-travelling" element in geography, thereby referring to the variable mobility of man, ideas, and materials over different parts of the earth's surface. Using the term *movement factor* as a translation of the French *circulation,* Jean Gottmann pointed out that "analysis of the movement factor as it applies to a position . . . helps us to understand easily the motives and imperatives of the policies . . . emanating from that position. Movement, however, makes for fluidity and change."[18]

Gottmann has presented movement and national ideas as the two main forces in political geography. Movement refers to current status in traffic, communications, transportation, and trade. Without movement, there can be no international relations.

We view the movement factor as consisting of three elements: the channel, the field, and the arena. Channel refers to pathway or means of movement; field, to the specific areas that include the origin, transit route, and destination of the channel; arena, to the general medium of space-land, sea, or air within which the fields and their channels lie.

CHANNELS OF MOVEMENT

Some channels are two-way; others are only one-way. Some channels can be used for a multiplicity of purposes; others have only

[18] Jean Gottmann, "Political Partitioning of Our World," *World Politics,* IV, No. 4 (July 1952), p. 515.

single-purpose functions. Some channels have no competitive channels; others have. What is important is first to recognize the nature of the channel and then to define the reciprocal impact that movement through this channel makes upon the fields within which the movement flows.

For example, pipelines are two-way; they are multi-purpose; they have competitors. Those pipelines that carry ocean-transported crude oil from the eastern seaboard to the interior of the United States can be reversed to carry products from the refineries of the interior to the east coast's cities. A pipeline that carries oil can be converted to carry natural gas, water, or powdered coal in slurry form. An oil pipeline has to compete with road-carried trucks and rail cars, and with water-borne tankers. On the other hand, a radio transmitter is only one-way; it has one purpose—to transmit sound; in underdeveloped countries where the percentage of illiteracy is high, the radio may have no competitors as a propaganda weapon.

We cannot disregard the possibility that geographical variability may loose its significance within or between specific channels of movement. Certainly, in the age of the intercontinental ballistic missile, there is no practical difference between a channel that extends for 4,000 miles and one that extends for 3,500 miles for rockets with a 5,000 mile range. The time lead that the latter distance presents to its user over the former might be no more than one minute. Also, electronically controlled automobiles traveling on expressways at 100 miles per hour could provide the traveler with the same ease and speed of movement as the crack express train or monorail. However, in most instances, movement channels have geographical variability owing to distance, physical features, and cultural distinctions.

In the case of the Soviet radio propaganda that is beamed to Latin America, it is not distance, but rather the amount of capital investment and broadcast time, and the choice of language and topic, that provide the advantage over the efforts of the United States Information Agency. The impact of the Soviet and American efforts can be compared by number of man-hour listeners; the relative effectiveness can be analyzed through public opinion polls. With American and Soviet technological capabilities assumed equal, it is possible to foresee a reversal of the present trend to one that is favorable to the United States, considering such other elements as distance, trade ties, availability of Spanish- and Portuguese-speaking peoples in the United States, and capital expenditure potential.

FIELDS OF MOVEMENT

Movement occurs within specific areas, and its effects are frequently felt outside these operational areas. Stephen Jones has suggested that such areas as are affected by movement be called "fields," and has pointed out that what occurs within the "fields" influences political units as a whole.[19]

We can cite, as an example of field, the area affected by the Mont Blanc Auto Tunnel. This includes Lyon and much of surrounding southeastern France, the tunnel itself, the Val d'Aosta, and Turin. The effect of the first all-weather auto-truck route across the Alps has been to increase the exchange of passengers and goods. Both Lyon and Turin benefit industrially. Many of the sleepy Alpine villages, too, realize new prosperity from the motels, gas stations, and restaurants built to serve auto passengers. Movement within this field is bound to affect the entire political area. For example, greatly increased trucking through the tunnel probably will come at the expense of traffic that moves in roundabout fashion via the ports of Genoa and Marseilles. Some provisions, in the form of subsidies or alternative sources of business, might have to be made by the states to the ports adversely affected by the tunnel. Another example would be the Lyon-Grenoble-Geneva region which has emerged with the help of modern transportation as a significant transnational field possessing distinct cultural and commercial unity.

ARENAS OF MOVEMENT

Arena of movement refers to the three space media (land, water, and air) through which movement takes place. As long as human habitation is restricted to land, our concern with the other two space media is as they are used for movement to the settled portions of the earth. From a political geographic standpoint, arenas of movement are important for their variable uses in projecting political, economic, and military power.

Previously, it was safe to generalize that land was the primary arena of movement for continental interiors, water for the Atlantic and Pacific shorelands and islands, and air for the Arctic. In fact, however, such a generalization is now apt to be misleading.

Land is the primary space medium for such continental interiors

[19] Jones, *op. cit.* In all, Jones sets forth five elements: political idea-decision-movement-field-political area, as a unified chain through which political ideas operate to affect political areas.

as Eurasia, North America, Africa, and Australia. However, water is a significant secondary medium in North America, and air, of some importance to all continental interiors, is heavily utilized in North America and in the U.S.S.R. While not nearly as important as to North America, water is becoming a tertiary medium for the Soviet Union—witness its fishing activities in the North Atlantic, its naval activities in the Eastern Mediterranean and Indian Ocean, its merchant shipping that plies the routes to southern and eastern Asia, and its stake in the reopening of the Suez Canal.

Water is the key medium interconnecting Eurasia's rimlands and the remainder of the Atlantic and Pacific ocean littorals and islands. But air has achieved significant stature as a connecting medium for the North Atlantic.

Finally, while the Arctic is almost exclusively the domain of the air space medium, we must look to the future when nuclear-powered polar submarines and Soviet Arctic surface vessels, spearheaded by nuclear icebreakers, will make water a secondary medium.

Unity or Change?

Basically, the movement factor exercises a unifying influence as men, goods, and ideas move via channels to connect fields. However, we should be mindful that movement can act as a unifying force upon one field at the expense of other, formerly unified elements. Specifically, movement that unites fields in different countries may divide fields within one country. Communism has unified some Russians, Italians, and Frenchmen, but at the same time has created greater cleavages within Italy (the Industrial North versus Rome) and within France (the rural countryside versus the industrial cities). The movement of Jamaicans and Pakistani into Liverpool and London may not be a factor that will lead to greater unity between the United Kingdom and Jamaica and Pakistan. The racial antagonisms that have been stirred up as a result of these immigrations can become, on the contrary, a source of friction.

Therefore, rather than state that movement exercises a unifying influence, we prefer to say that movement is the greatest inspirer of change, bringing with it unity to some fields, but disunity to others.

Because movement reflects change, the political geographer must be alert to the ramified political consequences of such movement— those tending to unite and those tending to disunite.

Let us take certain critical parts of the world and touch upon movement developments that have important political significance. First we can cite the 480-mile pipeline between Edjele in eastern Algeria (near the Libyan frontier) and the Gulf of Gabes port of Skhirra in Tunisia. The pipeline is the channel, and the field includes the Algerian oil deposits, Tunisia's ports and cities that benefit from transporting or using the petroleum, and France's refinery areas. The political areas affected include Tunisia, Algeria, and France. Arena in this case embraces land and sea. In agreeing to the decision to construct the pipeline and thereby give France a second and alternate oil-carrying route from the Sahara to the Mediterranean, the Tunisian government undertook certain risks. Algeria may some day undermine this venture in French-Tunisian co-operation, perhaps to the point of cutting the line. France, too, has assumed a political risk in handing to Tunisia a weapon—i.e., the threat of pipeline take-over—that can be applied against France. What were Mr. Bourghiba's motives in assuming such risks? Were they based on economic need and anticipated revenues from this line, as well as a counter-pressure against the French presence in Binzert? Or was Mr. Bourghiba so firmly committed to the concept of a French-Arab North African Community that he deliberately wished to tie his country more intimately with France despite the attendant risk of intra-Arab conflict and greater economic dependence on France? While it is only a thin line in the desert, this channel of movement reflects a reciprocal relationship between France and Tunisia that is fraught with dangers and yet with hope.

A second movement development that might be cited has to do with the construction of two railroads between the Soviet Union and China. The first, completed in 1955, from Jining in North China to Ulan-Ude (east of Lake Baikal) on the Trans-Siberian Railway, crosses Mongolia at Ulan-Bator. The second, interrupted before completion, would have connected Yumen in Kansu Province of Northwest China with the Turksib Railway near Lake Balkhash. This railway would cross Chinese Sinkiang at Urumchi and enter Soviet territory via the low, grassy Dzungarian Gate. The first line traverses 500 miles of desert; the second, over 1,000 miles of desert. These lines are strategically important because they represent the fastest and most secure routes for transporting bulk materials between the U.S.S.R. and China. Viewed in the context of Sino-Soviet friction, however, they suggest channels of tension, especially since they have attracted Chinese settlement near the Soviet borders.

All of the areas named are fields of movement. Chinese settlement in Inner Mongolia and the relative proximity of industrialized North China could place Eastern Outer Mongolia and the Lake Baikal region under considerable Chinese pressure (as these areas were once subject to Japanese threats). The proximity of a string of modern, industrialized Soviet centers along the Turksib Railway poses an equally strong threat to China's control of Sinkiang, most of which is more than 1,000 miles' distance from Lanchou—China's present northwest frontier. Expressed in different fashion, China's pioneer fringe in Inner Mongolia and the Soviet pioneer fringe of Turkestan are in a position to move forward along the new transcontinental railroads. The expansion of these respective frontiers poses mutual threats to the Soviet-dominated Mongolian People's Republic and to Chinese Sinkiang. It also heightens the mutual vulnerability and thus the interdependence of the two countries.

The twentieth century has given unprecedented breadth and sweep to the movement factor. As we have advanced from the automobile and radio age to the age of television, manned aircraft, and guided missiles, the political impact of events in one part of the world upon another has become more direct. However, our ability to predict the consequences of this impact is less certain.

Movement developments need to be considered in economic as well as technological terms. For example, jet aircraft make it possible for statesmen to span the North Atlantic in six hours. The effect has been to help to centralize power in the hands of the few, and personal diplomacy on the highest level has become the rule. However, jet aircraft play another vital role in movement.

Jumbos and other jets, charter flights and low-fare regular passenger fares, make it possible for hundreds of thousands of American students and middle income persons to become international travelers. They also perform the same role for Europeans moving in the other direction. One may be overly sanguine in predicting that this increased travel will facilitate acceptance of the concept of a North Atlantic Community by an American generation that knows Maritime Europe so well. On the other hand, the concept may be less readily acceptable to Europeans, precisely because of their disappointing experiences with this restless, rootless generation of American students who descend on their cities each summer "to live off the land."

An International University in Moscow or an African students' airlift to the United States are as important an element of the movement factor as is the prospect of increasing the range of radio-tele-communications through the use of earth-girdling satellites. If we accept a university and its environs as the field of movement, then we must be prepared to recognize that there is a geography to this field. Thus, the nature of the distribution of African students within American universities has important political implications. Where such students take up locations in small college towns, residing in dormitories with their White counterparts, they are most likely to be integrated successfully into the university milieu. Where they take up residence in large city-based universities where housing may be available only in segregated Black sections of the city, the results may be disastrous.

A Geographical Framework
for the Exercise of Political Power

To consider the exercise of power geographically, we should treat space (place, area, and landscape) as it interacts with political process, and the political systems which emerge from this interaction. We may, of course, take the position that the relationship among states is almost a random one; that the world is carved up into 140-plus national political systems, harmonizing with and competing with, interacting with and ignoring, remaining steadfast or changing overnight in relationship to one another without reference to such geographical qualities as distance, mass, resource, distribution, access or contiguity.

Or we may look at this world as one world, divided and polycentric—a world in which certain nodes (points or places) exercise or share primary power or influence over broader impact areas, shaping these areas, ultimately, into unique kinds of landscapes. In other words, we can find some logic to the ordering of the patterns of the relations among states. The major tensions of international relations occur when these nodes or places clash with one another as they interact in areas that are common ground.

Some of the traditional measures that we may use to forecast the ability of a place or node to influence the impact area are the mass of the place (its size in terms of population and area); the position of the place (location relative to the area); the resources of the place; the accessibility of the place to the area; and the cultural and ideological characteristics of the place, which influence its desire and ability to interact with the impact area.

We may view influence or power as radiating outward from the given place or node to a series of other, essentially recipient places. These lines, through their extent, direction, intensity, and linkages form that pattern for the area we have described as the Impact Area. One might use the term "sphere of influence," but this term is probably misleading, for it suggests monolithic impact, when, indeed, almost no part of the world is influenced by another place to the exclusion of other and often competing influences.

The notion of the existence of a number of places in the world, each of which has the capacity to forge impact areas, is at the root of polycentrism. The question that faces us now is not whether polycentrism exists, but whether it exists within some context of global equilibrium, or whether it is a portent of global fragmentation and chaos.

For theoretical support of the equilibrium position, we can turn to certain psychological aspects of group behavior. In studying small groups, we have learned that some measure of conflict and competition is vital to the emergence of a cohesive system. Translated to the nation state and conflict theory, this suggests that not only group dynamism, but also group cohesion, is increased through the tensions that forge the dialectical processes by which states interact.

Given this proposition, we must ask ourselves how many places or nodes the world political system can support. Is there a limit to this number beyond which the tension and conflict become so complicated that we have either chaos or complete standoff? And what of the relationship of major places or power nodes to secondary places? It would be helpful, of course, to be able to suggest that neat, hierarchical arrangements do exist (e.g., 3 major, 18 secondary, 108 tertiary places; or 4 major, 12 secondary, 36 tertiary, 108 quarternary, etc.). But the nature of our information system is too complex, far-reaching, and multivaried to hypothesize any neat hierarchical arrangements, within geostrategic and geopolitical systems or across them.

Suffice it to say that some broad hierarchical arrangement does exist—that as major or primary nodes increase in number (e.g., four at the moment, but surely five in the near future), impact areas change and the potential for overlap increases.

Moreover, the emergence of a system of world or global cities, stimulated by the growth of multinational corporations, must be considered in terms of its relationship to the national state system. The urbanized places of the world, in some economic and social ways, have more in common with each other than they do with their own national and other rural hinterlands. In seeking interdependence they might forge new patterns of impact areas that could compete with the social and economic patterns laid down by the present international political system. There are, currently, 130-plus cities with populations of one million and over, more or less the same as the number of national states. But these cities are distributed within only 30 per cent of all the national states. We cannot therefore assume that the global city system would ever include the entire political world. If great cities do become more dependent upon one another for goods, capital, ideas, and communications than on their respective rural hinterlands, then many of our current notions about the relationship among states, relationships that stemmed from traditional urban-rural interactions, will have to change. It is doubtful that such a system will emerge as a direct challenge to nationalism. Only if for other reasons (such as fears of mutual destruction, or economic advantages), nationalism begins to decline, can the global city system be expected to take on political significance.

Finally, two frameworks, one cognitive and the other based upon measurable data, are essential to understanding the spatial aspects of international power and influence. The first is *locational perspective,* that is, the locational value a nation or group or political elite attributes to its own place and to those other places that make up its impact area. The second is the degree of connection the political process allows a given place to interact with other places in forming impact areas. We can refer to this as the degree to which a political system is *open or closed* insofar as permitting itself to be linked to other places through the flow of men, goods, and ideas. This can be measured synchronically (i.e., comparing different systems at the same point in time) and diachronically (comparing the same system at different points in time).[20]

China and the U.S.S.R. may be used to illustrate the application of the two frameworks. Broadly speaking, the Soviet locational perspective is the MacKinder Heartland one. That is, Soviet leadership sees itself operating from a place that is central within Eurasia. What happens in Sweden, France, Turkey, India, China, or Japan is seen within the context of the assets and liabilities of Eurasian centrality. To this essentially landsman's view has been added the airman's polar view that brings Alaska and Northern Canada

[20] For full discussion see Cohen and Rosenthal, *op. cit.*

into focus as an impact area. However, this air perspective does not have the primacy that the Eurasian land one has, with all the attendant political risks that the U.S.S.R. appears to be prepared to take in Eurasia. Hence, the Soviet view remains land-based. This global view was a natural outgrowth of the historic Czarist regional posture (of being central in Eurasia, with major thrusts eastward into Asia and secondary thrusts into Europe). Under modern technological conditions, the Mackinder view of Eurasia leads directly to a global view, given the hypothesized relationships of dominance of Eurasia in the world.

The Chinese locational perspective is somewhat more ambiguous. On the one hand, it is highly regional (Sino-centric in Asia), concerned with its location in Eastern Asia and China's encirclement by the United States from the Pacific, and the Soviet Union from the Inner Asian borders. On the other hand, the perspective is global within the context both of the world rural-urban and the socialist-capitalist struggles. The former rural-urban view suggests China as focal to a rural world interconnected by water (although the Chinese have yet to articulate this kind of centrality); the second goes back to the MacKinder Heartland-World Island view and is predicated upon a long-term unity of the world socialist camp through establishment of party relations between the U.S.S.R. and China.

Compared synchronically, the U.S.S.R. has a more open political system than China's, using this term in the sense of measuring the degree of its external links, and especially contacts from the outside inward. Both the Soviet and Chinese are systems at the closed end of the spectrum. Considering matters diachronically, the U.S.S.R. has gradually opened its system since the Second World War (there was also a relatively open period during the late 1920's). China, on the other hand, has presented few opportunities for outside elements to bring their influence to bear on the Chinese political system, although recent events in Sino-United States relations, following President Nixon's 1972 visit to China presage a change.

Ancient and Recent

Frameworks of Analysis

The essence of geopolitical analysis is the relation of international political power to the geographical setting. Geopolitical views vary with the changing geographical setting and with man's interpretation of the nature of this change. On this last point, Mackinder commented: "Each century has its own geographical perspective. To this day, our view of geographical realities is colored for practical purposes by our preconceptions from the past."[1]

In this century, our view of the geographical setting, and hence of geographical "realities," is a combination of landform distribution and patterns of movement. In the nineteenth century, the prevailing view of the geographical setting was the distribution of continents. Previously, climate and regional landforms served as the basic framework. Current debates suggest that tomorrow's geographical "realities" will weight population distribution and resource complementarity far more heavily than has heretofore been the case.

What purpose does geopolitical analysis serve? Harold and Margaret Sprout feel that such hypothesizing "may serve purposes of contemplative research or of policy-making and propaganda, and that whatever the avowed interests of the authors . . . [their geopolitical writings] have tended to serve both kinds of purposes."[2] We could cite modern works, ones of a dispassionate geographic nature as well as those of the German geopoliticians, to prove this point. But let us reach back into antiquity to Aristotle, who held that their tem-

[1] Halford J. Mackinder, *Democratic Ideals and Reality* (New York: Henry Holt and Co., 1942), p. 29.
[2] Harold and Margaret Sprout, "Geography and International Politics in Revolutionary Change," *Journal of Conflict Resolution*, IV, No. 1, p. 152.

perate-zone location qualified the Greeks for world dominion over northern and southern climate people.[3]

Granting the truth of the observation made by the Sprouts, we would simply add that the geopolitical analyst is validly fulfilling this dual function so long as he does not deliberately distort the geographical setting as *he sees it* and as long as he does not lay claim to being the practitioner of an empirically based science.

Geopolitical analysis has two major aspects: 1) description of geographical settings as they relate to political power, and 2) laying out of spatial frameworks that embrace interacting political power units. It is more difficult to attempt such analysis today than in the past. Because of the hierarchical spatial overlap that exists among great power blocs and the process of constant political realignment, sharply defined global political divisions cannot be easily rationalized. Moreover, the exercise of political power may be the measure of a man's daring or a people's desperation, rather than a result of the cultural and physical setting.

Formerly, geopolitical analysis could be more safely attempted. Until the late nineteenth century, major power blocs were associations of European-based empires. The core of world power resided in a tightly compressed area—the European and Mediterranean maritime-influenced landscape. For over 3,000 years the nodes of this power were such localized points or areas as Mesopotamia, the Nile, Western Persia, Hellas, Carthage, Rome, Byzantium, Baghdad, Spain, Portugal, France, England, and Germany. This was "the world that mattered"—a world whose highly endowed geographical setting enabled its inhabitants first to develop their local environments in maximum fashion and then to reach out to less favored parts of the earth, exploiting their specialized resources for the benefit of the home base. Whether it was Aristotle referring to Athens, Polybius to Rome, or Pope Alexander VI to Iberia (at the promulgation of the papal bull dividing the Discoveries between Spain and Portugal), "the world that mattered" consisted of the coastlands that bordered the Mediterranean and the eastern North Atlantic.

With the latter half of the nineteenth century came a change. Some analysts felt that "the world that mattered" now had come to embrace the entire Northern hemispheric landmass, from 30° to 60° North Latitude. Others felt that world power was shifting to the

---

[3] Aristotle, *Politics*, VII, 7. Translated by B. Jowett (New York: The Modern Library, 1943), p. 291.

continental sectors of this belt only—i.e., to North America and to Russia.

James Fairgrieve, for example, used the term "the world that counts" to describe those areas to which *place* and *distribution of energy* have given power primacy. Fairgrieve pointed out that "the history of the world is mainly that between 30° and 60°, and the peoples of these lands have naturally taken the lead in the world."[4] Within these latitudes, the United States, Europe (including Russia), and China, interconnected by sea and land routes, constituted Fairgrieve's "world that counts." Interestingly enough, Fairgrieve, writing about future possibilities in 1915, did suggest that the intertropical latitudes might one day become the world that counts because "the nearer the equator one goes the greater are the potentialities of saving energy."[5]

Today, we are far less confident that any one part of the earth (specifically the "north temperate" zone) possesses the material and human advantages to monopolize world power. Such factors as population and national will are beginning to claim equal weight with location, climate, and resource patterns in the world-power ranking process. Thus, China, India, and Brazil have emerged as states that aspire to world power. And the temper of our times is such that the analyst who would suggest that these states lack the prerequisite geographical setting to compete with existing power nodes is apt to be accused of deterministic thinking.

The second aspect of geopolitical analysis—dividing the world into power blocs—is much more complex because of the spatial overlap of great power interests and the hierarchical nature of power relations. Because communication has conquered many of the restrictions formerly imposed by distance, West Berlin and Cuba can, at least temporarily, stand as enclaves within mutually conflicting power spheres, and Thailand and North Vietnam can belong to separate spheres.

In the light of the foregoing, can we no longer speak of "the world that matters" and "the world that does not matter"? Must we refrain from suggesting that certain parts of the earth's surface are destined to remain, essentially, within the spheres of influence or as impact areas of major powers?

---

[4] James Fairgrieve, *Geography and World Power* (University of London Press, 1915), p. 357.

[5] *Ibid.*, p. 358.

Our answer is "No." We believe that geopolitical analysis still retains its validity. Place, accessibility to resources, and qualitative use of these resources through historically derived cultural advantages continue to give power dominance to certain parts of the earth. If relatively weak and depressed states have begun to exercise considerable influence on the world political scene, it is not because they possess power, but because of the stalemate between the North Atlantic and Soviet blocs or between the United States and Mainland China. This stalemate has presented weak states with the opportunity to play one force off against the other. Abuse of this opportunity may well backfire, as the major powers come to realize that the issues between them will be solved only through their own actions.

A case in point is the attitude of the Soviet Union toward the sensitivities of others in such matters as the Hungarian and Czechoslovak revolts, and the resumption of atmospheric nuclear testing. When the U.S.S.R. concluded that its national interests would be best served by taking unpopular measures, it did so with complete disregard for what others might say. Whether the resultant propaganda "defeat" for the U.S.S.R. has been a real liability in the East-West conflict is doubtful. The U.S.S.R. suffered a propaganda "defeat" in Hungary and Czechoslovakia. The United States gained a propaganda victory among the Arabs with its anti-British-French-Israeli stance relative to the 1956 Suez campaign. Basically, these victories and defeats are only relevant as they affect Great Power relations.

It may well be that our reluctance to use such terms as "the world that matters" stems from the fact that the East-West stalemate has caused both sides to exercise power in halting fashion. However, this does not do away with the fact that the ability to exercise this power does exist, and that many nations do not have it.

Naturally, the ability of weak states to take advantage of the international stalemate and to exercise political voices far in excess of their power abilities is not without political significance. For this reason we might wish to revise our description of the divided world into "the world of direct power capability" and "the world of indirect power capability." Major power areas are capable of international action of their own initiative; weaker states can only act when the major powers afford them an opportunity.

With such a view of the world, a sense of political clarity can be maintained. Without it, we in the West run the risk of losing our sense of what is important to us and what is not. If we feel that every part of the earth is of equal weight in the power struggle, we shall exhaust ourselves economically and emotionally, as well as militarily, in the struggle to attain some form of global power equilibrium.

Geopolitical Perspectives of the Ancients

Geopolitical theories to explain the political partitioning of the earth or to rationalize a change in the existing pattern are as old as the Old Testament. When Abram and Lot, upon returning from Egypt, found that the land of Canaan could not support their combined flocks of sheep, herds of cattle, and tents, they agreed to partition the land.

The basis of partition was water. Lot selected the well-watered Jordan Valley, whose physical qualities were reminiscent of the favored Nile Valley; Abram retained the grassy hills of Canaan.[6]

In the ancient and classical times that followed, there developed wide cultural and technical disparities among peoples. Some became gifted irrigation farmers; others had horses, or used iron, or possessed location advantages; still others were driven by an especially harsh environment to conquer territories as a means of survival. Whatever the reason for their strength, the strong were able to press their political and military advantages over the weak, because the movement of ideas, men, and resources was so limited, and the advances made by one group were not readily acquired by another.

Geopolitical views, at first, were limited both as to the extent and the character of the geographical setting. The partition of Canaan between the Jordan Valley oasis and the western Palestine hills was quite representative of the times. River valleys like the Nile Valley and Mesopotamia were natural units, unified control of which was the major geopolitical objective. Adjoining landforms like deserts or hills were treated as separate areas, which at best served as barriers against invasion, and at worst as breeding grounds for warlike incursions.

When man began to seek broader geopolitical horizons, in this period, he did not consider as his major goal the combination of major valleys, desert, and mountain into one complementary unit. He sought rather to unite various river valleys and their divides into one geopolitical region. He was oriented to one major landform. Thus, three to four thousand years ago, Middle Eastern rulers

---

[6] Genesis 13.

aspired to unite the Nile and the Fertile Crescent, from Thebes to Ur. The setting for this unity of space was the irrigable lowland agricultural world, with primary land (the Fertile Crescent) and secondary sea (the Levantine ports and Crete) ties. The desert and mountain regions remained distinct and separate geopolitical units. When the Pharoahs of Egypt became locked in combat with the kings of Anatolia's Hittites, their goal was to clear the latter from the Syrian frontier—not to try to enter the Anatolian plateau and annex it to their empire.

The Greeks began to employ broad physical patterns as their bases for dividing the known world geopolitically. Hecateus, in the sixth century B.C., drew a map dividing the world in two parts: Europe (including Siberia) and Asia-Africa. Climate was the basis for this political partition, Europe representing the cold areas of the north and Asia-Africa the warm areas of the south. The Asia-African environment, more favorable for settlement, was considered the major power locale. A century later Parmenides proposed his theory of five temperature zones or belts, one torrid, two frigid, and two intermediate. Building upon Parmenides' temperature zones, Aristotle claimed power pre-eminence for the intermediate zone inhabited by the Greeks. Such a broader view tended to see in the geographical setting something more than unity of landform. However, the Greeks continued to explain local political partitioning by land-characteristic differences. Thucydides, for example, explains the rise of Attica as due to freedom from invasion. Attica's attraction is described as deriving from its qualities as a place of refuge, which stemmed from the poverty of its soils and its consequent undesirability to outside factions.[7] This Thucydides contrasts with the rich-soil parts of Hellas, which were caught up in continual strife because of their attractiveness.

Soon continental landmass was added to climate as a framework for the geopolitical setting. The Greek Polybius suggested that the Asian continent imposed boundary limitations on the Persian Empire, stating that "every time they (the Persians) ventured beyond the limits of Asia, they found not only their empire but their own existence in danger."[8]

The Roman geographer Strabo's view of the earth was continentally oriented, and European-centered. He divided the entire globe

[7] M. I. Finley, editor, *The Greek Historians:* Thucydides, Book I (New York: The Viking Press, 1959), p. 219.
[8] *Ibid.*, Polybius, Book I, p. 443.

into quadrilaterals, within one of which he placed the habitable earth. This habitable earth he described as looking like a soldier's cloak lying within a parallelogram and surrounded by water. The habitable land area consisted of three divisions, Europe, Libya, and Asia, whose forms were molded by the various arms of the ocean. Strabo viewed the European continent as being "the quarter most favorable to the mental and social ennoblement of man."[9] That Strabo wrote of a "world that mattered" geopolitically can be seen from the following: "Now the geographer should attend to none but our own habitable earth, which is confined by certain boundaries [from the Pillars of Hercules to the Eastern Ocean Bay of Bengal, and from Ierna (Ireland) to the Cinnamon (Ceylon) country]."[10] . . . "The countries which border on the regions uninhabitable . . . have no interest to the geographer."[11] . . . "It would not serve any political purposes to be well acquainted with those distant places and the people who inhabit them, especially if they are islands whose inhabitants can neither hinder us, nor yet benefit us by their commerce."[12]

The idea of there being more than one habitable world and therefore of multiple core power regions was not considered by Strabo or by the majority of the earlier Greek writers. However, Plato had introduced such a new dimension with his "lost continent." In *The Republic* Plato conceived of an ideal state, strong enough to repel any state and located on a new continent—Atlantis.[13] Later the Roman Mela asserted that the southern temperate zone was habitable and no doubt inhabited.[14] While the theme of a great *terra australis* persisted among the ancients, it was by no means commonly accepted and did not fundamentally shake the faith and resolve of European continental supremacists.

Whereas the ancient Greeks and early Romans regarded the inhabited world as an island, Ptolemy made it fade away in the north, south, and east into "unknown land," rejecting the continuous ocean as a mere assumption.[15]

---

[9] Strabo, *The Geography of Strabo,* translated by H. C. Hamilton and W. Falconer, Vol. I (London: Bohn, 1854-57), p. 191.

[10] *Ibid.,* p. 199.

[11] *Ibid.,* p. 203.

[12] *Ibid.,* p. 174.

[13] J. Oliver Thomson, *History of Ancient Geography* (Cambridge University Press, 1948), p. 91.

[14] *Ibid.,* p. 323.

[15] *Ibid.,* p. 342.

With respect to movement, classical geographers tended to think in single-feature terms, using either water or landforms as barrier boundaries. In the fifth century B.C., Herodotus subdivided Asia into *actae* (peninsular tracts of land), using the surrounding water bodies as boundaries. Strabo preferred to use land boundaries, such as the Isthmus of Suez to separate Libya from Asia, and the Taurus to divide Europe from Asia. But Pliny the Elder, in presenting a unique Roman geopolitical view of the world, employed a combination of movement channels—roads and sailing vessel routes—to map the Empire. He showed Rome as extending its regional influences in various directions around the Mediterranean in conformity with the extent of the Roman road system. In some cases these roads terminated at barrier rivers, such as the Rhine, Danube, Euphrates, and Nile. The terminating points of the Roman road system served as an outer-ring boundary for the Empire. However, surrounding the Roman core was another (interior) ring—the Mediterranean Sea. Complete control of the Mediterranean gave to Rome a unified, sea-based, open inner core.

Early Muslim geographers hewed closely to ancient Greek and early Roman geopolitical thought. Thus, the northern quarter of the globe alone was regarded as inhabited, and as being in the center of a vast uninhabited area surrounded by interconnected seas.[16] The continental framework was widely accepted by medieval Arab geographers, who regarded Asia–Africa as one unit and Europe as a separate unit guarded by water barriers at Gibraltar and the shores of Marmara. Islamic geographers were interested in provincial geography, as well as descriptive geography and astronomical-cartographic geography. Provincial geography, in this connection signified the political geography of specific countries, mostly within the Islamic world. The very division of the Mediterranean along north-south lines reinforced continental geopolitical orientation. Only Spain was an exception, and Moorish Spain, for much of its history, had little in common politically, and even ideologically, with the rest of Islam.

Perhaps the first major attempt to break the continentally oriented geopolitical setting of Christian Europe versus Muslim Asia is seen in the fourteenth- and fifteenth-century Portuguese efforts to circumnavigate Africa. Portuguese ambitions were to use the sea to gain the riches of Africa and India, and to surround the Muslim Middle East

[16] George Kimble, *Geography in the Middle Ages* (London: Methuen, 1938), pp. 51-55.

from East Africa and the Indian Ocean. Here was a new strategy, free of the bounds of continental thinking. Such strategy derived its inspiration from early Greek concepts of the insular character of the habitable world, and from the lessons of the Discoveries. This view matured into a truly global strategic view as Europe's national states began to carve out colonial empires, acquiring key islands and coastal enclaves in their drives to unite ocean basins.

Early Global Geopolitical Perspectives

With the development of modern geography came attempts to find an underlying pattern and unity of the geographical setting. Immanuel Kant expressed the belief that a "Universal International State" was founded upon the nature of things.[17] He held that nature 1) provided that man can live in all parts of the world; 2) scattered people by war so that they might populate the most inhabitable regions; and 3) by the same means, compelled them to make peace with one another.[18] Kant was European-centered. He felt that no European balance of power could be struck because the will of states to subdue each other was too great. On the other hand, he held that a peaceful European federation of free states could impose global peace.

While Kantian philosophy accepted no form of unity save a global one (i.e., the Universal International State), the founders of modern geography admitted the concept of regionality within their philosophical system of global unity. Regionality was based upon varying views of geographical patterns. Where these views had international political or strategic implications, they became the basis for modern geopolitical thought.

Contemporary geopolitical views of the earth take stock of the patterns of arrangements of land and waters and of their interconnecting lines. For example, one view centers on Eurasia and Africa, which constitute 56 per cent of the earth's total land area and include 86 per cent of the earth's populations. Encircling this huge landmass are open seas that are three times as vast as all of the land combined. Here, then, is a distinct view of what is called "World-Island." Its focus is the center of the earth's largest landmass. An-

[17] Immanuel Kant: "The Principle of Progress," *Eternal Peace and Other International Essays,* Vol. 3, World Peace Foundation, 1914, p. 66.
[18] *Ibid.,* p. 91.

other view centers on the Northern Hemisphere—i.e., Eurasia, North Africa, and North and Central America. This embraces 60 per cent of the earth's land area and 85 per cent of its people. The focus for this global view is the air and ocean space that links North America and Eurasia. There are other global views, such as the one that centers on the Atlantic, and views the adjoining Americas, Europe, and Africa as the key landmasses of the earth.

From these differing views of the earth's spatial patterns have evolved differing strategic theories. One is that control of the heart of Eurasia could mean world domination. Another is that control of those peninsular lands that rim Asia, such as Western Europe, the Middle East, and South and East Asia, could mean world domination. Another is that control of the Polar world by one power could spell world control. Still another is that a world of three to five Great Powers can achieve geopolitical balance.

Regardless of the various points of view, this much is clear. Strategists, today as in the past, ascribe varying degrees of importance to various parts of the earth, so that their political and military actions are greatly influenced by their geographical views.

While most of the geopolitical concepts with which we are concerned have been sketched out within the past seventy-five years, we can trace their geographical-setting base back to the beginning of the nineteenth century.

Alexander von Humboldt and Karl Ritter, whose first contributions appeared respectively in 1799 and 1804, founded modern geography in Germany. They held to the concept of the unity of nature, and to the reciprocal relations between man and the state, and the natural environment. Ritter elaborated a hierarchical system of regional divisions within the unified globe. First, he divided the earth into two: the land (continental) hemisphere and the water (oceanic) hemisphere. The boundary between the two was a great circle drawn through Peru and south of Asia. Then, within the land hemisphere Ritter saw two more subdivisions: the Old World and the New World. The former possessed considerable climatic similarity because of its great east-west extension. The latter displayed more climatic diversity because of its north-south extension. Further down the scale of size, Ritter conceived of each continent as a "natural whole." Finally, in some cases, he recognized divisions of continents as individual units.

Arnold Guyot, who introduced modern geography to the American public with a series of lectures delivered in French in Boston in

1849, did much to describe and interpret the work of Ritter.[19] Guyot presented the two types of global divisions: 1) the land hemisphere's Old World-New World landmass division, and 2) the water hemisphere's Atlantic-Pacific Ocean basin division. The Old World he described as the world of mountains, plateaus, and limited-use plains; the New World as the world of rich plains. In discussing the oceanic division, he referred to the Atlantic basin as the most maritime, where inland seas predominate and where bordering land slopes are all long and gentle. The Pacific basin is described as the most "oceanic," with land-locked seas predominating and rimming land slopes that are short and rapid.

Guyot was among the first modern geographers to stress the central position of Europe within "the ocean [that] is, in fact, the grand highway of the world."[20] While he constantly emphasized the oceanic unity of the globe, his two major geopolitical concepts stemmed from Ritter's view of continents as "natural wholes." The first concept held that the mantle of world leadership was passing from Europe to North America and its European-derived culture. The second concept sketched the grouping of continents in three double-worlds, with leadership resting within the northern continents. Each of the northern continents was seen as contributing to a "natural universal civilizing" order, with Asia as the cradle, Europe as the maturing ground, and North America as the culminating locale of this process.[21] In vague, mystical terms, Guyot saw the bonds of Christianity, race, and proximity of location as the basis for global unity of the northern continents.

The Landpower Setting

It fell to the German geographer Friedrich Ratzel to make the first systematic studies of political areas. Ratzel was not the first to recognize that differences in the physical and cultural environment contributed directly to the political division of the earth. He was, however, the first to treat space and location systematically in his comparative studies of states, and it is for this reason that Friedrich Ratzel is regarded as the founder of modern political geography.

[19] Arnold Guyot; *The Earth and Man,* translated by C. C. Felton (New York: Scribner's, 1889), p. 70.

[20] *Ibid.,* p. 316.

[21] *Ibid.,* p. 331.

Writing at the turn of this century,[22] Ratzel based his system on principles of evolution and natural science. He viewed political geography as a branch of natural science. The two essentials of Ratzel's systematic approach were space (*Raum*) and location (*Lage*). Space he regarded as contributing to and being dependent upon the political character of groups occupying this space. Location he viewed as giving particular uniqueness to the space occupied by the state.

Ratzel's evolutionary point of view was most clearly expressed in the "geographical laws" that he sought to establish defining the effect on states of their space and location. These laws stemmed from his organic view of the state. Ratzel considered the state as an organism fixed in the soil; a spiritual and moral organism derived from the imperfect combination of men; a spiritual tie to the land that derives from living together, from common labor, and from the need for protection against the outside.

Ratzel's "laws" were above all laws of space and location. The activities, character, and destiny of men and their states were held to be products of location, size, altitude, frontiers, and space. He placed special emphasis on frontiers, which he regarded as the peripheral organ of the state, and, as such, evidence of its growth or decline, strength or weakness.

Perhaps the most significant contribution of Ratzel to our ideas of the geographical setting lay in correlating continental areas with political power. Ratzel felt that man's need for large space, and the ability to utilize it effectively, would be the political dictum of twentieth-century international politics. In this he was most deeply influenced (as Guyot had been) by his studies of the United States—the first modern state to evolve within a "great space" framework. Relegating Europe, eventually, to a minor role in world politics, Ratzel felt that history would be dominated by larger states occupying continental areas, like North America, Asiatic Russia, Australia, and South America. In this continental approach there was, and still remains, the frequent contradiction between the advantages of large space and the disadvantages of location. This approach also is weakened when it fails to account for the qualitative and quantitative differences of man-resource ratios within comparable continental areas.

It remained for Halford Mackinder to combine great space and location in a view of the geographical setting that attributed pre-eminence to one continental portion of the world. Mackinder's geo-

[22] Friedrich Ratzel, *Politische Geographie* (Münich: R. Oldenbourg, 1897).

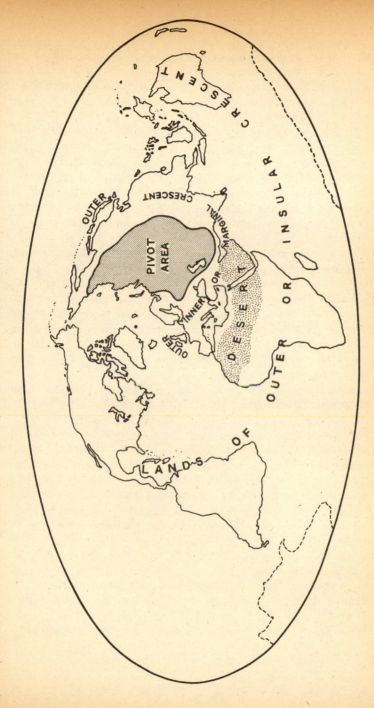

MAP 1. Mackinder's World—1904

graphic writings and lectures over the span of the first half of the twentieth century are best known for their influence upon German geopolitics and for the strategic counter-doctrines they inspired. Sir Halford can also lay claim to having established geography as a university field in Britain.

Mackinder was trained in biology, history, and law, as well as in topography, strategy, and geography. This explains his interest in historical analogies, as well as in the ecological studies that led him to geography and finally to diplomacy. Some measure of his philosophy can be discerned from the following quotation "Man and not Nature initiates, but Nature in large measure controls. My concern is with the general physical control, rather than the causes of universal history."[23]

Mackinder's theory, first propounded in 1904, was that the inner area of Eurasia is the pivot region of world politics. (See Map 1.) He warned that rule of the heart of the world's greatest landmass could become the basis for world domination. Mackinder felt that it was entirely possible for the land power that gained control of the pivot area (be it Russia, Germany, or even China) to outflank the maritime world. Eleven years later, James Fairgrieve was to point out even more forcefully that China was in an excellent position to dominate Inner Eurasia.[24]

It can be seen that the pivot area, as defined in 1904, was that part of eastern Europe and northern Asia characterized by polar or interior drainage.

What many critics have failed to note, as they have elaborated on Mackinder's theories, is that his views of the world kept changing. As a geographer, Mackinder was more aware than most of his critics that man's use of the physical environment constantly changes, and that even the environment itself changes, albeit at an almost indiscernible pace.

Mackinder's 1919 map demonstrates his changing views of the world. (See Map 2.) The Heartland, as defined in 1919, was revised to include the Tibetan and Mongolian upland courses of the great rivers of India and China. Also, while not labeled Heartland, Eastern and Central Europe were introduced as a strategic addition to the Heartland, and for all practical purposes are considered Heart-

[23] Halford J. Mackinder, "The Geographical Pivot of History," *Geographical Journal*, XXIII (1904), p. 422.
[24] Fairgrieve, *op. cit.*, p. 332.

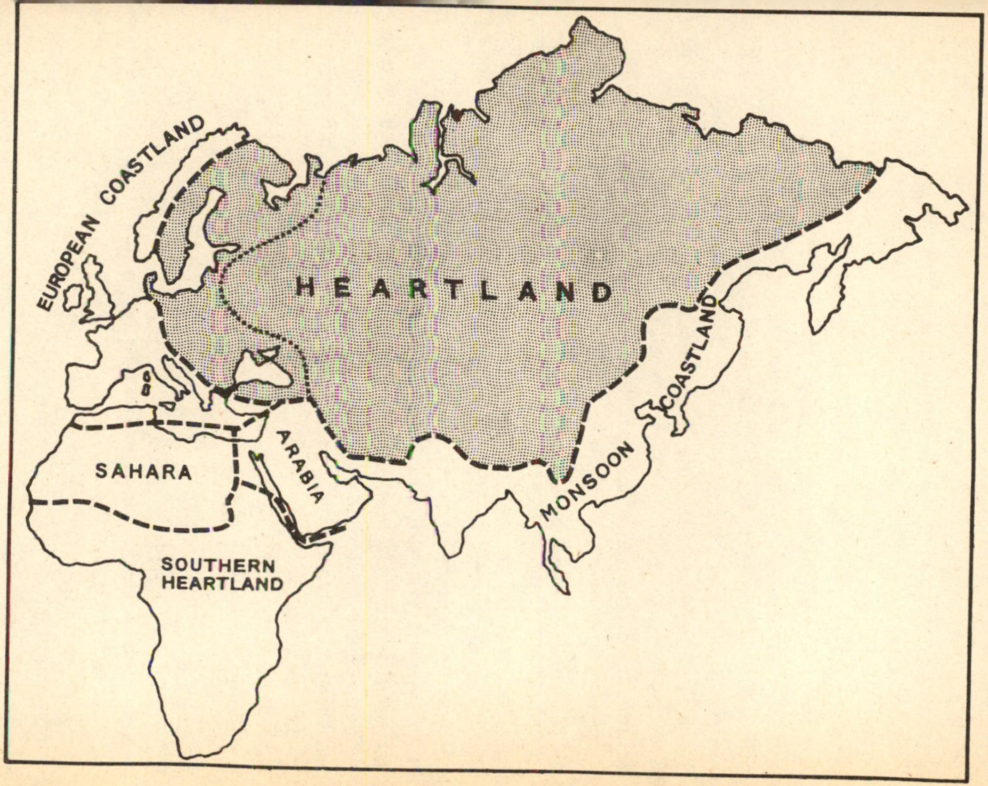

MAP 2. Mackinder's World—1919

land. Mackinder's new boundary took into account advances in land transportation, population increases, and industrialization. Because of these advances, he felt that the Baltic and Black Sea land areas had become strategically part of the Heartland. These areas essentially lie within the Eurasian Lowland Plain and within the winter snowline. The term *Heartland*, incidentally, was not actually introduced by Mackinder, but by James Fairgrieve in his 1915 work, *Geography and World Power*.

It was in Mackinder's 1919 volume that he enjoined the statesmen of the West to remember this saying: "Who rules East Europe commands the Heartland: Who rules the Heartland commands the World-Island: Who rules the World-Island commands the World."[25] Thus, the middle tier of German and Slavic states, from Estonia to Bulgaria, becomes, in Mackinder's opinion, the key to world domination—a key then as available to Germany as to Russia.

Seldom have one man's theories been so exposed to critical examination as have those of Mackinder over the past decades—after years of passive or uncritical acceptance. But when all is said and done, most Western strategists continue to view the world as initially described by Mackinder. American foreign policy of containment in the postwar era, with overseas alliances peripheral to the Eurasian landmass, was an attempt to head off Soviet-controlled Heartland's dominion over the World-Island. Containment of Mainland China by the United States has had, as its objective, the sealing off of the remainder of the East Asian maritime reaches of the World Island, given the major breach made by the introduction of Communism to East Asia.

German Geopolitics

German geopolitics adopted the word *Geopolitik*, and much of its organismic-Hegelian philosophy, from the Swedish political scientist Rudolph Kjellén. For its views of the geographical setting, geopolitics seized upon diverse and occasionally contradictory concepts that had been sketched out by Ratzel and Mackinder. Led by Karl Haushofer, the geopoliticians preached conflict, strategy, and total war. They made household slogans of such words as *Lebensraum* (living space) and *Autarchy* (economic self-sufficiency) in a post-World War One Germany which ached for the restoration of the *Reich* to world power status.

[25] Mackinder, *Democratic Ideals and Reality*, p. 150.

Three geographical settings kept recurring in the literature of German geopolitics: 1) Ratzel's large states, 2) Mackinder's World-Island, and 3) north-south combinations of continents. Haushofer, harking back to Ratzel's laws on the spatial growth of states, saw large states as the wave of the future. Mastery of Germany over smaller states to the west and the east within Europe was regarded as "inevitable," and the conflict needed to bring this about as completely justifiable, because continental mastery in Europe was the goal.

Haushofer saw in Mackinder's World-Island the spatial framework for German hegemony over the new World Order. The German geopoliticians had two objectives in World-Island: 1) dominance over Russia to achieve Eurasian mastery, and 2) destruction of British seapower to gain complete World-Island rule. Haushofer held that landpower possessed a fundamental advantage over seapower. He looked to a German-Russian alliance as the core of Eurasian union with a broader transcontinental bloc that was to include China and Japan. Indeed, during most of the 1920's and 1930's, Haushofer called for Japan to accommodate itself with China and the Soviet Union, just as he propagandized for German-Soviet friendship.

Ratzel's correlating of continental areas with world power status influenced the geopoliticians in two ways: 1) their Pan-European concepts, and 2) their pan-regional concepts in general. The geopoliticians spoke of Eastern Europe as lying within the "European law of geopolitics."[26] By so doing they claimed an inherent continental unity for Europe, whose eastern boundary was defined as a line running from Lake Peipus to the lower course of the Dneister River. The U.S.S.R. was considered Asian by Haushofer. Europe, including the Slavic lands of Eastern Europe, was to be unified under Germany as the prerequisite to achieving accommodation with the Russians over the fate of Eurasia.

Thus, Eastern Europe was to be the springboard for German ambitions in Eurasia. The German geopoliticians generally hoped to force the Russians into a voluntary agreement in the control of Eurasia. Military conquest of the Soviet Union was never wholeheartedly subscribed to by Haushofer, who doubted that blitzkrieg methods would succeed in conquering the vast Russian space.

A different form of continental setting was proposed by the geo-

---

[26] Derwent Whittlesey, *Germany Strategy of World Conquest* (New York: Farrar and Rinehart, 1942), p. 170.

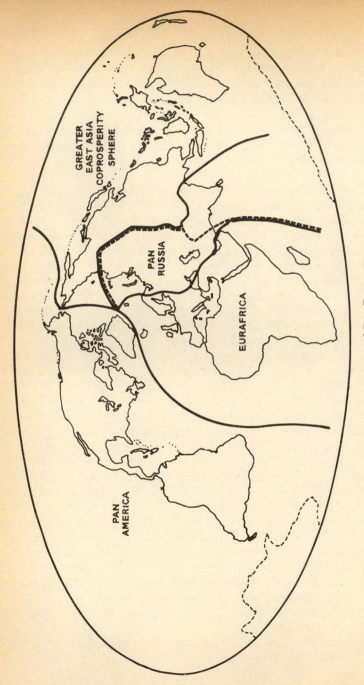

MAP 3. Principal Pan-Regions

politicians in their pan-regional concepts. Alternately suggesting three or four regions (Pan-America, Pan-Eurafrica, Pan-East Asia, and when matters suited them, Pan-Russia), the geopoliticians suggested that the world be organized along north-south double-continent lines. This was to provide for complementary products and peoples. Within continental boundaries, they argued, lay the vast, contiguous space and the self-sufficiency of economy that would enable world power equilibrium to be attained.

In theory, however, Haushofer could never reconcile this pan-regional subdivision with an Old World-New World geopolitical division, which he frequently proposed. For he felt that Pan-Eurafrica, Pan-Russia, and Pan-East Asia would have to combine to stand on a par with Pan-America. In this last geographical setting, the Old World-New World equilibrium, we find a contradiction to the Mackinder view, which had also been espoused by Haushofer. This latter view considered the Americas as separate continental islands, destined to remain satellites of the World-Island. (See Map 3.)

The inadequacies of the pan-regional concept have been pointed out by many. Pan-regions could only be achieved by war. They did not offer the world a strategic equilibrium, for the southern half of each pan-region is not sufficiently remote from the opposing northern core region to be free of its pressures, and will therefore remain in an exploited rather than complementary state, preventing internal harmony by inhibiting stability. South America is no closer to North America than it is to Africa or Europe; Africa is as close to the U.S.S.R. as it is to Germany; and India is not much farther away from East Asia than it is from most of the U.S.S.R.

Nonetheless, it must be pointed out that since the Second World War there has been a closer drawing together of the world on north-south lines, at least for economic purposes. Europe's withdrawal from South and East Asia has stimulated much stronger European-African economic contacts. Japan has increased its economic involvement with many of the lands to its south, and Mainland China has made strong inroads in part of Southeast Asia. Most recently, renewed United States concern with Latin America has redirected the thinking of many of our people along north-south lines. Whether economic lines necessarily presume or justify strategic ties, as suggested by the pan-regionalists is, of course, an entirely different proposition.

That German geopoliticians expressed such contradictory views of the geographical setting can be understood. *Geopolitik* lacked scientific limits. It was a normative rather than an empirical study. As a nationalist-propagandist doctrine in the Germany of the 1930's, *Geopolitik* did not have to meet standards of objective criticism, and thus lacked the basic elements of scholarly self-discipline. Also, with the launching of the Nazi attack against the Soviet Union, the geopoliticians dared not publish opinions that ran counter to Hitler's strategy of the moment. In fact, Karl Haushofer was imprisoned in the Dachau concentration camp in 1944, and his son Albrecht, also a geopolitician, was executed for having become implicated in the army plot against Hitler of 1944.

The Seapower Setting

We have thus far followed the line of Ratzel-Mackinder-Haushofer, with their basic emphasis upon the advantages of landpower within the continental setting. Now it is time to return to the evolution of views of the geographical setting that were ocean-oriented.

Alfred T. Mahan was not a professional geographer. He was a naval historian and strategist, a journalist, and the second president of the United States Naval War College. However, Mahan expressed a view of the geographical setting that was of pioneering geographical significance.

Admiral Mahan is best known for his analysis of the basis of seapower. When Mahan wrote of seapower, he was referring to sea-transported power. Control of the sea could only be achieved by controlling those land bases that had the advantages of strategic location, coastal shape, and defensive depth to their hinterlands.

It is Mahan's view of the world that makes his writings so significant to the geographer. This view, first expressed in *The Problem of Asia*,[27] was Eurasian-centered. Mahan felt that the northern land hemisphere was the key to world power, with Panama and Suez marking the southern limit of the most active commerce and politics. Within Eurasia, the most important component of the northern land hemisphere, he recognized Russia's position as the dominant Asian landpower, and felt that it was unassailable. Mahan pointed out, however, that this landlocked position presented certain disadvantages as well as advantages. He then described the zone between the thirty and forty degree parallels in Asia as the zone of conflict between Russian landpower and British seapower. Finally, he predicted

[27] Alfred T. Mahan, *The Problem of Asia and Its Effect upon International Policies* (Boston: Little, Brown, 1900).

that world dominance could be held by the Anglo-American alliance from key land bases surrounding Eurasia because of the inherent advantages of sea-movement over land-movement. Indeed, Mahan predicted that an alliance of the United States, the United Kingdom, Germany, and Japan would one day hold common cause against Russia and China.[28]

In a real sense, then, Mahan held a view of the world that anticipated Mackinder's World-Island view but culminated in diametrically opposed strategic conclusions.

Nicholas Spykman can be described as the direct heir of Mahan's strategic doctrines, in a geopolitical sense. However, Spykman's terminology, his detailed global geographical settings, and the political conclusions that he derived from his views of the world show that his basic inspiration came from Mackinder, whose strategic conclusions he attempted to refute. Essentially, Spykman sought to arouse the United States against the danger of world domination by Germany. He felt that only a dedicated alliance of Anglo-American sea-power and Soviet landpower could prevent Germany from seizing control of all the Eurasian shorelines and thereby gaining domination over World-Island.

What Spykman did was to suggest that the Eurasian coastal lands (Mackinder's "Marginal Crescent," including Maritime Europe, the Middle East, India, Southeast Asia, and China) were the key to world control because of their populations, their rich resources, and their use of interior sea lines.

In essence, Spykman had the same global view as Mackinder, but he rejected the landpower doctrine to say: "Who controls the Rimland rules Eurasia; who rules Eurasia controls the destinies of the world."[29] To Spykman, the Rimland, Mackinder's Marginal Crescent, was the key to the struggle for the world. (See Map 4.) In the past, the fragmentation of the Western European portion of Rimland and the power of the United Kingdom and the United States made unitary control of the Rimland impossible. Spykman feared that one power, such as Germany, might seize control of European Rimland and then sweep onto the other portions through various combinations of conquests and alliances, using ship superiority and command of a network of naval and air bases around Eurasia. Certainly there is still much to be said in favor of sea communication as far as the move-

[28] *Ibid.*
[29] Nicholas Spykman, *The Geography of the Peace* (New York: Harcourt, Brace & Co., 1944), p. 43.

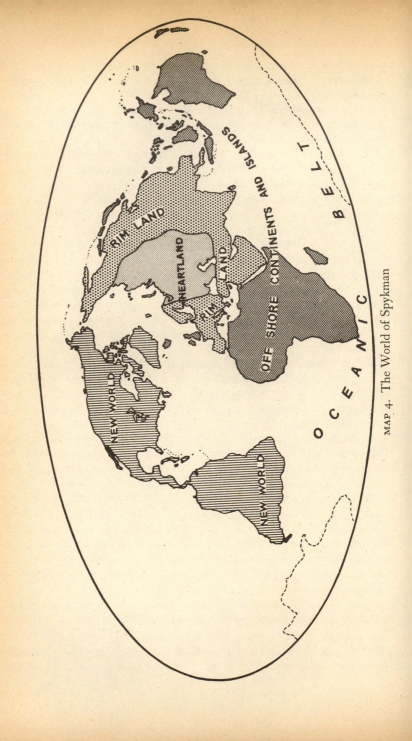

MAP 4. The World of Spykman

ment of goods is concerned. Also, aircraft carriers and submarines have given a mobility in the use of aircraft and missiles to ocean basin powers that fixed land air bases lack.

The inadequacy of Spykman's doctrine is today most clearly apparent from the fact that no Rimland power is capable of organizing all of the Rimland because of the vulnerability of the Rimland to both the Heartland and the Offshore Powers. A united Maritime Europe would have to have complete control of the Mediterranean, North Africa, Middle East, Africa south of the Sahara, and Australia, before it could attempt to exert its strategic dominance upon the remainder of the Rimland. It could succeed only if the Heartland or the Continental American power did not intervene. By the same token, a Rimland China that swept into control of South Asia would be at a disadvantage in seeking to control the Middle East against Heartland, Western European, or African-based pressures.

Today's realities are that Mackinder's Outer Crescent, or continental islands like the Americas, Africa south of the Sahara, and Australia; and the large islands off the Eurasian shore, like the United Kingdom and Japan, are in competition with the Heartland for the lands and the minds of Rimland peoples. In this struggle, Africa's role is unique. While we may hesitate to call Africa the "Second Heartland" (as Mackinder did) it nevertheless need not be permanently tied to the other Outer Crescent lands in a political-strategic sense. Complete control of Rimland by either side would mean world domination. A Rimland divided or partly neutralized means a world more nearly in power balance. It is important to note that just as rule of the Heartland does not automatically mean command of World-Island, so rule of Rimland would not mean automatic command of World-Island.

The importance of interior lines of land communication, even between parts of the Rimland, looms greater today than it did in Spykman's considerations. Thus, the China land base was able to sustain North Korea and North Vietnam in spite of the control of the seas and the air by offshore powers. Communist development of networks of rails and modern highways, in South China and North Vietnam, as the sinews of politico-economic penetration has put Laos—from which radiate the highly successful, primitive trails that have withstood American bombings and invasions for so many years—Cambodia, and South Vietnam in critical positions and threatens Northern Thailand. These are further examples of a Rimland power's use of land communications when denied access to connecting seas.

The development of railroads and highways in Sinkiang, Mongolia, and Tibet by the Chinese is an interesting example of a Rimland power penetrating parts of what Mackinder included in his 1919 Heartland. Indeed, as we have noted, he warned of a Chinese-dominated pivot area in his very first article. One might suggest that in the long run Sinkiang will be more easily controlled from the Heartland (Russian Turkestan) than from North China, by means of the railroad from Lake Balkhash to Lanchou, whose building was interrupted by Sino-Soviet tensions. But this is not the case for Tibet. China's vast space, population, and zeal to become a great power, as well as its bases in Tibet, North Vietnam, and Laos for several years foreshadowed the use of land connections to threaten India and Nepal as well as southeastern Asia. The outbreak of conflict over the Sino-Indian frontier in October, 1962, is doubtless only the forerunner of continuing military and political pressure by the Chinese against India. The Tarim Desert, the Karakorum Range, the Kun Lun Mountains, and the Tibet Basin are formidable barriers to competition from China's northern neighbor, as China strengthens its position in southern Tibet. The remainder of the Rimland (the Middle East and Maritime Europe) is less susceptible to landbase conquest from adjoining Rimland areas, but it is of course more susceptible to Heartland's pressures.

The Airpower Setting

The impact of the air age upon geopolitical thought has produced a variety of views. In 1942, Renner suggested that the air lanes had united the Heartland of Eurasia with a second, somewhat smaller Heartland in Anglo-America, across Arctic ice fields, to form a new, expanded Heartland within the northern hemisphere.[30] A major attribute of this new pivot area would be the mutual vulnerability of its Eurasian and its Anglo-American portions across the Arctic. Such a pivotal area would not only be a great Heartland in the power sense of the word, it would also afford the advantages of interior air, sea, and land routes across the polar world, which as the arena of movement might well be the key to Heartland and therefore to world control.

Another opinion, that of Alexander de Seversky, has been de-

[30] George T. Renner, *Human Geography in the Air-Age,* New York: Macmillan, 1942, pp. 152-54.

scribed by Jones as the "airman's global view."[31] De Seversky's map of the world is an azimuthal equidistant projection centered on the North Pole.[32] The western hemisphere lies to the south of the pole, Eurasia and Africa to the north. Here again is an Old World-New World division. North America's area of "air dominance" is Latin America (our area of reserve for resources and manufacturing); the Soviet Union's area of air dominance is South and Southeast Asia and Africa south of the Sahara. Where North American and Soviet air dominance areas overlap (this includes Anglo-America, the Eurasian Heartland, Maritime Europe, North Africa, and the Middle East), de Seversky considers this the area of decision. Here, according to this view, air mastery and therefore global control can be gained.

In one sense, this view is an extension of that of Renner. In another, however, it has led to two different, and highly questionable, conclusions. The first stems from the distortion of the map projection, which suggests that Africa and South America are so widely separated that they are mutually defensible by their respective "senior" partners—the Soviet Union and the United States. In actuality, Africa and South America are closer to one another than to their "senior" partners. And for all practical purposes, Africa and South America are equidistant from the United States.

Secondly, de Seversky's view was that air supremacy, and with it control of the northern hemispheric area of decision, could be achieved by one power through all-out aerial warfare. While he spoke of only the United States, the U.S.S.R., and perhaps the United Kingdom as having the potentialities of Great Power, in theory any country with the necessary military hardware, recuperative strength, and will, could achieve dominance. That country might be located within the northern hemispheric area of decision; but it might be located anywhere on earth, say Argentina or Australia, as the manned bomber and missile have become truly intercontinental. Thus de Seversky's views lead to two conclusions: 1) "air isolationism" that suggests a viable division of the world into two; and 2) "a unitary global view" that suggests that, in the event of all-out war, the power that leads in military hardware can dominate the world regardless of its location.

[31] Stephen Jones, "Global Strategic Views," *The Geographical Review*, XLV, No. 4 (July 1955), p. 501.
[32] Alexander P. de Seversky, *Air Power: Key to Survival* (New York: Simon and Schuster, 1950).

De Seversky's major work, written in 1950, did not anticipate that several powers might achieve the capabilities of mutual destruction. He felt that the strongest air fleet would be able to knock out its opponent's air fleet and thus achieve complete mastery of the world.[33] Today, we know that we may face a situation of mutual destruction in an all-out nuclear conflict, or of limited destruction in limited wars. However the case may be, comparative advantage of space owing to dispersal or time-distance re-emerges as a factor. While such advantage might be of small solace to the survivors of a nuclear war, it at least serves as a form of deterrent. In the case of limited wars and subversion, where air mastery in itself cannot play a decisive role unless coupled with land- and sea-based actions, comparative locational advantages certainly remain a key factor.

There are those who hold that air power has added, not a third dimension as such to land and sea movement, but simply a complementary dimension to each of these channels. Particularly if all-out warfare is eliminated, this view of what Jones calls the "air-first moderates"[34] suggests that air power can be decisive only as it lends a comparative advantage to land or sea powers.

Sir John Slessor is an exponent of air-borne nuclear weapons as "The Great Deterrent" against total war. Ruling out total war, Slessor concludes that air power's role is to supplement sea- or land-based forces. He holds that even an invasion of Western Europe could be countered by a limited type of air attack—land defense, to arrest invasion without all-out nuclear war. To Slessor, whose strategic doctrine follows a Rimland-Heartland equilibrium theory, the likely arenas for limited war are the Middle East and Southeast Asia, with air power being the key supplement to sea-supported land actions.[35]

[33] In a subsequent publication, *America: Too Young To Die* (New York: McGraw-Hill, 1961), de Seversky's views show little change. Thus he says: "One either controls the entire air ocean around the globe or one controls nothing [pp. 36-37] . . . Unless we take leave of our strategic senses we are not going to fight limited wars [p. 113] . . . The fact is that in any territories contiguous to Communist Russia or China, the Communist forces cannot be stopped by limited war. The same thing in reverse applies to Africa and other continents [there is a change from his previous "strategic assignment" of Africa to the U.S.S.R. (p. 118).] . . . it would be wise to look to the nations of Central and South America, our neighbors in this hemisphere, before we scatter largess over Asia and Africa [p. 134] . . . Our only hope is to make of our own heartland an invincible base from which we can project our offensive against any part of the world."

[34] Jones, "Global Strategic Views," *The Geo. Rev.*, p. 500.

[35] John Slessor, *The Great Deterrent* (New York: Praeger, 1957), pp. 264-85.

The Cultural Base Setting

Certain global strategic perspectives are derived, not from the movement factor, but from the grouping of elements that comprise the cultural environment, such as population or technology. The tendency to organize socio-political strategic grouping around such factors as race or population mass was given contemporary push by the Bandung Conference, which projected an era of world division between Colored and White races. Some analysts, including Arnold Toynbee, combining race and population weight, have suggested that the world is divisible into two: the Oriental and the remainder. Then there are views which utilize levels of technology as the criterion. George Kennan, for example, put forth a world organized around five major nodal regions, each capable of producing modern war-making machines.[36] The United States, the U.S.S.R., Japan, the United Kingdom, and Germany are advanced as the nodes, because they are capable of major nuclear weapons production and delivery owing to their advanced technology. These culturally derived views seem to ignore the complexity of the inter-relationship of military, economic, and cultural processes. They therefore suffer from being single-faceted views. By contrast, views based upon movement attempt to be comprehensive because they subsume these complex processes.

Mackinder's World War Two World

We have described the flexibility of thought that was characteristic of Mackinder in his 1904-19 period. That he continued to be aware of the implications of geographical change is even more apparent from an article written by him in 1943, in which he both reassessed the nature of the Heartland and reviewed his global views. It is ironic that much of what has been written about Halford Mackinder's views pays scant heed to his last published work.

At that time, at the age of eighty-three, Mackinder wrote an article entitled, "The Round World and the Winning of the Peace."[37] In this article he consigned to the ashes his famous 1919 dictum about the rule of the Heartland meaning command of World-Island.

[36] *New York Times,* March 29, 1966, p. 30.
[37] Halford J. Mackinder, "The Round World and the Winning of the Peace," *Foreign Affairs,* XXI, No. 4 (July 1943).

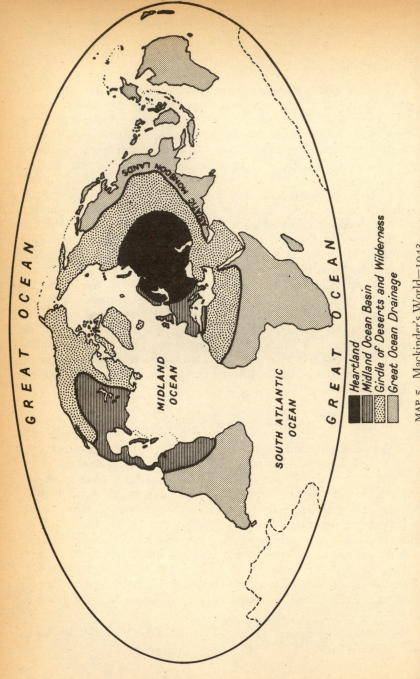

GREAT OCEAN

GREAT OCEAN

ARCTIC MONSOON LANDS

MIDLAND OCEAN

SOUTH ATLANTIC OCEAN

■ Heartland
▥ Midland Ocean Basin
▦ Girdle of Deserts and Wilderness
▨ Great Ocean Drainage

MAP 5. Mackinder's World—1943

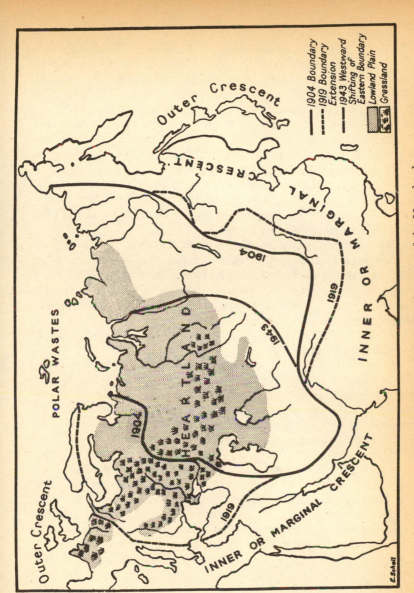

Outer Crescent

Outer Crescent

POLAR WASTES

HEARTLAND

1904

1943

1919

1904

INNER OR MARGINAL CRESCENT

INNER OR MARGINAL CRESCENT

1919

1904 Boundary
1919 Boundary
Extension
1943 Westward
Shifting of
Eastern Boundary
Lowland Plain
Grassland

E. Schell

MAP 6. Mackinder's Development of the Heartland

Mackinder drew no map to accompany his article. Therefore, a map which cartographically expresses what Mackinder wrote is presented here, as well as one which shows the new boundary of Heartland. (See Map 5.) First, Lenaland (the Central Siberian Tableland) is detached from the Heartland. Thus, Heartland now consists largely of the cleared forest and steppe portions of Eurasia. More important, Mackinder's concept of the map of the world had changed. He now spoke of a North Atlantic unit (the Midland Ocean) as being as significant as the Heartland—its transpolar counterpart. He also referred to Monsoonal Asia and the South Atlantic Basin as important units of the future. A fifth unit, described as a "Mantle of Vacancies," is the barrier zone that separates the Heartland and the Midland Ocean units from the others.

The changing yardsticks that Mackinder used in drawing the boundaries for Heartland indicate that the original concept of the pivot area of the world had changed from that of an arena of movement (i.e., as a region of mobility for land forces) to one of a "power citadel," based upon people, resources, and interior lines. The three boundaries (see Map 6) that reflect his changing views of the earth indicate that he was well aware of technological developments, including air power.

It is futile to debate the merits of Mackinder's views today unless we take into account the changes he himself made during his lifetime. There are, of course, certain weaknesses in the Heartland theory. One is that Heartland's centrality is not necessarily an advantage, because of the concentration of targets in the event of air attack from peripheral lands. Another fact, unforeseen up to World War Two's end, is that the Soviet Union is today far better equipped to control Eastern Europe's tidal lands than is Germany. Thus, while we might rephrase part of the 1919 dictum to state that who rules the Heartland commands Eastern Europe, it is now clear that rule of the Heartland (and Eastern Europe) does not mean automatic command over Maritime Europe or other parts of the Rimland. To put Mackinder in appropriate perspective, the post-World War Two American containment policy perceived his Heartland world of 1904 and 1919. Present American balance-of-power strivings are more in consonance with his 1943 global view.

3 GEOSTRATEGIC AND GEOPOLITICAL REGIONS

Alignments for Our Age

In the global strategic views that have been outlined, emphasis has been placed upon the strategic unity of space, organized through a single arena of movement. Unity of the landmass through the channel of railroads and highways is the basis of the Heartland concept. Unity of the sea through the channel of ships is the basis of the Rimland and North Atlantic Basin concepts. Unity of the air through bombers and missiles is the basis of the North Polar concept, and of the concept that brushes aside the variable significance of land and sea masses to say that the dominant airpower can command the world, regardless of the location of that power's land base.

A basic premise of these global strategic concepts is that the unity of one arena of movement is indivisible—that the dominant fleet can rule the entirety of the open seas; the dominant land army can rule all of the land space; the dominant airpower can rule all of the air.

But today's realities suggest otherwise. Unity of arenas of movement cannot be complete, and power within such avenues is therefore divisible. This is because complete dominance of one avenue of movement cannot be attained unless one power completely destroys another through nuclear warfare. Sea-controlling powers cannot prevent the landpower from building up its air and sea forces and continuously attacking the sea lanes via the medium of aircraft, missiles, and nuclear-powered submarines. A landpower cannot be impervious to attack from the sea, because of the striking capability that seapowers can exercise through aircraft, missiles, air-borne troops, and submarines. The basic advantages that these arenas offer to their prime users are, therefore, coming more and more to be shared by the secondary users. For example, sea lanes are not fixed and are thus more difficult to block. However, the seas are open and enable opposing nuclear-powered submarines to position themselves anywhere with increasing ease as range, depth, and time cease to limit submarine operations. Or, land lanes lie within territorial boundaries and are thus somewhat screened by distance from prying, hostile eyes. However, the fact that land lanes are far less variable than sea routes exposes them to the increasing accuracy of long range "zeroing-in" devices, as intelligence techniques make it possible to pinpoint the location of these land lanes.

Many in the Western World regard the sea as the most important arena of movement because it binds our global components. They seek to attain total control of the sea through control of key land bases. However, it is fallacious to think of the indivisibility of the seas, and to continue to assume that it is absolutely vital that the Soviet landpower be denied contact with any part of the open sea. The U.S.S.R. does not need a foothold on the open sea to threaten Western World sea lanes. This it is doing with missiles and submarines. Containing the U.S.S.R. in a spatial sense—trying to prevent Soviet influence from breaking into parts of the Rimland—does not safeguard our sea lanes. Soviet use of bases in Caribbean, Mediterranean, or Red Seas, Indian Ocean or Western Pacific waters does not create new threats to our global security; it only intensifies the basic threat. Whether or not the U.S.S.R. is denied further access to the Rimland, the shores of the United States will not be safe against Soviet nuclear submarine-based missiles.

In their uncritical acceptance of Heartland-Rimland views of the world, many American policy-makers have tried to maintain the status quo throughout the Eurasian Rimland, and drawn rigid political and economic battlelines everywhere, regardless of the specific territory, government, or people involved. In so doing they tend to accept obligations to compete everywhere and anywhere with the landpower, no matter how unfavorable the terms.

The Maritime World has become the victim of a myth—the myth of the inherent unity of World-Island, given the unity of Heartland in combination with part of the Rimland. An adjunct of the myth is that the sea-based powers cannot maintain their position unless complete command over all parts of the Eurasian littoral is maintained. This is the myth that stems from Mackinder's earlier writings and Spykman's rejoinders. It is especially ironic that so little attention was paid to Mackinder in 1943, when he suggested that the Maritime World was ultimately divisible into three units.

This is not to question the thesis that control of the World-Island by one power would ultimately spell world control, but rather the assumption that the Western World cannot stand unless it rigidly contains the U.S.S.R. from spilling onto the Eurasian littoral—that if parts of this littoral are hostile or neutral, our over-all position as an alliance of nations that are interconnected by the sea is untenable. We question the assumed need to try to contain Communist power at every point on the fringe of Eurasia, regardless of whether or not such a containment is militarily or ideologically tenable. Above all, we question the concept that it is strategically necessary to treat *all* of the ocean-rimming lands as part of one global strategic region, granted that the Maritime World must be in a position to maintain sea communications as effectively as possible.

We consider ourselves to be the Maritime World, and rightly so. Our difficulties stem, however, from a false image of the Maritime World. A maritime-oriented state must have more than a coastal location. It must have useful ports and harbors, access to the hinterland, sea-mindedness, and an economic structure that depends upon international trade, either because of the advantages of product specialization or because of the absence of a broad base for relative self-sufficiency. A maritime-oriented global strategic region can be globe-embracing without having to include all ocean-fronting countries and regions. It need include part, but not all, of the classical Rimland. Recognition of this would enable the Western World to choose its allies with more discrimination, to avoid international blackmail, and to select bases for their ideological as well as purely territorial significance.

Those who have accepted the Heartland-Rimland thesis have also accepted the "falling domino" game as applied to the Rimland. They have driven themselves into a frenzy of effort to plug all possible leaks in the Rimland dike, regardless of the risks involved in making commitments or the chances of success.

Let us illustrate this uncritical acceptance of the myth. The following report appeared in *The Stars and Stripes* for Friday, August 19, 1960, datelined Tokyo—UPI:

> Although Laos is not strategically important for its manpower or natural resources, it shares a 620-mile border with Red China and Communist North Vietnam. Loss of Laos to the Bamboo Curtain bloc would "pull the plug" so to speak, opening Communist floodgates to Southeast Asia.

We should not dismiss this piece of prose as mere reporting for our foreign policy has guided itself along such lines. We were told that

Southeast Asia would fall if France lost Indochina. We were told that Laos was necessary to safeguard Thailand, Cambodia, and Vietnam. But actually, Laos could have remained firmly in the Western camp and Cambodia could and almost did swing over to China. Or a *coup d'état* in Thailand could change that country's foreign policy. South Vietnam's fate depends essentially on its struggle with North Vietnam, and only secondarily on events in Laos and Cambodia. Indonesia came close to swinging into the Communist orbit in 1957 irrespective of events on the Southeast Asian mainland. And Malaysia, an important Maritime World link in Southeast Asia, ideologically as well as strategically and economically, will remain with us to the degree that its government succeeds in strengthening its central authority, improving living standards, and unifying its people. Having Thailand, Cambodia, and Laos as screens between Malaysia and China is a secondary consideration.

The same holds true for our ventures in the Middle East. We were once told that Iraq was the cornerstone of METO because it was the land link (and basically the sea link) between Turkey and Iran. We invoked the Eisenhower Doctrine to keep a pro-Western government from being toppled in Lebanon. In both cases our efforts were in vain; Iraq now holding a hostile, and Lebanon a quietly neutral position toward the West. We were told, during the critical period of intervention in Lebanon, that King Hussein of Jordan would have to be kept in power at all costs, lest the West be driven from the Middle East. Consequently British support was tendered the monarch. Then, to protect Kuwait against threatened Iraqi annexation, British troops entered that principality. Again in the 1970 Jordanian-Syrian crisis over Jordanian liquidation of the Palestine guerrilla movement, the specter of United States action was raised as part of the effort to keep Syria and Iraq from intervening against the Jordanian government. But direct intervention to favor pro-Western Arab leadership elements does not guarantee the maintenance of lasting ties with the Western World. Jordan, now so firmly in Hashemite hands, could easily fall prey to combined Egyptian, Libyan, and Syrian pressure, either through a Palestinian coup or through an agreement between King Hussein and the Republic of Arab States. And British withdrawal from the Persian Gulf accentuates the ephemeral nature of previous British commitments to that region.

Does this mean that it is not important to maintain Western footholds in the Middle East or in other critical regions? Clearly not. However, it is entirely possible to maintain such footholds without having blanket control of the region. At present, the keys to our

Middle Eastern position are Turkey, Iran, and Israel. Events in the Arab world need not and usually do not affect our ability to work out accommodations with these non-Arab states.

Regions

Geographers recognize two forms of subdivision, or regions. One is a single-feature region; the other is a multi-featured, or composite, region. The single-feature region may be an agricultural region, like the Commercial Crop and Livestock of the United States, or Amazonas' Shifting Cultivation region. It may be a climatic, or a physiographic, or a trading region. The multi-featured region is what geographers call the geographical region, or the *compage*.

The geographical region is the organization of space, based on both quantitative and qualitative criteria, and expressing associations of various elements. Non-geographers tend to think of such areal units as "total" regions which, while difficult to define in apprehensible terms, are nevertheless objectively real. The geographer rejects the "total" region. He considers the region to be merely a device for separating areal features. It is "a community of physical, biotic, and societal features that depict, or are functionally associated with man's occupance of an area."[1] To constitute such a geographic region there must be sufficient heterogeneous elements present capable of blending into a unity, but this unity does not achieve totality.

The geographical region may be a more clear-cut example, but no region, including the single-feature one, is finite, so regional boundaries can scarcely lay claim to universal acceptance. Thus Hartshorne has said, "Any regional division is not a true picture of reality, but it is an arbitrary device of the student . . . depending on what elements appear to him as most significant."[2]

[1] "The region that is defined in terms of the entire content of the human occupance of the area, is an association of interrelated natural and societal features chosen from a still more complex totality because they are believed relevant to geographic study." Whittlesey terms this the "compage." Compages differ, in size or rank, from the small locality (like the Damascus oasis) which can be represented on a map on a scale of one inch to the mile, to the large realm (like the Middle East) which can be presented on a scale of one inch to 80 miles. From "The Regional Concept and the Regional Method," by Derwent S. Whittlesey, Chapter 2 of *American Geography—Inventory and Prospect,* P. E. James and C. F. Jones, pp. 19-70.

[2] Richard Hartshorne, *The Nature of Geography* (Lancaster, Pa.: Association of American Geographers, 1939), p. 285.

It is easier to define single-feature regions. Among these, the political region can lay claim to being the most tangible and to having its roots in "reality." Political divisions, either by states, or by groups of associated states, are clear-cut. Their boundaries can frequently be seen on the ground, or at least they are mapped with precision. Moreover, these boundaries act as walls behind which differences within the national state or the association of states can be blurred or eliminated, and beyond which differences with other states or groups of states can be accentuated.

But how tangible or close to reality is the political region if we compare the world political map of 1939 with that of 1973? Those who recall the school texts of the 1930's can scarcely forget the spread of the British and French empires over approximately 35 per cent of the earth's surface. The political divisions were real—yet they have proved ephemeral. This is indeed the difficulty with political regions. They are real and tangible for the moment, but if they lack firm groundings in broader political, social, economic, and physical "realities," then they are fleeting.

It is to geography that we turn for a true appreciation of political realities. The geographical setting, both that which is fixed and that which is dynamic, provides us with a basis for understanding today's political map and for anticipating change. Therefore the geopolitical map is more closely attuned to reality than is the political map.

Geostrategic and Geopolitical Regions

A hierarchically-conceived framework for geopolitical analysis should distinguish between divisions that have global extent, and those that have regional extent. For this purpose, we shall employ the terms *geostrategic regions* and *geopolitical regions*.

The geostrategic region must be large enough to possess certain globe-influencing characteristics and functions, because today's strategy can only be expressed in global terms. The geostrategic region is the expression of the interrelationship of a large part of the world in terms of location, movement, trade orientation, and cultural or ideological bonds. While it is a single-feature region in the sense that its purpose is to embrace areas over which power can be applied, it is a multi-feature region in its composition. Control of strategic passageways on land and sea is frequently crucial to the unity of geostrategic regions.

The geopolitical region is a subdivision of the above. It expresses the unity of geographic features. Because it is derived directly from geographic regions, this unit can provide a framework for common political and economic actions. Contiguity of location and complementarity of resources are particularly distinguishing marks of the geopolitical region. Geopolitical regions are the basis for the emergence of multiple power nodes within a geostrategic region, as exemplified by the emergence of Mainland China as a second power center in the Communist world. Put another way, the geostrategic region has a strategic role to play and the geopolitical region has a tactical one. The geostrategic region is nodal in its structure, while the geopolitical is more nearly uniform.

It is important to keep clear the distinction between geostrategic and geopolitical units. Confusing their characteristics and functions may result in an overestimation of the capacity of geostrategic regions for political and economic unity, or in an underestimation of the capacity for unity within geopolitical regions. The attempt to convert the global Maritime World military alliances into a tightly knit political and economic unit, or the assumption that the political differences between Maritime Europe and the Maghreb, where basic geographic unity exists, cannot be reconciled, are examples resulting from such confusion.

The emerging concepts of geostrategic and geopolitical regions were a product of the rise of Europe's colonial empires and the drives to acquire key islands and coastal enclaves as a means of uniting ocean basins. The strategy of building the Portuguese, Spanish, French, Dutch, and British Empires, of carving out spheres of influence in the "exploitable" world, began to take on global or geostrategic connotations. And drives to expand the frontiers of the United States and Russia or to gain unified control over Maritime Europe and the Mediterranean sought to fulfill goals of political unity within and among geographical regions, and therefore took on geopolitical overtones.

Our scheme for the geostrategic partitioning of the earth rests essentially upon the yardsticks of *place* and *movement*. Place includes the location of regional population and economic cores, and great barrier zones; movement includes trade orientation and ideological cultural bonds.

There are, strictly speaking, only two geostrategic regions today: 1) The Trade-Dependent Maritime World, and 2) The Eurasian Continental World. Projecting our views into the future, we anticipate the eventual emergence of a third geostrategic region—the Indian Ocean realm. Such a region, likely to arise from the ashes of the British Commonwealth and other formerly European colonial areas, may not possess all of the qualifications for playing a truly global power role. Yet this former colonial intertropical world is likely to attain second-rank geostrategic status under certain eventualities that we will discuss in a later chapter.

The core of the Trade-Dependent Maritime World is the Maritime Ring of the United States; the core of the Eurasian Continental World is the Russian Industrialized Triangle. Thus both regions can be described as "nodal." Maritime Europe and Mainland China have emerged as second power nodes within these geostrategic regions.

The United States is thrusting its development energies toward its coastal rims, intensifying connections with other parts of the Maritime World. The Soviet Union's development thrust is landward, with its major direction into the Eurasian Heartland. The secondary thrust along the western and eastern frontiers is spearheaded by pipeline and railroad construction.

Geostrategic regions can be subdivided into various geopolitical regions. The Trade-Dependent Maritime World includes: a) Anglo-America and the Caribbean, b) Maritime Europe and the Maghreb, c) Offshore Asia and Oceania, and d) South America. The Eurasian Continental World includes: a) the Russian Heartland and Eastern Europe, and b) the East Asian Mainland. Between these two geostrategic regions lie Shatterbelts—the Middle East and Southeast Asia. (See Map 7.) Unlike the relatively uniform geopolitical regions, the Shatterbelts are nodal in structure.

Unaccounted for in this scheme are Africa south of the Sahara and South Asia. South Asia does possess qualities of geopolitical unity that make it likely to be recognized, in the near future, as a unit separate from both geostrategic regions. Africa, on the other hand, shows little sign of being able to attain continental geopolitical unity. This does not mean that Africa is not important to the sphere of influence of the Trade-Dependent Maritime World, nor is it outside of it. What is does mean is that Africa south of the Sahara is not likely to find internal geopolitical unity within the framework that has been outlined. If, however, the European footholds in Central and South Africa should be lost, then the entire eastern half of the continent might gravitate geostrategically to South Asia, especially and ironically if the "Asian Problem" that currently preoccupies

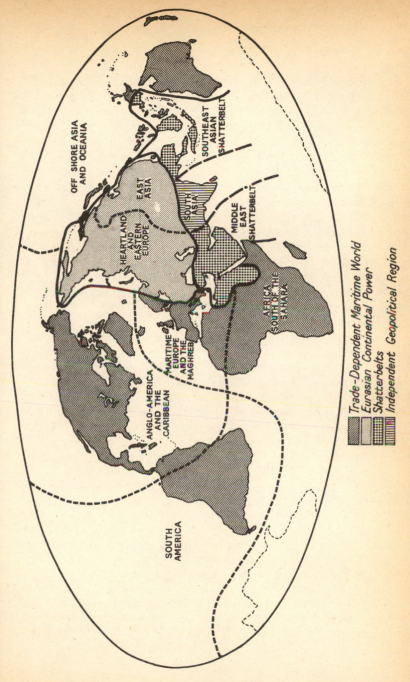

MAP 7. The World's Geostrategic Regions and Their Geopolitical Subdivisions

OFF SHORE ASIA
AND OCEANIA

EAST ASIA

SOUTHEAST
ASIAN SHATTERBELT

HEARTLAND
AND
EASTERN EUROPE

SOUTH
ASIA

MIDDLE
EAST
SHATTERBELT

MARITIME
EUROPE
AND THE
MAGHREB

AFRICA
SOUTH OF THE
SAHARA

ANGLO-AMERICA
AND THE
CARIBBEAN

SOUTH
AMERICA

Trade-Dependent Maritime World
Eurasian Continental Power
Shatterbelts
Independent Geopolitical Region

so many Africans is solved through emigration, expulsion or assimilation.

Several criteria have been used to define the Trade-Dependent Maritime geostrategic region. These include: 1) orientation to the Atlantic and Pacific Ocean basins, 2) primacy of sea communications in interconnecting this region, 3) distribution of raw materials and people so as to call for regional specialization and interdependence, 4) a band of white settlement across the temperate lands of the southern hemisphere, 5) trade-dependence with the North Atlantic Basin, and 6) highest levels of technology. The major ecumene[3] of this geostrategic region extends from the Northeastern United States through Northwestern Europe. This may soon grow to include the Southeastern United States and Cuba. The secondary ecumene extends from Los Angeles-San Francisco through Southern Japan. This is in the process of being extended to Taiwan and the Central Philippines. Although sea lanes tie these two ecumenes together, it is the combination of overland and coastal United States routes that directs these ties.

Ideological bonds, complicated by present or recent aspects of colonialism, are not as strong within the Trade-Dependent Maritime World as they are within the Eurasian Continental Communist World, despite the ideological schisms that plague the latter (revisionism *vs.* orthodoxy, Maoism, Castroism and National Communism). In part, these bonds will be strengthened as the "have" parts of the Maritime World share more of their wealth with the "have-nots." To help to describe this Trade-Dependent Maritime World, the dependence of nations upon sea trade has been mapped according to the ratio of imports to national income. This map (see Map 8) reflects a variety of factors, such as limitations of land bases, underdevelopment or absence of resources for manufacturing, colonialism, and alliances.

If we look at the world as seen on Map 8, we note that certain parts of the so-called Maritime World are far less dependent upon sea lanes than other parts. What we see are groupings of trade-oriented "islands," which we have called *Ocean Trade-Dependent*. A second grouping is trade-oriented, but to a lesser extent. This we have called *Ocean Trade-Oriented*. Lastly, we have the *Inwardly*

---

[3] *Ecumene* is used to describe the area of densest population in coincidence with rail, highway, ship or air networks or any combination of these. Variability and low costs for sea lanes and variability and speed for air lanes make it unnecessary for the ecumene to require the contiguity on sea that it must show on land.

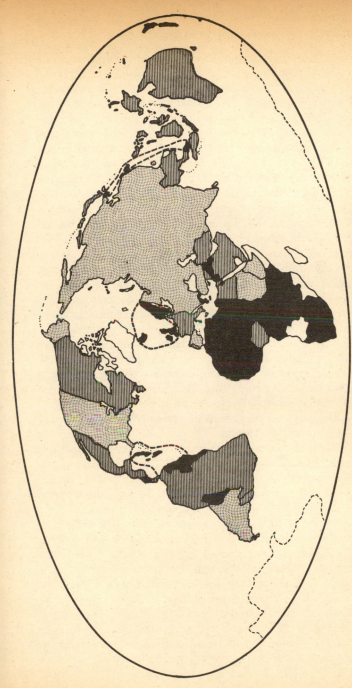

IMPORTS AS A PERCENT OF NATIONAL INCOME
1% to 10% Inwardly-Oriented Countries
11% to 24% Ocean Trade-Oriented Countries
25% and over Ocean Trade-Oriented Countries
Ocean Trade-Dependent Countries
No data on Angola, Mozambique, Malagasy,
Somalia, Yemen and Greenland

MAP 8. Geopolitics and Trade

Oriented countries, mostly within the northern hemisphere. The economic and the strategic interests of these groupings vary, but the trade "islands," above all, must be free to trade with one another and with the rest of the world. The global nature of the American commitment is readily apparent from this map. As long as its important allies are so heavily dependent upon overseas trade, the United States has to help them maintain their sea contacts. When this map is related to global location, contiguity, unity of arenas of movement, strategic raw material trade, population distribution, and ideology, we arrive at the Trade-Dependent Maritime geostrategic region.

The major ecumene of the Trade-Dependent Maritime Region consists of the Northeastern United States and Western Europe. This ecumene's components in Anglo-America and Maritime Europe are the cores of the two most richly endowed and strongest geopolitical regions within the Western World. Coordinated action between these two geopolitical units is imperative if the strategic unity of the Maritime World is to be maintained. Such action must be on a global scale, because the Maritime World's extent is global.

While warning Europeans against taking us for granted, we Americans have tended to take our European partners for granted. However, in most important European countries there exist strong forces that favor neutrality and Cold War disengagement. These forces, in combination with active Communist party cadres in Italy, France, and Greece, make it imperative for us to recognize that partnership must be genuinely reciprocal.

Much of Maritime Europe's disenchantment with American leadership stems from Washington's stand on the Suez Canal crisis of 1956, which effectively destroyed the Anglo-French position in the Middle East without offering adequate substitutes. Subsequently, such issues as the mishandling of the U-2 incident, the inability to formulate an effective NATO nuclear weapons policy, the *volte-faces* with respect to Laotian policy, the ineffectual stand on India's take-over of Goa, the American-influenced solution to the West New Guinea dispute, and above all Vietnam, have shaken many Europeans' confidence in their transatlantic partner. The merits of the specific issues are less important than the background to their emergence. In most cases, United States action has been taken without consultation with European nations or consideration of their sensitivities and needs. One can cite many examples of the failure of Western European countries to foresee the handwriting on their colonial walls; or, in their turn, to consult frankly and freely with the United States. But leadership of the Atlantic Alliance demands from us more than simply petulant reactions or playing to the galleries of world opinion. Our errors of omission are as serious as our errors of commission. The responsibility of leadership bears with it the responsibility for consultation with our partners.

The most significant geopolitical action taken by the United States since the Second World War was to take the initiative in supporting European economic recovery and in forging the North Atlantic Treaty Organization. If we should fail to follow up these accomplishments and lose our position as senior partner of the Atlantic Alliance, the Maritime World will become hopelessly divided through the shattering of its geostrategic framework. Moscow's road to victory lies, in the last analysis, not through Belgrade, Tirana, Saigon, or Delhi, but through Paris, London, Bonn, Rome, and, in the Pacific, through Tokyo.

To speak of the Eurasian Continental World as including Mainland East Asia may appear to some readers to be an overweighting of ideology—Communism—as the criterion, or an underestimation of the depth of the ideological schism between the U.S.S.R. and the Chinese People's Republic. Mackinder felt that the belt of deserts and mountains separating China from the Soviet Union would be a sufficient barrier to separate the Heartland from what he called Monsoonal Asia. And some contemporary observers, like George Kennan, hold that "If time was against him [Stalin] in 1927, so was space. He faced the fact that he was 5,000 miles from the scene of action, and a foreigner, whereas Chiang and Mao were Chinese, and were right there . . . there are geographic limits to the possibilities of military expansion"[4] (again with reference to Soviet relations with China). Kennan believed that the Sino-Soviet alliance was destined to break apart because of the cultural, racial, and physical differences that divide the two powers. That the alliance has broken down is indisputable. The real question, however, is whether the differences between the U.S.S.R. and China outweigh their common interests in remaining in opposition to and in undermining the Maritime World.

We may not be able to prove or to disprove the thesis that the gulf between a Westernized, Christianized Russia and Oriental China is too great to be bridged by Marxism. But we can challenge the thesis that China and the Soviet Union are too far apart

[4] George F. Kennan, *Russia and the West under Lenin and Stalin* (Boston: Little, Brown, 1960), p. 276.

to be able to operate within a unified geostrategic framework. While the distance from Canton to Riga is about 5,000 air miles, and that from Shanghai to Moscow is about 3,700 miles, the gap between Lanchou, China's "Chicago of the West," and Alma Ata, Kazakhstan's scientific university center, is only 1,500 miles. Paotou, the new steel city of North China, is but 900 miles from Irkutsk.

Admittedly, there are vast empty areas between the two states. Semipalatinsk, a site of Soviet nuclear testing, lies exactly midway between Peiping and Moscow and is surrounded by empty reaches. However, the true test of proximity in space is the distance that separates the two national ecumenes and the channels of movement that bind them together. Novosibirsk, a city of nearly one million people, and now the eastern edge of the Soviet ecumene, is 1,800 miles from Peiping, the focus of the North-Northeast Chinese ecumene. Moreover, Sinkiang, China's "New Frontier" of the Northwest for mineral and industrial development, adjoins one of the Soviet "New Frontiers," Kazakhstan.

Deep ideological rifts, such as those over Stalinism, coexistence, and the communes, exist between the Soviet Union and China. Moreover, China has challenged the position of pre-eminence hitherto held by the U.S.S.R. within the Communist bloc. The Chinese first issued this challenge in striving for regional hegemony over North Korean and Vietnamese affairs. Then they broadened this challenge through support of Albania and a show of diplomatic strength in such countries as Cuba and Egypt. What is probably involved is not a permanent splitting of the Communist World, but rather the emergence of multiple power cores within it. Such a course is to be expected within any geostrategic region, because of the cohesion and uniqueness of its geopolitical subdivisions. As serious as Sino-Soviet divergencies are, they are no greater than, and in many ways resemble quite closely, the divisions that exist among the geopolitical regions of the Maritime World. We view the Eurasian Continental World, then, as polycentric, with deep and unresolvable differences of race and culture. Strategically, however, the elements that lead to interaction, competitive as well as cooperative, make for a unity of the geostrategic region.

In viewing the ties of the East Asia Mainland geopolitical region to that of the Soviet Heartland-East European region, we can draw some useful parallels from the relations between two comparable units—Maritime Europe and the Maghreb, and Anglo-America and the Caribbean Basin.

First, the gap between the respective ecumenes is not substantially different. About 2,000 miles separate the Chinese and Soviet ecumenes, and 3,000 miles are needed to span the North Atlantic. In time-distance terms, the overland gap is shorter (three to four days as compared with five to six days). On the other hand, if we weight time-distance by cost of freight movement, we find that the advantage shifts to the North Atlantic sailing route and that, economically, the ecumenes that are the termini of this route are closer together. Sea routes also exist as links between China and the U.S.S.R. However, these (the 6,000-mile Northern Sea route and the 9,000-mile Indian Ocean route) are longer, slower, and less reliable, and should not enter this process of comparison.

Second, the mutual relations of these geopolitical regions are comparable in terms of size, population, and gross national product. Omitting from consideration all North American lands north of the Arctic Circle, we find the following:

TABLE 3

Selected Data—Major Geopolitical Regions

Geopolitical Region	Land Area (Sq. Mi.)	Population	Annual Gross National Product
East Asia Mainland	3,750,000	730,000,000	$50-80,000,000,000
Soviet Heartland and Eastern Europe	9,000,000	360,000,000	$300,000,000,000
Maritime Europe and the Maghreb	2,500,000	360,000,000	$700,000,000
Anglo-America and the Caribbean	8,000,000	320,000,000	$1.1 trillion

The land area ratios are quite similar: 1 to 2.5 for China and its neighboring Heartland unit, and 1 to 3 for Maritime Europe and Anglo-America. The population ratios are somewhat wider apart, 2 to 1 and $1\frac{1}{10}$ to 1 respectively, but maintain the same order. Gross national product ratios, again in the same order, show a wider disparity, 1 to 4 as against 1 to 1.6. However, if we give combined weight to population and gross national product, we find China's ratio to the Soviet Heartland to be 1 to 2, while Maritime Europe's ratio to Anglo-America is 1 to 1.5.

Third, just as the North Atlantic regions have become increasingly interdependent strategically and economically, so have the two Eurasian Continental geopolitical units. Traditionally, the U.S.S.R. has feared the pressures upon its Siberian lands that might be exerted from Chinese Turkestan, Outer Mongolia, and Manchuria. In recent decades these pressures originated from Japan and more distant Pacific-held bases of the Western world. Now such pressures emanate from Mainland Chinese areas that are within the strategic reach of Soviet landpower.

As Soviet agriculture and industry continue to spread into Russian Central Asia, Central Siberia, and the Far Eastern provinces, the U.S.S.R. will surely become more vulnerable to Chinese pressures. At the same time, the greater Soviet stake in Asia and increased Siberian self-sufficiency will both force and enable the U.S.S.R. to find a modus vivendi with its neighbor. Extension of the Chinese frontier northeastward (Manchuria) and northwestward (Chinese Mongolia and Sinkiang) is likely to have the same effect upon Chinese relations with the Soviet Union. The result, in our opinion, will lead to greater interdependence between the two, from the conditions of mutual vulnerability.

China has always had two faces—the Continental North and the Monsoonal South. It is our belief that Chinese industrial progress and agricultural developments will give primacy to the continental face. Therefore, in our geopolitical scheme, we have departed from Mackinder and Spykman, who considered China to be one of Eurasia's marginal regions—a monsoonal land, turned towards the Pacific, open to sea power and permitting the exercise of sea power from it.

In our opinion, China's ocean frontage is not first-class.[5] Without control of Offshore Asia, China will not be able to live apart from, let alone dominate, the Eurasian Heartland. And Offshore Asia, the combination of a populous string of island-nations and Australasia, buttressed by the North American landmass to the north, is not easy strategic game for Mainland China. On the contrary, it

---

[5] Fairgrieve, on this point, observed: "The position of China fronting the open ocean, on the road to nowhere by sea, and the absence of any Mediterranean Sea, are great, silent, negative controls which have . . . tended to confirm the Chinese . . . as landsmen, and to prevent them from becoming seamen." *Geography and World Power*, p. 242. A similar view of China as a Heartland-oriented power is presented by W. A. Douglas Jackson in his penetrating interpretation of the Russo-Chinese borderlands, *The Russo-Chinese Borderland* (Princeton: Van Nostrand, 1962).

constitutes a region that appears to be quite capable of shaping a unique geopolitical consciousness.

Boundaries of the Geostrategic Regions

The boundaries that separate the Trade-Dependent Maritime and the Eurasian Continental worlds next tempt our geographical appetites.

While Arctic wastes and mountains-deserts serve as broad boundary zones to the north and south, only thin lines separate the two geostrategic regions along the east-west axis. The boundary in Asia runs through the Sea of Japan, the East China Sea, and the South China Sea. It divides Mainland Asia from the great string of insular states from Japan to Maritime South Korea to Taiwan to the Philippines. Anchoring this offshore string is Alaska on the north and Australia on the south.

That such a boundary can be claimed for Mainland and Offshore Asia is more than simply an expression of current political realities and wishful thinking for the future. Mainland China is not maritime-oriented. Its most important and most rapidly expanding industrial areas lie in North China—a region that lacks good water communications. Even in South China, where fine ports are to be found, these ports are blocked from the interior by jumbled masses of hills and mountains. Moreover, South China's industrial potential is more limited than North China's.

On the other hand, Japan, South Korea, Taiwan, and the Philippines are part of the Trade-Dependent Maritime world. Their faces are to the sea, both in a commercial-technological sense and in a strategic sense. Japan is the core of Offshore Asia. Without Japan there can be no broad geopolitical region such as we have outlined. The fact that most of Japan's population, ports, and resources face the open Pacific and not the Sea of Japan is a further reflection of its maritime orientation. Korea, historically the buffer between continental Asia and the offshore islands, retains this function today. Its southern half serves to enclose the Yellow Sea and at the same time to bar Mainland China from Southern Japan.

Some geographers have held that Japan's location with respect to the East Asia Mainland is similar to the location of the British Isles with respect to Western Europe. If this were true, then the geopolitical relationships of each to its mainland would have to be similar. In fact, however, the parallel is a poor one. The British Isles are a single group of islands, 120,000 square miles in area, with 60 million people, and only 26 miles from the continent. They have no association with other offshore islands. In terms of culture and trade, Britain's fate is inextricably bound with that of the continent. Japan, with 142,000 square miles in area and 100 million people, is, at its closest, 210 miles from the continent and 450 miles from Mainland China. Japan has close associations with other, large offshore islands. Highly industrialized, Westernized, and ocean-oriented, Japan has demonstrated in the past decade and a half an ability to turn its back economically on the mainland. Indeed, even at the height of Japan's involvement with Mainland Asia, its trade with the mainland was proportionally only half that of Britain's with Western Europe.

As we look at Japan's associates in Offshore Asia, we find a similar picture of aloofness from the mainland. Taiwan is 100 miles distant from the continent, and the Philippines, 450 miles. With their trade interconnections and their general cultural-ideological orientation, these islands are closer to one another than they are to the mainland. If we extend the region to include Australian New Guinea and Australia-Oceania, there unfolds the concept of a Western Pacific geopolitical region that has moved rapidly in the direction of interdependence, both internally and with the rest of the Trade-Dependent Maritime World.

In looking at the Western Pacific boundary between the Trade-Dependent Maritime World and the Eurasian Landpower, we see that it has become a line within a rather narrow water zone. South Korea plays a most vital role in the establishment of this line. While Dean Acheson may once have felt that "Korea is of no strategic importance to the security of the United States," events that have occurred in the last two decades emphasize that the contrary is true. The security of Japan requires that South Korea remain within the Maritime sphere of influence and Japan's inclusion within the Trade-Dependent Maritime World is vital to the security of the United States. Korea is the only portion of the mainland that we have included within our Offshore Asian geopolitical region. Shannon McCune has pointed out Korea's historic and current role as contact zone between the Asian continent and seapower.[6] In modern times isolationism proved impossible for the "hermit kingdom." Japanese rule of Korea took place at a time of weakness for China and Russia. But the recent conflict has occurred at a time of balance be-

[6] Norton Ginsburg, editor, *The Pattern of Asia* (Englewood Cliffs, N.J.: Prentice-Hall, 1958), p. 130.

tween Sino-Soviet and Western forces. Political partition was probably the inevitable result of this stalemate. From a Korean standpoint
this partition is most assuredly unhappy because the two Koreas have
not found economic orientation to the Great Powers to be a substitute for prewar unity. On the other hand, the mutual needs of the
major powers require either bufferdom or division, and bufferdom
proved unfeasible. Under such circumstances Korea has become a
pawn in the global power struggle. Extraordinary American financial
aid to the South Korean economy is therefore not only strategically
vital and praiseworthy from a humane point of view; it is a moral
obligation that we must continue to honor. Many critics of the Korean War of 1950-53 have described this as the "wrong war at the
wrong time and in the wrong place." There can be no right war. But
the Korean War had to be fought where it was and when it was to
affix a Western Pacific boundary to the interests of the world's two
geostrategic regions. The boundary in Europe had been fixed by the
disposition of victorious allied forces in the wake of World War
Two, but the one in Asia was still fluid. When the Bamboo Curtain
was drawn on Mainland China, the Korean War became inevitable
and the resulting stalemate can be said to have met Maritime World
security objectives. Under the pressures of the Korean War, both the
peace treaty with Japan and the ANZUS Pact were signed. Then,
in 1954, SEATO was established. Thus was Offshore Asia's role
within the Trade-Dependent Maritime World geostrategically recognized in a formal sense. It is to our bitter regret that false analogies
were drawn by American statesmen between Vietnam and Korea.
For Vietnam, located within the Southeast Asian Shatterbelt, does
not occupy the same geostrategic boundary position between the
Maritime and Continental worlds that Korea does.

Turning to the European boundary that separates these two geostrategic regions, we find ourselves confronted with a clear, hard line
—the Iron Curtain. This is the boundary that divides Maritime from
Continental Europe.

Mackinder was, as we have noted, the first modern geographical
strategist to look at the world and its history from the "seaman's" and
the "landsman's" points of view. In recalling the various boundaries
employed by Mackinder to divide the Continental from the Maritime portions of Western Eurasia, we note three changes. In 1904,
the boundary was delineated by a line running from the Caspian
Sea to the White Sea. In 1919, it was shifted westward to include an
area bounded by a line cutting through the Anatolian plateau, the

Pindus Mountains, the Dinaric Alps, the middle Danube, central Germany, Denmark, and the Scandinavian peninsula. In 1943, Mackinder emphasized the difficulty of laying down a western boundary line. He spoke, rather, of a border zone, extending in general from the Baltic to the Black seas. Thus, in seeking a yardstick for the Heartland's western border, Mackinder finally fell back upon a broad strategic zone where Eurasian land power met European sea power supported from overseas. The delineation of a line within the zone was to be subject to revision in accordance with technological change and other developments.

The importance of this zone was not lost to the German geopoliticians who aspired to world domination. They viewed Germany's position as central, or intermediate, between Eurasian land power and Western sea power. Most, like Banse,[7] conceived of Germany as the European spearhead against the Russian landpower of the east. They preferred that Germany play this role, not through direct military conquest of the U.S.S.R., but through conquest of Eastern Europe and then through political and economic pressure upon the Soviet Union. To this way of thinking Germany's two wars in the west were "civil wars"; those in the east were considered ill-timed, but nonetheless these wars did express the fundamental clash between European civilization and the Slavic world. A contrary view that was voiced in the West during the Second World War was that German history, from the Teutonic struggle against Rome, through Luther's revolt against the Church, to Nazism, was fundamentally a revolt against Western civilization.[8] This was translated geopolitically into the thesis that Germany, with her historic strivings eastward, was essentially part of the Eurasian landmass. Appeasers of Hitler could see in this thesis a means of satisfying Germany's ambitions at the expense of the U.S.S.R. Opponents of Hitler who adopted this thesis saw Germany's invasion of Russia as Germany's major step toward world conquest.

Regardless of how we feel about such speculations, we can assert that Germany has been the land of geopolitical doubt, with both Continental and Maritime aspirations. It has had two components: 1) the Industrial West, with its urban concentrations, its dependence upon European and world trade, and its physical connections with

[7] Ewald Banse, *Germany Prepares for War,* translated by Alan Harris from the German edition of 1932 (New York: Harcourt Brace, 1941).

[8] Raoul de Roussy de Sales, *The Making of Tomorrow* (New York: Reynal & Hitchcock, 1942).

the Rhine, the North Sea, and the English Channel as outlets for its commerce; and 2) the Agricultural-Industrial East—home of the *Junkers*, the peasant farmers, Prussian militarism, and German *Kultur*. It is in the East that German aggression and dreams of world domination have traditionally flourished. The 1,100-year-old *Drang nach Osten*, and the more recent secondary pulls towards Western Europe can perhaps be said to characterize "landward" Germany. This eastern area has been the symbol of a landpower that has striven to add more and more space to its political bounds, but failed in its attempts to unite Eurasia because of its cardinal error of seeking to unify the Heartland by force while simultaneously striking out at the Western sea power area. The split personality that characterized pre-World War Two Germany can be seen in the alternate attempts to strike bargains with Great Britain and the U.S.S.R. Thus there were periods during which Germany saw itself as an ally of Britain and periods of furious naval building when it saw itself as a competitor for control of the Maritime World and world empire. Similarly, there was the experience of Germany's making common cause with Russia, including the Stalin-Hitler Pact of 1939 and the German-Soviet rapprochement of the 1920's, and the great wars between Germany and Russia.

Germany remains the question mark of Europe. Today it is divided along the Elbe. Eastern "landward" Germany is within the landpower orbit of the U.S.S.R.; western "seaward" Germany is highly dependent upon the rest of Maritime Europe and Anglo-America.

The boundary zone that divides the East from West Germany today is one of the oldest in European history. The eastern boundary of the Germanic tribes, as affixed at the Treaty of Verdun in 843, lay along the Elbe. The boundary between the East Frankish Kingdom of Louis and the Slavonic tribes included Holstein, and ran along the Elbe and Saale line to Erfurt, and from there southeastward along the Bohemian Forest. (See Map 9.) The Slavonic lands east of the Elbe were overrun by Germanic peoples in the following two centuries, and the subsequent unification of East Prussia with Brandenburg led to the eventual unification of all Germany.

The present political line between East Germany and West Germany runs from Lübeck south to the most northerly part of Bavaria, and eastward along the Ore Mountains to Czechoslovakia. This roughly follows the old Slav border line, although it includes portions of Thuringia that were never held by the Slavs.

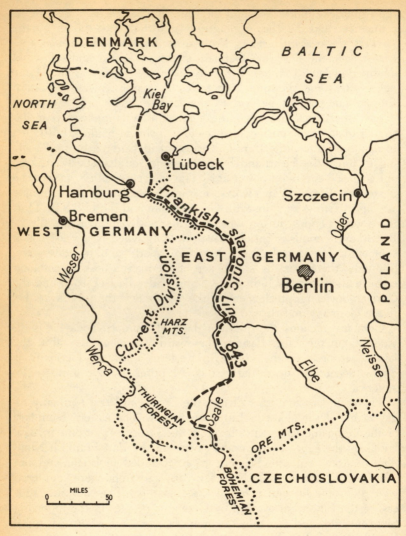

MAP 9. Ancient and Modern Divisions of Germany

The division of Germany into two, coming as it has with the reduction of the combined German territory by 24 per cent and the repatriation of twelve million Germans from Eastern Europe, has altered the Eurasian geopolitical map in a most fundamental manner. Prewar Germany was a balanced entity, which had a central location within Europe and possessed qualities of both a seapower and a landpower. It was, in this sense, a frontier state between the Eurasian coast and the interior. Today, the German Federal Republic is a remarkable reflection of Maritime Europe as a whole. It is the prime example of the seaward-oriented state, vying with the United States for first place in the international trade world. West Germany's manufacturing base has made unprecedented strides in the past two decades in steel, chemicals, textiles, automobiles, machinery, and ships. This has been accomplished through ever increasing dependence upon foreign raw materials like fuels, fibers, and iron ore; foreign labor; and foreign markets. Population density for West Germany is 630 persons per square mile (that of Prewar Germany was 355 per square mile)—certainly an indication of the highly urbanized state of the economy. In area, population and manufacturing, West Germany and the United Kingdom are now remarkably similar. Indeed, West Germany has outstripped the latter as an industrial power.

What has changed the face of West Germany even more is that agriculture has lost ground. Prewar united Germany produced, on an average, 80 per cent of its total food needs and was as close to being a balanced industrial-agricultural state as could have been expected. Today, only about half of the lands and crops that were available to Germany's 1937 population of 70,000,000 are available to West Germany's 66,000,000 people. The varied landscape of the country—plain, plateau, and mountain—makes possible the cultivation of only about one-third of the total land area. The attendant land pressure results in smaller farms, smaller cultivated acreage to agricultural population ratios (three-quarters that of East Germany), and high dependence upon imported foodstuffs, Germany's largest import item.

The increased dependence of West Germany upon international trade is reflected in its booming ports. Hamburg, Bremen, and Lübeck have become almost completely dependent upon the North Atlantic region, which accounts for about 70 per cent of all West German foreign trade. Where once Hamburg handled a good deal of Czech as well as East German trade, it now turns mainly to the

Atlantic for markets and raw materials. Bremen has lost the Central European hinterland to which it once sent cotton, rice, and jute and from which it received textiles and chemicals. Lübeck, formerly a Baltic trading *entrepôt*, has seen its eastward trade in timber, fish, coal, and cattle shrink.

West Germany is today an integral part of the Maritime World. There is little reason to suspect that the prosperity that has been won from this new-found association, as well as the political freedoms currently enjoyed, would be given up in return for unification with the East if this were the sole alternative laid before the West German people.

Meanwhile, Germany east of the Elbe has become even more inextricably part of the Continental Landpower Realm. Physically, politically, economically, and strategically East Germany has passed into the East European orbit.

While East Germany also is an urbanized, industrialized society, it is far more closely identified with the heavily agricultural East European plain than with the West European landscape. East Germany is an exporter of foodstuffs. Nearly half of the country's total land area is under cultivation, a figure that is the average for Hungary, Poland, Romania, and Czechoslovakia. East Germany's potato production is two-thirds, sugar and livestock is one-third, and cultivated land per capita is one-and-one-half times that of West Germany. The role of East German agriculture within its national economy is far more important than that of West Germany's agriculture relative to the West German economy.

Another mark of East Germany's mixed industrial-agricultural character is its population density of 390 persons per square mile. This is two-thirds the population density of West Germany. On the other hand, such a density is higher than that of the other East European countries, where agriculture has still greater prominence.

East German economic integration within the Soviet bloc began in 1949 with the formation of the Council for Mutual Economic Aid. Fully two-thirds of its trade today is with the Soviet bloc (and less than 10 per cent with West Germany). Almost all of the raw materials needed by its industry—such as rolled steel, iron ore, and oil—come from the Soviet Union. Communications, too, have been directed eastward through such devices as linking the television system to that of Poland, Czechoslovakia, and Hungary.

For our generation, at least, it would appear that the geopolitical dualism of the two Germanies has been established. Mackinder's boundary that divided the Heartland from Maritime Europe was given political status shortly after World War Two. Within a quarter of a century ideological and economic forces have given political reality to the distinction between landpower- and seapower-orientation in Central Europe.

The author feels that the current division of Germany is geopolitically sound and strategically necessary. From the standpoint of Eastern Europe and the Soviet Union, the loss of East Germany to a united, Western-oriented Germany would represent a security threat that could not be accepted and doubtless would bring on war. Not only would the U.S.S.R. be exposed once again to the Maritime World, but more important, such a step could only be brought about through the destruction of the unified Eastern European political and economic system, a system that the U.S.S.R. has shown it will maintain at the risk of war. But the other side of the coin is equally important. A unified Germany within the landpower orbit would destroy the economic and strategic being of Maritime Europe, whose current integration is dependent upon West German participation. Certainly the West would go to war to prevent this. What then of the prospects for a united "neutral" Germany? Uneasy would lie the heads of statesmen of both West and East if such a land were to re-emerge. Size, wealth, regained central position, and claims to the "lost provinces" would probably put Germany into the position of playing off both sides. To encourage ideas of a reunited, neutralized Germany would indeed be to play a game of "Russian Roulette" with all-out East-West war as the likely outcome.

Postwar German geopoliticians have not been so naïve as to suggest that a united Germany, by itself, can act as a third power to balance the scales between East and West. They have, instead, emphasized the role that a German-led, united Europe might play as a balancer or stabilizer, to act as a brake on the United States and the Soviet Union.[9] Germany in control of Western Europe, and in a position to throw its weight with either side, would be the logical outcome of the creation of a unified, neutral state.

United, and dominating Western Europe, Germany might be able to hold the balance of power between East and West. Divided, Germany remains an important element within both the Maritime and Continental realms, without the ability to disturb the security of

[9] E. W. Schnitzer, *German Geopolitics Revived: A Survey of Geopolitical Writing in Germany Today*, The Rand Corporation, 1954, pp. 34-37.

either realm. It is through partition that Germany can best separate the Great Powers.

What continues to be particularly disturbing to this viewer is the espousal of German unity as formal United States foreign policy. The Communist World has, during the years of Berlin crises, brought the issue to the forefront. Growing sentiment for Germany's division is to be found within the non-aligned states and the Maritime European World, as well as in the Soviet Union. The United States, by adhering to a policy that is geopolitically unsound, runs the risk of political isolation and strategic "brinkmanship." Granted that our foreign policy decisions should not be made as concessions to Soviet threats, are we prepared to accept a divided Germany, now that a detente over Berlin seems to be at hand? The American record of post-crisis foreign policy soul-searching is a dismal one. We have not wanted to negotiate on the Offshore Chinese Islands during periods of Communist Chinese attacks, and rightfully so. But as the crises have died down, so has our desire to consider the problem of these islands in a cold, dispassionate light. The same holds true for our attitudes towards Berlin and German reunification. In times of crisis we cannot negotiate for fear of giving in to Soviet pressures; in times of quiet we do not feel pressed to negotiate.

To date few clear voices in this country have challenged the German reunification policy of the United States. The fact that the division of Germany is favored by the Soviet Union need not mean that the West must favor unification. On the contrary, to continue to favor unification would be to fall into the gravest strategic trap of the twentieth century. For there will be no peace in Europe, and therefore in the world, unless we recognize the need to establish a clear boundary between Western sea power and Eurasian land power in Europe. Here we speak for the moment of de facto recognition, not de jure, for West Berlin must be kept free, and de jure recognition of East Germany by the United States is likely to make West Berlin more of a pawn in East German-West German politics. A realistic solution would be one by which both the division of Germany and the freedom of West Berlin were recognized and guaranteed by the Great Power blocs, perhaps through the mechanism of NATO and the Warsaw Pact countries.

While the division of Germany has been tacitly accepted both by the Soviet Union and by most Western European countries as being vital to maintenance of the current balance, there is one solution to the problem of a united Germany that might, in the future, be favored by France. If accepted also by Germany and the U.S.S.R., this could presage the destruction of the Western alliance. The Gaullist espousal of a United Europe, from the Atlantic to the Urals, might lead to acceptance of the notion of a United Germany by the U.S.S.R., given a situation in which a Franco-Soviet alliance would counteract possible German dominance. The impact of such a United Europe concept would be to bring about what war and revolution could not—the linking of the Heartland to the European Rimland, under the dominance of the U.S.S.R. With such a possible prize, Soviet foreign policy might well reverse itself and abandon support of East Germany in exchange for a European unity that would include the reunification of Germany. Thus, the Gaullist vision of Europe is one with far-reaching and dangerous consequences to the Western alliance. A stronger Maritime Europe that includes Great Britain within the Common Market is the surest guarantee of a polycentric Maritime World that will balance the Eurasian Continental realm.

Shatterbelts

Two Shatterbelts divide the Trade-Dependent Maritime from the Eurasian Continental geostrategic regions. These are the Middle East and Southeast Asia. A Shatterbelt is here defined as a large, strategically located region that is occupied by a number of conflicting states and is caught between the conflicting interests of adjoining Great Powers.

In his volume *Geography and World Power*, James Fairgrieve called attention to a "Crush Zone" of small states that had gradually come into existence between the Eurasian Heartland and the seapowers (essentially European, such as Britain, France, Portugal, Spain, and Italy, but also Japan). He spoke of these states as "largely survivals from earlier time, when political and economic organizations were on a smaller scale . . . each [with] characteristics partly acquired in that earlier time and partly natural . . . [each] with sufficient individuality to withstand absorptions, but unable or unwilling to unite with others to form any larger whole."[10]

Fairgrieve viewed these states as buffers, "precariously independent politically, and more surely dependent economically." He listed within this "Crush Zone" such states as "Finland, Sweden, Norway,

[10] Fairgrieve, *op. cit.*, p. 329.

Denmark, Holland, Belgium, Luxemburg, Switzerland, Poland, the Balkans, Iran, Afghanistan, Siam, and Korea."[11] He conceded that in a certain sense Germany, China, and even India might be expected to belong to this belt. However, their uniqueness, Fairgrieve recognized, lay in size, resources, and historic relationship to the encircling land and sea worlds. Above all their uniqueness lay in their roles as possible centers from which the Heartland might be organized.

Much has happened to this "Crush Zone" in the military, political, and economic sense since Fairgrieve described it in 1915. In Central and Eastern Europe, the "Crush Zone" has disappeared, replaced by political and economic blocs, clearly allied with the contending geostrategic regions. Buffers like Finland, Austria, and Yugoslavia exist. However, they do not form part of a continuous zone and are in the process of strengthening economic ties with larger, neighboring units.

Reflecting the elimination of the European "Crush Zone" are World War Two-inspired changes in boundary lines, political and economic consolidation of national states, integration of transportation along the North European and Danubian plains, and merging of economic core areas on a broad regional basis.

Mainland China is no longer even a possible part of the "Crush Zone" and Korea lies outside it. For Korea, as we have seen, is too small to provide elbowroom for bufferdom. Its partition serves as the line of contact between the two geostrategic regions. But elsewhere the zone described by Fairgrieve has retained its essential character. Indeed, the post-World War Two attainment of independence by many colonial peoples has tended to strengthen fragmentation in the "Crush Zone."

As we survey politically fragmentized areas of contact between the world's seaward-oriented powers and the Soviet bloc, we find, not a continuous zone, but two distinct belts. These are the Shatterbelts of the Middle East and Southeast Asia. Because they command strategic narrow seas and because of their specialized agricultural and mineral products, the political and economic fate of the Shatterbelts is of vital concern to the Trade-Dependent Maritime World. Because their land avenues project toward important parts of the Eurasian Continental World, their fate is of equal concern to this geostrategic region.

What is peculiar to the Shatterbelt is its fragmented political and

[11] *Ibid.*, p. 330.

economic character. Owing to physical, environmental, historical, cultural, and political differences, the Shatterbelt appears to be incapable of attaining political and/or economic unity of action. Parts of the Shatterbelts tend to seek neutrality and to lead the entire region into this path, but other portions are committed to external ties, either because of their self-interest or because of military and economic pressures from the external power centers.

Since the Second World War, both geostrategic regions have shown that they regard retention or establishment of spheres of influence within the two Shatterbelts to be strategically vital. In various discussions of the possibilities of reducing tensions in the Middle East and Southeast Asia through restriction of armament sales, the Great Powers have not been willing to restrict sale of arms to these regions in their entirety. Each of the Great Powers has allies which it insists upon strengthening.

A locational characteristic of these belts is that they are not caught directly between the United States and Soviet power blocs. The core area of the Eurasian Continental World (the Russian Industrialized Triangle) adjoins the Middle East, while the Maritime World's core (the Maritime Ring of the United States) is removed. The Middle East, then, is subject to the vicinal pressures of the U.S.S.R. and Maritime Europe, with the United States operating partly in tandem through the latter. In Southeast Asia, the powers with direct vicinal stakes are Mainland China and Japan. The United States Pacific ecumene serves as an adjoining, but not "near" neighbor, and the Soviet Union is a locationally-removed participant. The role of Japan as a base and rationale for American activities in Southeast Asia can scarcely be overestimated. Because Shatterbelts are easily accessible to a number of adjoining and even remote geopolitical regions (the latter functionally connected by water), they exhibit many extra-regional cultural and economic features.

Complete control of the Shatterbelts is no longer possible for either side, nor is it theoretically desirable, since this would mean an expenditure of energies in blanket fashion over an area of variable internal significance.

Each Shatterbelt offers footholds to the contending Great Powers. Footholds perform a variety of functions. First, these footholds can serve as bases in "cold" and "hot" war situations, checkmating adjoining areas which might be used as springboards for attack. Second, they maintain the buffer qualities of the Shatterbelt, insuring that one force will not swallow it up. If, for example, the Middle

East were to lose its current Shatterbelt characteristics and fall completely under Moscow domination, the arena of contention would shift directly to Africa, thereby placing Maritime Europe in mortal strategic danger. Third, the maintaining of Maritime World footholds within Shatterbelts clearly indicates, to Communist, neutral, and allied states alike, that we have no intention of withdrawing to positions that are so rigid and crucial as to leave no alternative but to wage nuclear wars. In other words, Shatterbelts offer the elbowroom for various forms of contention that other areas do not. Finally, footholds can better enable Great Powers to encourage genuine neutrals. But, for the Maritime World, these footholds would best be based upon stable alliances with internally popular governments. Otherwise, they become nothing but minority-controlled puppets and a constant source of weakness.

Conclusion

A policy of containment that views the world according to the Heartland-Rimland pattern draws us into grave strategic errors, for all parts of the Eurasian littoral are not of equal strategic significance to the Trade-Dependent Maritime World. Nor does a policy of complete disengagement from overseas areas meet the strategic needs of the United States and its major allies. We should, therefore, in our global approach distinguish between those parts of the world that: 1) warrant Maritime World support at the risk of total war; 2) warrant Maritime World support at the risk of limited wars, and therefore limited objectives; 3) warrant indirect military and diplomatic support; 4) warrant no Maritime World military involvement. The same applies to our economic competition with the Soviet bloc and China. Only if we do this can we form alliances that will carry out the objectives of our strategy, rather than dictate our strategy.

Broadly speaking, the lands that border the Atlantic and those that overlook the open Pacific are the lands that must be rigidly protected. Within the Shatterbelt areas, the Maritime World has the ability to choose its allies—and should not continue to try to involve countries or peoples whose motives are basically anti-Western or whose genuine aim is to achieve a position of neutrality in the world. There is a place in this world for neutrals, particularly in South Asia, Africa, and within the Shatterbelts. But at the same time we regard as critical the need to maintain Maritime World footholds within the Shatterbelts and Africa. In North Africa, in the Middle East, in Africa south of the Sahara, and in Southeast Asia, stable and long-lasting links must be forged with like-minded and interested nations. We cannot regard as suitable partners areas of limited space—such as small offshore islands, weak enclaves surrounded by stronger powers, or countries whose populations are basically opposed to Maritime World alliances.

In certain instances political partitioning along ethnic (or national) lines may be unavoidable if Maritime World links are to be assured. In this vein, racial separation along territorial lines and the setting up of independent White and African national states, rather than the apartheid policy, which seeks communal partition at the expense of the Africans, might offer the most realistic long-range solution in South Africa. Plans to partition Palestine and India were regarded by many as naïve and impractical, but they have been carried out and are, at a minimum, short-term solutions to "insoluble" problems.

Implicit in these observations is the fact that all geographic areas need not and should not be treated as strategic "wholes." In this respect, it is unsound to issue blanket invitations to countries of certain areas to enter defense pacts, or to ally ourselves with governments that are totally divorced from their people, when there is the possibility of our becoming committed to countries whose defense is not strategically vital to Maritime World survival. This, above all, is the lesson to be learned from Vietnam.

These views are some of the results that we have obtained from relating our knowledge of geography to strategy. Since geography, in its broadest sense, is constantly changing, and since movement mirrors these changes, we dare not rely upon concepts of the past, but must be continuously on the alert to examine the changing geographic scene, and to interpret the impact of this change in the formulation of strategy. This is the approach through which we can genuinely understand geography's influences upon strategy—an influence that we may try to ignore, but one that will not ignore us.

Part Two

POWER CORES IN
A WORLD DIVIDED

4 THE UNITED STATES

Change and Interdependence

This study of the world's geostrategic regions and their geopolitical subdivisions will focus upon the cores of the four major geopolitical regions: Anglo-America and the Caribbean; Maritime Europe and the Maghreb; the U.S.S.R. and Eastern Europe; and Mainland China.

The first of the divided world's power cores to be discussed is the United States. This selection was not made on the premise that a volume written by an American author for an essentially American audience should begin with the home front. It was based, instead, on the fact that the United States occupies the primary and central position within the Trade-Dependent Maritime geostrategic region. Further, the United States is the world's leading power, when the combination of economic and military strength within a unified central political framework is considered. Finally, much of what is happening within the Soviet Union, China, and Maritime Europe is based upon attempts to copy or to improve upon the American power position, and can therefore be better understood if the American geopolitical scene is first examined.

How we Americans occupy our landscape has much to do with the geopolitical role that we project for our country in world affairs. Three different orientations have characterized the changing landscape of the United States: 1) the Maritime, 2) the Continental, and 3) the Continental-Maritime. We have now entered the fourth stage—the Maritime-Continental.

The Maritime pattern prevailed from colonial times to the War of 1812. Whether acting in concert with or in isolation from Europe, we regarded ourselves as an Atlantic-seaboard people, deriving our sustenance from and, exposed to the political fortunes of, an Atlantic coastal location.

From 1812 to the Spanish-American War we were continentally oriented. The Louisiana Purchase heralded the beginning of this era, and the results of the War of 1812 assured our Atlantic, Gulf, and Great Lakes frontiers. A few years after the war, the Red River of the North was ceded by Britain, and Florida by Spain, to complete our ownership of the coast up to Texas. For nearly a century we concerned ourselves with continental expansion and political consolidation. By 1893 Frederick Jackson Turner was able to call attention to the passing of the American frontier. Statehood had been granted to the northwest and, on the continent, only Utah, Oklahoma, New Mexico, and Arizona remained to be admitted to the Union.

Outbreak of the war with Spain in 1898 heralded the era of involvement in both the Caribbean and the Pacific, and the beginning of the Continental-Maritime period. Hawaii, Guam, the Philippines, and Puerto Rico were annexed, and extensive political and military commitments were made elsewhere in Pacific and Caribbean waters. But the intensive development of the interior continued. These were some of the internal developments that occurred between 1900 and 1920: 50,000 miles of railroad trackage were constructed; 14,500,000 immigrants were admitted to the country; total population growth was 30 million; the majority of our national parks were established; farm acreage was expanded by nearly 100 million acres; and manufacturing increased substantially in the Middle West and the Pacific Coast, partly at the expense of the Northeast. Because of factors such as these, the Continental was dominant over the Maritime orientation. The period between the two World Wars was transitional. Its end marked the beginning of our present era—the Maritime-Continental. The geopolitical consequences of this shift in orientation have fundamentally affected our lives and those of generations to come. Our perspective of the Maritime period is one in which the colonies were part of the exploitable world. During the Continental period, the perspective was strongly Western Hemispheric, as the nation reached out for self-sufficiency. The Continental-Maritime period was one of search for overseas markets to add to the benefits of self-sufficiency. Its perspective was a modified global one, the "Manifest Destiny" concept inspiring the linking of the Caribbean and Pacific Ocean basins to the continent. Still in this period, World War One heralded the "rediscovery" of Europe.

Our present Maritime-Continental period is one of the abandonment of the concept of self-sufficiency, replaced by one of super-abundance based upon tapping the resources of the entire world. While Atlantic partnership remains the focus of this global view, controls in the Pacific, substitution for the European presence in the Middle East, and to a lesser extent Africa, and "rediscovery" of Latin America have characterized these views. The four periods may also be described in communications technology terms as the development shifted from schooners to clipper ships, to the Great White Fleet and the Pan-American Clipper piston airplane, and then to jet aircraft.

When we view the map of the United States today, we see, in effect, a Maritime Outer Ring and a Continental Inner Ring. The Maritime Ring faces the open water. Our ports and their dependent industries, our heavily urbanized population, our overseas political and trade involvements radiate outward from the Maritime Ring. The Continental Inner Ring, with a smaller population but with a surplus of material resources, helps both to support the Maritime Ring and to interconnect it via land lanes. Continental expansion is far from over. Growth is particularly rapid in the western parts of the Continental Interior, in contrast to the declining population of its central parts. However, the focus of human occupance in the United States lies within the Maritime Ring.

The United States in Its World Setting

The geographical setting of a state and its global outlook are interrelated. As settings change, so must these outlooks. When Arnold Guyot took a geographer's look at continental United States in 1849,[1] he regarded it as one of the three northern continental cores destined to control the world. Europe and Asia were considered as partners with North America in Guyot's three double-continent global view. Of the three cores, he felt that the United States would take the leading role because of two basic advantages over the others: 1) centrality within the northern hemispheric setting, behind a screen of ocean which possessed both isolating and interacting qualities, and 2) size and interconnectibility of the well-watered interior that was the challenge and the fulfillment of the United States.

Alfred Mahan had a different view of the geographical setting of the United States. He espoused a Maritime-Continental view, within

[1] Guyot, *op. cit.*

a twofold global framework: the Western and the Oriental halves. To Mahan, the United States was an outpost of European power and civilization. Its Pacific shorelands and islands were simply extensions of the Atlantic-oriented European realm.

Half a century later, Nicholas Spykman saw the United States in still a different setting. He divided the world into two:[2] 1) the Eurasian Rimland, and 2) the combination of Eurasian Heartland and Continental Islands. The latter, essentially, represented the circum-North Polar lands of Anglo-America, Britain, and the Soviet Union. Within this framework a Maritime United States held a central location, with sea lanes to Britain and air-sea lanes to the U.S.S.R. While bordering the Eurasian Rimland from the circum-polar northern position, the Heartland-Continental Island group also surrounded the Rimland from positions along the southern continents. From such a view, Spykman concluded that the United States should maintain Trans-Atlantic and Trans-Pacific bases within striking distance of Eurasia to control the balance of power along the Rimlands. This would have to be done in partnership with the Soviet Union and Britain, not in competition with them.

As opposed to Spykman's doctrines, Continentalist views during and after the Second World War presented a totally different case. James Malin, for example, took a "quarterspheric" approach to the world. He felt that the United States was a landmass state that should not extend its commitments across the Pacific and the Atlantic, or south of the Amazon.[3] He felt that there would be room in the postwar world for seven or more major powers (North America, Japan, China, Russia, Germany, Latin Europe, and the British Empire). Malin derived much of his inspiration from his studies of the American frontier and from his readings of de Seversky. His view was an amalgam of Continentalism, Northern Hemispheric supremacy, and circum-North Polarism.

Following the war, George Cressey suggested that North America had become the real Heartland of the world. Cressey redefined Mackinder's Heartland as a "World Citadel." He suggested that North America, not Eurasia, contained this citadel because the core of North America was the one area in the world that possessed all the advantages of interior space, size and resources, and access to the sea.[4]

[2] Spykman, *op. cit.*, pp. 51-61.

[3] James Malin, "Space and History," Part 2, *Agricultural History*, 18 (July 1944), pp. 107-26.

[4] George Cressey, *The Basis of Soviet Strength* (New York: McGraw-Hill, 1945), pp. 245-46.

Lest Cressey be regarded as a pure Continentalist, we should add that in other writings he presents the Continental-Maritime view. He links the United States to the Atlantic, suggesting that our Trans-Pacific commitments be limited to the Northeast Pacific,[5] and states that "the permanent assets of the Atlantic powers should always exceed the limitations of continental Eurasia."[6] Earlier American geographers like Semple held similar views: "The preëminence which the Atlantic has gained will long dominate the Pacific, and geographical conditions make it doubtful whether this supremacy will pass to the larger basin."[7]

Our view of the Maritime-Continental setting of the United States does not draw any geopolitical doctrinal conclusions from the fact that the center of gravity of the country's maritime orientation faces the Atlantic. However, we must look to all of the elements that unify a state if we are to project that state's world geopolitical position. The Pacific coastlands of the United States are today fast-growing, mature components of the Union. The conferring of statehood upon Alaska and Hawaii is an act whose geopolitical consequences must not be underestimated. The United States is now a Pacific power, no less than an Atlantic power. Alaska not only neighbors Siberia; its borders are a short 1,400 miles from Hokkaido. To talk of dividing the Pacific down its middle (the 180th meridian) as the westward boundary of American power[8] makes no sense politically or strategically today. The Northwest Pacific is as important to Alaska as is the Caribbean to Florida. Events in either sea affect the security of the United States as a whole.

As we picture the Maritime United States then, it is as an Outer Ring which surrounds and dominates the Continental Interior. (See Map 10.) Specialization increases the complementary nature of the various portions of the Maritime Ring. It is this Ring that gives to the United States both a central and an interconnecting position in relation to the rest of the Trade-Dependent Maritime World. This geostrategic region, as outlined in Chapter 3, includes two-thirds of the earth's water and land surface and one-third of its population.

[5] George Cressey, *Asia's Lands and Peoples* (New York: McGraw-Hill, 1951, rev. ed.), p. 17.

[6] George Cressey, *How Strong Is Russia?* (Syracuse: Syracuse University Press, 1954), p. 133.

[7] E. Semple and C. Jones, *American History and Its Geographic Conditions* (Boston: Houghton, Mifflin, 1933), p. 422.

[8] Cressey, *Asia's Lands and Peoples*, p. 17.

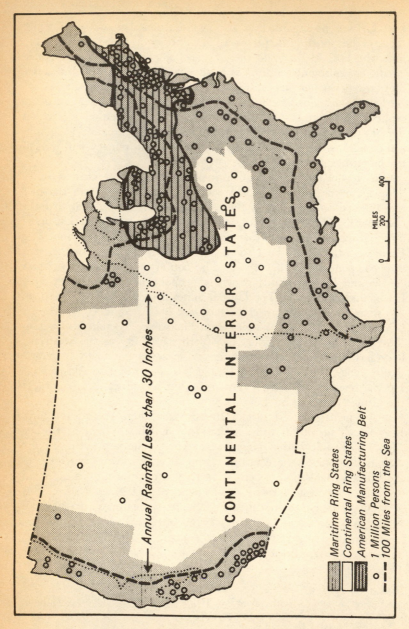

Annual Rainfall Less than 30 Inches

CONTINENTAL INTERIOR STATES

MILES
0   200   400

Maritime Ring States
Continental Ring States
American Manufacturing Belt
○ 1 Million Persons
100 Miles from the Sea

MAP 10. The Maritime Ring of the United States

The center of the region's surface area lies midway between the Hawaiian Islands and California. The center of its population (and land) area lies along the southeastern tip of the United States. Clearly, if any one part of the Maritime United States is at the center of the population and land area of the Trade-Dependent Maritime Region it is the Gulf-Atlantic coast. But without the unity of the Maritime United States, including its Pacific borderlands, the concept of American centrality within its broader geostrategic setting would become meaningless.

The Maritime Ring

America's experience with the development of the West set geographers to speculating on the relationship between Continentality and Seapower. Ratzel saw the two elements as complementary. To him and to his disciple Semple the conquest of the interior was made possible by the unifying qualities of the Mississippi drainage system, which had oceanic outlets. The vast North American Continental Interior could be viewed, not in land-oriented isolation, but in a maritime-connected framework. During this period, however, others tended to draw distinctions between the "closed space" of the coastlands and the "open space" of the expanding Continental Interior. When Turner called attention to the passing of the frontier, he wrote of the beginning of the era of "closed space" for the country as a whole. In a "closed space" era, new uses of and adjustments to the land would be necessary, both economically and politically. Malin, however, dissented, asserting that the "closed space" doctrine was related to the continental agricultural realm of the nineteenth-century United States, with little relevance to the urban industrial scene of this century.[9] He then proceeded to suggest that the Continental Interior holds the same wealth of raw materials for industry today that it held for agriculture in the past. In Malin's analysis, the "open space" of the interior can still be the dominant factor in American life. He drew the picture of a central power axis running north-south from Winnipeg to Dallas-Fort Worth, with "power potential distributed along the length of the axis with the effective center shifting to fit changing requirements."[10] Writing in 1944, Malin predicted that industry would migrate into the interior and that pop-

[9] James Malin, "Mobility and History," *Agricultural History*, 17 (October 1943), p. 117.

[10] James Malin, "Space and History," Part 2, *op. cit.*, p. 110.

ulation distribution would accompany the shift. In this scheme, population would move towards the supply of food and towards light-weight metals, alloys, plastics, and hydro-power, to find in the interior its most logical locational setting. Also, greater north-south mobility than now exists would be provided along the central axis by major air commercial centers.

Such a view of the interior is a synthesis of Continentalist-Isolation and Air Age views. Malin is not the only one to project a great future for the Great Plain states as the center of an industrialized continental interior. De Seversky placed his center of United States power in Kansas.

Events of the past two decades, however, belie the claims of the prophets of continental supremacy. Those states that lie along the central axis of the interior remain lightly populated and only moderately industrialized. The rate of growth for all states of the Continental Interior, 9 per cent for the past decade, has been below that of the entire country (13 per cent). Where there have been absolute losses in state populations, these have occurred in the Continental Interior. An indication of the political weakening of this Mississippi-Rockies Continental Interior is its 1960 loss of seven seats in the House of Representatives. The taking-over of the Continental Interior by large-scale, mechanized farming has been accompanied by a drop in rural population, for which population loss manufacturing has not compensated. Further Congressional losses in the Continental Interior took place as a result of the 1970 census, with Congressional gains accruing to the Maritime West and South. Of the eleven seats changed, California is the gainer of five, Florida of three, and Texas one. The Continental Interior was a net loser of two seats.

The unlocking of the mineral riches of the Continental Interior, the intensification of its agriculture, the populating of the great cities —in other words, the inward-turning of America—has not come to pass. Instead the coal of the Great Plains remains locked beneath the black earth, agriculture has become mechanized and increasingly extensive, market villages and towns have lost their traditional functions, and manufacturing cities have not grown as rapidly as their Maritime Ring counterparts. The cost and difficulty of developing broad manufacturing bases from which to urbanize the Continental Interior is proving substantially greater than is the case within the Maritime Ring, and the dreams of the Continental supremacists are far from realization. This is not to downgrade the major importance of the Interior's land base for agriculture—an agriculture whose productive capacities are of global significance and which may in the decades to come prove the single most important export factor in achieving a trade balance for the country.

To debate whether our Continental Interior is "open" or "closed" space today seems fruitless, for these terms are no longer expressions of what is meaningful in our land use patterns. Instead, the concept of the changing use of space must be substituted. Change is occurring in areas where land is in surplus as well as scarce, for change is as evident in the rural Continental Interior as it is in the urbanized Maritime Ring. Change in the use of space results from new uses of local resources or from the movement factor that allows distant resources to be brought to the scene.

In the Continental Interior, millions of acres may be involved in change. An example is the 25 million acres of grasslands that were converted to crop acreage in the 1920's and 1930's, or the similar amount of land that was recently taken out of production to be put into the conservation reserve soil bank. In urban areas change may involve only a handful of acres, but the impact upon society, economically and socially, is profound. When, for example, the Delaware-Lower Schuylkill became developed as the newest and second largest oil refining area of our country, only about 15,000 acres of land were involved. But the Delaware Oil Refinery District represents an investment of over $1 billion, and gives direct employment to 20,000 workers and indirect employment to twice that number in associated chemical industries. A far smaller tract of land, 80 acres, was involved when a regional planned shopping center was constructed in Metropolitan Boston. However, this center has one-fifth of the total retail space of the Boston central business district; its appearance on the scene has drastically changed suburban shopping and residential patterns. In Baltimore, architects and planners who are working toward the revitalization of a great city have fixed their attention on a mere 22-acre plot, a civic and office center of sufficient size and scope to change the form of the central business district by its presence and influence. Downtown Boston has been completely changed, architecturally, economically, and psychologically, by two projects that occupy only a handful of acres—Government Center and the Prudential complex. In perceptual terms, downtowns and areas adjoining them seem to be drawn closer as spot clearance, tall buildings, and clear fields of vision shrink distance and unite areas. Clearly, then, the considerations of vast space versus limited space are secondary when it comes to change in a modern society.

Since the Second World War, change in space has been most marked along our Maritime Ring, not within the Continental Interior. This Ring might well be described as the *United States of the Four Seas*—the Great Lakes, the Atlantic, the Gulf, and the Pacific. These coastlands vary in many ways: climate, elevation, landforms, natural vegetation, agriculture, and minerals. But they are unified in more important features: dense populations, high degrees of urbanization, large numbers of usable ports, and strong concentrations of manufacturing. Among the important physical elements of unity are humidity, natural harbors, and the barrier effects of the Appalachians and the Western ranges. Average annual rainfall for the Maritime Ring is over 30 inches (save in southeast Texas and along the southwest California coast). In most instances the rainfall is over 40 inches. Such precipitation is adequate for the water needs of both urban centers and productive agricultural hinterlands. The best natural harbors occur along the highland-framed Northeast and Pacific coasts, and where the Coastal Plain's Interior Lowland (the low-lying, eroded portions of the inner coastal plain) has been joined to the ocean through submergence—from Buzzards Bay to the James River. The South Atlantic, Gulf Coast, and Great Lakes have poorer natural harbors, which have required dredging, and, in many cases, upstream locations. Nonetheless, as we consider the Ring in its entirety we find that no single maritime state except perhaps Mississippi lacks a good deep-water port, be it natural or artificial.

While the mountains have not served as complete barriers between the sea and the interior, they have directed the alignment of land transportation lines along specific avenues. The Southeast Atlantic coast has poor overland connections with the Midwest. This has, in turn, given stronger impetus to north-south movement along the Atlantic Seaboard. Where the Great Lakes and the Atlantic come closest together (the New York, New England, Pennsylvania, and Maryland corridors), east-west land links are best. Because of the north-south trend of the West's mountain-desert-plateau reaches, land links between the Gulf and the Pacific Northwest coasts have been weak.

Complementary resources and products also help to unify the Maritime Ring. Petroleum, coal, forest products, sulphur, cotton, phosphates, iron and steel products, and canned fruits and vegetables are the sort of materials that are interchanged.

Some of the larger cities and population concentrations that are oriented to the Maritime Ring are as much as from 150 to 250 miles from the sea (the Inner Lowland cities of Texas and the "central place cities" of the farm belt of the Great Lakes states). The majority of the population, however, lives within three hours' automobile drive of open water. Indeed, the 100-mile contour from the coast includes 60 per cent of the entire population of the United States.

On Map 10 we have noted the states that are within the Maritime Ring. They total 30 of the 50 states, but include 80 per cent of the population. The ten states to achieve the largest absolute population growth within the last two decades were maritime states. Nine of the country's ten largest metropolitan areas and 29 of the 50 largest metropolitan areas are Maritime Ring ports. In percentage of urbanized population and manufacturing output, the Maritime Ring accounts for even more than its total share with over 90 per cent of the population and 88 per cent of the value added by manufacturing.

This same measure of preponderance does not quite hold true for agriculture and mining, where the Maritime Ring accounts for 64 per cent and 73 per cent, respectively, of our total national output. If the Maritime Ring were to balance its agricultural and mining outputs with its population, it would have to produce an additional $6.3 billion worth of agricultural products (over current output of $22.7 billion) and $2.2 billion worth of minerals (over current production of $17.5 billion). These figures emphasize the importance of the Continental Interior as the support base for the Maritime Ring. On the other hand, the fact that we import $5.3 billion worth of agricultural products and over $2.8 billion worth of minerals suggests that the role of international trade as a supporter of the Maritime Ring is substantial, if not actually comparable with that of the Continental Interior.

The earmark of the Maritime Ring is intensive movement of goods by sea. This movement is threefold: local, intercoastal, and foreign. Ship movements to and within the Ring account for about 40 per cent of all United States goods movement in ton-mileage, and for about 30 per cent in tonnage.

Trade among the states of the Maritime Ring is considerably heavier than trade between these states and the Continental Interior. This fact was first illustrated by data mapped by Ullman in his *American Commodity Flow*.[11] Analysis of selected maps dealing with rail commodity flows for three states (Connecticut, Washing-

[11] Edward Ullman, *American Commodity Flow* (Seattle: University of Washington Press, 1957).

ton, and Iowa) indicated that the two maritime states, Connecticut and Washington, did their overland rail trading overwhelmingly (96 per cent and 72 per cent, respectively) with other states of the Maritime Ring. Even Iowa, a part of the Continental Interior, did 67 per cent of its trade with the Ring.[12] Thus, the complementary nature of the highly specialized portions of the American Seaboard is a stronger inducement for land trade than the lower transport costs to the interior.

National political power in the United States resides within the Maritime Ring. In the 1960 presidential elections, the Democratic Party prevailed by winning 18 of the 30 Maritime states, even though it won in only 5 of the 20 Continental states. The gubernatorial elections revealed the same incidence of Democratic Party mastery within the Maritime Ring: 10 of 14 Maritime state contests were won by Democrats, but only 5 of 13 in the Continental states. In 1968, the Democrats lost the Maritime Ring, the victory of the Republican party in the presidential elections being assured when 13 of the Maritime Ring states shifted to the Republican camp, and 4 states were won by the States Rights party. In the same year, there were gubernatorial elections in 12 Maritime Ring states, 8 of which were won by Republicans, giving Republicans a substantial majority of state governments.

Political power; economic strength; urbanization; dense and well-integrated land, sea, and air links; foreign-trade contacts—these are all characteristics of the Maritime Ring. The Seaboard is the American frontier; it is the frontier of change and of diversity. The emptying out of the rural countryside, the decline of the central city, and the patterns of suburbanization are changing the face of the Maritime Ring. Human diversity, the feature of most borderlands because of their proximity to other areas, is also a feature of the Maritime Ring. The French-Canadian of the Northeast, the Puerto Rican of New York, the Latin American of Florida, the Cajun of Louisiana, the Mexican-American of the Southwest and California, the Black of the Great Lakes, the Atlantic, and the Gulf, and the Japanese- and Chinese-Americans of the Pacific, give to the Maritime Ring a highly diverse racial and ethnic flavor. To this may be added the diversities of religion that characterize the region. Of 14 states with estimated Catholic populations of over 20 per cent, only one—Montana—is non-

[12] The commodities that were analyzed were agriculture, manufacturing, and minerals (exclusive of petroleum).

Maritime. These diversities, with their attendant contrasts in standard of living, educational level, and socio-political outlook, form America's cultural pluralism of the mid-twentieth century. Since change is the most striking characteristic of a frontier, and since the Maritime Ring is the most significant area of change, then surely the "New Frontier" of the United States is the Maritime Ring. Here is the arena where our greatest challenges and fulfillments lie.

Geographical Regions

While we have divided the United States in two realms—the Maritime and the Continental—these realms are so vast that they need, in turn, to be subdivided into geographical regions. Ours is a country composed of smaller "countries" that differ from one another physiographically, climatically, agriculturally, culturally, and in degree of self-containment. These smaller "countries" and their differences can be described through the process of regionalism.

Often we equate geographic regions with the apparently rigid framework that characterizes the physical landscape. In fact, however, the geographic regions of the United States constantly change in their character and extent, because the geographic region is a combination of various physical, biotic, and cultural regions. As these latter change in relation to one another, the geographic region—which is something more than a simple sum total of a number of single-feature physical and cultural regions—also changes.

We can go back to Colonial times to find examples of regional change. In the early Colonial period, there were three geographical regions in the East: the Southern, Middle, and Northeastern. But while Maryland was regarded as a Middle Colony at the beginning of this era, it had become part of the Southern region by the end of Colonial times. This was because tobacco and slave culture gained a firm position, while manufacturing failed to entrench itself. The physical environment had not altered, but man's emphasis in the use of the environment had.

At the end of the nineteenth century, there was a radically different regional map. (See Map 11.) The Middle and Northeastern regions had merged. The Middle West—which had had such close ties to the Northeast during and before the Civil War—was now quite distinct; the old links of history, settlement, and land-use patterns that had tied the interior plains to northern New York and New England had lost much of their meaning. Perhaps the most impor-

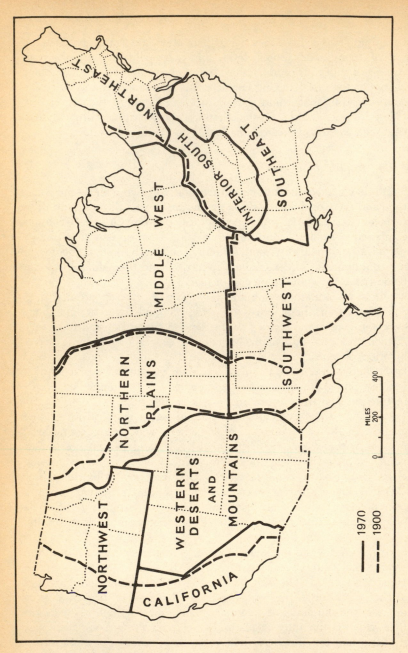

NORTHEAST

INTERIOR SOUTH

SOUTHEAST

MIDDLE WEST

NORTHERN PLAINS

SOUTHWEST

NORTHWEST

WESTERN DESERTS AND MOUNTAINS

CALIFORNIA

MILES
0   200   400

—— 1970
–– 1900

MAP 11. Changing Geographical Regions of the United States

tant conflicting set of interests among all of these regions stemmed from the dryness and land policies of the West as compared to the humidity and manufacturing interests of the East. The geographic regions of 1900 were closely framed by either landform or climatic features. But they were also framed by the limited use of the land. Thus, the Pacific coast was regarded as one region because man had not yet begun to develop his diversified activities to the point where the differences between the Northwest and the Southwest coasts had become geographically meaningful.

Today's regional map is the product of several factors, the more important of which are the physical environment, population growth, urbanization, agricultural shifts, and dispersal of manufacturing. The Northeast is the land of commerce, manufacturing, and recreation; the Southeast, of specialized agriculture, lumbering, and light industry; the Interior South, of specialized crops and manufacturing; the Southwest, of chemicals, light metals, and grazing. Many of these are activities that date back only two or three decades. The Middle West, while continuing to show strength in commercial agriculture, is increasing its manufacturing and commerce. But even agriculture is changing. Sorghum and soybeans are now as important as corn, and "Corn Belt" is a misnomer.

The Northern Plains, the lands of wheat and cattle, are still sparsely settled and have yet to solve their water deficit problems. But some of the commercial cities have become manufacturers also, as in farm implements and aircraft production. The Western Deserts and Mountains, traditionally a region of mineral production, are making extremely important advances in irrigated agriculture—fruits, vegetables, and cotton. In the Far West, the distinction between the Pacific North West and the California regions has become more marked, with lumbering, manufacturing, fishing, and interior dry farming in the north, and manufacturing, horticulture, and recreation in California.

An example of how regional change is brought about can be drawn from a study of cotton. The old cotton belt, from the Atlantic through Texas, with the Mississippi Valley as the center of gravity, has disappeared. Today nearly two-thirds of all cotton is being grown from the East Texas borders to California, and Texas and California are the two leading states in value of production. As cotton has declined in the South, the South has lost its common denominator and has become divided into three distinct regions: the Southeast, the Southwest, and the Interior South. The Mississippi, formerly the focal point for the South as a whole, is becoming a contact zone between Southeast, Southwest, and Middle West (as it was prior to the Civil War). In this valley, general agriculture and manufacturing are replacing cotton. South of Memphis, for example, depleted loessal soils are being scraped down and seeded with grass to sustain a new livestock industry. The Polled Hereford and the Black Angus are moving down from their cool Midwestern habitat to take up an "air-conditioned" life in the South (including ventilated barns and summer night grazings). Meanwhile, lacking the jobs formerly supplied by cotton, Blacks moved northward—to St. Louis, the Ohio River Valley, the Great Lakes area, the Northeast, and the West. Clearly, the migration of Blacks away from the South depends upon intra- as well as extra-regional factors. Industrialization of the South and breaking down of employment and social barriers in the cities have begun to influence recent Black migration toward Southern cities. While during the 1960-70 intercensal years, extraregional flows continued to the point where 47 per cent of the Black population is now outside of the South, it may be that the current regional distribution pattern of Blacks has reached a point of stability, with growth in the North to be anticipated mainly from internal growth, and in the South from rural to urban migration. Certainly, the economic growth of the South, now the nation's fastest growing region, will affect the migration patterns of the Black American, accelerating rural depopulation. Shorter distances and greater ease of diffusion can be expected to attract migrants more strongly in the future than has been the case to date.

Another element that has reshaped the South has been Drainage Basin development activities in the valley of the Tennessee. A third has been the growth of mining and manufacturing along the Gulf Coast. All of this has contributed to create three geographical regions where formerly there was one. The change in California is equally marked. Whereas in the past the region was limited to the California Mediterranean, today's region embraces desert and range areas as well. This is because recreation and manufacturing have developed as arid-land outliers of the southern California population and economic core.

What regional changes may we anticipate in the next half-century? The Northeast and the Great Lakes regions will probably come to be considered one region. Factors contributing to this will be the development of larger ocean ports along the St. Lawrence Seaway and filling in with population of empty or rural areas in New York State and Pennsylvania.

The Ohio, Tennessee, Mississippi, and Missouri basins may emerge in a single mixed agricultural and manufacturing region, embracing the present Northern Plains, western Middle West, and Interior South regions. This would, in effect, make a regional unit of the more populous half of the Continental Interior.

The improvement of highways, waterways, and air routes should cut down the current advantages that our long-haul East-West railroad system possesses and give more of a North-South axial characteristic to our interior. The Southwest and the Southeast we foresee as mature, distinct regions, with increased contacts with the rest of the Maritime Ring. The Western Deserts and Mountains Province will become more important as a support base for California. But distance and barriers to the West, as well as population orientation and accessibility to the Continental Interior, should allow this region to maintain separate identity. As Alaska matures, it will become more firmly embraced within the regional confines of the older Pacific Northwest.

Population Distribution

Several Western nations have experienced psychological shocks, and fear the loss of national dynamism with the slowdown of their population growth. Such a condition now appears to be facing the United States. The near-cessation of immigration and the decline in family size during the 1930's and early 1940's pointed to population decline as an element of American life. Post-World War Two demographic history shows an unexpected reverse of the declining population growth curve. Greater prosperity, better housing, improved transportation, social attitudes toward larger families, health and educational benefits, earlier family formations—all accounted for our population increase. For 1950 to 1960, the increase was 18.5 per cent—the highest increase for a decade since 1900-1910 (which was 21 per cent). This decreased to 13.3 per cent in 1960-70. The slowdown of population growth has resumed once again, fed by socio-economic conditions and by ideological forces favoring planned parenthood and zero population growth. All this reflects a basic national trend and concern to balance the population with the land base and other resources. Because the population and economic growth model has been widely challenged as a philosophical model for national well-being, Americans are increasingly willing to accept population stabilization as a desirable goal. Many do not see in such stabilization an accompanying decline in national vigor and dynamism, but rather view stabilization as an opportunity to experience greater satisfaction through harmony with nature.

To the geographer, major questions are: Where is this population distributed, and What are the trends in changes in distribution? First, the Northeast and North Central regions (as defined by the United States Bureau of the Census) are losing their overwhelming dominance as population regions. In 1930, they accounted for 64 per cent of the total population; in 1960, they accounted for only 54 per cent; and in 1970 only 51 per cent. The South and the West not only experienced far greater rates of population increase over the past ten years; they had greater absolute growth (13.5 million, against 8 million). By 1985, at current growth rates, the South and the West are likely to be more populous than the North Central and the Northeast regions.

TABLE 4

United States Population Density by Rings

	Sq. Miles Area (exc. Alaska)	1970 Pop. Density/ Sq. Mi.	1960 Pop. Density/ Sq. Mi.	1950 Pop. Density/ Sq. Mi.
Maritime Ring	1,492,000	113	100	76
Continental Interior	1,536,000	22	21	19
U.S.A. Total	3,028,000	66	59	50

Recasting these national population growth figures, in our broader division, we find that the Maritime Ring grew by 28 million, or 16 per cent during the past decade, while the Continental Interior grew by only 2.6 million, or 9 per cent. Population is spreading over the national map. This would seem, in a small measure, to be reducing our vulnerability to nuclear attack. However, two forces serve to concentrate this population spread: the Maritime Ring and urbanization. Actually, they are interlocking forces, for the Maritime Ring intensifies urbanized-industrial developments. Population density in the Maritime Ring has increased to the point of being 4.5 times that of the Continental Interior. Within the Maritime Ring, urban, and particularly metropolitan, populace dominates. Seventy-five per cent of the ring is urban, and two-thirds is metropolitan. Most of the population growth of the United States (85 per cent) occurs in Standard Metropolitan Statistical Areas (SMSA)—that is, in cities of 50,000 or more and the areas surrounding them; of this metropolitan growth about 85 per cent takes place within the Maritime Ring.

What is of strategic importance is the measure of concentration of our metropolitan population within a few metropolitan areas. First, over 60 million people live in only 15 metropolitan areas (each of which has a population of 1.5 million or more). This is about 45 per cent of the total metropolitan population of 130 million. Second, central cities within the metropolitan areas account for 58 million people, or less than half the total metropolitan populace. These cities are densely populated, many of the houses are old, and streets are narrow. Plans for successful evacuations of such areas in event of war are highly illusory; indeed, civil defense for those cities is no longer a viable policy in a nuclear age. By far the greatest concentration of our big central cities is in the North Atlantic-Great Lakes districts. Of 60 central cities of 200,000 population and over, 27 are in this region. The two other major clusters of central cities occur in the California and the Texas-Gulf areas, each with seven central cities.

Finally, let us consider population concentration within the American Manufacturing Belt. This belt of 400,000 square miles, which extends as a modified rectangle from the Eastern Seaboard to Milwaukee to St. Louis, contains two-thirds of our manufacturing output (and one-third of Canada's). Here are 61 central cities with populations of 100,000 and over, totalling over 30 million people. Moreover, 53 of the 100 largest SMSA's, with combined populations of 75 million, are located within the belt. Population density for the American Manufacturing belt is 225 persons per square mile. By contrast, the Soviet Manufacturing Belt is two and one-half times the size of ours, and contains within it 148 cities with populations of 100,000 and over. Their combined population is about 70 million. Evenly spread over the Soviet belt are another 100 million rural folk. Population density for the Soviet Manufacturing belt is therefore somewhat less than ours, with 170 persons per square mile. And when we consider that we have as many people in urban areas of 100,000 and over in one-third as many cities, and in two-fifths as big an area, the greater dispersal of the Soviet population becomes readily apparent.

Suburbanization

Were the urban populace of the United States to continue to concentrate in central cities, the social and strategic outlook would indeed be bleak with respect to the stress and vulnerability that come from over-concentration of people, manufacturing, and distribution facilities. However, suburbanization is the major feature of our modern urban life; and suburbanization means population dispersal. By 1960, 47 per cent of the total metropolitan population was suburban, the great majority living in small, scattered towns, villages, and subdivisions, rather than in suburban cities of 50,000 and over. The 1960 suburban population represented almost a 50 per cent increase over the 1950 population and a rate of growth that was five times that of our large central cities. By 1970, suburban population well exceeded central city population.

With our suburbs accounting for three-quarters of the country's entire population increase, the effects upon the landscape have become marked. Dispersal is the essential feature of America's population distribution pattern. Attendant upon this dispersal is the multiple-core character of such aspects of urban life as manufacturing, retailing, transportation, and government. There are those who criticize suburbanization as being wasteful of land, materials, transportation, and human energies. They advocate, as an alternative, the renewal of the central city. But renewal can no longer be seriously posed as the alternative to suburbanization. Renewal can only preserve part of the functions that have been left to the central city in the wake of the unprecedented suburbanization movement. Rather than bemoan suburbanization because of its imperfections, it is time to maximize its potential. If our country can find the financial and administrative resources to initiate vast central city renewal programs, then we can certainly allocate part of those resources to guide suburban growth.

Where suburban dispersal is carried out within limited forms of self-containment, we make the most efficient use of our space and of the transportation channels that link this space. In this context, the roles of industrial parks and planned shopping centers assumes crucial importance, insofar as they, along with highways and residences, mold the shape of our urban areas. Up to now, American cities have been star-shaped, with major arteries radiating from the single central core. The urbanized area of today is assuming a multiple-core form. The cores are set within a form that resembles a series of concentric wheels, connected by spokes. These cores are located at strategic intersections of the wheels and spokes. The rims of the wheels are the highway belt systems, many of which are part of our national Interstate Highway program. The spokes are the older radial arteries, developed initially as railroad and streetcar lines. Duplicatory public transport facilities along these radial arteries are gradually being eliminated, to be replaced, probably, by rapid transit lines.

This new pattern of urban areas is molding and being molded by the location of industrial parks and planned shopping centers. Seeking cheaper land, parking space, and intersecting circumferential-radial highway routes, such centers have stimulated residential building and feeder highways in their vicinities. If the highway is the pioneer of development, then its intersections dominate the location strategy of that development.

Suburban industrial park and shopping center growth has taken place most rapidly in the Middle West, Southwest, and California. Where flat terrain is encountered, as along the Great Lakes outwash plain or the Texas prairies, suburbs tend to adjoin one another. The fact that relatively few unplanned secondary business and industrial districts exist in these areas, as compared to the Northeast, is due to the ease of public and private transit connections to the downtown area in the 1920's and 1930's that concentrated retailing and manufacturing there. Now, with the great surge of suburban growth, new industrial and shopping centers find that they can tap virgin territory because of lack of competition. In the Northeast, on the other hand, older outlying towns still represent formidable competition to various new planned enterprises.

If dispersal is in keeping with desires for rural environment and with national security needs, the location of new population centers on the periphery of urbanized areas is desirable. On the other hand, transportation costs and the convenience of labor force or of customers frequently dictates that these centers be located on the more heavily populated side of the suburbs in the direction of the central city. To reconcile these two forces—peripheral strategic dispersal and "inboard" orientation—is not easy. But planning agencies might well pay greater attention to the need for such a resolution, and federal, state, and city groups might employ the power of tax inducement more widely than they have heretofore. The location of new planned cities will provide a unique opportunity to eliminate haphazard sprawl and to concentrate critical masses of people in the outer sections.

The channeling of people between their places of residence and the new industrial and shopping centers has increased the strain upon our highways, necessitating the creation of a new highway system. At the same time, however, these patterns of work and shopping trips continue to decrease the strain on arteries leading into town. In the burst of highway building that is only now tapering off, it is as important that we avoid overbuilding as underbuilding. In this last phase of highway building, we must avoid the temptation to "finish the job" by bulldozing excess radial highways leading into central city downtowns, merely because plans look "incomplete" without them. This is a human issue in terms of hardship of the people displaced and the priceless residential areas sometimes destroyed, and an economic issue in terms of the waste of resources. The need is now for rapid transit lines which will not require the massive parking structures in the downtowns that radial highways generate, and which are likely not to be used to full capacity a decade or so hence, as the suburban cores reach their full maturity.

Urbanization and the Black American

To prevent sprawling suburbs from atomizing, intermediate centers and efficient means of transportation can be forged. But another form of atomization is with us, which is social and political in nature. It threatens to split central cities away from their suburbs. This is the fact that northern cities are becoming Black, as the growing suburbs remain White. Such a phenomenon weakens the socio-economic strength and cohesiveness of the United States. It may also have an important impact upon our relations with other parts of the world, especially the non-White sectors.

The South is no longer the exclusive habitat of the Black. On the contrary, about half of the 22 million Blacks of the United States now live outside the South. With an annual migration northward in the 1950's and 1960's of 200,000, and a rate of increase that is one and one-half times that of the White population, the American Black, who was a rural Southerner two generations ago, has become to a large extent an urban Northerner or Westerner.[13] So dramatic has been the change-over for the Black from farm to city that today a higher percentage of the non-White population (72 per cent) than the White population is urban. Now that the Southern city has reached new heights of industrial prosperity and barriers against

[13] J. F. Hart, "Changing Distribution of the American Negro," *Annals of Association of American Geographers*, 50, No. 3, September 1960, p. 260.

racial discrimination are being broken down, especially in such centers as Atlanta, New Orleans, Houston, Dallas, Memphis, and Miami, the rural Black migrant is turning to nearer urban centers. The Black migration of the 1970's is likely, then, to focus on the urban South, a trend not supported by the U.S. Bureau of the Census 1970 statistics, but one which can be expected nevertheless. De facto discrimination in the North, the widespread enactment of residential requirements for welfare recipients, unspeakably bad ghetto housing conditions, and lack of central city job opportunities, all point to a lessening of the "push" to the North and an increase of the "pull" to the Southern city. Given the current trends, including the growing attractiveness of the urbanized South, the Black American is likely to be 90 per cent urban by the end of the 1970's. Segregation, as practiced by Whites in the North, coupled with the economic and cultural status of the Black migrants, has confined the Black of the North to the central city. The suburbs are, with only a few exceptions, closed to him. Charting the racial characteristics of large central cities in the United States presents the problem vividly. Northern central cities have as high a proportion of Blacks as do Southern cities, but the Black proportion of total metropolitan area population is relatively smaller in the North. (See Figure 12.) This is because of two characteristics of Southern urbanized areas: suburbs tend to be annexed by central cities, and suburbs are more open to Blacks. Most central cities continue to show net population loss but to gain hundreds of thousands of Blacks in the process. Washington, Baltimore, St. Louis, Newark, Gary, Cleveland, Detroit, Chicago, and Philadelphia have Black populations that range from 70 per cent to 33 per cent of the entire population. Cleveland, for example, which had only 87,000 Blacks in 1940, now has 288,-000. Within 10 to 20 years, Cleveland could have a Black majority. As the central city becomes "black" and the suburbs remain "white," there is the grave danger that a political-cultural iron curtain will be rung down between the two. Are we to renew our central cities physically without taking into account the implications of the demographic pattern? If Black migration can be channeled into the suburbs, then this new form of spatial segregation can be broken. But if not, we are going to have to devise radically new political and administrative frameworks to prevent racial walls from dividing our metropolitan areas to the detriment of all concerned. The forces behind metropolitan government will have to act more vigorously and with greater federal support if maintenance of the central city is to

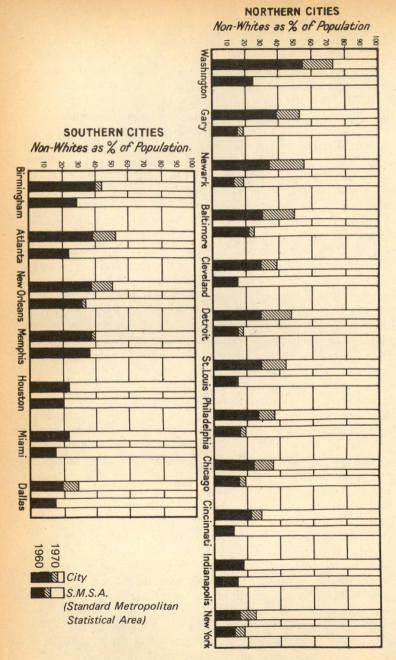

FIG. 12. Blacks and Other Non-Whites as Per Cent of Urban Population in the United States

be shared by the entire metropolitan populace. Unless action is swift we may not be able to avoid a new and ugly political phenomenon —the division of the metropolitan area along racial lines.

Some have felt that the election of Black mayors, symbolizing the enfranchisement of the Black people, would be a major step forward in solving the racial and economic problems of central cities. And with Black majorities in six major cities, or with populations of over 40 per cent in eight others, Black control of big city government can be anticipated. But whether it is Gary, Newark, Cleveland, or Washington, D.C., clearly the political victories of Black leaders are not enough. The decay of the schools, crime, drugs, the breakdown of essential city services, the erosion of the tax base—these are not problems that are essentially the product of racial tension or that can be cured by "power to the people"—in this case, Blacks. To gain power over a declining body politic is a hollow victory. What is required is clear-cut separation of functions at the metropolitan and central city level, with educational and social services lying within the province of smaller, manageable units (say at the 50,000 to 100,000 population level), and transportation, utility and industrial development services being performed at the metropolitan level. Community control is a slogan that has considerable power and logic to it, but must stop short of tax-levying capacity if equalization of city services is to come about for all of the population, irrespective of race or class.

What has been said about Blacks can be said, too, for Puerto Ricans. Indeed, the problem is more complex because it is regional as well as metropolitan. About 80 per cent, or over one million, of all mainland Puerto Ricans live in New York City. This places an overwhelming burden upon one city's economic-cultural absorption capacities, as well as adding to the plight of the Puerto Ricans themselves. A major national effort is required to encourage the dispersal of Puerto Rican immigrants throughout the country. Federal planning to stimulate the creation of job opportunities in urban areas of various sizes and functions, and the offer of travel, housing, and social inducements to the immigrant, appear necessary to resolve the problem. Our country will be poorly served if the present trend continues. Indeed, the economic, moral, and social climate of New York City is a national, not a local, problem, and the measure of success that we meet in absorbing our Puerto Rican citizens on the mainland or in developing the island has great repercussions throughout Latin America.

The Urbanized Region

A final aspect of this discussion of population distribution is the urbanized region. Metropolitan areas have begun to overlap one another, leapfrogging and bypassing rural areas to form continuous regions. The largest of these regions is the Eastern Seaboard, or Megalopolis. It extends from north of Boston to Fairfax County, Virginia, with a population of over 36 million. Megalopolis arose as a grouping of the country's major seaports, commercial centers, and manufacturing activities. Its future growth is uncertain—some feel that it will continue to grow, but only along the coast, north to Portland and south to Norfolk; others feel that the region will expand westward along the New York and Pennsylvania corridors, to include the Great Lakes areas; still others feel that the New York corridor will become so heavily filled with transportation lines that it will lack the room for sufficient people to warrant the area's inclusion within Megalopolis.

A major significance of Megalopolis lies in its impact upon population distribution. Megalopolis, today, expresses a relatively even distribution of our increasing population, with densities of 100 to 250 persons per square mile. If Megalopolis were to expand across the New York and Pennsylvania corridors to the Great Lakes, then adjoining areas in upper New York, central Pennsylvania, and eastern Ohio would probably become emptier. In the face of this possibility, there is need to plan for an even distribution of the incoming people. This will call for the development of well-spaced, medium-sized central cities, with their surrounding rings of suburbs and agricultural areas—all tied together by an adequate land and air transportational net. By dispersing the population within the urbanized region, we shall enhance our national well-being and security. On the other hand, poor planning that permits an imbalance of population within such regions will heighten our vulnerability to ecological, social, racial, and defense pressures.

Planning for new towns has just begun to catch the imagination of the public as well as to command the attention of the professions. The few current examples, such as Columbia, Md., and Reston, Va., may be too narrowly based upon upper middle class commuting residents to serve as an adequate guide for the future. Certainly if the American planned city turns out to be nothing more than an escape from the big city by people of one narrow socioeconomic class and a form of twentieth-century "urban estatism," it will not be addressing itself to the problem of dispersal.

The City-Region

Two centuries ago, we emerged as a federal nation through a compact that developed a unique hierarchical relationship between central government and the individual states. Over time, the central government has tended to assume powers never contemplated by our founding fathers, in part because the necessary functions to be performed could scarcely be imagined. For the first time in four decades, a serious challenge to the centralization process has been posed by President Nixon's commitment to shift initiative to the states and to regionalize federal administrative mechanisms. Given the national needs to integrate the planning of our social and economic resources base, this strategy would appear anachronistic. While the tugs between federal and state government continue to occupy the attention of our politicians and the courts, the emergence of a potential new element in the hierarchy, an element that currently derives most of its legitimacy from the states, requires immediate attention.

It is not enough for big city mayors to trek to Washington and to appeal for direct federal support that will circumvent state channels. And it is sidetracking the issue for Norman Mailer and others to insist that New York City's problems can be solved by granting it statehood. We are faced with a large number of City-Regions, mostly sprawling across state lines, for which there must be found a place in the political hierarchy that is coordinate with and not duplicatory of states. Of our twenty largest SMSA's, thirteen sprawl across or have influences that extend beyond state or national lines. Their problems cannot be solved within the context of state government. But beyond this, a group of City-Regions needs to be developed with appropriate political powers to take its place within the political hierarchy. Logical candidates are the greater areas of New York, Los Angeles-San Diego, Chicago-Milwaukee, Philadelphia, Detroit, Providence-Boston, San Francisco, Washington-Baltimore, Pittsburgh, St. Louis, Cleveland, Houston, Minneapolis-St. Paul, Dallas, Cincinnati, Seattle, Atlanta, Buffalo, Kansas City, Miami, Denver, New Orleans, Phoenix, Salt Lake City, and Portland Oregon.

The criteria which might be employed to designate such regions could be absolute size or degree of dominance within a state (e.g., 25 per cent or more of the total population). To distinguish between the functions of the City-Region and the state, we could very broadly allocate service powers to the former and development powers to the latter. Thus, City-Regions would establish regional educational, transportation, social service, police, and employment agencies. States would handle utilities, environmental control, industrial development, agricultural, consumer protection, recreation, and labor relations functions. In some instances there would have to be overlap. But the City-Region would have to have coordinate taxing power with the state. With populations that have per capita income that are about one-fifth greater than the national average, these City-Regions can afford to tax themselves differentially to supply the higher level of services that they want and need.

Manufacturing and Resources

The map of American manufacturing is undergoing change, although this change has not yet produced the dispersal of facilities that strategic planners would like to see. As of today, the American Manufacturing Belt shows only slightly less relative strength than it did three decades ago. Sixty-three per cent of the value added by manufacturing is generated by factories located within the Belt. A major reason for this continued dominance is the industrial strength of the Pittsburgh-Cleveland-Detroit, Chicago, and Miami Valley districts. Government-financed industry was heavily built up in these areas during the Second World War, and the momentum of this industry in attracting all forms of supplementary and by-product industries has been maintained, and accelerated during the Korean War, and again during the Vietnamese War. Of the six states with the largest absolute amount of annual capital expenditures, four (Ohio, Pennsylvania, Illinois, and New York) are located within the American Manufacturing Belt.

However, outside manufacturing districts are on the upswing, and are gaining an increasing share of national manufacturing. The bulk of this activity is taking place in other parts of the Maritime Ring. Some examples are 1) aircraft, electronics, shipbuilding, petroleum, and chemicals in California; 2) aluminum, chemicals, petroleum, metallurgy, shipbuilding, electronics, and aircraft in the Gulf Southwest; 3) textiles, paper and pulp, fertilizers, and food processing in the Southeast; 4) aircraft and aluminum in the Pacific Northwest; and 5) electronics in New England. Outside the Maritime Ring, aircraft and petrochemicals are on an increase in the Great Plains, and steel and electronics in the Western Deserts and Mountains.

To appreciate trends, we can note that expenditures for new plants and equipment in the Southeast, Southwest, and Far West regions are now 30 per cent of total capital expenditure for the country as a whole. Current manufacturing output in these regions is 28 per cent of the national output. In other words, rate of growth based upon capital investment has caught up with current output, denoting economic maturing of these regions. Texas leads the states in annual capital expenditures for manufacturing; California ranks fourth; and Texas and Louisiana show the highest growth rates for such expenditures.

Why is manufacturing spreading over the United States landscape, and what are the prospects for the eventual creation of a new and larger American Manufacturing Belt? Growing population, improved transportation and communications, and discoveries and new uses of raw materials are responsible for the growth and dispersal of our manufacturing plants. As examples of new major sources of domestic raw materials we can cite magnesium along the Gulf Coast; wood pulp in Tennessee; open-pit coal mines in eastern Oregon; coal in Utah, Colorado, and Wyoming; petroleum in California, Alaska, Wyoming, and offshore Louisiana; phosphates in Tennessee and Idaho; natural gas in New Mexico and Wyoming; and even deposits of iron ore in Colorado and southern California. These minerals have stimulated local manufacturing and, at the same time, have attracted allied industries that require raw materials from other parts of the country.

Another reason for manufacturing dispersal lies in the greater use of imported raw materials. One such resource, which is reshaping the map of the American iron and steel industry, is iron ore. As we look back we recall how the industry developed in Pittsburgh, and then followed the Ohio River-Youngstown corridor to Cleveland, Lorain, Detroit, Chicago, and Buffalo. In shifting toward the Great Lakes, the steel industry took up a position intermediate between Appalachian coal and upper Great Lakes iron ore and limestone. Today the southern shores of the Great Lakes account for 40 per cent of United States steel capacity. Pittsburgh accounts for only about 10 per cent.

Despite impressive supplies of domestic iron ore and taconite, we have had to begin to exploit new deposits of foreign iron ores. Moderate resources were first tapped in Chile, Cuba, Sweden, North

Africa, and Liberia. Then vast deposits were uncovered in the Guiana Highlands of Venezuela, and along Canada's Quebec-Labrador border. We now import one-third of our pig iron from foreign areas.

Over the past twenty years steel mills with coastal locations have had high growth rates. The continuing emphasis upon iron ore imports should maintain this growth in the years ahead. The Great Lakes steel centers, including the Canadian one at Hamilton, are likely to continue to increase their capacity faster than the national rate of increase. Since 1960 two major companies, for example, have developed sites for new plants in the Chicago area. The Atlantic Seaboard should also continue to grow more rapidly than the national capacity. Sparrow's Point and Morrisville have plants that can now produce over 11 million tons of steel, and a site for a new plant at Camden has been acquired by a major company.

Birmingham is using more and more Venezuelan ores because of the low iron content of its local ores. Rate of growth for Birmingham steel over the past decade has not matched the national rate. This can be attributed not to location factors but to company policy. The Birmingham steel industry is owned by the United States Steel Corporation, whose general rate of expansion has been relatively low because of its already high share of the market. Nonetheless, the rate of expansion at Birmingham was considerably higher than U.S. Steel's total rate of expansion.[14]

Improvement of the waterways to allow shipment of Southern Appalachian coal to Mobile might stimulate the growth of a steel industry there. Plants along the lower Mississippi using Ohio River coal may also be anticipated. Finally, the plants along the Gulf, such as those at Houston and in California at Fontana, can be expected to increase their capacity. These, incidentally, experienced the fastest rate of growth in the past decade. While the center of gravity of the steel industry will remain along the Great Lakes, the increase of capacity along the entire Maritime Ring will be economically—as well as strategically—beneficial to the nation as a whole, for a dispersed steel industry means greater dispersal in the transportation, construction, machinery, fuel and mining equipment, and non-durable consumer goods industries.

Aluminum manufacturing is another example of a change in an industry's location that is dependent in great measure upon foreign

[14] Gunnar Alexandersson, "Changes in the Location Pattern of the Anglo-American Steel Industry: 1948-1959," *Economic Geography*, Vol. 37, No. 2 (April 1961), pp. 95-114.

raw materials. In the last few years, this industry's location concentration has shifted from the Northwest to the Texas-Louisiana-Arkansas-Alabama area. It is also growing along the St. Lawrence and Ohio Rivers. The major sources for our bauxite are in Surinam, Jamaica, Guayana, Ghana, Brazil, and Hispaniola. As Pacific Northwest hydroelectric power has become scarcer, the Gulf's natural gas has taken on new importance in aluminum reduction. In this context we should note that the cost of fuel, in making aluminum metal, is 20 per cent of the total cost—higher than the fuel cost involved in extracting alumina from bauxite. We should also note that the growth of the industry in Canada, first at Arvida on the Saguenay and most recently at Kitimat, British Columbia, is largely aimed at the United States market, and is located accordingly.

Many other industries are taking a coastal location because of their dependence upon such imported materials as wood pulp from New Brunswick, petroleum from Venezuela and the Middle East, and natural gas from the Peace River in British Columbia. We could add food, wool, hides, cement, manganese, cobalt, uranium, abrasives, mica, chrome, copper, tungsten, and tin to this list of raw materials that affect plant location. It adds up to the fact that today's rapid industrial growth and dispersal is in part a product of our interdependence with other portions of the Maritime World, especially the Atlantic Basin through which pass over 75 per cent of our imports. The changing significance of areas from which our imports are obtained is shown in Table 5.

Over the past quarter of a century, Maritime Europe has become increasingly important as a source of United States imports. So has Canada. Maritime Europe, Canada, and South and East Asia together furnish 80 per cent of our imports. Latin America has dropped substantially in its share of United States imports, while the other regions show little change.

In examining the role of individual countries, however, we find some deviations from the regional import trends. While Canada is by far our most important source of imports (twice the value of the next supplier), Japan now ranks second, with 14 per cent, having slightly outstripped the United Kingdom and West Germany. Within the various import regions we find that the United States is overly dependent upon one country in some regions, but has a more balanced number of suppliers in others. In Latin America, Mexico and Venezuela supply us with half of our imports from the region. In South and East Asia, Japan is even more dominant, supplying us

TABLE 5
United States Imports by Region

Region	Per Cent of United States Imports, by value			
	1969	1960	1955	1937
American Republics	12%	26%	32%	24%
Canada	29%	20%	23%	13%
Western Europe	28%	30%	20%	
Eastern Europe	1%	—	1%	26%
Middle East	1%	2%	3%	
South and East Asia	23%	16%	14%	32%
Australia and Oceania	3%	2%	2%	2%
Africa	3%	4%	5%	3%

with about 60 per cent of all of our imports from the region, or six times that supplied to us by the next ranking, Hong Kong. On the other hand, while the United Kingdom sells us 20 per cent of the imports received from Maritime Europe, West Germany accounts for another 25 per cent, and France, Belgium, and Italy combined account for another 27 per cent. With generally competitive economies, therefore, no single Maritime European country can achieve a position of monopoly within its region as a seller of goods to the United States. This is not true in the case of Venezuela, Mexico, or Japan. With Venezuela's oil, Mexico's minerals, and Japan's manufactures, these three countries lack regional competitors for the sale of commodities to the United States. With Britain's entry into the Common Market, that trade bloc will dominate Europe's export trade to the United States.

Another measure of association is the degree to which other regions are dependent upon the United States for their exports. This is shown in Table 6.

It can be seen that the dependence of Canada upon the United States is very heavy, and that of Latin America, and South and East Asia moderately so. If, however, we look into the details of this regional dependence, we find some highly revealing national relationships. In the Western Hemisphere, countries like Canada, Colombia, the Dominican Republic, Ecuador, Guatemala, Mexico, and Panama send up to 40 per cent of their exports to the United States, and Brazil, Bolivia, Chile, Costa Rica, El Salvador, Haiti, Honduras, Peru, and Venezuela, a minimum of 30 per cent. Elsewhere, other closely associated traders are the Philippines, which sends us nearly

TABLE 6
Regional Exports to the United States

Region	Per Cent of Exports to the United States, by value (1969)
Latin America Republics	33%
Canada	70%
Western Europe	8%
Middle East	9%
South and East Asia	26%
Australia and Oceania	15%
Africa	8%

50 per cent of its exports, and Japan, with about one-third of its exports. On the other hand, countries like the United Kingdom, West Germany, and India ship 10 per cent or less of their exports to us.

While the political association that stems from trade dependence can change almost overnight for any single country, it is far less likely that such associations could change quickly with regions as a whole. It is in this context, therefore, that the trade ties of the United States with Canada, Maritime Europe, Latin America, and Offshore Asia take on such mutual long-range strategic importance.

We have thus far dealt in general with imports to the United States. The import of specific commodities that are crucial to the workings of our manufacturing economy and the sources of these imports further amplify the picture. Table 7 lists a few of the more critical materials and their chief suppliers.

Some of our supplementary imports are added to the output of materials in which we rank as the world's number one producer, such as iron ore, copper, lead, zinc, petroleum, and uranium. Nevertheless, we have become such hungry consumers that we still must import up to one-half of our production of these commodities to fulfill our needs. As we continue to consume more than we produce, our dependence upon foreign imports mounts. Since most of these imports enter by sea, the continued development of manufacturing within our Maritime Ring seems assured. In the long run, we believe that the new American Manufacturing Belt will extend from the Great Lakes-Northeast Region through the South Atlantic and Gulf (both the coastal strip and the inner strip from the Southeast Piedmont to the Texas prairies). Of this area, only the Carolinas and Georgia will not be strongly influenced by direct access to the

TABLE 7
United States—Selected Imports and Major Countries of Origin

Materials That Are Mainly Imported

Materials	Suppliers
Abrasives	Canada
Antimony	Yugoslavia
Bauxite	Jamaica, Surinam
Chrome Ores	U.S.S.R., Turkey
Cobalt	Congo, (Kinshasha) Belgium-Luxembourg
Hard Fibres	Mexico, Philippines
Manganese	Gabon, Brazil
Mercury	Canada, Spain
Nickel	Canada, Norway
Platinum	Republic of South Africa, U.S.S.R.
Tin	Malaysia, Thailand
Titanium	Japan, Australia
Tungsten	Canada, Peru
Natural Rubber	Indonesia, Malaysia

Supplementary Imports

Iron ore	Canada, Venezuela
Copper	Chile, Canada
Lead	Australia, Mexico
Zinc	Canada, Mexico
Petroleum	Venezuela, Canada
Potash	Germany, France
Sawmill products	Canada
Silver	Canada, Mexico
Uranium	Canada, Republic of South Africa
Wool	Australia, New Zealand

sea. California, from San Francisco to San Diego, will be a separate but closely interrelated part of this belt. A second district—the combined Ohio, Missouri (up to Omaha), Tennessee (up to Knoxville), and Mississippi (north of Memphis) rivers—is likely to emerge as the river-oriented manufacturing belt of the Interior. The latter, however, will be partly dependent upon the open ocean, as its components are today, because of the advantages in using barges to move bulk products.

The creation of a global network of military and political alliances stimulated the United States to increase international trade, strategic materials stockpiling, and capital investment, as a means of strengthening this network. In turn, the greater role of international trade and foreign investment within the United States economy has made the maintenance of these alliances more vital. The net effect of these causally related forces has been to increase the measure of interrelationship between the United States and the rest of the Trade-Dependent Maritime world. This represents a fundamental change in the U.S. global position—a change which is most clearly expressed in America's role as the central and leading component of a thoroughly interdependent geostrategic region.

Of course, American dependence upon an international trade economy is not without its attendant difficulties. The trade imbalance of the last few years is a problem, steps toward whose resolution involve delicate political maneuvering. Thus our relationship with Japan, which continues to pile up dollars by exporting widely to the United States and only grudgingly lifts certain restrictions upon imports from America and upon American investment capital, is threatened by the absence of unhampered economic complementarity.

An even more serious problem, strategically and fiscally, looms should we allow ourselves to become increasingly dependent upon imported oil and natural gas. The proposed import of liquefied natural gas from Algeria, and negotiations to invest several billion U.S. dollars in Soviet Siberian natural gas resources to be imported by the United States in liquified form, would in and of themselves not raise serious strategic problems. But should such importation be coupled with the growing dependence upon petroleum imports, the repercussions would indeed be serious. The financial drain on our balance of payments would be over $10 billion annually. Current oil import trends suggest that by 1980, 30 per cent of all petroleum used in the United States would be imported—and half of this from the Middle East. To be so dependent upon oil imports from Arab countries (e.g., half of the Middle East imports might come from Saudi Arabia) could be a grave strategic mistake, and we must take steps now to avoid such a condition.

Changing American energy policies and practices can reverse the tide. For example, conservation of energy resources can be encouraged by raising the cost of certain fuels (e.g., gasoline or natural gas for electricity use) so that the increasing rate of energy use will be arrested, or alternative sources will be used. Also, synthetic oil and gas from coal, sandtars, and shales can be introduced into the market. Finally, restraints on the development of breeder nuclear reactor plants can be lifted by developing a more rational set of political licensing controls.

A major energy policy that seeks to decrease dependence upon imports requires that the policy be developed in consonance with Canada's capacities and needs. It also requires a willingness to accept a higher energy cost structure. In the latter connection, the escalating prices of crude oil created by the policies of producing countries (OPEC) actually serves American national interests, for the day is brought closer when U.S. energy resources will not be at a competitive disadvantage with foreign resources.

An added dimension of the problem is that decreased dependence by the United States on Middle Eastern imports will enhance the position of Maritime Europe and Japan. For while they will continue to be heavily dependent upon the Middle East, U.S. needs will not increase the drain. But for Europe and Japan, too, the need for developing alternative sources of petroleum (Latin America, the North Sea, the Maghreb, Indonesia, Australian and Japanese off-shore waters), as well as alternative sources of energy are immediate. All this is not said to challenge the wisdom or almost inevitability of interdependence, but rather to stress that it is a delicate process that in some instances must be pursued cautiously and not foolhardily. Moreover, interdependence for the United States within the Trade-Dependent Maritime World poses less security risks strategically than dependence upon other geostrategic regions or Shatterbelts.

The United States and Canada

We have, in Chapter III, represented Anglo-America and the Caribbean Basin as one geopolitical unit. The ties between the United States and Canada are such that the geopolitical destiny of the two can hardly be separated. Neither Commonwealth status nor French-Canadian culture are sufficient bars to this common destiny.

Five elements combine to unify Anglo-America geopolitically: 1) the distributional pattern of Canada's population; 2) the United States-orientation of Canada's major geographical regions; 3) the extractive and primary-producing nature of Canada's economy; 4) Canada's position along the Arctic, facing the Soviet Heartland; and 5) the overwhelming dominance of the United States within this Anglo-American partnership.

Arctic and subarctic climates and soils confine Canada's 22 million people to a narrow population band that faces the United States border. Much of this band is within 50 miles of the international boundary and two-thirds live within 100 miles; almost none of it is beyond 300 miles. The population band is not continuous. It is interrupted in its east-west extent by barrier areas that break across the border into the United States. These are the Rockies, the Appalachians, and two prongs of the Laurentian Uplands—the poorly drained Upper Great Lakes-Superior Highlands and the Algonquin Park-Adirondacks districts. The result is a fivefold clustering of Canada's population—along the Pacific Coast, in the Prairie Provinces, in the Ontario Peninsula, the Middle St. Lawrence, and the Maritime provinces. Each of these clusters is more remote from its Canadian neighbor than from its counterpart in the United States. The Prairie and Maritime populations are relatively dispersed.

The association of Canada's population clusters with areas across the border is not exclusively due to east-west distances and north-south breaks. It is also due to the fact that Canada's geographical regions are northern extensions of United States regions. That the Canadian sections are generally complementary, not competitive, with their United States counterparts is due to the abundance and supplementary function of Canada's raw materials, the extractive nature of the Canadian economy, and the differences in age and rate of economic development between the two countries. Rail, highway, air, water, and telecommunication ties show marked north-south trends reflecting the movement of goods, men, and ideas across the border.

Save in Quebec, Canada's main manufacturing centers are contiguous with those of the United States. They are strongly tied to American manufacturing in that they depend upon United States factory-made machinery and other goods. Many of these factories are United States branch plants. Also, Canadian consumer products tends to follow the style and trends set by United States products. Mining, too, shows strong orientation to the south. Since the annual output of Canada's manufacturing and mining is over four times that of agriculture in value, the first two industries are the key to Canadian-United States economic associations. Such leading Canadian manufactures as pulp and paper, nonferrous metal smelting and refining, and sawmills, are largely noncompetitive with United States industry. Petroleum refining and natural gas can serve those areas of the United States that lack petroleum, like the Pacific Northwest and the Northern Plains. Canada's mineral production is therefore either complementary or supplementary. Occasionally, however, temporary gluts in production create financial distress for Canadian suppliers of such minerals as petroleum, uranium, or gold.

It is only in agriculture that the two national economies are competitive. When we consider that farm products account for 18 per cent of Canada's exports we can understand how competing farm export policies can irritate but cannot fundamentally alter the economic associations of the two countries. The same can be said for divergent farm policies which motivated Canada to sell vast amounts of wheat and barley to Communist China in the time of United States refusal to do so.

The location of Canada athwart the Arctic, facing the Soviet Heartland and separating Alaska from the United States, has made joint defense an absolute necessity. Much has been written about American bases on foreign soils peripheral to Eurasia. But we seem to take for granted the fact that some of our most crucial bases, both defensive and offensive, are on Canadian soil. There is no alternative to NORAD (the Canadian-United States North American Air Defense Command).

The size, wealth, and general nature of United States life tends to shape Canada's economic and cultural patterns. Frequently Canadians resent the various forms of pressure that result from their associations with Americans. But this resentment is tempered by the realization that the alternative would be economic disaster and military helplessness. Over 70 per cent of Canadian foreign trade moves across the border; $20 billion of United States investments are in Canada (30 per cent of total United States private investment abroad); such industries as petroleum and natural gas, aluminum, iron mining, and pulp and paper have been developed by United States market needs.

It is argued by some Canadians that the runaway exploitation of Canada's resources, owing to United States financial pressures, will one day bankrupt Canada. Their call is, therefore, for a form of economic nationalism that will conserve these resources. This fear of overexploitation is a valid one. The answer, however, does not lie in restraints on United States trade and investment. For the Canadian citizen does not live in isolation from life to the south—he lives in close proximity with it. He seeks the same living standards and consumer comforts that Americans seek. Choking off the output of Canada's raw materials would cause a radical, and politically unthinkable, drop in living standards.

In fact, the danger of the depletion of raw materials is common to both the United States and Canada. It can best be averted through joint economic planning. It is this type of planning that is so necessary in other fields as well. A smoother flow of raw materials to United States factories is needed to prevent sudden dips in Canadian employment opportunities, as is joint action on agricultural surpluses, to convert the farm economies from that of national problem to national asset.

United States-Canadian relations can proceed in only one direction—toward greater interdependence. As the United Kingdom has chosen Continental Europe over the Commonwealth from an economic standpoint, even greater economic unity between the United States and Canada may be the consequence. Even if this should not be the case, joint agencies for economic and military activities will require continued strengthening. The freest possible use of each other's territory should be encouraged to spearhead the closest relationships between the two countries. There already exist such links as the St. Lawrence Seaway, crude oil pipelines from Alberta to the United States continental interior and Pacific Northwest, and pipelines for refined oil from Portland, Me., to Montreal. There are also natural gas pipelines from fields in British Columbia to the United States Pacific coast and the northern continental interior. Moreover, Canadian territory may prove a feasible route for shipment of United States Alaskan petroleum to the major markets. The future is likely to bring an integration of electric grid and water supply systems. It may see the construction of a modern water route from Montreal to New York City, via the Richelieu River and Canal, Lake Champlain, and the Hudson; or it may see the development of a submarine tanker route across the Canadian Arctic to connect the east and west coasts of North America.

Mutuality of interests means, above all, mutuality of understanding. Because northern British Columbia and the Yukon Territory lack Canadian access to the Pacific, some Canadians have called for the granting of a corridor across Alaskan Panhandle territory. We may pass this off as being neither economically nor strategically important to Canada. However, the decision of 1903, which confirmed the landward boundaries of Canada so as to deny access to the sea, "is still a sore point in certain Canadian circles."[15]

Canadian interest has centered on the Chilkoot and White Passes, which link Whitehorse in the Yukon to the Lynn Canal and the

[15] Norman Nicholson, *The Boundaries of Canada, Its Provinces and Territories* (Ottawa: Department of Mines and Technical Surveys, 1954) pp. 40-41.

sea via the Skagway. The latter is American territory. The granting of a corridor to Canada would not affect the strategic or economic position of the United States, because our major land link, the Alaskan Highway, passes through British Columbia for 634 miles before even entering the Yukon Territory. A far-sighted American policy that respected Canadian political-psychological yearnings in this particular instance would be a minor, but significant, expression of mutual understanding.

Nowhere else in the world should the United States be as sensitive to political developments as in Canada. Were political neutralism to take over in that country, it would represent our most serious international political setback. Strengthening the geopolitical unity between the United States and Canada is crucial to the well-being of both peoples. To this end, the closest economic and political planning is both necessary and possible.

Surely Canadian fears and resentments of the United States are to be taken seriously. "Economic imperialism," a charge widely leveled against Americans by Canadians, cannot be dismissed out of hand. Until there is genuine complementarity in terms of the sharing of value added by manufacturing, the basis for the charge remains. Moreover, specific Canadian industries, like fisheries and petroleum deserve free access to United States markets, given the significance of these industries to the Canadian economy. Also, even slight dollar exchange rate differentials in favor of the United States dollar, even though eased by the "floating" of the Canadian dollar, create unnecessary resentments.

Particular strains that stem from United States energy needs require that positive steps be taken by American-controlled industry and the American government to counteract the negative impact of major development projects in Canada initiated to send supplies to the United States. For example, any major pipeline project (be it to carry oil from the Alaska North Slope or the Athabaskan tar sands, or natural gas from the Prairie provinces or the Canadian Northwest) would cause a major inflation problem for Canada. Also, opening up new Canadian natural gas resources on a large scale to serve the American market could have the negative effect of a price rise for Canadian home and industrial consumers because of the higher cost of exploiting and transporting the product. Moreover, profits made by the producing companies would largely accrue to American shareholders; benefits from increased costs would not accrue to Canadians.

We cannot call for new Canadian efforts to help increase the flow of natural or synthetic oil and gas to the United States without recognizing the costs to Canadians and being prepared to cover them. Subsidization of prices to the Canadian consumer and aid to the Canadian government in coping with the inflationary effects of too rapid a capital investment inject are examples of what can be done. Similarly, United States pressures upon Canadians to build deep-water oil ports along the east coast for handling foreign crude must recognize that oil port investments alone are not a sufficient quid pro quo. Genuine complementarity requires that U.S. capital investment be directed to refineries and petrochemical industries as well—i.e., a "value-added" orientation, if Canada is to enjoy fair and equal benefits.

For a few years, Canadian alienation from the United States increased as many Canadians tried to reject "Americanization," and looked with some measure of comfort at the specific problems—Vietnam, race relations, drug culture, etc.—that plagued their neighbors to the south. But this smugness has been dispelled as Canada has found itself racked with divisions resulting from the violent actions of the French Canadian separatist movement.

In the challenge to Canadian cohesiveness, ironically, may lie the seeds of deeper American-Canadian understanding, given neither nation can now afford self-satisfaction. The federalism that characterizes Canada's body politic has always been reinforced by the pull of the United States. But today this federalism may need the sympathetic support and politico-economic backing of the United States for survival itself. For example, the industrialization of Quebec, a sine qua non in removing the issue of economic exploitation in the relations of French and English-speaking Canada, is not likely to take place if left to the freedom of the market mechanism. To compete effectively with the scale of American manufacturing and to serve both marketing forces and managerial convenience, Canadian industry has concentrated in the Lower Ontario section of the American Manufacturing Belt. To reverse this trend will require not merely Canadian federal governmental intervention, but conscious steps by American industry, supported by United States federal incentives. Only through the concerted action of the pertinent forces in both nations, will Quebec be able to industrialize successfully.

A new element in the issue of American-Canadian relations is the one that has changed the demographic balance in Canada itself—the immigration from central and eastern Europe that has entered since the Second World War. This immigration (16 per cent of Canadians are foreign-born) has altered the internal scene, decreasing the French Canadian percentage of the total population (now about 30 per cent) and constituting a powerful force, potentially, for reconciliation of English and French Canada. Granted that these immigrants have been "Anglicized," class and culture differentiate them from English Canadians and may serve as a balancer in the conflict. This immigrant group also does not possess the historic fears of the United States held by older Canadians. For the new immigrants, the class-leveling effects of Americanization may constitute a significant pull.

Canadian nationalism is an extremely significant factor in United States-Canadian relations. Partially because so much of Canadian industry (60 per cent of manufacturing, two-thirds of mining and smelting, 60 per cent of petroleum) is foreign-controlled, mostly United States; partially because so much of Canadian real personal income growth is attributable to United States foreign investment; and partially because Canada's resources exploration and market requirements are skewed by American influence—fears of economic and possible political domination are powerful. History, in the form of United States aggressive actions, pressed Canadians to form the Federation. Fear of the United States has helped keep the Federation together. The relationship is indeed one of "enmity-amity." But the influences are too strong, the ties too close, the interaction too great, and the United States mass too preponderant for there to be any turning back. Although not one nation, the relationship of these two communities is too unique and the destiny too interconnected for anything but further geopolitical integration.

The United States and the Caribbean

The Gulf of Mexico—Caribbean basins have often been described as the "American Mediterranean." Ratzel and Semple were among the early ones to note geographical similarities between the interior seas of the Old and the New worlds, and Spykman used the term in a geopolitical sense, describing the American Mediterranean as the area over which the United States held absolute hegemony. He defined it as a tropical raw material zone lying between the continental masses of North and South America, and providing a transit zone between them and between the Atlantic and the Pacific.[16]

[16] Spykman, *America's Strategy in World Politics* (New York: Harcourt, Brace, 1942), pp. 48, 49.

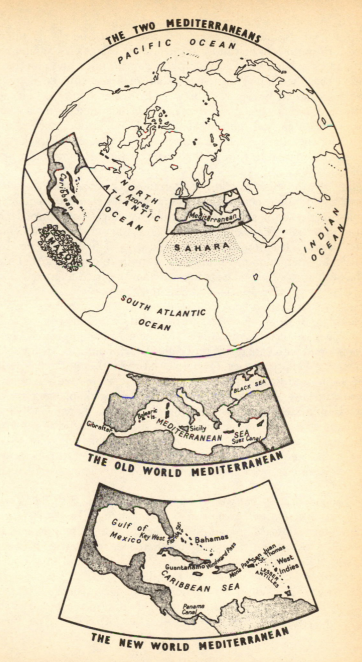

MAP 13. The New and Old World Mediterraneans

The "American Mediterranean" is indeed a useful term for geo-political analysis, but its geographical setting must be clearly under-stood if the term is to be validly applied. (See Map 13.) Examination of the maps of landforms, demographic characteristics, and movement tells us that the Old World Mediterranean Sea is situated between North Africa and Europe, *not* between Africa and Europe. The sea is the intermediate that links two northern hemispheric territories—temperate Europe and subtropical North Africa. It does not link the two continents, for the Sahara bars the way. Most of Africa has an Atlantic orientation to Europe that bypasses the Mediterranean alto-gether.

Similarly, the New World Mediterranean is not situated between North and South America. It lies between, and connects, temperate Anglo-America with subtropical Middle America—both the islands and the Central American Mainland. The Amazon bars continental South America from the Caribbean, and most of South America has an Atlantic orientation to Europe or to eastern Anglo-America. Thus, both southern continents are removed from the Mediterraneans and lack close geopolitical associations with them.

Such a view places the Mediterraneans in their proper geographi-cal settings—those of inland seas, surrounded by littorals whose north-ern reaches are disproportionately larger, more populous, more favor-ably endowed with varieties of raw materials, and more technologically developed. The ecumenes of both Maritime Europe and Anglo-America are being extended southward toward their Mediterraneans. These ecumenes obtain supplementary, as well as complementary, re-sources from their southern, neighboring lands. Thus, Caribbean petroleum and iron ore supplement the Anglo-American resource scene, while sugar, bananas, and bauxite complement it. North Af-rican grains, grapes, iron ore, and phosphates supplement Maritime Europe's resources, while citrus, cotton, and petroleum complement them.

Physiographically, the two regions are subdivided—the Old World Mediterranean into two basin-rimming shorelands; the New World Mediterranean into Mainland and Island groupings. In this, and in a general location sense, lie subtle differences, of course, between the two regions. The open North African coast, devoid of water or forest barriers, can be more easily unified by a dominant power. Moreover, the Old World Mediterranean's western reaches lie under the influence of Maritime Europe, while its eastern reaches are sub-ject to pressure from Asia (specifically, the U.S.S.R.). The New

World is bordered by only one power core—the United States. Finally, the Suez Canal is an extra regional link for its Mediterranean. While performing a similar extraregional function, the Panama Canal also serves as an internal link between and within American Mediterranean countries.

These differences notwithstanding, the analogies between the two regions are the more important elements of comparison. Geopolitical associations within the basins depend, essentially, upon the course of events along their northern shores. When most of Europe was unified by Rome, North Africa, too, was brought within the framework. When Europe became split and totally disorganized during medieval times, the Arab corelands to the east seized the opportunity to unify North Africa. Eventually, the revival of European power that began with the Discoveries returned North Africa to the European-oriented fold, but not within a unified framework, because Europe itself lacked unity.

The New World Mediterranean's history shows some striking parallels as well as obvious differences. As long as the North American Mainland remained underdeveloped and disorganized, unity of Middle America was supplied by an extraregional core—Spain. The emergence of European competitors to Spain brought those states into the American Mediterranean also. From the end of the seventeenth to the nineteenth century, Middle America lay divided, strategically and politically, because Europe was divided and because North America was geopolitically immature. Finally came the rise of the United States as the unified, mature overlord of the northern littoral. For over seventy years, command of the American Mediterranean has been held by the United States. The European footholds that remained after the displacement of Spain are only relics. Strategic unity of Middle America has been enforced by the power from the north.

United States hegemony over the Caribbean lands did not follow the course of modern European hegemony over its southern Mediterranean littoral. The United States has fostered the development of formally independent states within a unified strategic framework. North Africa, on the other hand, was developed through a colonial-imperialist process and independence has come in the face of European opposition.

We have used the term *hegemony* to describe North-South power relations in the two Mediterraneans. In the past, military and economic preponderance was equated with political and social attraction, and strategic dominance forced geopolitical cohesiveness. To-day this is not necessarily the case. Strategic dominance can assure geopolitical cohesiveness only if the stronger power is prepared to apply naked force in the formation and control of political and eco-nomic processes. This European powers have done in North Africa and the United States has done in Middle America for most of the first half of the twentieth century. This, too, is the path that the U.S.S.R. has taken to create conditions for geopolitical unity with Eastern Europe. But if the use of direct and unremitting force is re-nounced, if continuous intervention in foreign political and economic processes is repudiated, then something in addition to strategic domi-nance is needed to assure geopolitical unity.

We have elsewhere described Anglo-America and the Caribbean, and Maritime Europe and the Maghreb, as geopolitical regions. This they have been in the recent past, this they are today, and this they are most likely to be in the future. But such regions will only stand as meaningful cohesive units if their northern littorals succeed in finding a new political and social modus vivendi with the lands to the south. The exercise of strategic power in finding this modus vi-vendi certainly cannot be renounced; it is a fact of political life! But its direct application will have to be in consonance with political and social objectives that are mutually desirable, not as a substitute for such objectives.

Since the Second World War many Americans have sat back and viewed France's agonizing entanglements in the Maghreb as the just deserts of a colonial power. The inevitability of the fall of colo-nialism was trumpeted and the rights of colonial peoples to inde-pendence was championed. But we have not really felt morally and politically bound to concern ourselves with the future of European-North African relationships. We buttressed France's position in Maritime Europe, but considered that locale as totally separate from the North African scene. What we have failed to recognize is that just as it is inevitable that colonialism-imperialism must end, so is it absolutely essential that a new form of geopolitical association should emerge in its place within the Old World Mediterranean. Much of our lack of understanding of the problem stems from our compla-cency about our own stake in the American Mediterranean.

This complacency was rudely shattered by Cuba's defection to the Soviet camp, and by gathering storms in the Dominican Republic, Guatemala, Haiti, Nicaragua, and Panama. Our leaders are seeking to reappraise past attitudes and to develop new forms of political and economic accommodation with the Caribbean. A by-product of this reappraisal will be to make the American public more conscious of Maritime Europe's analogous position in North Africa. The latter is as much a part of the European Inner Security Zone as the Caribbean is part of the United States' Inner Security Zone, and Algeria may be France's Cuba. So long as Maritime Europe remains dependent upon Middle Eastern petroleum the Suez Canal or its pipeline bypass is Europe's Panama Canal. The problems that the northern powers face in their relations with their southern Mediterranean littorals are analogous; the stake in their resolution is equally great.

The involvement of the United States in Caribbean Basin affairs can be divided into three phases of geopolitical association:

1) *The Period of Defensive Posture.* Americans had a legitimate fear of European states using their Caribbean island bases and Mexico to dominate the Gulf and the Mississippi, thereby confining the United States to the eastern seaboard. Moreover, Americans were attracted by the wealth of the Indies—sugar, rum, and slaves—to which the subsistence colonial economy stood in marked contrast.

2) *The Period of Emotional Aggressiveness.* With the slavery issue resolved by the Civil War, northern as well as southern voices could now be raised in favor of United States expansion in the Caribbean. The interests were commercial, humanitarian, and strategic. By the turn of this century, military and economic considerations had become sufficiently forceful to inspire a series of interventions in Cuba, Haiti, the Dominican Republic, Nicaragua, and Panama. With the growth of population and industry in the Gulf states and in California, the extension of United States interests into the open Pacific, and the cutting of the Panama Canal, strategic considerations became especially pressing. The Good Neighbor Policy represented a less emotional and more sympathetic approach to our relations with Latin America, but without any essential change in our aggressiveness toward the rest of the hemisphere.

3) *The Fear of Counter-Encirclement.* Today, while continuing to recognize the significance of the Caribbean Basin to the United States in a strategic-economic sense, we have also begun to consider the implications of our being cut off from Middle America in a political sense. While we continue to encircle the Soviet Heartland, we fear counter-encirclement from the Soviet Arctic and from the south for the first time in almost a century. The actual military threat posed by one hostile country like Cuba is negligible, but the success of its revolutionary policies could tap widespread anti-United

States sentiment in Mexico, Panama, Venezuela, Hispaniola, and even Puerto Rico. The emergence of political systems radically opposed to United States political and social ideals, coupled with Soviet bases in Middle America, is not entirely inconceivable. The fears that we in the United States had of the implications of the Cuban situation are, in this sense, not unlike the fears of the Soviet Union at the time of the Hungarian revolt. In both cases the major powers felt compelled to resist political and military encirclement. The Soviet Union's solution to the problem was, and remains, continuous force exercised directly and through puppet regimes. The United States, as yet, has found no clear-cut answer to the question of how it will maintain its primacy of influence in the Caribbean. Agreement between the United States and the U.S.S.R. over removal of Soviet nuclear missiles from Cuba was a recognition of United States primacy of interest in the region. The agreement did not, however, eliminate the possibility of the spread of the revolution. On the contrary, it provided a guarantee that the United States would not intervene by force to overthrow Castro, a guarantee which we have not been able to exact from the Russians in terms of their potential reactions to hostile regimes in eastern Europe.

FORCES OF ATTRACTION AND DISRUPTION

Assessment of Middle America's geopolitical features shows that, while the majority of them serve as forces of attraction toward Anglo-America, some are disruptive forces.

Location is the most compelling force of attraction. Location has two faces: strategic and economic-demographic. Strategically, the Caribbean islands can be viewed as the northern and eastern sides of a frame that encloses the interior sea. The northern side is of particular significance to the United States. It consists of two "walls"— the Bahamas, which are the outer one, and the Greater Antilles, which are the inner one. Through this part of the frame traffic is channeled in two major passageways: the Florida Straits and the Windward Passage. These passageways route the shipping of the Maritime Ring of the United States—Atlantic-Gulf movement via the Florida Straits, and Atlantic-Pacific movement via the Windward Passage and the Panama Canal. Venezuelan-United States traffic can use the Mona Passage, between Puerto Rico and Hispaniola. The eastern edge of the frame consists of the Lesser Antilles. These smaller and less populous portions of the Caribbean are mostly European dependencies, although American bases are spotted throughout. Shipping to Europe moves via St. Thomas at the northern end, and Trinidad at the southern end, of this island string. From such bases as Key West, Florida; Guantanamo, Cuba; San Juan, Puerto Rico; Panama; and Chaguaramas, Trinidad, the United States navy has traditionally guarded the waters of the American Mediterranean. There are those who today suggest that such a guardian role is unrealistic, in the face of the threat of intercontinental nuclear war. If we were to abandon our Caribbean naval-air defenses, however, and to ignore the threat of submarine attack upon the southern shores of United States territory with either nuclear or conventional warheads, would we be more realistic? Should we leave interior sea lanes, including the Panama Canal, unprotected from petty harassments during times of local flare-ups? Should we abandon bases from which we supervise South Atlantic missile-testing shoots and rocket launches, and rely upon more remote Mainland staging points? The Caribbean defense system may not have much strategic value in the face of all-out war, but in terms of limited arms engagements, and of economic and political contention, its significance to the United States can scarcely be questioned.

Another aspect of location is the proximity of the major part of the insular Caribbean's population and resources to the southward-expanding United States ecumene. This population proximity is a relatively recent geopolitical phenomenon. To explain why Cuba had been able to remain politically free of the United States, despite very early interest in the acquisition of the island on the part of Thomas Jefferson and John Quincy Adams, Semple cited its physical isolation from the mainland during the eighteenth and nineteenth centuries:

> The peninsula of Florida . . . was in fact almost wholly inoperative as a connecting link because of its extensive swamp lands, which render the lower third of the peninsula almost uninhabitable. There was here, therefore, no chance of an increasing population which should outgrow the narrow limits of a peninsula and overflow into adjacent islands, as emplified everywhere else by peninsula history.[17]

But the unprecedented growth of Florida in the last four decades has removed this element of isolation. The normal spillover from Florida and the steady flow of tourists and businessmen from all points of the east coast to Havana in pre-Castro times, and the large Cuban and

[17] E. Semple and C. Jones, *American History and Its Geographic Conditions*, p. 441.

Puerto Rican populations of Miami and Tampa, attest to this new proximity.

As we view the unprecedented strides made by manufacturing, mining, and diversified agriculture from Florida through the lower Mississippi to Texas, we are reminded of Semple's statement that "the United States has a greater claim to strength as a Gulf power than as a Pacific,"[18] and that Ratzel long ago stressed the leaning of the United States toward the Gulf.

The change-over of the United States Plantation South to a modern, urbanized, industrial-agricultural region can have great impact upon Middle America's economy. The availability to the Caribbean lands of raw materials like phosphates, sulphur, cotton, refined petroleum, of a variety of manufactured items, and of a large consumer market from the United States Gulf region, could stimulate Caribbean economic developments.

Certainly the fact that half of Middle America's trade is with the United States, and Middle America ranks second only to Canada in United States foreign investments per capita, is a force for unity. In the past, the complementary resources of the temperate and tropical parts of the world were regarded as a major element in geographical attraction. Today, however, this is not necessarily the case. The traditional pattern of tropical raw materials and finished United States goods exchange is a geopolitically disruptive force. This is because the price of raw materials has failed to keep pace with those of manufactured articles, and "the rich have gotten richer, while the poor have gotten poorer." Moreover, national pride impels underdeveloped states to become manufacturers, whether or not they can financially justify such a position. What this means with respect to the Caribbean is clear. The people of this region will not be content to exchange their sugar, tobacco, cacao, henequen, bananas, iron ore, bauxite, nickel, lead, zinc, and petroleum for United States finished goods. And they will not accept their present status of one-crop or one-mineral countries, dependent upon political and market conditions that they cannot control. Instead, they desire diversified agriculture and consumer industries to supplement their extra-active economies. Puerto Rico, with its cement, textiles, shoes, plastics, and glass is an example of the sort of economic diversification for which the others yearn. If the United States can spread the concept of "Operation Bootstrap" through all of insular and mainland Middle

18 *Ibid.*, p. 403.

America, broadening the economic base without undercutting the present specialized economic resources that the Caribbean possesses, then economics will again become a force of attraction, rather than a disruptive force.

Genuine complementarity means a two-way, not a one-way street, with each side obtaining its fair share of value added by manufacturing. Such complementarity will exist when Venezuelan crude oil and iron ore, Jamaican bauxite and alumina, Honduran timber and bananas, Cuban sugar and Guatemalan coffee are exchanged along with Latin American steel wire, fine furniture, veneer panels, chocolate, frozen fish, banana cake, fishing nets and shoes—in return for United States raw materials as well as finished products.

The prospects for rapid change are remote. The more mature Puerto Rican economy is the result of a special set of relations with the United States. How well would "Operation Bootstrap' have succeeded without the immigration valve of New York City, let alone tax subsidies and a favorable and protected climate for United States investment?

As much as has to be done by the United States to stimulate genuine complementarity, action must be taken by the Caribbean countries among themselves. To talk of a Caribbean Common Market is no longer pure fancy. With outside assistance, regional planning and harmonious resource allocation, much can be done through internal efforts. We are not speaking of sophisticated items of exchange, but rather of mundane articles like food, clothing, furniture, building material, soaps, shoes. These can be exchanged within Caribbean America, given the proper political, economic, and psychological milieu.

Two other major disruptive elements are political and social. The United States position in the Caribbean cannot be based upon dictatorships of the Right or of the Left. For if United States-style political and social democracy is to have any influence upon the Caribbean scene, it must be able to influence day-to-day events there. Until now we have depended upon small elites, backed by our economic and military force, to maintain our hegemony. The wave of today in the Caribbean calls for reform and our mission is to encourage this reform openly and wholeheartedly—to lead, not to follow. While this, too, would be a form of intervention in Caribbean affairs, intervention is likely to occur in whatever relations we possess with the American Mediterranean.

Another highly disruptive force in United States-Caribbean relations is racial discrimination in the United States. The Caribbean is a region that is Negro, White, Indian, East Indian, and mixed. Islands like Cuba, Haiti, Jamaica, Puerto Rico, and many of the eight smaller West Indies are heavily Negro. So are sections of the mainland, like British Honduras, the Nicaraguan coast, and Panama. The historic impact of plantation agriculture made much of the American Mediterranean (including the United States South) a "Negro Lake." While we have become aware of the complications that racial discrimination within the United States creates for our foreign relations with Africa and Asia, we overlook its effects upon the Caribbean. So long as we dealt with small, white oligarchies in most Middle American countries, we could be oblivious to the sensitivities of their non-White inhabitants. Now we will have to deal with "the people," and unless we can do so with clean hands, our hopes of leading the reform wave in the Caribbean may well founder on the rocks of domestic racial discrimination. One of the keys to our Caribbean policy, then, lies in the rapidity with which the American Black is able to take his place as a full and equal member of our society. We must also be prepared to meet a reverse form of racist discrimination within the Caribbean itself. For a people long subject to White oppression will, given the opportunity, turn on Whites with hostility and rancor. The jibes and discrimination faced by White tourists in many a Caribbean isle is likely to increase in intensity until general economic and social conditions improve. So will the treatment of White businessmen. We can, in the face of such sentiments, turn away in pique, or we can accept these strains as the inevitable price of normalization of United States-Caribbean relations.

Certainly the stark contrast in living standards between the United States and the Caribbean is a disruptive force to geopolitical unity. Rapid population growth, limitations of water and arable land, dependence upon a few commodities, and absence of manufacturing are all responsible for the Caribbean's plight. The region's current population of 95 million is more than triple the 1920 population, and growth is nearly three per cent annually. Fresh water has to be shipped to some West Indian islands because storage facilities are so limited. In Haiti, for example, land redistribution is no solution because most of the land is not arable. Haiti, a nation of small landholders, is one of the most poverty-stricken countries in the world. Urbanization within the essentially rural Caribbean has solved few economic problems and created many new ones. One single city in each of the following countries holds one-fifth of that country's population: Cuba, Venezuela, Panama, and Costa Rica. However, urbanization has not alleviated poverty. Instead, hundreds of thousands have crowded into urban centers that lack manufacturing bases. The result is a declassed urban people with little to do but to respond to revolutionary slogans.

Under such economic conditions, the contact that we make with Middle Americans through such forces of attraction as tourism, trade, baseball, and widespread use of the English language, are often turned against us.

Geopolitical unity between Anglo-America and the Caribbean is a logical, but not an inevitable, consequence of the geographical relations between the two regions. Forces of attraction are greater than the forces of disruption. And United States strategic needs are not among the least important of these attraction forces. Certainly the Caribbean is as vital to the military and psychological security of the United States as is Eastern Europe to the Soviet Union or the Maghreb to Maritime Europe. What we cannot afford to do, however, is to take the American Mediterranean for granted. Geography proposes; man disposes. Only a vigorous response to the challenges presented by the various disruptive elements that have been noted can provide the geopolitical unity that is so logical and so necessary.

The process of change and interdependence is the most striking characteristic of the geopolitical landscape of the United States and the rest of the Maritime World. Perhaps we are too close to the scene to appreciate the full implications of this process. Domestically, political and economic power is being reconcentrated within different portions of the Maritime Ring. Internationally, dependence upon foreign raw materials and foreign markets may necessitate sweeping changes in the production and marketing of American goods. For example, the subsidization of American manufactures for export may be no more far-fetched a proposal than were agricultural subsidies half a century ago. Also, on the international plane, a genuine partnership with Maritime Europe would have far-reaching effects upon our global foreign policy and our current controls over nuclear weapons. As with any other major nation, the posture of the United States in international affairs cannot be examined through a series of discrete, isolated actions in diverse parts of the world. This posture has global earth-space parameters, and indeed, outer-space ones as well.

Geographical analysis usually begins and ends with place. But place becomes geographical only when recognized as a particular part of the earth's surface within which certain processes interact spatially to create unique area associations. To evaluate these area associations, insight into the dimensions of scale, time, and movement are necessary. Thus, in considering the United States within a national scale as the amalgam of diverse internal regions, what is measured and analyzed is quite different from analysis of the country at the international scale. Since process change occurs over time, all geographical problems have a temporal context. To think of America's changing position in world affairs, from the context of the self-sufficient country of pre-World War Two to the globally interdependent one of today, or of the shift of Black America from its exclusively rural Southern locale of the 1920's and 30's to the great urban centers of the North, is to utilize the time scale as an aid in evaluating special trends.

Movement, the third dimension, is the vehicle through which the dynamism of earth-man relations is established. Movement involves men, goods, and ideas and includes such diverse processes as immigration, trade, exchange of ideas, weathering, shrinking of water bodies, or port and railway construction. Jet age movement, including long-distance travel with the assistance of mid-air refueling, travel in outer space, or the use of communications satellites for news and other television purposes, is a dimension of major proportions in understanding America's ability to reach outward today.

There is no single view of the global setting that would be accepted without qualification by all nations as a view of reality. For each nation is egocentric, and reality is *its* reality. Geographers have held views of the earth since the times of Hecateus and Strabo, and will continue to expound them, subject to the influence of scale, time, movement, and of course, personal background and outlook. Thus, when an American geographer looks at the world at large, he looks at it from a particular and undeniably nationally oriented vantage point. This does not, however, imply an inevitably narrow, partisan base, for recognition of one's own perceptional background can help the observer to maintain a modicum of balance and objectivity.

To speak of the United States as part of a distinct geostrategic world is to recognize a state of global interdependence. Such a state is part of a continuing process which has led America from its periods of isolationism, continental expansion, and global egocentrism to the present era of global interdependence. With the help of vast space, abundance of natural resources, a unique economic system, and open immigration, the United States achieved self-sufficiency and an economy of abundance. But no means has been found to restrain this abundance. Because of the competitive nature of the domestic economy, the chemical-technological-automation revolution, the commitments that arose from involvement in two World Wars, and the perceived need to help rehabilitate or develop other nations, the United States has found itself plunged into an era of super-abundance—an era which builds upon and yet partly weakens the base of self-sufficiency, in return for a broader base which depends upon international exchange to maintain economic and political momentum. Super-abundance is a mixed blessing. With super-abundance also come problems of environmental deterioration, energy supply drain, the poverty gap, and the economic exploitation of other parts of the world.

Whether other nations, like the Soviet Union, once having achieved the goal of abundance through self-sufficiency, can and will move into this subsequent phase, remains to be seen. But certainly America's super-abundance is inextricably intertwined with her global strategic posture.

It has been posited that the Anglo-American and Caribbean geopolitical region is part of the Trade-Dependent Maritime World. The step-up in the regional hierarchy from the geopolitical to the geostrategic represents an enormous leap in scale and range of complexity. It is within the context of this complexity that United States relations with South America, Maritime Europe, Offshore Asia and Africa can be most clearly appreciated. For the United States today, various alliance problems that may arise within the Organization of American States, the North Atlantic Treaty Organization or the Southeast Asian Treaty Organization cannot be regarded as independent and isolated. Certainly, when it comes to the weighing of American capabilities and needs, the issue is not a North Atlantic Alliance versus an Alliance for Progress, nor is it a Maritime Pacific Concord versus a Maritime Atlantic Concord. The issue is not *either/or*; it is *both*. Japan, Brazil, Spain and Argentina, Canada and Jamaica—and yes, the United States and Cuba. These are parts of one Trade-Dependent Maritime World. The concept of a Trade-Dependent Maritime World including, as it does, not only Anglo-America and the Caribbean, but also Maritime Europe and the Maghreb, Offshore Asia, South America and Africa South of the Sahara, represents a level of spatial generalization that must allow for non-conformities and for differences in degree of association. To speak of the American power core as occupying a central position within the region is to refer, above all, to central responsibilities in working with the other power core, Maritime Europe, and with Japan in achieving prosperity and equality within the entirety of the realm.

In summary, U.S. foreign policy goals may be considered within two contexts—strategic and tactical. At the strategic level, maintenance of a global posture means retaining our perspective of being central to the Maritime World through a series of collective and bilateral alliances. The ability to apply power overtly in the Maritime World and covertly elsewhere is essential to realization of the posture. Because we have espoused an open political system that is based upon international freedom of movement and interaction, conditions for this freedom need to be guaranteed. They cannot be assured through the exercise of power alone, but require readjustments in the international economic balance as well. This may very well affect our current living standards, for no nation can or should hope to exhaust so much of the world's natural resources to pursue an escalating G.N.P. growth as has the United States. The strategic goal requires changed priorities. Complementarity with Canada and the Caribbean, partnership with Maritime Europe, the strengthening of the alliance with Offshore Asia—these, in order, are the tasks.

Tactical goals to accomplish the above, require reevaluation of the relationship between ideology and foreign policy, the strengthening of national cohesiveness and territorial consolidation. The myth that American-style democracy is good for all and need be a sine qua non for trade or aid has long been debunked. We have been trading with the Soviet Union; trade with Communist China has begun, and we have granted aid to a variety of states, irrespective of their ideological nature, such as Spain, Portugal, the Arab dictatorships, and Taiwan. The question of when to apply trade or aid as a weapon to influence the establishment, maintenance, or overthrow of regimes is a very delicate one. In general, where we can do nothing about the character of regimes, little is to be gained by manipulating the economic situation in the name of democracy. Where our direct responsibility lies is in our relations to allies with duly constituted democratic regimes. We are justified in making a value judgment in favor of representative government and of applying economic power to preserve or enhance democratic states.

Strengthening our national cohesiveness involves facing up to and seeking remedies for the feelings of alienation that grip segments of our society. Steps in this direction have been taken by ending discrimination against minorities, lowering the voting age, and seeking a more dignified system of aiding the poor. We have just begun the task, and many more steps are necessary before the fabric of our national life is repaired. Our democracy must be sufficiently broad of base so that never again will large segments of that society—the minorities, the youth, the poor, the students—feel estranged from the goals of the nation, including its foreign policy. In this connection, technical changes in the system of foreign policy decision-making are called for, including a revamping and democratizing of the State Department, with a more direct responsibility for making decisions than it has enjoyed under our past six Presidents, and a more open relationship to the public through the Congress. Above all, open channels of communication are required, which permit a variety of inputs and feedback to allow the decision-making process to weigh the various perceptions that individuals and organizations bring to bear on the problem.

Finally, readjustment of the structure and outward form of the body politic is needed. Reorganization of internal administrative lines to give voice to our great, interstate City-Regions will provide internal geopolitical balance. Reconsideration of the parameters of the nation by redefinition of the "organic" United States is also overdue. Specifically, the ambivalent roles of Puerto Rico, the Virgin Islands, Guam, and the Trust Territories need reappraisal. In the last analysis, a federal society based on states (or, for the future, States and City-Regions) ought to include all of the administered territory within the same hierarchical framework, and not leave some parts in semi-colonial status.

5   MARITIME EUROPE

The Emergence of
a New Type of Superstate

Today's superpowers, the United States and the Soviet Union, have in common that they are political unions of diverse physical and cultural landscapes. Because of historical circumstances, racial and ethnic groups in the United States are not the basis for separate, internal, political components as they are in the Soviet Union. However, as we have noted, America's minority groups are concentrated in specific areas, and this concentration does have political and economic consequences. In addition, the superpowers have the following in common: 1) large, well-knit, and densely populated ecumenes; 2) vast areas of moderately populated, exploitable national territory in which extensive farming is carried on or extractive industries are pursued—such lands we will call "effective national territory"; and 3) huge tracts of unpopulated, barren land, both frozen and desert wastes—the empty spaces.

Both the effective national territories and the empty spaces provide abundant sources of raw materials and the bases within which to conduct many of the scientific activities of the nuclear age. They also offer in their subhumid-continental and subtropical-arid sectors a long-range outlet for expanding populations. These vast tracts of land situated outside of the ecumene are national morale boosters; their environment provides continuous challenge to the national spirit and genius.

Maritime Europe is a third major power region of the globe. But Maritime Europe is different from the other two and from the fourth major power, Mainland China. It is not a superpower because it lacks political unity. It is also not a superpower because it lacks the vast effective national territories and the empty spaces of the United States and the Soviet Union.

Is it too late for Maritime Europe to copy the geopolitical structure of the superpowers? A unity of Maritime Europe, western North Africa, and the Sahara would present a diversified political landscape that would have much in common with that of the other two. Until the end of the Second World War, suggestions for the creation of such a structure would have been regarded as sheer fantasy. This was because of 1) the stalemate stemming from the nearly balanced strength of Maritime Europe's separate core areas; 2) the interests of Germany in Eastern Europe; 3) the extraregional associations of the United Kingdom and France. Today none of these three factors is of sufficient objective validity to deter Maritime Europe's geopolitical unity. The biggest obstacle is the problem of achieving geopolitical union with the Maghreb. Had such a federation been proposed forty years ago, its realization would have been relatively simple. At that time the ratio of Europeans to the Muslims of the Maghreb was 15 to 1. In contrast, the ratio of Slavs to non-Russians in 1917 Russia was only 3 to 1. Replacing European colonial rule with a genuine federation might have met with enthusiastic Muslim response. At worst, no greater force and pressure would have had to be applied than was applied by the Russians against native peoples in the conversion of the Czarist Empire to the Union of Republics.

It is pointless to bemoan what might have been. Today's problems will not be solved with yesterday's methods. European-North African geopolitical unity must now be achieved by subtle economic and political persuasion—not naked force; by appeal to the self-interest of each side—not one-way economic exploitation. Such a unity remains a practical possibility, if only because it is so sorely needed by both Europeans and North Africans. Realization of the union hinges, first, upon a speedy unification of the West European core without interim loss of the Maghreb to the Communist world. If unity of the European core is too long in coming, then the opportunity for the broader geopolitical structure will probably be lost.

In this chapter we shall discuss the prerequisites for a European superstate. Such a state would have, in common with the other superpowers, a large, well-developed middle latitude ecumene of 480,000 square miles, compared with 500,000 square miles for the United States core and 600,000 square miles for the Soviet Union. It would also have vast empty space—the Sahara. (See Map 14.)

However, the geopolitical structure of this European-North African state would differ in comparison with the others in five ways: 1) its ecumene would be far more densely populated; 2) it would lack ex-

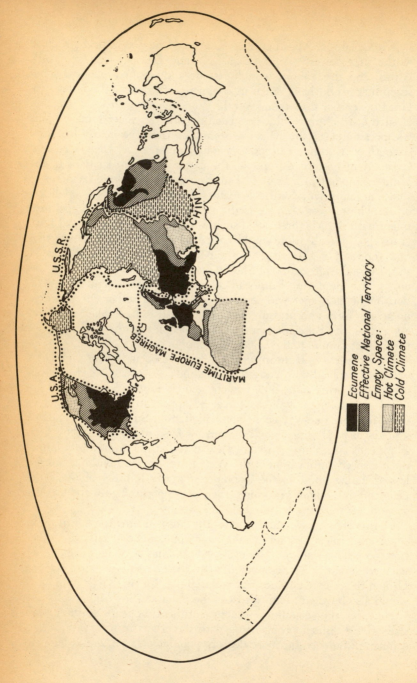

MAP 14. Geopolitical Features of the Four Major Geopolitical Regions' Power Cores

tensive effective national territory outside the core area; 3) it would continue to suffer from its locational-strategic position of being caught between the other two superpowers; 4) it would maintain intimate ties with other parts of Asia and Africa that could not be altogether discarded in any superstate-building process; 5) its empty space would be considerably less accessible to the rest of the country than is the case with the American desert or Soviet Central Asia.

Maritime Europe's ecumene has a population of about 215 million and consequently a population density of 465 persons per square mile. This is more than twice the densities of the ecumenes of the superpowers, the United States ecumene having a population of 95 million and a population density of 225 persons per square mile, and the Soviet ecumene having a population of 130 million and a density of 220 persons per square mile. China's ecumene has a population of 250 million and a density of over 500 per square mile.

Contrasts in effective national territories are vivid. For Maritime Europe, only the Mediterranean shorelands are effective national territory—i.e., the "exploitable" lands outside the ecumene, which possess raw materials and offer favorable milieu for settlement. But these shorelands are not highly mineralized and agriculture suffers from absence of level land and lack of summer rainfall. Also, most important, these areas are already densely populated relative to their resource base. Spain alone might be described as lightly populated (170 persons per square mile), though its lack of water limits population growth potential. Thus, Maritime Europe and North Africa do not possess the effective national territory with limited populations that the U.S.S.R. possesses in Siberia or the United States has in its central and western interior reaches.

The geologic fates have not been kind to this part of the Old World. The land that might have been Europe's exploitable national territory lies covered by the Mediterranean's waters. In the Soviet Union and the United States, such lands were covered by inland seas in the geologic past, but they have since emerged in their present dry-land form.

With respect to its locational strategic position, the ecumene of Maritime Europe is open to the Soviet core via the North European plain and to the American ecumene via the North Atlantic. Thus the Maritime European core lies wedged in between those of its neighboring superpowers. Their ecumenes, in turn, lie adjacent to only one superpower core.

Another measure of difference is extraregional links. The associations that European countries have in Sub-Saharan Africa, Asia, and Oceania help to mold the position of European uniqueness. Both the United States and Russia evolved in relative isolation. Their maturing economies rested on self-sufficiency. A European superstate will have to emerge from an already mature core. Consequently, existing extraregional ties such as those held by the Commonwealth or France cannot be snapped, but will have to be reshaped to accommodate changes brought on by the political unity of the core area.

Finally, inaccessibility of the Sahara is a handicap to Maritime Europe that neither the United States nor the Soviet Union has to face with respect to its desert area. Like the Sahara, the deserts of the latter two superpowers can be approached directly from the ecumene and the effective national territories. Unlike the Sahara, however, these deserts can also be approached from their far side. The Pacific coast and its bordering mountains constitute a forward point of population and surface water supply which has enabled Americans to support desert developments from an adjoining base. In the same manner, the peoples, resources, and surface waters of the Soviet Central Asian mountains and the industrialized centers of the Caspian Sea adjoin the Soviet Central Asian deserts, affording greater ease of development. South of the Sahara lies no modern European outlier, but Black Africa.

Mainland China, more similar in geopolitical structure to Europe than to the two superpowers, has the most densely populated of all major power ecumenes. Clearly, the transportation network that supports the industrialized populations of North China is far more limited than the networks of the other powers. The major form of transportation, the railroads, trend north-south; water communications are less adequate than they are in South China because of flooding and shallow waters. The ecumene extends from Manchuria (Haerbin, Changchun, Fushun, and Shenyang) through Peking, Tsinan and Tsingtao to Nanking and Shanghai. Its population densities range from 250 to 1,000 per square mile. The belt of Effective National Territory is relatively narrow. It includes northern and western Manchuria and the lands of North and Northwest China within the great loop of the Hwang Ho that lies south of the Great Wall. In general these are areas with population densities of from 25 to 125 persons per square mile. These "exploitable" lands are lands of intense colonization, the rapid growth of the steel center of Paotou and the industrial development of Lanchou exemplifying the trend. The

Effective National Territory is endowed with minerals (coal, iron, petroleum), but lies within the marginal rainfall belt of ten to twenty inches annually, thus offering grasslands that are convertible to a grain-growing economy (wheat, millet).

China's Empty Space is vast, and is populated either by nomadic herders or is empty. These lands of Inner Mongolia, Sinkiang, and Tibet wrap themselves around the Effective National Territory in a belt that stretches for over 3,000 miles and that is up to 1,000 miles in width. Inner Mongolia and Tibet especially are in the cold climatic regions. Both in the Effective National Territory and in the Empty Spaces, the Chinese are settling rapidly and diluting the national minorities of these lands with Han peoples. Ten times as many Chinese as natives live in Inner Mongolia, and the Tibetans have become a minority in their own land.

In consideration of all the above factors, we must conclude that a unified Maritime European-North African union would lack the completeness of geopolitical structure possessed by the two superpowers. Conceivably, a unified Maritime Europe might try to take up a third and balancing position in the East-West struggle. Should China also take up a balancing position, there might be symmetry through pairing, or equilibrium through individual standoff, among the four. Such a position has, as we have pointed out earlier, been projected by contemporary German geopoliticians, as it was by Charles de Gaulle. But, without unity with Eastern Europe as well, the "balancer" would not be powerful enough to remain truly independent. Once committed to casting its weight with one superpower against the other, Maritime Europe would probably not be able to reverse its position. Most logically from a political-strategic and economic standpoint, and most probably from an historic-cultural orientation, Maritime Europe will continue to maintain its close ties with the rest of the Atlantic Basin. Continued external pressure from the Soviet Union and internal pressure from national Communist parties, as well as the counterweight of Mainland China as a global force, suggest that a unified Free Europe would not take up a posture of third force isolation. Far more likely, such a geopolitical region would play a reinvigorated role as a full partner in the Atlantic Alliance.

The Locational Perspective

Europe is not a clearly defined continent; it is a part of the Eurasian landmass. Moreover, its links southward via the Mediterranean

Sea have brought it into close association with the North African littoral. To delimit Europe precisely is a matter of some difficulty, because Europe is not only a piece of land; it is a cultural concept. Europe is a place, but it is also civilization, history, land-use, urban patterns, trade, and above all, people. When European culture spills over into areas that are physically contiguous to what was traditionally known as Europe, the boundaries of Europe tend to change. Europe has expanded beyond its Urals boundary into Siberia, and across the Mediterranean into the Maghreb and the Levant. The English geographer Lyde aptly expressed this by saying, "The separation of Europe from Asia is, therefore, historic rather than geographical, political rather than physical . . . the weakness of any politico-historic influences is shown by the fact that the nominal frontier in the east runs neither along the Urals . . . nor along the Caucasus."[1]

In this chapter our concern is not with Continental Europe's eastern boundaries, but rather with the eastern borders of Maritime Europe. It is the separation of seaward from landward Europe that is the crucial geopolitical problem of the continent. For hundreds of years this boundary has lain along a belt of political instability, extending from Finland to Greece. North-south trade lines united the belt, but they were more than offset by clashes along the east-west axis. Lyde called that portion of the belt from the mouth of the Danube to the mouth of the Vistula "Isthmian" Europe.[2] The belt, in its entirety, has been called the Eastern Marchlands of Europe.[3] Mackinder described it as the "middle tier of states between Germany and Russia."[4] Now this belt of instability has shifted westward, from the Aegean and Black seas to the western end of the Baltic, to include the area known as *Mitteleuropa*, or Central Europe. Gottmann calls these combined central and eastern European lands, the Tidal Lands of Europe.[5] We have, in Chapter 3, discussed the problem of drawing a boundary line through the Tidal Lands of Europe. Whereas in the past the balanced strength of Germany and Russia made it necessary to draw the boundary somewhere within Isthmian

---

[1] Lionel W. Lyde, *The Continent of Europe* (London: Macmillan & Co., 1926), p. 7.

[2] *Ibid.*, p. 394.

[3] H. G. Wanklyn, *The Eastern Marchlands of Europe* (London: Philip, 1941.)

[4] Mackinder, *Democratic Ideals and Reality*, p. 161.

[5] Jean Gottmann, *A Geography of Europe* (New York: Holt, 1954), p. 333.

Europe, today's realities place all of the European Black Sea littoral and the Baltic within the orbit of Soviet landpower. Soviet-dominated Communism in Isthmian Europe represents a radical departure from older forms of extraregional controls, because it involves large cadres of national elements together with foreign Soviet forces in an enterprise of joint control.

In this chapter we shall focus our attention on Maritime Europe— that part of Europe that includes its western reaches, most of its northern reaches, part of its central reaches, and the Mediterranean reaches: all oriented toward the sea.

To Americans, the future without a free Maritime Europe can scarcely be contemplated. Maritime Europe is more than simply part of our past. Our association with it is an essential ingredient of our present and future. It was in Maritime Europe that the modern national state arose and industrial and agricultural specialization evolved. The cultural-political mold of the United States was Western European-inspired. With the maturing of our national state has come the desire to strengthen our bonds with Europe, not to weaken them. For along with the recognition of the significance of past ties has come an appreciation that our fate is inseparably linked with Maritime Europe's security. From its end of the North Atlantic Basin, Europe faces the heart of North America, and is as near to most of South America as is the United States. Of equal locational significance is Europe's position at the center of the Old World Parallelogram. From there, it is the staging area that overlooks much of Asia and Africa. Finally, we can note Europe's central location in a global sense. Most of the world's landmasses lie within one hemisphere, called the "land hemisphere," and the center of this hemisphere lies in France.

When we view this strategic location along with the size and quality of Maritime Europe's population, its productive capacity and political and economic links to the rest of the world, then we can only conclude that it is destined to remain the most important extraregional associate of the United States.

Background to Maritime Europe's Integration

If Asia is the most senior of the continents historically and culturally, then Maritime Europe is the most senior politically and technologically. From the Atlantic to the Elbe, little in the physical environment has been unaffected by this technology, whether applied through agriculture, manufacturing, or transportation. And little of this technological application has been unaffected by political boundaries.

Nowhere else has man, through changing machines and ideas, effected such a variety of stages in landscape development—some totally new, others recurring as higher levels of previously known stages. Thus, in Maritime Europe, soils have been chemically altered through intense application of fertilizers; forests have been restored over vast areas once stripped of their tree cover; streams have been canalized and flows regulated; mountain valleys have been inundated and embayments drained; coastlines have been reshaped. Some minerals have been exhausted (the iron ore of England's Cleveland hills) or have been considered too expensive to continue to be intensively mined (Sicily's sulphur). Others, however, have recently been discovered (North Sea natural gas and oil) or have been taken out of economic obscurity (Ireland's peat). Areas where settlements have been abandoned have been restored. New lines and systems of transportation have been formed, some on recent, others on ancient traces.

Age and diversity present certain obstacles to continued development of the landscape but at the same time afford dramatic opportunities. One obstacle to development is that technically advanced industries have large-scale commitments in capital investment (machinery and men), and that it may not be feasible to shift to an even more advanced stage because of the attendant economic and social disruption. Another obstacle lies in the sharp differences in rates of development that exist both within and between countries. While in theory, the surplus from more advanced areas could be used to build up the more backward ones, in practice, this surplus frequently is invested to accelerate the progress of the more advanced area.

Countering these general obstacles to continued economic development are two important forces: 1) the destruction of plants and machinery during World War Two and the disruptive effects of the postwar division of the continent, which forced a good deal of Maritime Europe to renovate its manufacturing plant, and 2) the opportunities for progress that are presented by an advanced, highly diversified landscape through area specialization and area interchange. Intimate inter-area associations stimulate less developed sections to intensify their rate of progress, because of their desires to emulate the advances that are being made by neighbors. In Europe, economic decentralization does not carry with it the risks of political separatism, as in larger, more dispersed regions. On the contrary, the economic buildup of southern France or southern Italy enhances the strength of the central government. In modern European experience, therefore, economic decentralization and political centralization fortify one another.

The diversity that characterizes Maritime Europe is to a great extent the result of the responses of different peoples to different physical environments. But some of this diversity has been politically inspired or intensified. It is with politically inspired differences, if they do not serve valid economic and social uses of the landscape, that today's proponents of European integration have their strongest quarrels.

We might divide the entire European geopolitical scene into two periods: 1) pre-World War Two separatism and 2) post-World War Two integration. In the first period, starting with the emergence of Europe from feudalism and culminating in the modern national state, differences within the physical environment served to set European peoples apart from one another. The divides between river valleys, in particular, served as barriers. Within river valleys, concentrations of population and economic activities constituted core areas for the emergence of national states. Some were along middle and upper river valley crossings, such as Augsburg (Lech-Danube), Vienna (Danube-Morava), Belgrade (Danube-Sava-Morava), and Paris (Seine-Marne). Others were at the lower courses of rivers or at the key coastal plains, such as London (Thames), The Hague (Rhine), Bucharest (Danube), Copenhagen, and Stockholm. Although the contemporary map of Europe indicates that inland seas and gulfs serve to separate states, these have not been historic barriers like the land divides. Indeed, the North, Baltic, and Mediterranean seas, and their various arms, have had a longer history as connectors than as separators. These seas began to be used as political boundaries in the seventeenth century, but only in the nineteenth and twentieth centuries did they take on their significant present forms.

The political-barrier qualities of land divides in Europe are perhaps best underscored by the fact that the boundaries that follow them have tended to remain fixed over longer periods of time than those that cut across broad plains areas. In this context, compare the greater permanence of boundaries that have followed the Swiss High Alps, the Pyrenees, the Carpathians, and the Transylvanian

Alps with those that have cut across the North European or Danubian plains.[6]

It is not simply the negative qualities of nature as a barrier to movement that has helped to frame the European national state. In Maritime Europe, access to the open sea from a state's core area enabled small territories to compensate for limited hinterlands by acquiring extensive colonial forelands across the waters. Indeed, a small land area could sometimes be turned to advantage in that short land frontiers required limited armies, while fleets, with minimal manpower requirements, could compete for world power.

We can therefore explain the map of national state Europe both in terms of the influence of the landmass and in terms of relationship to other parts of the world by sea. The deeply embayed submerged Atlantic coasts and the multiplicity of key river valley contacts with the sea contributed to the relatively large number of European states. Particular note can be taken of the role of glaciation in this context. Continental glaciation and its meltwaters provided the fjords and submerged the nonglaciated embayments which opened much of the landmass to the oceanic world. The young rugged ranges of the Alpine period and the mountain glaciation formed in these Pluvial times have formed convenient national boundaries. Even the land features associated with continental glaciation, such as the morainic ridges along the Baltic coast or poorly drained marshes have, by their barrier nature, served as boundaries. The hills and swamps of the southern Baltic coast, not the sea, barred Sweden from Poland and Germany. Also, as land communications improved, a power invading from the sea, like Sweden, lost much of its former mobility advantage, because opposing land forces could now concentrate with greater speed to oppose the sea invasion.

Differences in the physical environment, then, served to set Europeans apart from one another during medieval and early modern times. These differences formed frameworks for emergent national states. These states have since taken on political, economic, military, and psychological features, which have fortified the differences stemming from the physical environment. What intensified this process was the carving out of colonial empires, which compensated for domestic resource limitations and dispensed with the need for European states to act in consonance with their neighbors.

[6] For an appreciation of this, cf. figures 15 and 16 in S. Whittemore Boggs, *International Boundaries* (New York: Columbia University Press, 1940), pp. 114 and 116-117.

Jean Gottmann has suggested that *iconography*—the ideas that men hold about political units, especially the national state—constitutes one of the two principal forces that operate in the political partitioning of the earth. The second and contrary force is the *movement* of men, goods, and ideas across state lines.[7] Iconography seeks to maintain the status quo; movement reflects the dynamics of man's use of the land. It challenges the status quo because it puts pressure on the barrier features of existing political units.

In pre-World War Two Europe, when the age of political separatism prevailed, the national state was used as an instrument to interrupt movement from one part of Europe to another. Iconography was oriented to the national state, and stood in contrast to movement forces. Since the Second World War a regional iconography has appeared. *Integration* has become the motivating economic and political spirit within Maritime Europe (and also Eastern Europe). Broad patterns of unity within the landscape, such as the running together of national ecumenes and the building of efficient avenues of transportation and communication, are now held up as rationales for the framework of integration. Movement and iconography are now no longer contrary forces.

Specific factors promoting Maritime Europe's integration are:

1) Common economic recovery problems;

2) Common fear of military and political pressure from the Soviet Union, directly or through local Communist parties;

3) Loss of many dependent areas and consequent reduction of over-all commitments;

4) American support of European integration concepts and programs;

5) Economic specialization;

6) Counter-moves to East European integration programs;

7) Counter-moves to the U.S.-owned multinational corporations;

8) An inward, or more European, orientation by European statesmen and peoples. This is in part due to the factors listed above. In great measure, however, it is due to changes in world power status. The two greatest powers in the world that emerged in the wake of World War Two are non-European. For Europe to gain a similar position, individual national state activities are inadequate, and some form of integrated action has been proposed as a substitute.

[7] J. Gottmann, "Geography and International Relations," *World Politics*, III, No. 2 (January, 1951), pp. 153-73.

The integration of Maritime Europe is, in one sense, a vague concept because it means different things to different persons. To some Europeans it means political integration; to others, economic integration; to the U.S.S.R. it means the crystallizing of an anti-Soviet bloc as a satellite of the United States, in more or less the same relationship that the U.S.S.R. has with its Eastern European satellites. To many Americans the integration of Europe conjures up the picture of a United States of Europe. An integrated Europe could, as we have pointed out, evolve into a superstate, but it would have to have new forms and geopolitical goals.

The Physical Framework

Proponents of European integration point out that Europe has a unity that stems from the interaction of its physical and cultural diversities. These diversities are not hard and fast barriers, because they blend into the greater whole that is Maritime Europe.

Among the physical elements that favor unity is size. Maritime Europe is quite compact, with a land area of approximately 1,220,000 square miles. Its national ecumenes merge, and it is possible to travel through many countries and cultural areas in a very short time. To many Europeans, certainly, the provincialism of peoples in other parts of the world is unknown. Maximum distances in Western Europe, as from London to Munich or from Paris to Rome, are under 700 miles. One of the longest conceivable intra-European journeys, from Madrid to Hamburg, is only 1,200 miles.

Another unifying element is shape. Most of the land is never far removed from the ocean or the interior seas. Irregular coastlines have stimulated settlements, shipping, and fishing. Moreover, the long northeasterly trend of the coast from Portugal to Norway increases the extent of the area served by the warming and moistening westerly winds and currents. Even that small part of Maritime Europe that lies north of 60 degrees north latitude is warmed by the Atlantic, so that, unlike other parts of the earth in similar latitudes, it is habitable.

Although climatic differences are to be found in Europe, they are not sharp, but grade into one another, acting as complementary units. In this sense, climate can be considered a unifying element. Western Europe's west coast marine climate (mild winters, cool summers, and well-distributed rainfall) grades into that of Central Europe (where cyclonic winds are weaker, rainfall maximum is in the summer, and the winter frost period is longer). The Mediterranean climate is distinct from these other two climatic regions, but there are transitional zones that interconnect Europe's south and north. These are the climates of the Po Basin, the southern edge of the Massif Central, and northern Portugal. They are characterized by summers that are cooler than those in the Mediterranean and by slight cyclonic activity that brings late spring and early fall rain. Thus, in those countries where the Mediterranean climate and agricultural patterns prevail, especially in France and Italy, there are transitional physical and human-use areas, like the central Rhone and the Po, that serve to link their countries to the Europe north of the Alps.

Although physiographic regions are diverse, there is nevertheless a pattern to these distinct regions that makes interconnection easy. The outstanding physical feature is the North European Plain, with its associated lowland basins in France and England. This plain is surrounded by highlands. These include the north Scottish and the Fenno-Scandinavian Massifs to the north and the various Alpine ranges to the south. Associated with these Alpine ranges are enclosed or outlying plateaus, like the Spanish Meseta, the Massif Central, and the Bohemian Massif. Also enclosed within these ranges are such basins as the Po and the Upper and Middle Danube. The Alpine ranges, from whose crests streams flow either north and westward to the Atlantic, North, and Baltic seas, or south to the Mediterranean, serve as the main water divide for Europe. East-west travel has always been easy, in conformity with the North European and Danubian Plains. North-south or northwest-southeast movement has to be channeled through key pass routes in the Alps or along such river valleys as the Rhine-Moselle-Rhone, Rhine-Doubs-Saone-Rhone, and the Rhine-Main-Danube. Railways, roads, and navigable waterways occupy most of these passageways and many European cities have grown up at shipping points along the transcontinental routes. Thus, mountain barriers, while sufficient to discourage political intercourse, have never discouraged economic and cultural ties. This can be seen by examining the extent of the European ecumene, which stretches from the Scottish Lowland to the Rhine, the Pyrenees, and northern Italy—with gaps only in the Alps and central France.

Movement and Integration

Maritime Europe's inland transportation system has undergone radical changes. The system has been modernized, rationalized, and unified, furthering the general cause of economic and political integration. Movement, as we have noted, succinctly expresses the dynamics of man's changing use of the landscape. Prior to World War Two, railroads accounted for most of the goods shipped within Maritime Europe. Today, rail accounts for less than half of the ton-mileage, road for about 40 per cent, and water for the remainder. This trend is continuing. The fuels, ores, and building materials tra-ditionally handled by the European railways often can be moved more cheaply by water. Moreover, roads are capable of competing with rails for food, agricultural products, manufactured goods, and in some cases building materials, partly because of the short hauls for which railroads are used. For example, in the United Kingdom, West Germany, and Italy, highway hauls average up to 150 miles—or more than the average for railway trips. Railroads are being improved by integrating various national systems in rate-fixing and in handling, and by changing coal-burning locomotives to diesels and electrics. However, the railroad has had its period of dominance. A by-product of reduced railroad trackage should be the conversion of this valu-able space for new highways, as in urbanized portions of the United States.

The entrance of Maritime Europe into the automotive age came with breath-taking rapidity. Motor vehicles now carry most of the passenger movement, and annual motor vehicle production (over ten million) exceeds that of the United States. The use of motor vehi-cles can be reckoned as an important integrating factor. There are now over 60 million registered vehicles in the region (four times the 1954 number), or one vehicle for every five persons. In the United States the ratio is one for every two persons.

Production of automobiles on a per capita basis in such countries as France, West Germany, and the United Kingdom, is fast ap-proaching that of the United States, and the ratio of automobiles to persons is rapidly rising. This ratio probably will never match that of our country; because of excellent public transportation systems and less sprawling cities, fewer families in Europe need two cars than in the United States.

If such indices as automobile accident deaths and chronic traffic jams can be used, then Maritime Europe is already in the automo-tive age with a vengeance. With half as many automobiles, its traffic death toll exceeds that of the United States. Poorer roads and denser populations make driving relatively hazardous in Europe, and the building of modern highways in large, urbanized areas like London,

Paris, and Rome is extremely expensive. The net result of the desire of Europeans to have automobiles is forcing them to suburbanize at a rapid rate—more rapid than some planning authorities may wish to see. Also, because it is financially and socially easier to build modern highways in less populous areas, the frontiers between different European countries are likely to receive new highway construction more rapidly than some of the older big cities. The attendant problems notwithstanding, Maritime Europe has benefited increasingly from the automotive age. Not the least of these benefits will be derived from the role of the automobile as a social and economic force for European unity.

The map of European movement is undergoing change in intensity, quality, and directional flow of passengers and goods. (See Map 15.) Several projects which show the scope of this change are under way or have been completed. These include 1) *The English Channel Electric Grid Link.* This enables hydroelectricity that is surplus in France during the rainy winter to be sold to the United Kingdom. During the summer, surplus English coal-generated electricity is sold to water-short France. 2) *The Mont Blanc Auto Tunnel.* This is the first automobile tunnel through the Alps. It connects France to Italy by funneling traffic under the northern flank of the highest mountain in the Alps and through the Val d'Aosta. The Mont Blanc tunnel handles hundreds of thousands of vehicles annually, connecting Turin with both Geneva and Chamonix-Paris, and is an important stimulus to tourism and business, cutting time distance from Paris to Rome by about one-fifth. This tunnel seven miles long was built at a cost per mile that is in actuality less than the cost of highway construction in built-up areas like Greater London. 3) *The Great St. Bernard Auto Tunnel* is a further spur to German-Swiss-Italian traffic. 4) *The Moselle Canal.* Canalization of the Moselle River, from Thionville to Trier along the Rhine was carried out by France, Luxembourg, and Germany. Use of the canal enables Ruhr coal to be shipped to Lorraine at about half its previous cost. Its use has effected similar savings in the shipment of France's iron ore to the Ruhr and enables French steel to be exported via the Rhine. 5) *Transcontinental Pipelines.* The appearance of transcontinental pipelines is part of a revolutionary shift in the location of petroleum refineries toward the center of the European markets, not along Europe's coasts or at the sources of supply. Lines from Lavéra, west of Marseilles, to Strasbourg and Karlsruhe, and from Wilhelmshaven to Cologne, pipe petroleum to inland Rhine refineries. Other pipelines

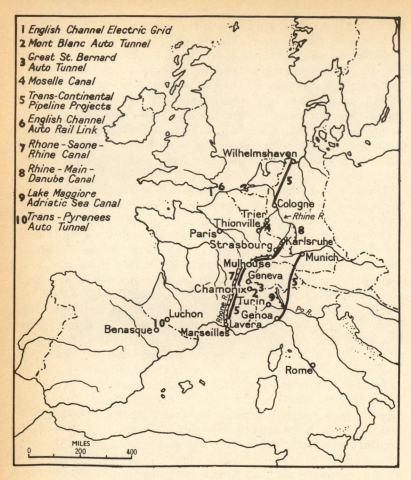

1 English Channel Electric Grid
2 Mont Blanc Auto Tunnel
3 Great St. Bernard Auto Tunnel
4 Moselle Canal
5 Trans-Continental Pipeline Projects
6 English Channel Auto Rail Link
7 Rhone - Saone - Rhine Canal
8 Rhine - Main - Danube Canal
9 Lake Maggiore Adriatic Sea Canal
10 Trans - Pyrenees Auto Tunnel

Wilhelmshaven

Cologne
← Rhine R.

Trier
Thionville
Paris
Strasbourg
Karlsruhe
Munich
Mulhouse
Geneva
Chamonix
Turin
Po R.
Luchon
Genoa
Benasque
La Vera
Marseilles
Rhone R.

Rome

MILES
0   200   400

MAP 15. Maritime Europe's Movement Links

are aimed at moving petroleum from Genoa northward to Switzerland and northeastward to southern Germany. Lines from Italy to Austria are also under consideration, and Vienna is already connected to the Soviet pipeline system. 6) *The English Channel Auto-Rail Tunnel* is under way. More than a conduit for goods and people, it will be a link to the Continent which has considerable psychological and political significance.

Other movement links are indefinite but nonetheless worthy of mention. These include 1) *The Rhone-Saone-Rhine Canal* (from Marseilles to Mulhouse), which may have to await greater political stability in the Mediterranean; 2) *The Rhine-Main-Danube Canal*, whose building would only be warranted by large-scale East-West trade; 3) *The Lake Maggiore-Adriatic Sea Canal*, which would utilize the Ticino-Po riverways; and 4) *A Trans-Pyrenees Auto Tunnel* under the Pic de la Glère to link Luchon in France to Benasque in Spain. The Spanish are interested in such a mid-Pyrenees Tunnel to connect industrialized southwestern France with Madrid.

Internationalized waterways are also a Soviet-bloc concern (links between the Danube and the Oder and between the Oder and the Vistula have been proposed), as are east-west pipelines from Soviet petroleum sources to Central Europe and to the Baltic. The future for innovations in Europe's land and water traffic links appears bright. When the expanded Common Market Europe and Free Trade Europe succeed in bridging their differences, some of the projects that have been mentioned may materialize more quickly than expected.

Ideological and political interaction is also an aspect of movement. In this respect, the inter-European ties of various National Catholic and Socialist parties can be regarded as forces for European unity. So is the mobility of labor, which brings with it a need on the part of the host country to fulfill the cultural as well as the material wants of the immigrant worker. The settling of people of different national origins, not in frontier zones, but in the very center of European states, is still another trend to be noted. No longer must we look to Alsace, Savoy, Provence, and southwestern Sweden for the zones of cultural contact that have developed as the result of movement of people. Now, Paris, London, Liverpool, Liège, Düsseldorf, Frankfort, Zurich, and smaller, more isolated manufacturing centers all contain sizable nonindigenous populations. Since national boundary zones are no longer the only cultural frontiers, their barrier qualities tend to lessen. Considering the general examples set by Maritime Europe since the Second World War, the Austrian-Italian dispute over "Italianization" of the German-speaking Tyrol would appear to be an unpleasant throwback to the prewar Europe.

The Resource Base

Many of Maritime Europe's economic problems are related to the resource base. Two questions arise with respect to this resource base: 1) what are Europe's raw materials? and 2) if distributed rationally, would these resources be able to build up the present national economies in a substantial manner?

In answer to the first question, it can be said that Maritime Europe is moderately wealthy in domestic raw materials, not in comparison with Anglo-America or the U.S.S.R., but with a more varied base than that of any other similar portion of the earth. If we compare the raw material base of the ecumenes only, Europe is not far behind the two superpowers and is ahead of China. Among the important raw materials that are available in ample quantity in Maritime Europe are the coal of Germany and the United Kingdom, the iron ores of France and Sweden, the potash of Germany and France, the petroleum and natural gas of the North Sea, the mercury of Spain, the sulphur of Sicily, the magnesium of Austria, the timber of Scandinavia, the water-power of the Alps and Scandinavia, and the specialized foodstuffs of the North European Plain and the Mediterranean (dairy and horticultural). The fact that the region has an increasing agricultural deficit must be noted. While rapid agricultural expansion is under way, especially in the Common Market-stimulated French sector, this is an expansion oriented to specialty crops. Consequently, relative self-sufficiency, even as practiced by the United States and the Soviet Union, is impossible. Only a revolutionary development of the Sahara as an agricultural storehouse for fruits, vegetables, and industrial crops could alter this picture. In the Sahara, however, surface, subsurface, and shallow waters are generally lacking and large-scale irrigated farming would have to depend upon desalted water from the sea or from deep subterranean sources that are claimed by some to exist.

Among the minor supplies of raw materials available to Maritime Europe are such minerals as manganese (Sweden and Italy), chrome (Greece), molybdenum (Norway), vanadium (Norway), copper (Norway, Sweden, Spain, Germany), lead (Germany), phosphates (France and Belgium), and petroleum (Austria, Netherlands, Germany, France, Italy). Again, limitations of petroleum frustrate possibilities of regional industrial self-sufficiency, unless Saharan oil and natural gas are assured.

All of these raw materials provide a substantial base for industry and it is easy to see how greater exchanges of materials within an integrated Europe have facilitated rises in production. For example, coal from Germany has been used to boost nitrogen output for fertilizer industries in Belgium, France, Italy, and Switzerland. Ruhr coal has also helped Italy and France to increase caustic soda production. Small amounts of surplus hydroelectric power are being sold by Luxembourg to surrounding localities in France, Belgium, and West Germany. The Dutch steel industry has been expanded with the aid of Luxembourg iron ores. Norway, whose hydroelectric potential is estimated at five times present capacity, could sell its surplus to Denmark. French bauxite and the currently un-mined Sicilian sulphur, are other materials that could be more fruitfully exploited by other European countries under the new production and marketing conditions.

Obviously economic integration has affected some industry more than others. These include steel, petroleum, chemicals, and power. In such industries, greater exchange of raw and semi-finished materials means higher production of finished products also. In the power industries, a wider European market continues to stimulate hydroelectricity developments and has hastened the exploitation of Saharan petroleum and natural gas. Even atomic power, although initial opinions of its potential have been tempered by rising cost estimates, is likely to experience more rapid progress because economic integration will enable smaller countries to benefit from the know-how and facilities of their larger neighbors.

The free interchange of labor has been an important factor in the greater exploitation of Europe's domestic raw materials as well as in its ability to process foreign materials. Mining in France, Belgium, and Germany, agriculture in France, and forestry in Sweden, have been expanded with the help of foreign labor. This manpower has also benefited the Belgian building industry, Germany's steel and chemical manufacturing, Sweden's machine making, and Switzerland's tourism. The European exporters of manpower—Italy, Spain, Portugal, Yugoslavia, Greece, The Netherlands, Denmark, Finland—and the Mahgreb and Turkey, have in recent years contributed most of Germany's 600,000, France's 500,000, Switzerland's 500,000, and Sweden's 100,000 foreign workers. Indeed, Italy is now so concerned with the outflow of its citizenry that its northern factories are trying to entice some *émigrés* to return. Spain, which has replaced Italy as the chief labor recruiting area for other European countries, is beginning to anticipate domestic labor shortage as a crucial block to its own industrialization. We may foresee the day when North African, West Indian, Hong Kong, Black African, and South Asian areas will become the major sources of European labor recruitment, in the absence of a sufficiently broad regional labor pool. A significant counter to the trend of freedom of mobility has developed in Switzerland. There, with 25 per cent of the labor force foreign (mainly Italian), a major national debate has broken out over decisions to halt the additional entry of foreign workers and, indeed, to roll back the numbers. The issue has been joined as a choice of decreased national self-reliance or a slowdown of economic development, with possible inflationary consequences.

Europe's experience with the labor market offers lessons to outsiders. Thus, the successful techniques employed by Europeans in stimulating people to move from depressed, overpopulated areas to labor-deficit areas, and the solutions of chronic depressed-area problems, have been studied by American experts who are concerned with the depressed areas of the United States.

Greater population mobility in the current context cannot help but act as a unifying element within Maritime Europe. The present population is growing slowly as compared to population growth in other parts of the world. In 1940 the population was 257 million, while today it is 325 million. This represents an annual increase of about 0.6 per cent over the past three decades. However, since the end of the Second World War the rate of growth has tended to increase in key European countries at an annual rate of 0.9 per cent for France, 1.3 per cent for The Netherlands, and 0.9 per cent for Germany. This increase is important to the Western European countries, where production growth has tended to outstrip population growth. Moreover, the Mediterranean countries have been unable to absorb their increasing populations, despite the fact that the increase is under one per cent. Consequently, countries like Italy, Portugal, Spain, and Greece, whose economic bases are narrow are still able to export labor in small but highly significant quantities.

Organizational Frameworks

Various organizations are working at different levels to integrate Maritime Europe. Some are functional; others are political. The functional organizations attempt to unify Maritime Europe for specific purposes, economic and military. Among them are: W.E.U. (Western European Union—the European component of NATO); O.E.C.D. (Organization for Economic Co-operation and Development); E.C.S.C. (European Coal and Steel Community); E.E.C. (European Economic Community—the Common Market); Euratom; E.F.T.A. (European Free Trade Association); and C.E.R.N. (European Organization of Nuclear Research). Among the organizations devoted to the creation of a united Europe through political means are the Council of Europe and the European Movement.

Unlike most of the functional organizations, the Council of Europe is not an intergovernmental agency, because its Assembly of Members of Parliament from the represented countries speak only for themselves. When efforts to turn the Council of Europe into a Federal Union failed, its leadership began to spur the idea of supranational specialized authorities possessing treaty powers granted by the participating states. The Coal and Steel Community was the first such supranational body, since followed by the Common Market and Euratom.

The most important act that occurred in the postwar European integration process was the creation of the E.E.C.—the Common Market of the Six. The founding countries—France, West Germany, Italy, and the Benelux states—became the core of Maritime Europe. The Common Market, when organized in 1957, had as its purpose the extension over the entire economic field of the type of co-operation that was already being realized within the Coal and Steel Community. In these few years, the pace of reduction of internal customs dues and quotas has been more rapid than projected, labor has achieved free mobility, and capital movement-restrictions have been mostly eliminated. The market free from national discrimination is emerging. On the other hand, tariffs toward third states can be increased, and this is a major fear of the United States as well as of the rest of Maritime Europe.

Certainly Common Market countries could impose tariffs against outside raw materials and foodstuffs. If the 190 million population of the European Six were, in itself, the only market with which E.E.C. industry had to be concerned, higher tariffs upon outside materials might not have far-reaching internal effects. But to continue to prosper, Common Market Europe has to continue to export. Wherever higher-cost domestic raw materials are used behind a protective tariff screen, the advantages in foreign trade that have been gained with such remarkable success are likely to be thrown away. If, for example, low-cost American coal is excluded by tariffs from Belgium to protect the Belgian coal industry, will Belgian wire be able to maintain its current price advantage that has given it half of the total U.S. market?

In general, the advantages that the Common Market offers its members in supplying a big internal market and an unrestricted flow of domestic raw materials should be sufficient to afford the import of foreign materials and products without economic discrimination. But specific industries could suffer if they sought tariff advantages, either from driving up export prices or from provoking foreign tariff retaliation.

Perhaps more than any other industry, agriculture has been represented as seeking to protect itself by Common Market walls. Small-scale, relatively inefficient German farming, especially in the South, is rapidly disappearing in the face of the onslaught of French agricultural competition within the Common Market's unified farm-pricing structure. Moreover, Italian products are eliminating more and more of the small vegetable farms of Belgium and southwest France. But France has been accused by critics of hoping to isolate its relatively high-priced farm products from the competitive effects of external competition. While such an eventuality is by no means impossible, there is no reason to assume that France's Common Market partners will blithely accept higher food costs and consequently lower living standards. Nor need we assume that French agriculture cannot follow the path of French manufacturing and adjust itself to both the demands and the opportunities of the Common Market. Indeed, the modern agricultural revolution that has swept over the American farm since 1940 has every possibility of capturing France's peasant base. True, deeply ingrained local practices and customs have kept French agriculture in a self-satisfied, static state. But part of the reason for the failure of the French farmer to modernize has been lack of market incentives and absence of pressures from forms of urban competition, like job opportunities and city-life amenities. The Common Market is changing the situation. New incentives represented by a European market that is four times the French market is inspiring a chemical and mechanical revolution in French agriculture. Fast trucks, modern food processing, supermarkets, and home refrigerators are creating new demands for the mass production and marketing of foodstuffs, which provides tremendous opportunities for French agriculture. With its rich and varied soil and climatic base, this agriculture should prove no less capable of responding to the challenge than French manufacturing has proved. At the same time, new employment opportunities in manufacturing and improved housing conditions in urban areas are luring increasing numbers away from the farms and spurring the social land-use revolution that is bound to accompany the chemical-mechanical farming age.

Does all this mean that outside farm products would lose ground in their fight for the European Common Market? Not necessarily. Europe can well become self-sufficient in food grains and dairy products if it so desires, but the fertile "limon" soils of the Beauce need not remain essentially in cereals and in sugar beets. Under more intensive farming conditions, they can, in part, be converted to horticulture (though probably at the expense of Belgian and German farm interests). Extensive grazing in the Massif Central may lose out to intensive cattle rearing and fattening along the Loire and the Garonne. Viticulture may disappear from parts of the humid east in response to the pressure of horticulture and dairying. Growth of the domestic rice market reduces Italian exports to other parts of the Common Market and gives scope to other European producers, like Spain, or to extra-European producers. Intensification and change in French agriculture could well affect the competitive position of outside dairy and meat-producing countries, but is less likely to affect outside cereal and sugar producers (who might partly shift their market emphasis from food to feed grains). And in the long run, the modernization of horticulture, not only in France, but in Mediterranean Europe, could shift the internal emphasis from livestock also, increasing the market potential for outside producers.

Maritime Europe is now 85 to 100 per cent self-sufficient in agriculture, with current surpluses in the Common Market in butter and wheat. This self-sufficiency is likely to decrease to 75 to 85 per cent within a few years as living standards improve. It is understandable to find the European Community going through a period of agricultural protectionism. But agricultural protectionism will prove no more valid for Common Market Europe than it has for most national states. Given the greater return on investment rewards that industry can offer, and a decrease in socioeconomic pressure from a shrinking farm group, the agricultural tensions between Common Market Europe and her neighbors will decline. Already countries related to the Common Market as associate members or special trade partners have found such ties to be boons to developing certain sectors of their agriculture. This is true for Greece, Spain, and Israel in citrus, for example. In the long run, even a country like Italy, now 90 per cent self-sufficient in agriculture, will require an increased food import budget for feed grains, oil seeds, fats and oils, wheat (durum), and tobacco, because local agricultural production will not keep pace with the demand of an industrialized, urban society. While there is currently great concern in Britain over the problem of finding a protected place for New Zealand and Australian agriculture in the expanded Common Market, and reluctance on the part of France to offer too great a set of concessions, we believe that the issue will be resolved by the eventual need of Maritime Europe for additional food imports from these Commonwealth countries.

The E.F.T.A. (European Free Trade Association, initially with seven members) and the O.E.C.D. (the Organization for Economic Co-operation and Development) were formed in response to the Common Market's emergence. The latter organization, including the United States and Canada as well as nineteen European countries, was conceived by the United States as a replacement for the O.E.E.C. Its goal is greater North Atlantic economic co-operation and co-ordinated aid to underdeveloped countries. The E.F.T.A., initiated by Britain, was designed to secure greater economic co-operation among its participants, while maintaining existing external associations. For while tariffs among member countries are to be eliminated, separate tariffs can be leveled by individual states upon third parties.

The fear voiced by many that E.E.C. and E.F.T.A. would crystallize as separate and rival blocs in Maritime Europe were exaggerated. Certainly Britain's decision to enter the Common Market, and France's agreement to welcome this entry, reflects the preponderant strength of the forces that are driving toward economic integration. E.F.T.A., in particular, may be viewed in an historical light as a stepping stone to the broadening of Common Market Europe. With expansion of E.E.C. in 1973, to add the U.K., Ireland and Denmark, E.F.T.A. has not withered away. It has regrouped with eight members to organize itself in relation to the Common Market. Now all of Maritime Europe's states belong to either of the two associations.

We may well view the present trade conflicts and negotiations between E.E.C. and E.F.T.A. as an important stage in an evolutionary process. Integrated Maritime Europe needs a core. This was initially provided by the Europe of the Six and now has been expanded into the Europe of the Nine. Integrated Europe also needs to maintain strong associations with the outside world. E.E.C., through France, developed extra-regional ties with the former French colonies; Free

Trade Europe, which had been formed around Britain and its Commonwealth, had even stronger extra-regional bonds.

If the core can be firmly consolidated around the Europe of the Nine without destroying outside associations, the results will be mutually beneficial to Maritime Europe and to those former colonial countries that maintain close economic and cultural ties with Europe. In the event that these ties cannot be maintained, the rupture will have grave political-ideological consequences. For the Commonwealth and the Francophone countries represent the best chance that the Western world has for maintaining sound global contacts that cut across racial and religious lines. Without such ties, our divided world might well become an assortment of hopelessly isolated blocs.

A European Capital

"Wanted—a capital city: centrally located, good accessibility, cosmopolitan in flavor, spacious, moderate climate, economically and politically stable, and with a 'European' tradition." Europeans have been searching for such a city since 1950.

As the number of organizations charged with integrating Europe proliferates, administration and personnel overlap. To help achieve co-ordination and rationalization of the integrating activities, their localization in one city seems highly desirable. Beyond the economic-social aspects of such localization, a central seat can fulfill broader political-psychological functions. If Maritime Europe is to be united it needs a capital to symbolize this unity, as well as to centralize it.

At present, the chief European organizations are located in four cities—Brussels, Luxembourg City, Geneva, and Paris. The Common Market organizations and NATO are in Brussels; the European Parliament and the European Investment Bank in Luxembourg City; E.F.T.A. and *CERN* in Geneva; and O.E.C.D. and certain space research agencies in Paris.

Table 8 is a selected list of major European organizations. Some, like E.C.E. and the European W.H.O., are United Nations-sponsored agencies; O.E.C.D. includes, as associated members, the United States and Canada. The European Organization for Space Research includes one non-European state—Australia. This addition makes available to Maritime Europe the Australian empty space. To European countries, France as well as others, the use of the Sahara is politically complicated as long as France's relations with North Africa remain in their present uncertain state. On the other hand, the

TABLE 8

Maritime European Organizations Headquarter Cities

Name	City	Number of Participating States
CERN (European Organization of Nuclear Research)	Geneva (Meyrin)	13
Council of Europe	Strasbourg	18
E.C.E. (Economic Commission for Europe)	Geneva	31
E.C.S.C. (European Coal and Steel Community)	Brussels	9
E.E.C. (European Economic Community)	Brussels	9
E.I.B. (European Investment Bank)	Luxembourg City	9
E.F.T.A. (European Free Trade Association)	Geneva	8
E.L.D.O. (European Space Vehicle Launching Development Organization)	Paris	7
E.S.R.O. (European Space Research Organization)	Paris	10
E.N.E.A. (European Nuclear Energy Agency)	Paris	21
Euratom (European Atomic Energy Community)	Brussels	9
European Conference of Ministers of Transport	Paris	18
European Movement	Brussels	15
European Parliament	Luxembourg City	9
European World Health Organization	Copenhagen	30
Eurovision (European Broadcasting Union)	Geneva	25
NATO (North Atlantic Treaty Organization)	Brussels	15
Nordic Council	none	5
O.E.C.D. (Organization for Economic Cooperation and Development)	Paris	21
Western European Union	London	7

Australian range at Woomera affords its European users the room for launching satellites, without attendant political problems.

It is one matter to describe the qualities needed by a national capital; it is quite a different matter to sketch out United Europe's requirements for a capital seat.

The chief function of a national capital is to unify the state. The capital city is the center from which radiate the various political and cultural influences that have "nationalizing" effects. Generally, capitals are found within the historic core of the state—that is, within the area of political and population concentration from which the state evolved. Paris is one such example; ancient Rome provides another. Historic cores tend to be centrally located within their states. Where they have been eccentric, capitals have often shifted from them to a more central location, such as in the case of Madrid. Sometimes centrality of location corresponds with the compromise choice of a site against two or more competing cities. Warsaw is an example, chosen over two former capitals, Poznan and Cracow. All capitals, whether central or eccentric, seek easy accessibility to the entire state.

Defensive qualities have been important considerations for locating capitals, as far as both specific sites and general locations are concerned. Budapest is the defensive point where the Danube enters from its last gorge onto the central plain. Ankara was chosen by Ataturk because of its remoteness from the sea.

Border capitals have fulfilled both defensive and offensive functions. Vienna was essentially a frontier-defender from its foundation to the late seventeenth century. Then, with the decline of the Turkish threat, it began to take advantage of its situation's excellent accessibility to three natural passageways: the Austrian, Moravian, and Hungarian gates. Other frontier capitals have been assigned offensive-colonizing roles. These are the *Wachstumspitzen* or forward points, like fifteenth-century Berlin and modern Jerusalem. Rawalpindi (Islamabad), the new capital of Pakistan, is another example.

Once a city becomes a capital, it generally grows rapidly because of its political importance to the state. Rome's growth was supported by the tribute of an empire, Washington's by the taxes of an entire nation. As Whittlesey put it, "the capital city reflects the wealth, power and political organization of the state of which it is the administrative center . . . [capitals] incarnate the corelands that have evolved as nationalities."[8]

However, Europe is not looking for the capital of a nation—it is looking for the capital of a group of nations. Perhaps Europe's capital should possess the locational qualities that federal capitals possess. Federal capitals have been located so as to avoid ill-feeling and jealousies between constituent units and to be as neutral of regional politics as possible. Washington, Ottawa, and Canberra are such cities. Brasilia, chosen partly for such a purpose, was also chosen as a frontier focal point which could unite Brazilians in a drive to conquer the interior.

When we consider Maritime Europe's needs, there is no interior frontier that requires the development-assistance of a capital. Nor is there much enthusiasm over the advantages of an extraterritorial middle-ground type of location, such as has been suggested for a 100-square-mile area along the German-Dutch-Belgian border, an

8 Whittlesey, *The Earth and the State*, pp. 159, 196.

area that has been in dispute. Many Europeans feel that it is more important to locate the capital in a country that is lukewarm about unity than to select a country or an area that is a small intermediary. This is not unlike the thinking that strongly favored locating the United Nations headquarters in the United States to keep the interest of the American public in the United Nations at a high pitch. Whether or not to seek a frontier capital along the Iron Curtain represents still another challenge to the location-seekers. The defensive liabilities of such a measure are obvious; on the other hand, it might be argued that the forward thrust of a European capital could have political-psychological advantages in maintaining close physical contact with Eastern Europe.

Among the cities that have been considered likely candidates for the capital seat are Brussels, Strasbourg, Milan, Nice, Luxembourg City, Paris, Geneva, and Saarbrucken. How closely they meet locational needs can only be judged by matching their qualifications with a list of "ideal" prerequisites. A European capital should, in our opinion, possess the following characteristics: 1) centrality within the European ecumene; 2) accessibility of air, rail, and highway routes; 3) size and economic diversity sufficient, not simply to "house" the capital, but to develop large and rich "European" cultural and economic institutions befitting a capital; 4) architectural blend of traditional Europe and the modern; 5) political and economic stability within the city so as to isolate the governing institutions from mob violence, terrorism, and more subtle forms of pressure; 6) high degree of multilinguism, a feature that is prevalent in many of Europe's cities.

Of the cities that have been considered, neither Saarbrucken nor Geneva has strong backing today. Had the Saar become an autonomous district within the Western European Union, the choice of Saarbrucken would have appealed to many. Rejection of a Europeanized Saar in the referendum of 1955 left Saarbrucken with few of the necessary qualifications for the capital. Geneva's location, facilities, and traditions as an international center are well known, and the city is busy absorbing hundreds of United Nations and European civil servants. However, Switzerland has remained aloof from the Council of Europe, Western European Union, and E.E.C., in an attempt to maintain neutrality in political and military matters. Its strongest concession to joint European action, to date, has been membership in E.F.T.A.

The nucleus of an integrating Europe is now the Europe of the

Nine. This is the Europe that has the greatest immediate need for one capital, and it is from within this Europe that such cities as Brussels, Strasbourg, Milan, Nice, Luxembourg, and Paris have been suggested as capital sites. Today's capital of Europe's Nine is likely to be tomorrow's capital of Maritime Europe and eventually of Maritime Europe and the Maghreb, London, Copenhagen, and Vienna are probably too eccentric to fulfill the function of a capital, and the latter two are overly exposed frontier cities besides. The choice of a city should be made within the core and with an expanded, unified Europe in mind.

Cities like Nice, Luxembourg City, and Strasbourg lack some of the necessary qualifications. Nice appears to be too small, too eccentric, and too one-sided in its economy. Luxembourg City, while more central, is nonetheless not especially well served by road or airplane. Moreover, it is a very small city (only 75,000 population). Strasbourg reflects much of the north-south unity of Europe in its location and architecture, and is on good east-west rail and automobile lines. The Mont Blanc and Great St. Bernard Auto Tunnels have improved road accessibility from the Mediterranean. Strasbourg is also multilingual. It is, however, a small city (under 250,000 population), does not have a broad economic base, and is not quite as well served by air as are larger European cities. While the Council of Europe's Parliamentary Assembly continues to meet in Strasbourg, the decline in vigor of the unity movement and the negative attitude of France toward direct election of representatives to the Assembly by peoples of the member-states have deprived Strasbourg of the likelihood of becoming the European capital.

Brussels and Milan, the cities with over a million in population among core cities thus far mentioned, have many desirable qualities as capitals. Milan, the trade crossroads of the past, is both an ancient and a modern city. It has a strong, vibrant, diversified economic base and many cultural attractions, and it is close to the Alps, which provide recreational amenities. With access to the entire Mediterranean, Milan would be able to symbolize the need for European-Maghreb unity. The city does, however, have some liabilities. It would be eccentric to the broader North Atlantic region; it is not multilingual; and it is a city in which industrial tension and Communist party strength can pressure governing bodies.

Brussels is perhaps the most central of all large cities within the European ecumene; it is highly accessible to the United Kingdom, the North Atlantic, Northern Europe, and Europe north of the Alps; it possesses beauty, culture, and economic strength; its industries are light and spread throughout the suburbs; and it has not been especially subject to industrial strife. While the Flemish-Walloon tensions that have plagued parts of Belgium are present in Brussels, such tensions are sporadic and not serious enough to jeopardize the normal workings of government. If the recent violence should persist or intensify, this would diminish the desirability of Brussels as a capital site. While it is a North European city by virtue of its location in Flemish Belgium, Brussels is French in character and multilingual in speech. Flemish, akin to Dutch, is a Germanic tongue spoken by many. The majority of the city, however, speaks French and is attractive culturally to all of the Mediterranean region. Finally, Brussels is representative of a zone that has been Western Europe's neutral zone in the past, while now serving as headquarters for NATO.

No European city has to grapple with the problems of racial discrimination that beset cities like Washington and New York, hindering their functions as national and international capitals. On the other hand, cities that can be subjected to violence and terrorism, like Paris of the 1950's and 1960's, and which have very large depressed and discontented minorities in their midst (again like Paris with its hundreds of thousands of North Africans), may not be the most feasible candidates for the capital of Europe. In part, of course, France under de Gaulle spurned the opportunities to take a more positive role to reinforce European unity, with its negative attitudes toward the European Movement, NATO, and expanding the Common Market. A change in these attitudes could reopen the question of Paris's suitability as the European capital. This choice could become especially pertinent should the restoration of a full-scale alliance between Maritime Europe and the Maghreb give to the French the possibility of leading the way in forging a broader geopolitical unity. For the present, however, given the trend to concentrate the Common Market organizations in Brussels and the shift thereto of NATO, Brussels would appear to be the leading candidate for the capital seat.

Relations with the Maghreb

The relationship of Maritime Europe to North Africa can, in part, be explained by the form and vicinal location of the Mediterranean Sea. The Mediterranean is an interior arm of the Atlantic. Structurally, the basin consists of four distinct units, exclusive of the Black Sea. In form, however, geographers have considered the

sea as having three basins: the Western, the Eastern, and the Black
—or two: the Western (to be precise, the Northwestern) and the
Eastern (Southeastern). The latter division omits the Black Sea.
Whichever the case, the Mediterranean is not a unit, structurally or
morphologically. Moreover, the character of its littoral is quite varied.
Newbigin has said, "The Mediterranean Basin is not a unit; its shores
belong here to the desert area, and there to Central Europe; only at
intervals are they truly Mediterranean."[9] The coastlands are diverse,
and the relationship of their parts to adjoining power cores adds to
this diversity.

When we consider the above factors, it is little wonder that political separatism, not unity, has characterized the Mediterranean basin.
Only Rome succeeded in unifying the sea completely. The Phoeni-
cians, Greeks, Carthaginians, Moors, Turks, and West Europeans
failed to do so, although the Greeks and Turks did unify the Eastern
basin geopolitically. France, now that it acts in harmony with its
European Mediterranean neighbors, can be said to have unified the
bulk of the Western basin strategically, for the time being.

For most of its history, the Eastern Mediterranean has been under
Middle Eastern-Asian influences. Unlike its western counterpart,
this basin possesses several major passages into the interior lands.
The Black Sea provides the opening into the Ukrainian steppes and
the Lower Danube; Asia Minor's coastal streams into the Anatolian
Plateau; the Syrian Saddle and Syrian Gate into Mesopotamia; the
Isthmus of Suez and Red Sea to Arabia; the Nile Delta into the Val-
ley proper; the Vardar-Morava Rivers into the Middle Danube; and
the Gulf of Trieste-Klagenfurt and Ljubljana passes into the Upper
Danube Valley.

Because it is accessible to these populous and well-endowed interior reaches, the fate of the Eastern Mediterranean has been tied to
the rise and fall of its hinterland powers. Unity has been imposed
from all sides of the basin—from Egypt, the Levant, and the North,
as the core of power has shifted along the littoral. Balanced strength
among these bordering nations has meant political separateness
within the basin.

The Western Mediterranean basin has experienced a different history of political development. With the line from Sicily to Cape Bon
as its boundary, the Western Mediterranean's narrow coast is, for
the most part, encircled by young, fold mountains. There are few

[9] Marion Newbigin, *The Mediterranean Lands* (New York: Knopf, 1924),
p. 211.

breaks across these mountains and no significant ones through the desert, such as the Nile. In addition, the Western Mediterranean contains a number of islands that are accessible to both northern and southern coasts (the Balearics, Corsica, Sardinia, and Sicily). Long ago settled by Europeans, these islands are outposts for European states in their strategic relationships with the southern shores.

The absence of effective breaks across the surrounding mountains has, until modern times, made the issue of control an internal or "family" matter within the Western basin. Thus, Carthage, Rome, North Africa, Spain, France, and Italy vied for control of the basin, with little outside interference. Because of the weaker North African support base, the Moors (as well as the Carthaginians before them) did not penetrate effectively beyond Spain, Sardinia, and parts of Sicily. During the Middle Ages, Spanish-French-Austrian rivalry over Italy diverted the attention of the European powers from the North African coast. With modern times came two changes: 1) improvements in land communications across Western Europe to the Mediterranean, and 2) the Anglo-French alliance, which controlled both the western entrance to the Mediterranean and the trans-Mediterranean sea lanes. As a result, France was enabled to attain strategic control over most of the Maghreb, entering Algeria in 1830, Morocco in 1875, and Tunisia six years later. However, Spanish and Italian counterinterests, as well as recurrent strife with Germany, prevented France from gaining unchallenged mastery of Western North Africa. Moreover, the geopolitical patterns of colonial association that France forged with this part of the Muslim world proved incompatible with Muslim demands for equality and political self-determination.

France's greatest omission, from the standpoint of its need to forge enduring geopolitical ties with North Africa, was that it did not populate the region adequately with Frenchmen or other Europeans, nor at the same time offer equality to the indigenous population.

During the European conquest of Africa, many Europeans saw in the southern continent an outlet for mass settlement, as well as a source of raw materials and potential markets. The fact is, however, that not even a favorable settlement locale like Mediterranean North Africa, let alone the unfavorable tropical reaches of most of the continent, succeeded in attracting mass European migration. North Africa measured its annual immigration in the thousands, not the tens or the hundreds of thousands. After the first fifty years of French colonization in Algeria, the European population numbered only about 400,000. A half-century later, this figure had increased to 800,000, with natural increase accounting for the major share of the growth. Prior to Algerian independence the figure was about 1,000,000. France did not populate Algeria on a larger scale for two reasons: 1) France lacked surplus population at home and 2) France was not suffering from the hopeless economic plight that had driven most of its neighbors to generate millions of emigrants. French farmers and workers were reluctant to move to Algeria as colonists, where they had to face the competition of cheap Muslim labor.

It is always tantalizing to speculate how different the geopolitical map would look today had European cooperation been as advanced a century ago as it is today. Had there been joint action on colonization even between France and Italy during the great period of emigration, North Africa today might be part of Europe. This presupposes that the increased immigration would have been more adequately supported by manufacturing than it has been in the actual course of North African economic development. A broader resource than is available within most of the European Mediterranean, a European laboring class, and greater pressures on France to support North African industrialization, would have favored such a process.

Leon Gambetta, France's Prime Minister during the occupation of Tunisia, is quoted as having said in 1880 that the configuration of the French coasts and the establishment of French rule in Algeria had made the Mediterranean, and especially the Western Mediterranean, France's "scene of action."[10] History has borne him out, but not in the geopolitical form that he had envisaged. For after 125 years of colonization and acculturation activities, France's political influence in the Maghreb is still tenuous. From recent events it has become apparent that France alone cannot maintain the necessary European association with North Africa. A united Maritime Europe, however, could assert its strategic dominance over the Maghreb if driven to take such a step—a situation that is quite similar to Soviet-Eastern European and United States-Caribbean geopolitical relations. It would utilize its control over Atlantic and trans-Mediterranean sea lanes and the Mediterranean islands to do so. Then applying its economic strength and cultural attraction, it could organize the geopolitical framework within which to unify the Western Mediterranean.

The participants in such a geopolitical program would be Mari-

[10] Quoted in Norman Harris, *Intervention and Colonization in Africa* (Boston: Houghton, Mifflin, 1914), p. 238.

time Europe and the Maghreb—not outside forces. For outside intervention could be attempted from distant bases only. The nearest are
militarily weak and economically underdeveloped states in West Africa and the Middle East. These states lie across broad desert barriers. This is not to say that such states *must* play a negligible role
in the Western Mediterranean. Egypt was a prominent sponsor of
the Algerian revolution, and Black African support of the F.L.N.
was a significant factor in the halls of the United Nations. But these
outside areas can only influence the situation when the leaders of the
Muslim Maghreb wish to invite such influence. In comparison with
either West Africa or the Arab Middle East, the Maghreb can more
than stand on its own feet in leadership cadre, cultural levels, military forces, and stage of economic development. Ultimately, this
should prove the decisive element in fashioning an accommodation
within the Western Mediterranean.

The initiative for such geopolitical accommodation must come
from the European side and, under the leadership of Charles de
Gaulle, the first such steps were taken with the granting of independence to Algeria and the subsequent economic agreements between France and the Maghreb. A unified Maritime Europe would
possess the capacity to formulate a political and economic agreement
that could satisfy the pressing interests of the Muslim Maghreb,
without sacrificing European strategic requirements.

Can Europe and the entire Free World afford anything short of
such accommodation? Were the Maghreb to turn away from the
West and become a Soviet base, the wartime defense of Western
Europe would be nearly impossible. Attack upon Europe from the
East by conventional land and air assault would be difficult enough
for NATO to repel. Were it to come from the Mediterranean as
well, the attack could hardly be stemmed. Foreseeing such an eventuality, the alternative left to Europeans would be either nuclear
holocaust or surrender. Even without war, an encircled Maritime Europe would be subject to currents that would expose southern Europe to extreme pressures of subversion, as well as isolate most of the
African continent from Europe. Spain, Portugal, France, and Italy
would become targets of individual and group activities that could
operate with relative impunity from North Africa, unless Europe
should draw a new Iron Curtain across the Mediterranean.

Another aspect of strategic location, empty space, has already been
mentioned. To France today, as well as to United Europe tomorrow,
the availability of vacant reaches for nuclear bomb testing and for

missile shoots is strategically important. Reggan, in the central Algerian Sahara, has been the site of French nuclear bomb testings, and their shift to Pacific sites has created considerable international problems for France. Even if underground testing of such devices should be banned, the need for use of such a vacant area for other military and civilian space-age projects would be no less.

To distinguish economic from locational strategic necessity is not easy. For what makes an area important is not simply where it is, but what it contains. To imperial Rome, North African wheat became a strategic necessity because of the remoteness of the Egyptian supply and the exhaustion of Sicily's grain lands. Centuries later, France returned to North Africa, where she developed its wheat, vine, and citrus products. Considering the wealth of the Metropolitan French agriculture, these commodities can scarcely be described as strategically vital. Indeed, until 1959, arguments as to the strategic economic importance of North Africa to France were spurious. North Africa's role as a breadbasket, a supplier of iron ore and phosphates, and a source of manpower for the French armed forces was more than counterbalanced by the French expenditures in social services and in policing the area. As a protected market, North Africa and other parts of the French Empire acted as "opiates" to French factories, which did not feel bound to modernize and to innovate as rapidly as many of their European neighbors. Only after Tunisia and Morocco had gained their independence and Algeria had been torn apart by revolt was the strategic-economic element injected into the conflict—the discovery of petroleum, which began to flow in significant commercial quantities from the Hassi Messaoud fields in 1959.

The need for petroleum is of the highest strategic order for France. In the past decade, dependence upon Middle East oil has been replaced by dependence upon Maghrebian resources and Libya. Thus France is no longer subject to the pressures of interdiction of its supplies either at the Suez Canal or along the overland pipeline routes. On the other hand, its dependence upon Algeria is not without difficulties. The rapid development of Algerian petroleum (at Hassi Messaoud, Edjele, and Zaraitine) was made possible by huge French outlays of capital, both in the fields and in three pipelines leading to the coast. The terminals are at Bejaia and Arzew, and Skhirra in Tunisia, with a fourth terminal under construction at Skikda. In addition, very rich deposits of natural gas at Hassi R'Mel have been connected to Oran and Algiers by pipeline, and the export of this gas in liquid form (LNG) to France and Spain has begun.

Despite the attempts of the de Gaulle government to safeguard the French investment and interests in the Saharan Algeria through special agreements and temporary stationing of troops, Algerian controls were steadily reimposed. Most recently, the Algerian government has exercised its authority by nationalizing 51 per cent of the French-owned oil industry, a step to which France has reluctantly acquiesced. Algeria fully nationalized all foreign non-French companies that account for approximately one-third of the total production. It is clear that partnership is the only basis on which France can hope to maintain its economic relationships with Algeria. Annual Algerian oil production of approximately 50 million tons meets France's consumption needs, and together with Libyan imports, provides France with a re-export potential in refined products. Oil also provides 80 per cent of Algeria's exports. In this connection, too, greater attention will have to be placed on building up Algeria's production of refined products, now only negligible. Indeed, the 1970 Algerian four-year development plan gives priority to basic industry that will manufacture semi-finished or finished products from Algerian resources. Algeria will not be content to permit France to monopolize the value-added by concentrating refining capacity on French territory. The over-all trend is clear—France has passed from a strategic dependence upon Middle Eastern oil to an era of oil partnership with the Maghreb.

Less significant strategically, but of great economic potential value, is the iron ore of the Sahara. Fort Gouraud in Mauretania has hematite reserves for 200 million tons, but Gara Djebilet, in Western Algeria, has reserves that are estimated at three billion tons. This is a surface deposit that is considered to be larger than any other single deposit in the world. Smaller desert deposits of manganese at Guettara and copper at Akjouit (in Mauretania) add to the favorable picture of mineralization. Finally, the Saharan environment could become the world's major base for solar energy production.

Although France temporarily detached the Saharan departments, administratively, from Algeria, the political future of this area could not be left in limbo, and with independence was integrated with the rest of the country. Morocco claims much of the Western Sahara, including Mauretania's portions, and has already encroached upon Algerian territory. Tunisia has sought a frontier change along the Algerian border, the gain of which might touch off further claims upon oil-bearing territories farther south at Edjele. To compound the complications, France and Spain have failed to agree upon accessways for transporting the mineral wealth of the Western Sahara. Fort Gouraud's iron ore needs an outlet to the Atlantic. The French-proposed rail line to Port Etienne would have to pass through southeastern Spanish Sahara. The Spanish counterproposal is to build a railroad half as long as that suggested by France to the Spanish Sahara's port of Villa Cisneros. If the vast iron deposits of the Algerian Sahara are to be exploited, then the logical outlet for them might be via rail to Agadir in Morocco, or through Moroccan territory to Ifni, which was returned to Morocco by Spain, in 1969. In 1970, the Algerian and Moroccan governments settled the border dispute that led to the War of 1963, agreeing to accept the original French-drawn boundary. As part of this agreement, it was decided to form a joint company to exploit and market the Algerian iron ore.

Without the Saharan lands, Algeria takes on most of Mediterranean California's physical characteristics. Containing two-thirds the population and land area of California, Algeria has a threefold climatic and landform division: 1) A semihumid zone—the densely settled coastal plain, rolling hills, and Tell Atlas Mountains. The climate is Mediterranean, with from 30 to 60 inches of winter rainfall; 2) a semiarid zone—the high intermontane plateau, with 12 inches of rainfall, or less; and 3) the Saharan Atlas Mountains, with 20 inches of rainfall on the northern-facing slopes and desert on the southern side.

Productive land in Algeria covers 17,000 square miles, or about four-fifths of California's crop land. Sizable deposits of iron ore, phosphates, and manganese, when added to the oil, natural gas, iron, and copper of the Sahara, provide Algeria with as favorable a mineral base as California's.

However, the two regions differ fundamentally in several respects, mostly related to human use. Among the major differences are these: 1) cultural and technological level of the bulk of the inhabitants in agriculture as well as manufacturing; 2) high degree of urbanization and industrialization in California, whereas 70 per cent of Algeria is rural; 3) availability to California of water resources from the humid portions of northern California and the Rockies-fed Colorado River system; 4) difference in political status of the two units.

Algeria requires both farm reform and a broad manufacturing base to lift its thirteen million Muslims out of their present poverty. Algeria also needs increased possibilities for large-scale emigration to help relieve its population pressures. Not only France, but all of Maritime Europe can provide such an outlet. Agriculture, especially, was molded to the desires of Europeans, not to the needs of native farmers. Over 500,000 acres, for example, were in vineyards, producing 500 million gallons of wine annually that were mostly sent to France as cheap table wines. These are among the best lands and ought to have been in food crops. The French do not need additional wine and the Muslims do not want it. Grains are grown on nearly 80 per cent of all farm land, mainly under primitive, dry farming conditions. While cereals are badly needed locally, an increase in their production can undoubtedly be accomplished through intensification and modernization, while at the same time some of the acreage currently in grains can be turned over to vegetables, citrus, and livestock. While the French put forth land reform as one of their major goals (the Constantine Plan of 1958), it has only been with independence that major efforts have been made to introduce co-operatives, modern farm techniques, land redistribution, and crop change-over. The role that French advisors now play as "guests" and hired consultants in Algeria has been a positive one and has contributed to the normalizing of Franco-Algerian relations. However, agrarian reform still suffers from lack of adequate skilled personnel, conservatism of the peasantry, insufficient land to go around, and an overpopulation that is the result of an annual birthrate of 3 per cent. Twenty-five per cent of the land is still owned by big farmers (3 per cent of the total farmers) and 300,000 small peasant farmers have only 10 per cent of the land.

Lack of industrial opportunities in the cities means that emigration to France and the rest of Europe is the only recourse. There is an analogy between the Algerian outflow to France and the Puerto Rican outflow to the United States, both in terms of the population pressure that generate the outflow and the concentration of the émigrées in low-paying city service jobs. Without the funds accumulated by the émigrées and remitted to the home country, the future would be dire in both cases.

The Algerian referendum of July 1962 confirmed the Evian agreements between France and the Algerian nationalists on Algerian self-determination. While the basis for agreement was co-operation and economic association between Algeria and France, the schism within Algerian nationalist ranks over this issue is deep. If Algerian nationalists choose association with France, the future can be bright economically. Such a choice, however, will mean clear-cut political-military identity with Maritime Europe and with the latter's global views and commitments.

The driving forces behind association are diverse. They include the strategic, political, economic, and cultural-psychological elements that have been noted. Petroleum and natural gas, especially, can serve as unifiers between France and Algeria, provided that the Algerian economic stake is not relegated to the production and transportation of these minerals. If Algerian industrial and consumer wants should become highly dependent upon an uninterrupted flow of these fuels, then the Algerian need to maintain a common front with France will become a matter of practical politics. Syria had little to lose (save a small transportation royalty) when as a reaction to the Anglo-French intervention in the Sinai campaign, and again in 1967, it cut the petroleum pipeline from Iraq to the Mediterranean. Syria also cut the Saudi Arabian TAP-line in 1970. Its economy was not directly related to the "black gold" that flowed across its territory. An Algerian economy that uses revenues from Saharan fuels to the point where it could not survive without them, would be a strong element for political, as well as economic, association with France.

The second outstanding force for association, as has been noted, is emigration; nearly three-quarters of a million Algerians have emigrated to France. Industrialization cannot solve the Algerian overpopulation problem in this generation. Indeed, the very wealth of Algeria's minerals and the availability of large amounts of French investment capital could stimulate the development of a high value, modern, manufacturing economy in Algeria that would not be able to absorb large numbers of workers. Oil refineries, chemical plants, steel mills, construction materials factories—the reflections of Algeria's specialized mineral base—are likely to be built in modern, automated forms, especially if Algeria seeks to keep pace with Common Market Europe. If manufacturing should be based upon a small, skilled, well-paid group, in contrast to the broad, rural population base, with its limited income, then financial and social friction would become sharp. The Algerian manufacturing base cannot absorb hundreds of thousands of workers. Emigration to Maritime Europe is necessary to absorb this surplus population and to contribute financial support to the Mother Country. Without association with France, and through France with the rest of Maritime Europe, such an outlet will not be available.

Perhaps the leadership of Algeria will reject the road of association because of the bitterness of the Algerian-French conflict and the desire to steer a course that provides options for an opening to the U.S.S.R. In our opinion, Algerian plans for neutralism are likely to prove illusory. For there is no possibility that an Algerian neutralism that might open the gates to hostile forces from the East could be left unchallenged by Europe. If association between France and Algeria should be rejected, what then?

Our reaction to a temporary turn to neutralism by Algerian nationalism should not be passive acceptance or "hands-off" disillusionment. Instead, such a term should be accepted as a challenge to the determination and ingenuity of France and its allies to create the geopolitical unity of Maritime Europe and the Maghreb that is so vital to the well-being of both parties and to the Maritime World as a whole.

If the efforts to integrate Maritime Europe and the Maghreb were to have as their goal the creation of a superstate that would duplicate and compete with the other two superstates, the goal would prove illusory. Because of its limited size, its lack of effective national territory, its agricultural deficiences, and its intermediate location between the ecumenes of the United States and the U.S.S.R., the European superstate cannot be an imitation of the others. Nor is Mainland China an appropriate model for Europe.

Moreover, Maritime Europe has to be unique because it is a world trader, not a continental or a pan-regional one. Half of all international trade is carried on by Maritime Europe, and over half of this region's trade is conducted with non-European areas. Even within the Common Market, where trade among the founding six members has increased by 225 per cent in the past ten years, 55 per cent of the international trade is carried on outside their Common Market framework. Finally, historic-cultural bonds within the southern hemisphere and strategic involvements in Anglo-America and Africa south of the Sahara make any form of "superstate self-containment" unthinkable.

If Maritime Europe has a new destiny to fulfill, it will fulfill it through internal consolidation together with reinforced external associations. European unity cannot be achieved behind economic and military frontiers. It can only be achieved along a new pathway, which will combine historic benefits of regional specialization stemming from global associations and the modern advantages of regional consolidation emerging from the breakdown of national differences. Maritime Europe and Maghreb's geopolitical structures, when viewed dynamically rather than statically, reflect or energize these developing forces of integration that are both regional and world-wide.

Frontiers and Their
Geopolitical Dynamics

Two basic locational conditions characterize the geopolitical positions of the U.S.S.R. and the United States. First, these two
superpowers have grown up in physical isolation from one another.
They are still physically remote, save in a time-distance, air-and-space-
age sense. Second, the Soviet Union lives in direct land or narrow
seas contact with a large number of sovereign states; Americans have
few neighbors.

The first condition may help to explain why the Cold War has
not erupted into a shooting war. The second condition underscores
the fact that the U.S.S.R. places a very high priority on its military
relations with its neighbors, while the United States cannot find
security through military hegemony over its neighbors alone.

The Arctic is the major barrier between the two superpowers. It
is, in a sense, the political "refrigerant" of today's divided world,
helping to keep the Cold War "cold." Because of polar seas and
peripheral frozen land masses, the United States and the U.S.S.R.
have no common area, either land or narrow seas, sufficiently endowed with people and raw materials to serve as a major arena of
Cold War conflict. True, Soviet and American territories are separated by only 26 miles of water in the Bering Straits, and the polar
air and waters are arenas of friction and sources of potential conflict
for air and submarine forces. But the mutual strategic threat posed
by the Arctic is as the arena of Hot War, not Cold War.

The major sphere of East-West contention today is the Old World
Rimland, where the land and sea boundaries of the U.S.S.R. meet
those of fifteen diverse national states—allied, opposing, and neutral.

To the U.S.S.R., regional security with respect to bordering states could in effect mean global security, because of the size and diversity of its economic base. If such security were to be obtained on Soviet terms, however, it would mean United States global insecurity. In contrast, United States boundaries, which meet only three different national states outside of the Arctic, present relatively minor security problems. Regional security for the United States, even when fully attained, cannot possibly mean global security. The wheel therefore has turned. American regional security, the prized goal of our Founding Fathers, to be obtained through enforced isolation from Europe, has lost its meaning. We continue to guard our frontiers, and this can be easily accomplished, for such security can be attained without infringing on other powerful national states. But this security, in isolation from what occurs in other parts of the world, has little significance.

Thus, while many geopolitical similarities may be nteod between the U.S.S.R. and the United States, particularly those stemming from land-resource use and development, a fundamental difference remains—the comparative outlooks on regional and global security. We shall deal in this chapter with the changing geopolitical map of the U.S.S.R. as related to this security outlook.

The Soviet Union is in the process of altering its landscape, both by making new uses of it and through territorial additions. This process affects both the internal and the external scenes. No longer does such a geographical quality as continentality alone serve to shape the U.S.S.R.'s geopolitical character; nor do the traditional ideas about Russia's drive to the seas fully explain her needs and aims.

Continental expansion of the Soviet Union has led to borders that are either wastelands or heavily populated marginal seas. Continental expansion of the United States has led to well-endowed, relatively empty coastlands and oceanic contacts with distant lands. To the United States, then, oceanic borders have been suitable, both for drawing up defensive national boundaries and for launching expansionist international contacts. To the Soviet Union, land and marginal sea frontiers have not been able to serve this dual purpose. Where, as in Central Asia, the frontiers have been the basis for defensive boundary lines, they have not been useful international contact zones. Where, as along the marginal seas, the frontiers have provided good international contact zones, they have not been adequate defensive boundaries.

The Changing Political Environment

The U.S.S.R., like all states, is the expression of the interaction of its people and the landscape which they occupy. The political marking off of this landscape produces a national landscape—the arena of the people's activity; changes in this area cause or reflect changes in national characteristics and objectives. A national landscape becomes altered in two ways: vertically, or through new internal uses, and horizontally, or through the addition of external areas or loss of territory. Vertical changes cut across the existing grain of the national landscape. They occur as new sets of physical, environmental conditions emerge (as through climatic desiccation, soil erosion, rising water tables, and forest removal), or as new uses of the physical environment are conceived (as through mining, new crops, or urban sprawl). The Netherlands, Japan, Sweden, Israel, Malaysia, and Finland furnish examples of both changes. Through specialized concentrations of national energies, increasing populations can be supported.

Horizontal change does not affect the existing grain of the national landscape; rather, it produces a new national landscape by annexation, loss, or substitutions of national territory. East Germany, without the former agricultural areas east of the Odcr, has become more manufacturing-oriented within its reduced field of activity. Jordan, when it annexed Eastern Palestine, diversified its national agricultural base without any fundamental changes in the separate parts of the landscape. However, annexation upset the political stability of the former desert kingdom by adding an ambitious, sophisticated, Palestinian leadership elite and a dissatisfied refugee element. Israel, having occupied the West Bank territories, now finds the Arab labor pool crucial to the development of Israeli territory, especially Jerusalem. The upsurge in urban building is particularly helped by this labor source. Arab agriculture serves as a complement or extension to the existing Israeli farm scene, by its emphasis on citriculture, fruits, and vegetables.

Historically, national states have matured, first through enlarging their territorial bases—that is, through horizontal change; and then through intensifying the use of this base—that is, through vertical change. Today, because of the pressure of population and because of the ease of transmitting technological experience, the two processes tend to occur simultaneously. As a state alters its character through boundary changes, it also alters its character through new uses of the landscape.

It is to this dualism in geographical change that we can look for a greater understanding of Soviet national interests. The following three topics have been selected as the basis for an analysis of the implications of geographical change within the U.S.S.R.:

1) The expansion of the national territory.
2) The response of the challenges of frontier areas.
3) The development of the national territory, not solely through progressive advance from the primary core of the state, but also from secondary core areas along the borders.

TERRITORIAL EXPANSION

The territorial expansion of the Russian Empire and its twentieth-century heir is a centuries-old process that may well not have run its course. Certainly, memories of Soviet annexations effected during and in the wake of the Second World War are fresh enough to cause us to speculate about future expansion. While one might suggest that the projection of ideological power through international Communism minimizes the importance of national boundaries in many ways, there is, nevertheless, a profound distinction bteween an area that has been internally absorbed within the boundaries of a state, and a satellite state. In the case of the Soviet Union, the annexation of specific areas within its territorial framework has converted these areas into internal components whose political relationship to the remainder of the state is quite stable. Such stability stands in contrast to the volatile nature of ties between the U.S.S.R. and its satellites.

The boundary of any national state marks the limit of its internal political authority. Such a line is more than a mark of sovereignty. It becomes a symbol, orienting the landscape towards the national core, and is thus a powerful centralizing element. Because it functions as a separator of one state from another, the boundary has strong defensive qualities.

A boundary line also cuts through frontier zones. Political frontiers tend to be intermediate, or transitional, human-use areas between adjoining political units. Usually, the very process of moving a boundary within a frontier zone affects the character of the zone as a whole. For what happens to the portion of the zone that becomes included within the new boundary cannot help but alter the political value of the remainder of the frontier. This, in turn, becomes more strongly attracted to, or repelled by, the power that has changed the boundary, depending upon the counterforce that can be exerted by the neighboring state.

As the Soviet Union has annexed territory, it has made every effort to convert these newly acquired areas into inwardly oriented, integral parts of the state. By the same token, however, these borderlands cannot be rigidly separated from contiguous non-Soviet territory, because of the goal of regional integration that the U.S.S.R. seeks with its satellites, especially those to the west. The result is, therefore, that the annexed lands serve both defensive and offensive functions. As they have been absorbed within the Soviet state, and tied to Soviet core areas, some of their former transitional human-use characteristics have been eliminated. Such integration is not part of a simple, monolithic state-building process, for many of the annexed areas have been added to non-Russian Union republics rather than to the Russian Soviet Federated Socialist Republic. The net effect of this annexation is to strengthen the country's defensive posture. These new lands are also being used as political and military spearheads for the external application of Soviet power towards the satellite states—and this is essentially an offensive posture.

As many states have expanded territorially, they have rationalized this expansion in terms of their need for "natural" boundaries. The term "natural" boundaries usually means physical features that can serve as the framework for political boundaries. The concept of "natural" boundaries as an historic necessity has frequently been repudiated by geographers and historians.[1] While nature provides us with features that can effectively serve as political boundaries, these features are our servants, not our masters. They become political boundaries only when we choose to make them serve this function. Herbert Luethy, in his lucid study *France Against Herself*, has this to say on the subject:

> . . . the natural frontiers of France are nothing but a figment of the jurists—entirely devoid of reality. Centuries of mole-like advance were required of the French monarchy before it could think of, let alone come anywhere within sight of, the Pyrenees, the Mediterranean, the Alps, the Jura, and the Rhine. Until the end of the Middle Ages, it was concerned exclusively with its own vassals, and those fron-

[1] Jan Broek, "The Problem of 'Natural' Frontiers," *Frontiers of the Future* (University of California, 1940), pp. 3-20.

tiers never provided it with security. They represented a claim, not a line of defence.[2]

The problem of "natural" boundaries is not, however, to be resolved simply by dismissing it as a pseudoscientific concept. If a people believes in "natural" boundaries, and ascribes to certain features of the physical environment a mystical, irrational function, then this belief becomes an unshakable basis for national action. At various periods in the development of the United States, such physical features as the Mississippi-Missouri watershed, the Sabine River, the Rio Grande, the Continental Divide of the Rockies, the Pacific shoreline, and the islands of adjoining oceans were designated as "natural" boundaries. These boundaries were attained through settlement, negotiation, or war. They were accepted by the public as providing the prerequisite territorial framework for geographical unity and military security. These features became part of the expansionist myth. For six million people living along the eastern seaboard in 1800 to begin a process of expansion that would lead to an ocean-to-ocean setting may not have been reasonable or necessary. But some men believe that states, like nature, abhor vacuums. As the myth of continental expansion became a national ideal, it acquired real substance. In these terms, the illogic of the following quotation from A. E. Parkins is the logic of United States history:

> Disgraceful as the Mexican War seems to us, three-quarters of a century removed from the spirit of those times when territorial aggrandizement was the factor that dominated our national policy, we must confess that American expansion to the Rio Grande and the Pacific was in full accordance with the laws of geographic adjustment that a virile nation makes when its potential economic energy is devoted solely to land-using occupations. . . . Coastlines that give ready access to the world ocean, mountain ranges, and desert tracts are the logical geographic locations for national boundaries.[3]

German geopoliticians were not unaware of the theoretical deficiencies of "natural" boundary concepts.[4] On the other hand, they were quick to point out the inconsistencies and unacceptability of many "artificial" (political) boundaries. The solution of the geopoli-

[2] Herbert Luethy, *France Against Herself* (New York: Praeger, 1955), pp. 10-11.

[3] Almon E. Parkins, *The South* (New York: Wiley, 1938), pp. 114-15.

[4] Andrew Gyorgy, *Geopolitics* (Berkeley: University of California Press, 1944), p. 228.

ticians was to introduce a vague term—the "organic" boundary. This was described as a political boundary set up in accordance with the geopolitical character of the state and shifting as the needs of the state dictates. Such boundaries were expected to function within their border zones as either offensive or defensive tools, depending upon the state's needs. The German geopoliticians made a unique contribution to the discussion of boundaries by emphasizing certain anthropogeographic elements—especially race, language, and culture—as being the most important element of the "organic" frontier.

Does Soviet geopolitical theory or practice seem to have derived any inspiration from such myths as "natural" or "organic" boundaries? Soviet geography rejects environmental determinism, as is illustrated by the following: "Economic geography of the U.S.S.R. is an active geography; it narrates about conscious and planned transformation of nature carried out by socialist society on the basis of advanced science under the leadership of the Communist Party of the Soviet Union."[5] Certainly such a philosophy is not likely to conjure up "natural" or "organic" boundaries as Soviet foreign policy objectives. Indeed, the violence of Marxist-Leninist attacks by Soviet geographers upon "environmentalism" in European and American geography seems to dispose of this as even a remote possibility. Moreover, the thesis that the "urge to warm waters" has been a persistent geopolitical aim in Russian history has been effectively discounted by students of the topic.[6] It is true that the acquisition of certain corridors to the sea was a persistent aim of some of the Czars who were in search of trade outlets and other forms of contact with Europe. But the approach has been pragmatic and opportunistic, concerned, above all, with lands athwart Russia's interior and marginal seas. It has not been based upon appeals to geopolitical deterministic slogans.

St. Petersburg, founded by Peter the Great in 1703; Odessa, first taken by Catherine II in 1774; and Vladivostok, founded in 1860 after annexation of the Amur provinces from China, spearheaded Russia's marches to the Baltic, Black, and Pacific waters. Significant earlier footholds on the sea had been Archangel in 1584 and Okhotsk, the first Russian settlement on the Pacific, in 1649. None of these coastal footholds, however, were to lead, ultimately, to broad openings on the world oceans, partly because of Russian defeats in

[5] N. Baransky, *Economic Geography of the U.S.S.R.*, translated by S. Belsky (Moscow: Foreign Language Publishing House, 1956), Preface.

[6] John Morrison, "Russia and the Warm Waters," *U.S. Naval Institute Proceedings*, 1952, pp. 1169-79.

the Crimean and Russo-Japanese wars, and partly because of the distance and physical barriers that separated the Russian ecumene from such waters.

Since 1939 the U.S.S.R. has acquired new lands on the Baltic, Black, Okhotsk, and Barents seas. These acquisitions have been on interior and marginal seas, and consequently have defensive rather than offensive significance. New footholds on open seas have been developed through the medium of political satellites—an important strategic gain for the U.S.S.R., to be sure, but not indicative of the launching of a full-scale "warm waters offensive." (See Map 16.)

Soviet territorial expansion has three objectives as its basis: strategic, economic, and nationalistic. Historic claims seem to be important only as they relate to the above factors and play an unimportant role within the Soviet propaganda mechanism. The strategic objective is defensively motivated in seeking to assure command of interior and marginal seas and land gateways. It also serves an offensive function in increasing the vulnerability of neighboring states to Soviet pressures. Economic objectives play a major role in providing the Russian ecumene with improved port facilities in the Baltic for foreign trade. They play a minor role with respect to the needs of specific localities. Thus Leningrad uses the hydroelectric stations of territory annexed from Finland, and Kiev takes natural gas and petroleum from Western Ukrainian lands formerly belonging to Poland. Nationality objectives relate not only to Pan-Slavic ambitions but also to the unity of minority peoples that operate within the Soviet nationality-administrative framework. Not only were Russian-inhabited parts of Latvia annexed to the R.S.F.S.R., and Ruthenian portions of Poland to the Ukraine, but much of the Karelian-inhabited portion of east central Finland was added to Soviet Karelia.

To weigh the relative importance of these objectives in assessing the motives behind Soviet territorial annexations is difficult, and it is complicated by the fact that two or three of these objectives can be simultaneously served. If, however, we were to single out two overriding elements, one would be the strategic needs of some of the most important cities of the U.S.S.R. for defensive depth, and the second would be fear of invasion from Germany.

Consider the fact that the principal international ports of the U.S.S.R., in 1939, were Odessa, Leningrad, Murmansk, Archangel, and Vladivostok. Of these ports, all save Archangel were frontier cities. Odessa was twenty miles from the Romanian border, Leningrad twelve miles and Murmansk fifty miles from Finnish territory,

MAP 16. Soviet Boundary Changes in Europe Since 1939

and Vladivostok thirty-five miles from Japanese Manchuria. Soviet Harbor, developed during the Second World War on the Gulf of Tartary as a deep-water naval base and commercial port for the Amur Valley, was only seventy miles from Japanese-held southern Sakhalin. With the territorial changes that have since occurred, Odessa is now fifty, Leningrad ninety, and Murmansk eighty miles from the borders of the Soviet Union, and Vladivostok is shielded by both southern Sakhalin and the North Korean satellite.

That this security problem is completely resolved from a Soviet point of view is questionable. Batumi, the Black Sea port terminal and refining center for much of Baku's petroleum, is only seven miles from the Turkish border. Baku itself is about fifty miles from Iran. Until the emergence of the U.S.S.R. as one of the great world powers with nuclear bomb capabilities, Soviet fears as to the exposure of her ports were realistic and well founded. Today, what security fears may motivate her to seek defensive depth for Caucasus oil ports or others would seem to be highly irrational. Indeed, had the U.S.S.R. held her present position of power eminence three decades ago, it is unlikely that she would have had to seize the territories that she did, at least from the standpoint of security motivation.

The second major element in Soviet territorial annexations was fear of invasion from Germany. Hitler's first plans for "Operation Barbarossa," for example, were to strike the Soviet Union simultaneously through several corridors: 1) Northern Finland against Murmansk and Archangel; 2) the Baltic, via southern Finland and the Baltic states towards Leningrad; 3) White Russia, from along the Warsaw-Bialystok-Minsk land corridor north of the Pripet Marshes and thence northward to Leningrad; 4) Southern Poland and the Donbas; 5) Romania to Odessa and the Black Sea.

Table 9 and Map 16 show how most of these approaches to the U.S.S.R. have been annexed as Soviet territory since 1939.

These land acquisitions represent an area of 265,000 square miles. They have increased the size of the Soviet Union to 8,606,300 square miles, which is 50,000 square miles more than the territories held by the Czarist Empire at its 1904 zenith. But far more than additional land, they represent significant strategic, economic, and nationality acquisitions.

Annexation of the Pechenga district in northern Finland, including the western Rybachiy peninsula, provides greater security to the ice-free port of Murmansk and nearby Kola Peninsula apatite resources. The latter mineral has freed the U.S.S.R. from its de-

TABLE 9

Survey of Soviet Land Annexations Since 1939

Area	Former Owner	Present Soviet Status
Pechenga District	Finland	Murmansk Oblast (R.S.F.S.R.)
Karelia (Salla)	Finland	Karelian A.S.S.R. (R.S.F.S.R.)
Vyborg District	Finland	Leningrad Oblast
Northern East Prussia and Memelland	Germany	Kaliningrad Oblast (R.S.F.S.R.) and Klaipeda Oblast (Lithuanian S.S.R.)
Estonia	Independent	Union Republic
Latvia	Independent	Union Republic
Lithuania	Independent	Union Republic
Eastern Estonia and Latvia	Estonia and Latvia	Pskov Oblast (R.S.F.S.R.)
Eastern Poland (Western Belorussia)	Poland	4 oblasts in Belorussian S.S.R. and Vilna Oblast (Lithuanian S.S.R.)
Transcarpathia (Ruthenia)	Czechoslovakia	Transcarpathian Oblast (Ukrainian S.S.R.)
Western Ukraine	Poland	6 oblasts in Ukrainian S.S.R.
Northern Bucovina	Romania	Chernovtsky Oblast (Ukrainian S.S.R.)
Central Bessarabia	Romania	Moldavian S.S.R.
Southern Bessarabia	Romania	Izmail Oblast (Ukrainian S.S.R.)
Tannu Tuva	Independent	Tuva A.S.S.R. (R.S.F.S.R.)
Southern Sakhalin	Japan	Sakhalin Oblast (R.S.F.S.R.)
Kurile Islands	Japan	Sakhalin Oblast (R.S.F.S.R.)

pendence upon imported phosphates. South of Pechenga lies Russian Pasvik, which was annexed by Finland in 1920 to provide access to Pechenga. This corridor and its nickel resources are now in Soviet hands; as a consequence, Norway possesses a common border with the U.S.S.R. Its taconite ore mining town of Kirkenes lies exposed, and the population of northern Norway as a whole is subject to strong Communist propaganda pressures.

Despite all these changes in the north, the entrances to the Barents Sea are still not in Soviet hands. The Svalbard island group is owned by Norway, which has rejected Soviet claims to this coal-mining Arctic archipelago. Soviet denunciations of NATO exercises off North Cape suggest that the possibility of efforts to seek further territorial accessions from both Norway and Finland should not be dismissed. In addition to Svalbard, we should recall that Finland's Inari district, once common to Sweden, Russia, and Norway, became Russian in 1809 and was joined to Finland, then under Russian control, in 1833. Were the U.S.S.R. to find a means to absorb Inari, Norway's Finnmark County, including the coastal reaches of Hammerfest and North Cape, would become exposed to increased' Soviet pressures.

The most important boundary change that occurred was the annexation of the Baltic republics. A Soviet geographer sums it up aptly: "Owing to its geographical position, the Soviet Baltic region is of prime importance for the external connections of the U.S.S.R. . . . [it is] a natural harbor which serves the Central U.S.S.R."[7] Although not entirely ice-free, Riga, the largest city and a major rail terminus, presents the Soviet Union with its best Baltic port. Klaipeda (Memel), and Ventspils (Windau) have newly developed oil ports, and Tallin has become a natural gas terminus. Kaliningrad (Königsberg) is an important ice-free addition to the eastern Baltic ports. Slight internal territorial changes have strengthened the Russian position in the Baltic, vis-à-vis both satellite states and non-Russian Soviet republics. Most important, the Kaliningrad Oblast, cleared of Germans and populated by Russians, is part of the R.S.F.S.R., and provides direct access to the Polish and East German satellites' ports of Gdnask, Szczecin, and Rostock. A portion of Estonia lying along the right bank of the River Narva has been detached to be added directly to the Leningrad Oblast. Finally, Russian-inhabited rural districts of Estonia (Petseri) and Latvia (Abrene and Kačanava)—east of the Gulf of Riga—were detached, and added to what is now the Pskov Oblast within the R.S.F.S.R. Pskov, at the southern end of Lakes Peipus and Pskov, is a key to Leningrad. Also following the principle of nationality boundaries, a Lithuanian-inhabited strip of Belorussia was added to the Lithuanian S.S.R., which had reincorporated Vilna from Poland. With Vilna and Pskov now both Soviet territory, the "Vilna Corridor" that follows the high Baltic end-moraine northeastward to Leningrad, is more secure. Soviet actions in the Baltic, in a broad sense, can be described as defensively oriented, owing to the exposure of the Russian core to the European lands to the west.

The westward shift of the boundary in Belorussia has brought the Pripet Marshes completely within the Soviet fold. This boundary

[7] Baransky, *op. cit.*, p. 384.

follows the "Curzon Line" of 1919, east of which Poland pushed after its 1920 war with Russia. Return to the Curzon Line has completed Russian control over the Vilna Gap, as well as occupying the high ground from Brest to Minsk that skirts the Pripet Marshes' northern edge. Moreover, Western Belorussia was claimed on nationality basis, White Russians being in the majority over Poles.

The Western Ukraine lands that have been taken from Poland include Lvov and Drogobych. The former is a rail hub on the upper Bug River whose industries serve the agricultural areas to the east. The latter is a district on the northern slopes of the Carpathians that used to be Poland's major petroleum-producing region. Its denial to Poland as well as its availability to Kiev has strategic economic implications. In the case of the Western Ukraine, unity of the Ukrainian people was an important basis for the claim, although the fact that the Soviet border is now but 130 miles from Krakow and just another fifty miles from industrialized Upper Silesia would seem to be another basis for Soviet interest.

With the absorption of Transcarpathia, the Russians accomplished much more than the union of Ruthenians with their kindred Ukrainians. This land annexation has given to the Soviet Union complete control of the Eastern Carpathian Mountains and a base on its southern slopes from which to overlook the Tisa River and all of the Hungarian Plain. Czechoslovakia and Hungary have common borders with the U.S.S.R., and Budapest lies exposed to a Soviet border that is only 150 miles away. And Belgrade and Vienna are not unaffected by this new Danubian position of the U.S.S.R.

The border changes in Northern Bucovina and Bessarabia also were justified in terms of absorbing predominantly Ukranian peoples, but, again, they serve broader Soviet interests. For now the lands between the Dneister and the Prut are Soviet, as is the northernmost mouth of the Danube. The Ploesti oil fields and Bucharest are about 125 miles from the Soviet border—still another example of the vulnerability into which a satellite state has been pushed.

Recent boundary changes in Siberia have been far less important than those in Europe. Sakhalin and the Kuriles point a double dagger towards northern Japan, and enclose the Sea of Okhotsk. However, these annexations have not affected Russia's Sea of Japan coast and Vladivostok. In the case of the latter regions, the Sovietization of North Korea is likely to be regarded as a security goal for Vladivostok, irrespective of Soviet-Chinese relation in Manchuria.

Annexation of nominally independent Tannu Tuva in 1944 may

well have been desired as a precedent for eventual Soviet annexation of the Mongolian People's Republic. A lightly populated and under-developed land, the Tuva A.S.S.R. is at the headwaters of the Yenisei and overlooks Irkutsk and the Trans-Siberian Railway from the eastern end of the Western Sayan Mountains.

It would be unwise to assume that territorial annexations along the periphery of the U.S.S.R. have run their course. The Soviet Union has shown itself quite capable of reviving territorial claims previously renounced. In the past, Russia's borders have included the upper Aras, upper Kura, and middle Çoruhk river basins. These are now in Turkey and claims to their major towns, Kars, Ardahan, and Artvin, as belonging to Soviet Armenia and to Georgia, were revived in 1945, at the time of Soviet demands for control of the Straits. Indeed, claims of Soviet Georgian professors for all of north-eastern Turkey up to Samsun, on the grounds of its once having been Georgian, were given wide publicity at that time.[8]

Iran, too, is not free of Soviet land annexation pressures. For a brief period (1723-32), all of the southern shore of the Caspian Sea was held by Russia. Soviet interests have been somewhat more re-stricted, to date, encouraging separatist movements in Persian Azer-baijan and in Kurdish Iranian areas south and west of Lake Urmia. From such positions, Turkey would be hemmed in on two sides, and northern Iraq would be directly exposed to the Soviet Union. In Chinese Central Asia, the Dzungarian Gate—the grassy plain head-waters region of the River Ili that connects Chinese Turkestan and Russian Central Asia—was once briefly occupied by Russia (1871-81). While present circumstances hardly suggest the raising of a claim to this region, it might be reactivated as a counter-claim to Chinese demands or simply as part of a strategic-area "swapping" process.

Whatever the future territorial claims of the Soviet Union may be, their formal basis is likely to continue to be on nationality lines. Natural features and historic claims become objectives as they coin-cide with nationality frontiers. Demands based upon nationality can be a very effective weapon for territorial expansion, for within the border reaches of the U.S.S.R. are many minorities with ethnic ties to peoples in neighboring states.

These include Armenians (with kinsmen in Turkey); Kurds

[8] *The Middle East—A Political and Economic Survey* (London: Royal Insti-tute of International Affairs, 1950), p. 46.

(with fellow-Kurds in Turkey, Iraq, and Iran); Azerbaijanis (with counterparts in Iran); and Tadzhiks (with related tribesmen in Afghanistan). Soviet minorities also have kindred groups in Outer Mongolia (the Mongols) and in Chinese Turkestan (the Turko-Tatars). Sustaining exiled groups who have kinsmen within U.S.S.R. border areas is an advantage that the Soviet Union has never been loath to exploit, and the demographic pattern that finds minority groups overlapping borderlands fits in well with programs of internal subversion within neighboring states. Only along the Manchurian border are significant border-overlapping minorities absent.

To secure one of her most vulnerable areas, the Far Eastern provinces, Czarist Russia for decades sought a position of influence in Manchuria. Security of the lands of the Amur Valley is certainly endangered by Chinese expulsion of Soviet influences from Manchuria and of claims to Soviet territory. In this connection, Soviet influence in North Korea may be seen as a counterweight to Chinese pressures, and an example of the mutual vulnerability that is so characteristic of Sino-Soviet relations.

Growing Soviet influence in Afghanistan appears to offer little serious threat to South Asia in and of itself. For Afghanistan is a dead end in terms of economics and transportation. We disagree with those like Toynbee who, harking back to that period in history when a disorganized Northern India fell prey to Afghan chiefs, consider Afghanistan to be one of the key powers in the East-West power struggle. This would be so only if Afghanistan, as a Soviet satellite, were able to further the cause of Pashtunistan, inciting the Pathans to open revolt against Pakistan. An open Soviet-Afghan alliance coupled with the Soviet-Indian alliance, and aimed at dismembering Pakistan by establishing an independent Pashtunistan, would in all likelihood be perceived by Mainland China as a threat to her regional interests and opposed as such. Probably (and ironically in terms of the historic British-Russian clash over the "roof of Asia") the Maritime World led by the United States would not take direct action because of South Asia's limited strategic significance to its security. Three forces dismembered Pakistan: West Pakistani exploitation of the East; Indian support of Bangladesh; and Soviet desires to undermine Pakistani-Chinese and Pakistani-United States links. A force for further dismemberment could be Pathan or Baluchi nationalism; the latter consists of Baluchis in Pakistan, Afghanistan, and Iran, who seek to create an independent Pakhtoonistan.

The region that is likely to remain the most persistent focus of

Russian pressure is the Middle East. In addition to the specific land claims on Turkey and Iran already discussed, the broader problem of the Straits remains a major concern to the Soviet Union. Soviet support of renewed Bulgarian demands for Greek Thrace territory could be conceived of as one way to outflank the approaches to the Dardanelles. From 1956 to 1967, with the elimination of the Suez Canal as a Western base, and with various Soviet port activities along the Mediterranean (Latakia and Alexandria) and the Red Sea (Hodeida and Port Sudan), Russian interests in the waterways to the Far East took on new vigor. Since 1967, Soviet military and naval presence has become direct in the Eastern Mediterranean, along the west bank of the Suez Canal, and in such countries as Syria, Egypt, and Iraq. Certainly the opening of the Suez Canal is in the primary Soviet interest, perhaps more so than for the West, which may find the oil pipeline route paralleling the Canal and other pipelines, as well as giant tankers, more desirable economic alternatives. Past emphasis upon the Black Sea and the straits was essentially defensive, for Soviet fear of attack through the water routes was well founded. Today's emphasis, however, is far more offensive, in the total political-economic-military sense. Never before has Russia had so large a potential stake in the Suez Canal-Indian Ocean-Far East sea route.

In a handful of years, the U.S.S.R. has installed its military presence in Suez and has shown itself prepared to play a "brinksmanship" game in supporting its Arab allies against Israel, to the point of escalating the struggle into a direct American-Soviet confrontation. Granted that such a confrontation may not be desired, it could come about accidentally or incidentally, given the weight that the Soviet Union attaches to its new gains in the Middle East. The link between a Suez-Red Sea and a Persian Gulf strategy is clear. Soviet control of the former will establish the Gulf as a new strategic goal. All of this, in turn, relates back to the Turkish Straits. The more the Soviet stake in Suez and the Persian Gulf, the more pressure will mount for full control of the Straits. Expulsion of Soviet military advisors and technicians from Egypt by President Sadat in 1972 was an action of pique by the Egyptian leader and certain army circles that placed a strain upon, but did not fundamentally alter, the Soviet-Egyptian alliance. Egypt is too dependent militarily upon the U.S.S.R. to seek to eliminate Soviet influence.

Here, then, is an historically new phenomenon unfolding—the Soviet drive for waters that heretofore have been desirable, but not strategically essential. Key to this drive is the Suez Canal. Should it be reopened under Soviet domination, the U.S.S.R.'s maritime offensive can be expected to escalate. Only reopening of the Canal under joint Egyptian-Israeli or international auspices is likely to reverse the trend. For the present, then, the danger of Soviet activities to the security of Turkey and Iran and to the survival of Israel revolves strongly around "Canal politics." The Black Sea-Mediterranean-Red Sea has become the Soviet "offensive zone," in contrast to the Baltic "defensive zone."

Vladivostok and the land routes thereto could become less important to the Soviets than the sea route around South Asia. Many have heretofore considered the Soviet northern sea route as the "Mediterranean" or Panama Canal of the U.S.S.R. Its limitations, however, are perfectly well known. In the long run, a combination of the European Mediterranean and Indian Ocean sea route, and the overland rail routes to China, will probably be the key to the U.S.S.R.'s contacts with the Far East. As we have said, this will increase the Soviet Union's appetite to secure control of strategic approaches, like Suez, the Persian Gulf, and the Strait of Malacca. But there is another lesson to be learned from this. As long as the Maritime World retains control of the key points along peripheral Eurasian sea lanes, ever increasing Soviet trade dependence upon these routes will make her more aware than ever of her strategic vulnerability to Maritime World counterpressures. If we are to counter the Soviet threat, we can do this most effectively by strengthening our control of the Black Sea approaches and Indian Ocean and Far Eastern lanes, and by denying the U.S.S.R. control of Suez through the agency of her Egyptian ally.

CHALLENGE OF THE FRONTIER REGIONS

The challenge of the frontier is far older in the Russian experience than in the American. By 1533, the northern Urals had been crossed, as Ivan IV broke the Tatar power that had confined his predecessor to Muscovy and Novgorod. Soon after, the fall of Kazan on the Volga opened the gate through and around the southern Urals. Finally, in 1581, Sibir, capital of the Siberian Khanate, was taken and sixty-eight years later a Russian settlement was planted on the Sea of Okhotsk. Thus a people of less than ten million had spanned the 4,000-mile gap to the Pacific. By the end of the seventeenth century, colonizing families extended from above the mouth of the Amur to the northern edge of the Bering Sea.

This early start in Russian colonization was accomplished with the help of Cossack tribesmen and in the face of the limited opposition offered by the few, weak, indigenous people of Northern Siberia. But Northern Siberia was a land valuable for its fur, lumber, and minerals. It could not attract large farm and commercial centers. Siberia's promising pioneering regions were at the southern edge of Northern Siberia, in the Caucasus, in Central Asia, and in the Far Eastern provinces. The military fate of these more populous native areas, bordered by such powers as Turkey, Persia, and China, was not resolved until 1860-65. Without a Russian military victory, not only would there have been little Russian settlement in Central Asia and along the Amur, but the Tomsk-Lake Baikal-Chita strip at the southern edge of Siberia could not have been fully developed.

But more than weapons were needed to colonize Soviet Asia. A national pioneering effort was required. Czarist Russia never wholeheartedly favored and supported pioneering in Siberia, save during the period 1891-1911. Even when government policy favored colonization by farmers, fishermen, and lumbermen, the Czars opposed industrialization outside of the European Russian and Ukrainian cores. Immigration came, not in waves, but as a "groping forward";[9] it occurred in the form of seasonal labor as well as permanent settlement. Increasing population pressure in rural Russia finally combined with political considerations to convince the last of the Czars that settlement in Asia should be encouraged. Heavy colonization then took place in the Western Caucasus, northern Central Asia, and—above all—in Siberia. Following the revolution, this process became more thoroughly planned and directed, for industrial as well as agricultural purposes. Moreover, while Czarist settlement in Asia was primarily for the purpose of exploiting the resource base so that its materials could be processed in Russia, today's settlement is directed toward partly self-contained, agricultural-industrial, regional complexes within a broader framework of national interdependence.

Much has recently been said by Soviet leaders about colonialism. That the word is frequently misused is clear. Strictly speaking, a colony is a territory of which the soil is principally owned by settlers from the mother country. Colonialism, as a process, involves settlement from a mother country, generally into empty lands and bringing to these lands the previous culture and organization of the parent

[9] Georges Jorré, *The Soviet Union,* translated and revised by E. D. Laborde (London: Longmans, 1960), p. 162.

society. Imperialism, as distinct from colonialism, refers to rule over indigenous people, transforming their ideas, institutions, and goods.

Where colonialism occurred in relatively empty lands, it has been described as "secondary colonization." Where it occurred in settled areas, being superimposed on indigenous societies, it has been called "primary colonization."[10] Primary colonization means, in effect, Colonialism-Imperialism, because it involves both settlement from the outside and the transformation of the native society as a result of the pressures of the colonists.

Most of the United States frontier was settled by a colonial process, because the American Indian population was so limited in number and because most of the land lay in a virgin state. Only in Texas and California was Colonialism-Imperialism operative, when English-speaking minorities settled and imposed their rule upon Indian-Spanish majorities. But the numbers involved were, again, quite small. Texas had 90,000 Indians and Spanish, and 30,000 Americans in 1840, and California had a total of 92,000 people, mostly Indians, when it joined the Union in 1850.

As practiced by the Czars and their Communist successors, however, Colonialism-Imperialism has been imposed upon millions of people. Certainly, this is a distinction in frontier development that is as important as any historic parallels that we may care to draw between the American and the Russian experiences.

No other people have colonized so extensively, in so heavily and indigenously populated an area, as have the Russians throughout their empire. From 1859 to 1897, six million Russians migrated, to increase the total of Russians east of the Don to 16 million. At this same time, there were approximately 25 million indigenous inhabitants in the area. Today, east of the Don, there are over 50 million non-Slavs. They are not only clasped to the Soviet Union in an iron grip; they are often locally outnumbered by the 35 million Slavs who live in their historic homelands. On a regional basis, Russians are the majority in the Trans-Volga steppes, the western Caucasus, and Siberia. Natives predominate in the rest of the Caucasus and in Central Asia.

In addition to such factors as national policy and the opposition of native groups and nearby foreign powers, physical environment has influenced the character of frontier development in Czarist Russia

[10] S. Herbert Frankel, *The Concept of Colonization* (Oxford: Clarendon Press, 1949).

and the U.S.S.R. It is estimated that about seven and a half million square miles (87 per cent of the total land area) present serious limitations to settlement, particularly farming. As a result, these lands of deficiency either have been bypassed, or have inspired revolutionary changes so as to become opened up to farming, manufacturing, mining, and transportation.

In his essay *Orographie de la Sibérie* Prince Kropotkin noted the similarities in landforms of the Russian Empire and Canada.[11] He compared the traverse from the Baltic across Central Russia, the Urals, the Middle Siberian plains, and, finally, the mountains and plateaus of Transbaikal, with a trans-Canadian traverse. Canada's maritime coast was likened to Russia's Baltic; her eastern forests to Central Russia's forests; her Great Lakes to the Caspian Sea; her Laurentian uplands bordering Lake Superior to the Urals; her prairie provinces to the Siberian steppes; her barrens to the Siberian tundra; her Rockies and Pacific ranges to East Siberia's mountains. Kropotkin observed that there was one fundamental distinction between the two: beyond North America's Pacific coast mountains there was no broad coastal plain, while beyond the Transbaikal Mountains lay the broad plains of the Amur, Manchuria, and North China.

Kropotkin's distinction failed to take into account California's potential for supporting a large population through agriculture, mining, and subsequently manufacturing. In contrast to the American Pacific, the broad Asian Pacific shorelands did not prove susceptible to large-scale Russian settlement. Because of the existence of wastelands or heavily populated, foreign-controlled areas along the Pacific, the "sea-to-sea" goal could not have the same meaning to Russians as it had to Americans. More significant a goal has been the settling of the Continental Interior, as a means unto itself, not as a stepping-stone to the Pacific. And the waterways that have the most geopolitical meaning to the U.S.S.R. continue to be the Baltic and Black seas—not the open ocean. If we characterized the United States as a Maritime-Continental nation, then we must characterize the Soviet Union as a Continental nation with the beginnings of a Maritime personality that is not likely to compete with the state's continental outlook for many years to come.

Canada does not, by itself, provide an adequate analogy to the Soviet Union. We would have to add to this picture the Great Lakes-

[11] Pierre Kropotkin, *Orographie de la Sibérie,* Institut Géographique de Bruxelles, Publication 9, 1904, pp. 40-42 (translated from the Russian, originally published in 1876).

Middle West industrial-farm belt of the United States, which can be likened to the Ukraine; the Western Desert and Mountain province, which can be likened to Central Asia; and the Californian Mediterranean, which has similarities with Trans-Caucasia. Such a composite view provides the American reader with a clearer idea of the immensity and diversity of the Soviet landscape.

NATURE'S LIMITATIONS

Because of latitude, remoteness from open seas, the barrier effects of mountains, and continentality, the U.S.S.R.'s climate leaves much of its territory too cold or too dry for large-scale permanent settlement. Permafrost alone covers three and a half million of the eight and a half million square miles. Not only is the subsurface frozen solid in the winter; in the summer the thaws tear up roads, railway beds, and building foundations. Most crops cannot grow in the permafrost area because of the cool, short summer, which also lacks adequate moisture. Farther south, in the brown soils and the chernozems of the wooded steppes, when the growing season does permit agriculture, the 10 to 15 inches of annual precipitation are highly effective because of low evaporation.

The second area of climatic deficiency embraces two million square miles of desert and semidesert lands in Central Asia. With 8 to 12 inches of rainfall annually, mostly in the spring and summer, intense evaporation reduces effective moisture to a minimum. These lands differ from the cold areas in that they can be made highly productive under specialized conditions of irrigation farming. An important feature of Soviet agriculture has been the large-scale development of industrial crops, vegetables, and fruits in the oases of Central Asia.

In addition to climatically deficient areas, there are two million square miles of rocky, mountain forest soils, immature hill soils, and peat bogs that are unsuited to cultivation. Although drainage is being expanded, less than 5 per cent of all Soviet crop land has installed drainage.

Within this framework, 10 per cent of the U.S.S.R. (900,000 square miles) is devoted to crops, and 16 per cent to permanent meadow and pasture. Of the crop lands, the most important area is the wedgelike triangle from Leningrad to the Black Sea to Krasnoyarsk along the Yenisei River at the edge of the Central Siberian Plateau. This triangle contains mixed forest podsolic, deep chernozem, and brown soils. East of the Urals, the triangle becomes quite narrow, and rainfall is marginal. But along this belt lie the manufac-

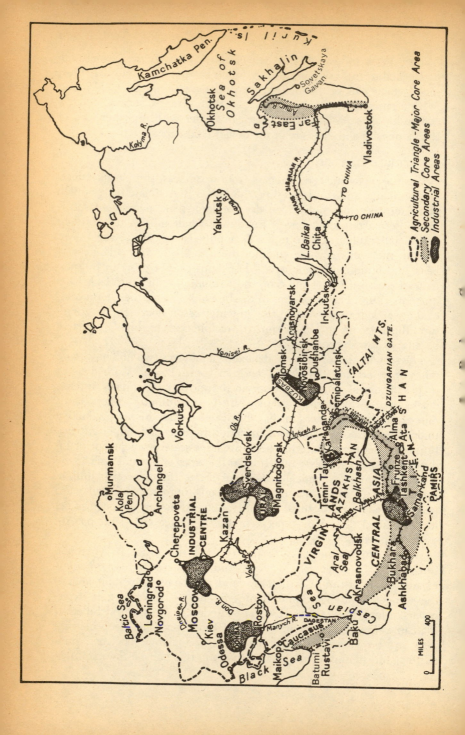

turing cities and farmlands of Siberia—a belt which, along with the Amur Valley, Central Asia, and, to a lesser extent, the Caucasus, represents the Soviet Frontier Region. (See Map 17.)

SOME INTERNAL CHANGES

We turn to some examples of internal change, not because these are sharply differentiated from the external affairs of the U.S.S.R., but precisely because they affect them so profoundly. First, with respect to agriculture, we are aware of the priority that is being given to increased agricultural production in the U.S.S.R. today. This cannot be otherwise in a country whose rural populace is 45 per cent of the total, and whose agricultural workers are 25 per cent of all workers. The primary aim is to improve the lot of a rapidly urbanizing Soviet society. If the result also achieves an agricultural surplus, the U.S.S.R. will have added an important economic weapon. To date, large-scale export of farm commodities has been carried on by the Maritime World, and particularly by the United States. In the long run, Soviet exports like cereals and industrial crops could become as significant a weapon in the race for the support of the uncommitted world as machinery and manufacturing know-how. For the moment, however, Soviet leadership continues to grapple with farm problems that partly stem from the development lag between modern industry and modern agriculture.

To recognize nature's limitations is not to succumb to them, but merely to take advantage of such knowledge. While Stalin showed little such recognition, Khrushchev did, albeit belatedly, and certainly his successors now do. Thus, limitations arising from climatic deficiencies (desert and permafrost), soil inadequacies (peat), and mountainous terrain can be overcome provided that adequate attention is placed upon irrigation, drainage, storage, and distribution. As long as investments remain inadequate, farming must represent a major economic, social, and political problem to the U.S.S.R.

Agriculture suffers from an economic development lag—not, to be sure, in a few favored areas such as the industrial croplands of Central Asia and Trans-Caucasia, and the grain lands of the Ukrainian steppe, but elsewhere—in the Baltic, in Belorussia, in the old Muscovy Center, in Polesye (the northwestern, forested Ukraine), and in Western Siberia.

Agriculture is a social problem because of the social backwardness of most rural populations. It is well to remember that there are actually more rural people in the U.S.S.R. today (110 million) than there were in Czarist Russia of 1914 (100 million). While these farm families now support a total population double that of 1914, they can be said to have only doubled their agricultural productivity in the face of five- and six-fold productivity increases in the Western World during the comparable period. A nation with such a large number of low-income farmers as the Soviet Union will face increasing social tensions as the living standards of urban dwellers improve, unless rural standards can be substantially elevated.

We have mentioned the agricultural triangle that extends from the Baltic and Black seas to Krasnoyarsk. In this area, 600,000 square miles are under crop cultivation. Here two revolutionary land-size changes have been made in the past two decades: 1) the pushing of grains to the north and the southeast, and 2) the relocation of certain crops and the planting of new ones.

It has been quite some time since the Ukraine—the historic center of the agriculture of the Russian Empire—has led Soviet republics in the production of any commodity save sugar beets. After the First World War, agricultural expansion occurred in the coarse grain and dairy lands of White Russia, and in the grain and root crop districts of Moscow. Then came the extension of cereal farming to eastern European Russia, especially the Volga lands, and finally into Siberia. There, spring wheat has been cultivated in the Yakutsk area, various cereals in Kazakhstan, and fruits and industrial crops in Trans-Caucasia and in Turkestan.

With agricultural expansion has come diversification. Grain production today accounts for 60 per cent of the total crop area, while in 1914 it covered 90 per cent. While significant increases in yields and acreage have been made along many lines, relatively little headway has been made in dairy and meat production. This has occasioned the launching of a grandiose plan for new farm expansion and crop diversification. The first phase of this plan dealt with growing wheat in the subhumid and semi-arid "virgin lands" in the east, from the Volga to Karaganda to Tomsk. The other phase consisted of converting coarse grain lands west of the Urals to corn and hogs. One hundred and fifty million acres are involved. Despite climatic liabilities, poor drainage, the need for summer fallow acreage, inadequacies of transportation, and labor shortages, progress was made in the first stages of the plan, but then setbacks occurred owing to the drought and reduced yields.

Because of the lack of sufficient large-scale investment in chemical fertilizers and irrigation works, these plans have failed to reach anticipated norms. Indeed, the failure of the Virgin Lands Scheme, which occasioned the Soviet import of wheat and triggered new debates and political tensions within the Soviet Union and was an important ingredient in Khrushchev's downfall, may have long-term, serious national psychological implications. For about a decade, the corn program of the U.S.S.R. experienced violent fluctuations in production, suffering alternately from declines due to moving into unstable and marginal climatic areas, to excesses in production due to Khrushchev's overly zealous pressures for increasing production norms. Dry farming is a gamble unless it includes the use of chemical fertilizers or fallow land. Otherwise, periodic disaster may be anticipated. The meeting of production targets in meats, dairy, and vegetables will, of course, affect domestic events. Success in grains and industrial crops will also have bearing upon foreign affairs. The 1970 grain target was 180 million tons. Wheat is by far the leading grain —half of the total now grown. Rye, oats, barley, millet, and corn complete the picture, save for modest production of rice. In recent years, grain production has varied between 140 and 160 million tons. The real question is not whether the goal can be reached but whether it will have to be reached at the expense of energies that could be devoted to livestock or vegetables, or even industrial capacity.

Irrigated land is only 5 per cent of total plowland and since 1957 costly irrigation projects have been reduced. Only cotton and sugar beets are being emphasized in new irrigation programs. Even here, in a water-conservation effort, some cotton is being grown without irrigation in a belt extending from the Eastern Ukraine to the Caspian Sea. Soviet cotton is now about one-fifth of the world production, and more and more of it is of the long-stapled Egyptian variety. It is small wonder, then, that cotton imports from Egypt are being resold to Maritime Europe at less than the purchase price. We can assume that the Russians will continue to dump cotton if they deem it economically necessary or politically desirable to do so. With over 10 million tons of raw sugar there is an ample supply of sugar and its by-product, and sugar dumping also occurs as a result of Soviet-Cuban trade. At stake is more than domestic economic prosperity, for Eastern Europe and much of the developing world are still in need of grains and industrial crops, despite some remarkable gains from their own increased farm productivity as a result of the so-called "green revolution." In its initial zeal for agricultural self-sufficiency, the Soviet Union gave up the political advantages that might have accrued from agricultural specialization and international exchange. The Western world has embarked on this course of international trade and is better equipped to meet the deficit food requirements of the developing world. Foreign trade in food becomes even more important as the distributional and storage capacity of developing countries improve. This gap between the U.S.S.R. and the Maritime World as food exporters may well increase when the West introduces new packaging and distributional means to reach what is today the highly undeveloped consumer market of the tropical and subtropical world. The United States, Canada, Australia, and New Zealand, have the ability to export foods in bulk to China and to the developed Socialist world, especially the U.S.S.R. This further demonstrates the gap.

The vicious circle in which the U.S.S.R. is caught is further underscored by the fact that spectacular advances in agriculture depend upon investment in machines, chemicals, and irrigation works. These investments will not create better employment opportunities for the bulk of the agricultural workers; instead, investments will displace workers—or, at best, simply widen the gap between the well-to-do, scientifically-run farms and the older villages. The surplus farm labor problem that could be triggered by a chemical-mechanical revolution will have to look to manufacturing for its resolution. This, then, is the dilemma. Agricultural investment will increase productivity, but not solve the attendant surplus farm labor problem. This can be resolved only by simultaneous industrial investment.

Industrialization

The abundance and variety of mineral and forest resources, stemming from the size and diversified geologic structure of the U.S.S.R., give to its industry a most significant advantage. No other political area is, potentially, so self-sufficient. The shortages that may exist in tin, cobalt, molybdenum, and tungsten are supplemented by the resources of satellites. The Soviet Union is better provided with mineral resources than any other single country, and new reserves are constantly being uncovered. Also, together with Eastern Europe's forests, the forests of the Soviet realm form more than one-third of the world's total forest areas, and timber is important as an exportable commodity.

But if space provides an advantage in the variety of resources that it has to offer, certain disadvantages stem from the distances between raw materials and markets. Manufacturing in the U.S.S.R., even more than agriculture, has to contend with transportation costs and problems that few other parts of the world must face. The mineral resources of the U.S.S.R. are spread much farther than are its people. Where one resource and a market may coincide, the other resources vital to the manufacturing process may be hundreds of miles distant. A classic example is the Urals-Kuzbas Combinat, wherein coal and iron ore are exchanged over a 1,200-mile distance.

An example of the magnitude of the transportation problem can be seen in the building of a huge, integrated steel plant at Cherepovets. This plant, with an annual output of 5,000,000 tons of steel, furnishes Leningrad's machinery manufacturing plants with their major source of steel. The steelworks have been located 300 miles east of Leningrad in a position intermediate to raw materials and market (from here, Moscow can be supplied, if necessary). The coal comes by rail from the rich Pechora-Vorkuta fields at the northern end of the Urals—a distance of 1,200 miles. Iron ore is shipped by sea from the Yena mines in the Kola Peninsula to Archangel, and then by rail for 500 miles to the steel plant. New plants like those at Cherepovets, Temir Tau (Kazakhstan), Magnitogorsk, and Rustavi (Georgia) have raised Soviet steel production to 117 million tons. But the cost of producing steel under such conditions is high, and the drain on transportation is considerable. Certainly, the export of steel under completely competitive circumstances, cannot meet the export prices of steel made in equally modern Western European or American plants.

The basic solution to the problem of distance is not only to move factories to the resources, but also to create markets nearby. The process of successful industrial decentralization is tied to that of population decentralization, and the Soviet government is making energetic strides in this direction. One of the consequences of such a process is the trend to decentralize economic planning and bureaucratic controls. Stalin decentralized plants and markets, but kept a highly centralized control of the various regions in Moscow. Khrushchev recognized the strangling effects of centralization and turned over planning as well as production to the regional centers. His successors have followed suit, though pulling back from certain economic liberalization policies, like incentives.

THE ADVANCE OF THE RUSSIANS

Plans that are concerned with developing mineral resources, decentralizing industry, or opening up new lands to agriculture have political as well as economic significance. Because this diversification is being spearheaded by Great Russians, a profound change in the population distribution map is taking place. Great Russians, who are 55 per cent of the country's total population, occupy key urban and mining areas in Kamchatka, Northern Siberia, the Amur Valley, the Kolyma Basin, the Siberian Wedge, the Ob and Yenisei valleys, Turkestan, the Western Caucasus, Karelia, and Kaliningrad. This population is in a position to submerge many small nationality groups, especially of the Turkic and Mongol stocks. Some idea of the trend can be seen in the fact that from 1955 to 1958 about two million young people alone, mainly Russians, migrated to the "virgin land" areas of Northern Kazakhstan.

The major Russian colonizing thrust was, and still is, an eastward one into Siberia. Settlement efforts by Russians in Central Asia and the Caucasus have had to contend with both existing native populations and less favorable physical environments. Nonetheless, over the broad sweep of time the process of Russian dispersion throughout the land seems inevitable. The Middle Volga, once Asiatic, is now two-thirds Russian. The Lower Volga and Ural River valleys, still largely Asiatic, contain growing Russian industrial centers. North Kazakhstan, the contact zone between Siberia and Central Asia, is now mainly Russian, as are areas in eastern Central Asia, like Semipalatinsk and Alma Ata, which have been opened to development by the building of the Turksib Railway. Farther north, the mining areas of the Western Altai Mountains are mainly Russian. The Trans-Caspian railway, which traverses southern Central Asia, has touched off Russian settlement along the eastern Caspian Sea, at Ashkabad and at Samarkand.

While Western Ciscaucasia (the Kuban) has long been Russian and is part of the R.S.F.S.R., the Caucasus as a whole remains essentially native. There are, however, Russian enclaves in Dagestan and Baku. Along the country's western frontiers, there have been significant population changes in Karelia and Kaliningrad (formerly northern East Prussia), which now have Russian majorities, and in Western Belorussia, where, in the wake of the emigration of Poles and the extermination of Jews, White Russians now predominate. Even where Russians are not in the majority, the introduction of Russian settlers into selected localities where industry, mining, or farming is being developed injects a Russian influence that cannot be measured in mere numbers. Urbanization means Russian settlement throughout the Soviet Union—a phenomenon that Harris first observed from his studies of Soviet census data nearly three decades ago.[12] For example, recent Soviet policy has been to set industry in the countryside, away from the major manufacturing centers. In many instances, these new centers have replaced older market towns, whose function has long since disappeared as a result of the collectivized agricultural framework. These new industrialized cores are Russian enclaves within the rural native habitat, setting the pace for the modernization that affects farming as well as the city.

It is true that political and cultural recognition of the 169 nationalities was a farsighted response by Soviet leadership to the problems created by the cultural diversity of Czarist Russia. The political-administrative framework that has evolved is based essentially upon this heterogeneity of nationality. But both strategic and economic needs motivate the Russians and their allied Slavic groups to continue to spread throughout the land. The very fact that the technical and administrative know-how needed to exploit the raw materials of the Soviet Union's frontier lands resides essentially in Russian minds and hands, makes immigration necessary and endangers the cultural position of national minorities. The construction worker, the foreman, the plant engineer, and the administrator are all needed to develop backward rural areas, and most of these are drawn from the older, industrial centers. The success of this exploitation of resources, in turn, makes the European Russian corelands increasingly dependent, economically, upon the frontier reaches. This is because regional interdependence, rather than regional self-sufficiency, is the basic goal of Soviet planning.

The Industrial Center represents, as it were, the main knot which ties up the principal threads of the country's inter-regional connections. . . . As a result of this construction (in industry, agriculture and transportation), the U.S.S.R. could develop its productive forces to such an extent that it is now no longer dependent on foreign countries both for industrial equipment and raw materials. . . . The rapid development of industry in the regions of the Volga, the Urals, Western Siberia, Kazakhstan and Central Asia . . . has greatly strengthened the ties of these regions between themselves and with the Industrial Center.[13]

[12] Chauncy Harris, "Ethnic Groups in the Soviet Union," *The Geographical Review,* July 1945, pp. 466-73. For a recent treatment of Soviet urbanization, see Chauncy Harris, *Cities of the Soviet Union,* A.A.G. Monograph Series, No. 5 (Chicago: Rand McNally, 1970).

[13] Baransky, *op. cit.,* pp. 406-11.

Interdependence is something more than dependence, to be sure. Nonetheless, each day brings with it greater Russian need for raw materials and products of national minority lands. As a consequence, nationality distinctions and freedoms are likely to yield increasingly to the centralizing forces and pressures of the Russian majority. Slogans of political autonomy and economic self-sufficiency may have little practical significance to the nationalities of this federal state in the face of centralized Russian controls and Russian population dispersal.

SECONDARY CORE AREAS

The lands of the Czars were harsh, somber, and untamed. So is much of the present Soviet landscape. When we think of the conquest of the frontier, we should not think of this advance into the wilderness as a slow, evenly paced advance from the primary core. Frontier settlement consists rather of a multitude of developments of various sizes and types. It consists of dots on the landscape, like mining towns; of ribbonlike stretches of farms and cities along railroads and rivers; of clusters of urbanized, industrial complexes; of broad sheets of plowland. The high proportion of territory that is in Arctic tundra, northern coniferous forest, mountains or deserts, has only superficial value to our assessment of Soviet national power. What is important is the specialized economic qualities of these distinct landscapes, and the manner in which they are being exploited. This can be measured by the numbers and sizes of the various points or locales of exploitation, and by the type and quality of lines of transportation.

In the development of Anglo-America, settlement did not occur through a uniform westward progression. Footholds were established along the mouth of the Mississippi (New Orleans), the southwest Pacific coast (San Francisco, Los Angeles), and the Columbia River basin, to support settlement back into the interior. These footholds were in areas sufficiently well endowed by nature to become rapidly self-supporting. As we contemplate the American scene, we see that the process of filling in the United States from these secondary core areas has been intensified in the past three decades.

In the same manner, the Far Eastern, Caucasus, and Central Asian regions of the Soviet Union serve as secondary core areas to supplement the extension of the frontier from the main European core. The progressive movement of Russians from the Don to the Kuzbas is therefore the major, but not the only, direction of frontier development. For the specialized resources of the Amur Valley and the Pacific coast, and of the mountains and adjoining plains of southern Central Asia and the Caucasus, have provided a basis for agricultural and industrial activities that can also help push back the frontier.

The Far East, historically, has been the strategic Russian key to the Trans-Baikal region. When it could not deny its enemies the use of Vladivostok as an ocean-supported base, the Soviet government of 1918 was helpless to take counteraction against the Czech-Japanese forces in Eastern Siberia, nor could it influence events in northern Manchuria. On the contrary, the four-year stay of the Japanese in Vladivostok was the key to Japan's control of the Chinese Eastern Railway and North Manchuria. Although lightly populated today (under six million), the highly urbanized Soviet Far East has a manufacturing and mineralized economy, with petroleum, machine tools, transport equipment, building materials, and fish as items that can support developments in the Trans-Baikal sector of Eastern Siberia. Moreover, grains and livestock are shipped to all of Eastern Siberia from North China via Vladivostok.

Another secondary-support core region is the Caucasus. For the most part, the Caucasus has remained quite distinct from the rest of the U.S.S.R. in a physical and cultural sense. However, Western Caspian and Maikop petroleum has been an important factor in the industrialization of the lower Don (Rostov and Kamensk) and the lower Volga. Also, Caucasus timber and farm production have played an important role in the emergence of Rostov as a great, national farm machinery producing center.

Underway in the North Caucasus is a large river canal project, designed to connect the Manych River, which flows into the Don at the Sea of Azov, with the Caspian Sea (following the remnant of an old watercourse). The riverway will be used for irrigation, as well as navigation. The Manych was traditionally regarded by Russian geographers as the boundary between Russia and Asia. With the completion of the project, the poorly developed "White Steppes" that border the northern Caspian Sea will gain support for irrigated agricultural development from the Caucasus base.

By far the most important of the secondary core regions is Central Asia. It is no accident that powerful, Central Asian, Turkic Khanates were able to resist the Czars until a century ago. For these Muslim empires lay at the mountain foot of Central Asia. Waters from the Pamirs, Alai, and Tien Shan supported large oasis civilizations in Bukhara, Samarkand, and Tashkent. Besides, the Aralo-Caspian desert served to bar the way from the north. But today these southern oases and many newly founded towns have become important Soviet agricultural and industrial centers. River waters have been stored and canalized to become the basis for the country's cotton-growing industry. Fruits and vegetables, sugar beets, rice, and tobacco are also important. Industry has kept pace with the modernization of agriculture. From Krasnovodsk (oil terminus and chemicals), to Ashkabad (textiles, glass, food), to Dushanbe (textiles, tannery, food), to Alma Ata (chemicals, food, publishing), to Frunze (textiles, cannery, food), vital industrial activities have been developed. Tashkent, the railway junction of the Turksib, Trans-Caspian, and Trans-Aralian lines, is the leading center, with large textile, machinery-making, and food-processing plants. Its satellite towns have developed hydroelectric power and copper refineries.

From these industrialized oases flow materials and market potential that aid significantly in the development of Northern and Central Kazakhstan, and of Western Siberia. Railways that converge on these southern cities (like the Turksib along the east, the Trans-Caspian along the southwest, the Karaganda-Balkhash cutting north-south through the heart of Kazakhstan) have attracted settlers and furthered industrial developments. At the same time, the railroads have made it possible for these southern oases to help support the development of the desert and steppe portions of Central Asia.

Secondary core areas attract pioneering activities, because of economic considerations and also to fulfill political-military needs. This is true in the case of the U.S.S.R. (See Map 17). The Caucasus and Central Asia are accessible to several older industrial areas. The development of these two secondary cores has stimulated the development of regions that are intermediately located between them and the older areas. This is a filling-in process, especially for the "White Steppes" and northern Kazakhstan. The Far East remains a more difficult forward development area to support because of its limited resource base, because of the harsh environment of the area to its west, and because of the lack of adequate interoceanic connections with the major core area (in contrast to America's Panama route).

Eastern Europe

Europe outside of Russia is divided into two parts, West and East. Central Europe is no more. It is a mere geographical expression that lacks geopolitical substance. The disappearance of Central Europe was foreshadowed by the dismemberment of Austria-Hungary in

1918, when the dual Empire, with 51 million people and 141,600 square miles fell apart, its lands being allocated to seven different states. The conquest of Austria and Czechoslovakia by Germany in 1938 and the Nazi-Soviet Nonaggression Pact of the following year led to the division of Central Europe between German and Russian power. The war, and Germany's defeat, brought on the sweeping changes in the ethnic and national boundary maps of Europe that have culminated in today's crushing reality—Central Europe is gone. Its eastern two-thirds belong to Continental Europe; its western one-third belongs to Maritime Europe.

Central Europe generally was taken by geographers to refer to that part of Europe lying between the Rhine on the west and Russia and the Balkans on the south and east. Eastern Europe meant, essentially, European Russia. It is instructive to recall that, while most geographical works following the First World War continued to speak of, and to regionalize in terms of, a Central Europe, Halford Mackinder, in 1919, spoke of the real Europe as being divided between East and West Europe.[14] To Mackinder's incisive mind, East Europe included the area from the Elbe to the Urals. Its Tidal Lands, or Middle Tier of states that lay between Germany and Russia, were, in his eyes, the key to control of all of Eastern Europe.

What Mackinder assumed was that Europe between the Rhine and the Volga must not be permitted to unite, and that it could be prevented from uniting by the creation of a tier of independent states from Finland to the Black Sea. Mackinder wrote, "You must have a balance as between German and Slav, and true independence of each. . . . The condition of stability in the territorial rearrangement of East Europe is that the divisions should be into three and not into two state-systems. It is a vital necessity that there should be a tier of independent states between Germany and Russia."[15] Mackinder pleaded for what he called an "adequate" subdivision of East Europe with a Middle Tier of "really independent" states. He called for seven states based upon the seven different Middle Tier peoples (Poles, Bohemians, Hungarians, Romanians, Serbs, Bulgarians, and Greeks), totalling more than sixty million in population, interconnected by railways, and having access to the Adriatic, Black, and Baltic Seas.[16]

[14] Mackinder, *Democratic Ideals and Reality,* map on p. 21.
[15] Mackinder, *Ibid.,* pp. 157, 158.
[16] Mackinder, *Ibid.,* p. 171.

Hindsight tells us that the *cordon sanitaire* failed for two major reasons, the hopeless divisions among these Middle Tier states, and the need of these countries for co-operation with and support from the Soviet Union. Without this support they were helpless against German economic and military pressure. Conversely, without German support they were helpless against Soviet pressures. Even a united Middle Tier could not have resisted simultaneous pressure from both powers. Yet no less a geopolitical observer than Isaiah Bowman was moved to state that extension of Poland through Galicia, and of Romania through Bucovina, linked these countries as a continuous belt from the Black to the Baltic Seas, enhancing their ability to stand together as a bulwark against Bolshevism.[17]

Opposition to Germany and the Soviet Union was not an adequate basis for the emergence of the Middle Tier as a third and balancing force in Eastern Europe. The antagonisms within and among the states concerned were too great to be surmounted by common fears of outside pressure. On the contrary, the various small states concerned sought support from either Russia or Germany in their schemes against their neighbors. Thus it was that these tidal lands of the German, Slav, Magyar, Romanian, and Jew—from the Oder to the Dneiper—sought to devour one another when Nazi Germany broke the status quo in the east. Capitalizing on the Munich Pact, Poland seized the Teschen area and Hungary absorbed the Magyarized southern border of Slovakia's Hungarian Plains, from Ruthenia almost to Bratislava. Later Ruthenia was turned over to Hungary by Hitler. In 1940 Hungary was further rewarded by its Nazi ally with Northern Transylvania. At this same time Bulgaria seized southern Dobruja from Romania. After the German invasion of Yugoslavia, both Hungary and Bulgaria were awarded spoils. Hungary took two portions of the southern Danube Plain, the Baranja (along the Middle Drava) and the Bachka (the Danube-Tisa "Mesopotamia"). Bulgaria seized Macedonia. It also occupied sections of Greek Thrace, from the Struma River to Alexandroupolis, in pursuit of a long-desired outlet to the Aegean Sea via the Maritsa River.

The ideal of national self-determination that was sponsored by the victorious allies after the First World War meant self-determination for some, but not for others. In every newly created state the national majority had to contend with large minorities that were frequently in the majority in specific cities or portions of the country. The

---

[17] Bowman, *The New World* (Yonkers, N.Y.: World Book, 1922), p. 294.

Czechs and Slovaks were only two-thirds of their country's population, the Serbs half of theirs, the Romanians three-quarters of theirs, and the Poles two-thirds of theirs. The extermination and deportation of millions during the Second World War, and the population transfers that followed, have made Poland Polish, East Germany German, Czechoslovakia Czechoslovak, Romania Romanian, and Bulgaria Bulgarian. Germans, White Russians, Ukranians, and Jews are to a great extent gone from Poland; Poles from Germany; Germans, Ruthenians, and Jews from Czechoslovakia; Germans, Slovaks, South Slavs, and Jews from Hungary; Germans and Italians, from Yugoslavia; South Slavs, Jews, and Bulgars from Romania; and Turks from Bulgaria. Many Magyars were expelled from Slovakia and from the Voivodina, especially the Yugoslav portion of that region. A new type of political boundary has been created—*a culture-molding boundary*—by which the demographic characteristics are reshaped to conform with the political boundary. We could, modifying Hartshorne's suggested terminology,[18] call this a "superimposed-subsequent" boundary. The boundary is marked off without regard to the original cultural landscape, and is therefore "superimposed." Then the cultural landscape is completely altered by population movement, and new cultural features emerge with which the boundary now conforms. What Europe has practised on a mass scale occurred earlier in Turkey, and has since been followed in India-Pakistan, Israel, Korea, Vietnam, and Dominican border areas, among other places. This twentieth century phenomenon has its roots in European expulsions and exterminations in the Middle Ages; and in Assyrian, Babylonian and Roman dispersals, of conquered peoples in ancient times.

This coincidence of nationality and national boundary is one condition of East European geopolitical life. Nationalism, in its National Communist form, has a more striking role to play than it could have in the historic past. Only Yugoslavia still faces problems of heterogeneity and nationality rivalries that threaten to weaken the state now held together so much by the personality of one man, Marshal Tito. A second is the far-reaching effects of regional economic integration that has been brought about both by Communist cooperation and by external pressure from the U.S.S.R. Economic life in the Soviet satellites has been transformed, particularly through heavy in-

[18] Richard Hartshorne: *Suggestions on the Terminology of Political Boundaries*, Leipzig, 1936.

dustrialization. Intraregional trade is quite heavy, though still less than the trade of individual countries with the Soviet Union.

In the first stages the rapidity of the drive to industrialize Eastern Europe follows Soviet patterns quite closely. However, it must be pointed out that industrial strength was and still is uneven. East Germany and Czechoslovakia are industrial countries, Hungary and Poland are partly so, and Romania and Bulgaria are still agricultural. The problems of industrialization are therefore not uniform throughout Eastern Europe.

Steel production was made the measure and guidepost of Eastern European industrial development, as it was in the U.S.S.R. Today's steel production for Eastern Europe is over 38 million tons, or five times the 1938 output. The heart of Eastern European steel production lies in one great complex, the Silesian-Moravian coal, iron ore, and zinc region. Here 70 per cent of all of Eastern Europe's steel is made. The Polish and Czech industrial areas have been connected by railways and canals, and iron ore from Krivoy Rog in the Eastern Ukraine has largely replaced the supplementary iron ore that was formerly imported from Sweden. Countries like Hungary and East Germany must rely upon imported raw materials for their steel. Heavy industry's expansion in Eastern Europe rests, therefore, upon two pillars—greater intraregional trade, and greater dependence upon the Soviet Union.

A reflection of the industrial dependence on the U.S.S.R. is the development of an extensive pipeline system from Soviet territory, bringing petroleum and natural gas to Czechoslovakia, Hungary, East Germany, and Poland. Warsaw and Krakow have for some time received natural gas from the Western Ukraine, and now petroleum is being pumped from the Caspian and Black Sea areas to East Germany and to the Danube Valley.

Nonferrous metals, coal, pig iron, industrial raw materials for light industry, and timber are other imports from the Soviet Union. Only in chemical fertilizers, soda, and sulphuric acid, does the U.S.S.R. lag in supplying its satellites with raw materials for heavy industry. The net result is that two-thirds of the foreign trade of individual Eastern European countries is with fellow satellite neighbors and the U.S.S.R., and there is little to suggest that this trend will be altered.

While growth characterizes heavy industry, light industry has made relatively little headway save in already advanced countries like Czechoslovakia, Hungary and East Germany. Trade patterns with the U.S.S.R. are in complementary industrial raw materials and heavy industrial products, not in consumer goods. Because of this, the bulk of whatever products Eastern Europe does import from the West are engineering supplies, chemicals, drugs, consumer goods, and foodstuffs.

Reaction to the policy of regional economic interdependence and national specialization came with the first stages of development. Romania, as Yugoslavia previously, sought to develop more compatible national industrial goals. Resistance by the Romanians has dampened, but not eliminated this Soviet industrial grand strategy. But the clash of interests, regional versus national, should be regarded from within the framework of an evolutionary process within which the forces of regional interdependence and national self-containment must come to grips with conflicting needs. There are, doubtless, minimum levels of national self-sufficiency which, for reasons of prestige, national psychology, and economics will continue to be pursued by the East European nations, especially those which possess a fairly diversified raw material base that encourages greater independence from the U.S.S.R. and trade with the West and China.

Eastern Europe has lost its traditional role of food exporter. Czechoslovakia and East Germany are major food importers today, and even Poland must import some grain. The stagnation of agriculture in Eastern Europe has left townspeople in a worsening situation of less available stocks at higher prices. Failures of the region's agriculture can be partly attributed to peasant resistance to collectivization, and partly to unbalanced emphasis on investment in manufacturing and transportation at the expense of agriculture. Essentially, however, it is the inevitable consequence of the change-over from a subsistence, national, agricultural economy to an industrial-commercial, agricultural economy, based upon regional specialization. If the U.S.S.R. can succeed in building up exports of grain and industrial crops (the latter, directly or through barter with third parties), then Eastern Europe's dependence upon Moscow will be further heightened.

The final condition of Eastern European geopolitical life is its strategic dependence upon the U.S.S.R. Between the Black and the Baltic seas, the Soviet Union has common borders with Poland, Czechoslovakia, Hungary, and Romania. As we have already noted, all of these countries are subject to pressures and the threat of instantaneous reprisals from Soviet soil. In addition, because of post-World War Two boundary changes and population expulsions, Poland and Czechoslovakia seek security from future German demands; Bulgaria from Romanian counterclaims in Dobruja; Czechoslovakia from Hungarian counterclaims in Slovakia; Yugoslavia from Hungarian counterclaims in Voivodina; East Germany, from West Germany's unity efforts; and Romania from Hungarian ambitions in Northern Transylvania. Even if local Communist parties did not require Soviet assistance to maintain their control over the satellite countries, or if such parties become or are replaced by nationally oriented parties, the strategic dominance currently exercised by the Soviet Union makes independence of action in the face of Soviet opposition highly unlikely.

Historically speaking, the shift in locational perspective of Eastern Europe has taken place with unprecedented speed. From a Shatterbelt with portions strongly oriented to the West (especially Czechoslovakia, Hungary, Poland, and East Germany), Eastern Europe has become absorbed within a geopolitical region dominated by the Soviet Union. The Iron Curtain is a reality and, for the foreseeable future, the two Germanies an established fact. The 1971 agreement over Berlin, assuring as it does Western access to the city, also recognizes the special character of West Berlin as not fully integrated politically within the Federal Republic. It makes it possible for the Federal and Democratic Republics to enjoy more normalized relationships and to anticipate greater degrees of interaction. Such a condition, however, takes into account the specific orientation of East Germany to Eastern Europe, and West Germany to Maritime Europe.

Within Eastern Europe, there are significant patterns that suggest a dynamism of relations. The Inner East European belt consists of East Germany, Poland, Czechoslovakia, and Hungary; the Outer East European belt consists of Yugoslavia, Albania, Romania, and Bulgaria. The Inner Belt plays a strategically more sensitive role than does the Outer, although the increased Soviet offensive posture in the Black Sea and the Eastern Mediterranean suggests that there are limits which it will impose on Romanian nationally-independent action.

Movement-orientation that existed prior to the Second World War has altered drastically. Then, Czechoslovakia was oriented to the Elbe River and the North Sea; Hungary, via Austria and Yugoslavia, to the Adriatic; Poland, via the Baltic Sea, to Germany, the U.S.S.R., and Sweden, and via the North Sea to France; and Romania and Bulgaria via the Black Sea and the Aegean to Turkey. Today's orientation is as follows: the Baltic Sea axis of East Germany and Poland to the U.S.S.R.; the Carpatho-Land Corridor of Hungary and Czechoslovakia to the U.S.S.R.; and the Black Sea orientation of Bulgaria and Romania to the U.S.S.R.

Relatively or moderately extra-regionally open systems developed in Yugoslavia, are being tried in Romania, and were attempted but failed in Poland, Hungary and Czechoslovakia. From a regional point of view, the system is relatively closed intraregionally from one state to another and closed to the outside world. But it is open in terms of relationships with the U.S.S.R. We may anticipate a gradual opening of the system intraregionally, as national confidence builds up, old rivalries die out, and political polycentrism within the Communist world becomes an accepted fact. Such polycentrism can emerge provided that it does not take military and strategic paths independent of Soviet interests.

Trade as an Economic Weapon

Much of the struggle between the Maritime World and the Communist bloc manifests itself in economic clash. The Soviet bloc has already enjoyed considerable success in capturing overnight much of the foreign trade of a few neutral, and even Western, nations. Egypt, Cuba, and Guinea are prime examples, but Afghanistan, Iceland, India, and Turkey are cases where a substantial share of the business has turned to the Soviet Union and its satellites. Through extending credits, grants-in-aid, and barter, and through buying up large quantities of raw materials like cotton, coffee, sugar, wool, and fish, a major power can redirect the foreign trade of subsistence or single-commodity countries.

On the other hand, states that suddenly shift to the Soviet market have reason to be cautious. Unless the U.S.S.R. has a long-term need for the commodities it decides to import, it may suddenly reverse its decision to make such purchases, leaving the supplier without alternative markets. Moreover, Soviet purchases of commodities that are already produced in quantity in the U.S.S.R. is apt to lead to "dumping." Cotton from Egypt has already been dumped on the European market. In the future, machine tools, paper, pulp, and petroleum could be dumped.

With respect to petroleum, it should be noted that from the tanker ports on the Baltic, Caucasus, and Emba, crude and refined products can be shipped to northern and western Europe. Also, from Danube Valley pipelines there can be connections to Italy to bring petroleum to the Mediterranean. Currently the Soviet Union has the capacity to export substantial amounts of oil and natural gas to Maritime Europe (although not to the point of becoming the dominant supplier). Potentially it can export oil and gas to Japan and gas to the United States. Some modest "dumping" in Maritime Europe can temporarily disturb the Western-controlled petroleum marketing mechanisms. But the greater the desire of the U.S.S.R. to gain influence within the Arab oil-producing states, the less likely it is to practice "dumping," especially as the share of revenues and ownership by Arab governments increases and as the Arab stake in high market prices is raised. Indeed, if "dumping" should become a conscious long-term Soviet policy, the target is more likely to be Arab governments than Western oil companies, in a policy designed to undermine these governments and create economic chaos favorable to Soviet-oriented Arab revolutionary forces.

A greater danger lies in the possibility that Arab oil-producing states might be taken over by Soviet-oriented regimes and that Soviet policy could then be to use potential denial of Middle Eastern petroleum as pressure against Maritime Europe and Japan. For the Maritime World to rely upon the enlightened self-interest of Arab leadership to maintain the flow of oil is not warranted by past performance (cf. Iraq, Syria, and Libya). The only credible defensive Middle Eastern petroleum posture is a large-scale, co-ordinated program by the Maritime World to develop alternative sources of energy, to reduce wasteful consumption practices, to increase oil and gas synthetics, and to press forward with increasing vigor for alternative oil and gas sources, including and perhaps especially in offshore areas.

The U.S.S.R. can be expected to apply its economic advantage with considerable vigor so long as it uses foreign trade selectively as a weapon. The Maritime World cannot duplicate this procedure because it is committed to spreading assistance throughout most of the world, out of economic, strategic, and humanitarian considerations.

We need not assume that, in the long run, the economic path of the U.S.S.R. will be smooth. The Maritime World's advantage in terms of capital accumulations, know-how, and present near-monopoly on international trade will be enhanced by certain permanent Soviet international trade liabilities that derive from its landward orientation:

1) The development of Soviet resources is moving manufacturing farther and farther into the interior of the country. The more successful the development of the Siberian and Central Asian frontier, the greater the distance from the export market. This means in-

creased transportation costs and a permanent disadvantage vis-à-vis ocean-located states, neither railroads nor pipelines being as effective as sea lanes. Despite substantial improvements in efficiency, Soviet railroads (which carry 80 per cent of all goods, compared to less than half that percentage for the United States), remain the most heavily loaded in the world, with attendant problems of wear, maintenance, and delays. Moreover, absence of a first-class road network means absence of the flexible type of transportation service that a specialized national economy should have—a factor of time-cost as distinct from distance-cost.

While the new pipeline grid has recently been laid down from the Urals-Volga to the Baltic and through Eastern Europe, and another system has been constructed eastward to Eastern Siberia, there are severe limitations to its effectiveness for international oil trade. Pipeline costs are not strictly competitive with waterborne movements. In the United States, where about one-fifth of all tonnage is moved by pipeline, most of this movement is either of the feeder variety or of specialized projects (refined) and natural gas. Bulk movements of crude oil go by sea where possible—a significant contrast to the Soviet system which continually contends with the friction of long-distance land transportation. In brief, then, the farther eastward the extension of Soviet development areas, the longer the average distances over which goods must be hauled, and the higher the cost.

2) The diversity of the raw material base of the U.S.S.R. means that, in the long run, large-scale purchases of minerals and industrial crops from underdeveloped countries will only duplicate Soviet resources. In the absence of major Soviet consumer goods imports, these are the only types of imports that can be brought in. Soviet self-sufficiency, in other words, is a long-term hindrance to international trade.

A shorter-term liability to trade stems from the lower living standards in the U.S.S.R. This makes it unlikely that large-scale capital surplus will be exported on a sustained basis during this period of Soviet development. On the plus side, the landward push is making for a more intimate set of contacts with bordering Asian countries, including northern Iran, Afghanistan, and China. These contacts bring with them the pressure to exercise greater degrees of Soviet strategic power in the borderlands. In the case of China, the landward growth of the U.S.S.R., as well as the counterpart Chinese growth, makes for tension and conflict. But the mutual vulnerability that arises from the landward meeting of the two nations suggests that this condition, as well as basic ideological ties, create a "love-hate" dynamic that will eventually lead to greater cohesion between the two.

The National System—from More Closed to More Open

Relations among states revolve around the nature of the system which characterizes particular states. Whether we speak of ideology or economics or cultural values, the issue of how the national system is organized politically vis-à-vis the outside world is crucial, and the geographical impact of this political system upon the landscape is profound. Generally, all states are organized along a broad continuum that might be described as ranging from an *open* to a *closed* *system*. By an open system we refer to one in which the state is open to all forms of external contact—i.e. movement of people, goods, and ideas (free *circulation*, to use the French term). A closed system is one in which national political boundaries are used to bar all circulation with the outside world. Obviously, no state can have a fully open or a fully closed system, and nations also alter their policies of systems over time. The U.S.S.R. during the late 1920's was more of an open system than it was during the 1930's, when it was tightly closed. Since the 1950's there has been a steady continuum in the re-opening of this system—first to Eastern Europe, then to the underdeveloped world, and recently to the Maritime World (Japan, Italy, the United States, and the United Kingdom). If we continue to describe the U.S.S.R. as a more or less closed system today, surely its system is far more open than that of Communist China, which is just beginning to open its system. So the issues of time, maturity, economic, and strategic needs as they relate to the nature of the system all come into play in the review of the geopolitical character of the Soviet Union.

In a sense, Soviet short-term objectives and Soviet tactics are interchangeable terms. If we consider Soviet tactics within the closed-open political system context, the focus upon their geographical consequences becomes clearer.

Key items within the tactical sphere have to do with economic development, the integration of transportation and communications, and the equalizing of socioeconomic conditions. During the closed system (the Stalinist period), we find the following characteristics:

1) *Drive for agricultural self-sufficiency to free the Soviet Communist state from dependence upon the outside world.* Czarist Russia, a

grain exporter, was supplanted by the Soviet Union, a grower of cotton, sugar beets, etc. Urbanization of the Soviet population, with its increased food requirements (higher living standards and distribution losses), further accelerated the drive for self-sufficiency.

2) *Development of small-scale industry to serve the purposes of regional specialization.* This served the double objective of reducing transportation costs and of improving the economic conditions of the national minorities. It meant, however, small factories, use of local fuels, including lignite and peat, and in general, a retreat from Lenin's early calls for large-scale industrialization and electrification.

3) *Move of industry to the Urals and eastward.* The pull of resources, the impetus of Russification, and the impact of war all contributed to the eastward move. It is noteworthy that Communist thoughts of relocating industry eastward began during the conflict with the White Russians. At one time Lenin felt that the Ukraine might have to be written off because of the threat that it might cut loose. First the Urals, then the Kuzbas, then Lake Baikal, the Soviet Far East and Central Asia became significant industrial landscape elements.

4) *Barring the Soviet Union to inflow of foreign capital, foreign travelers and foreign ideas.* This was, in effect, the period of the one-way street. More roads led into Moscow than radiated outward, including the long-term residence taken up by foreign Communists in the Soviet Union and the complete dominance by the Soviet Communist Party of foreign Communist parties. Landscape reflections included such elements as the lack of connection between Russian broad-gauge and East European standard-gauge railways, the development of socialist realism architecture, and the time lag in the adoption of certain Western technologies.

The Second World War and its aftermath have seen a significant opening of the Soviet system. Eastern Europe, first and on the largest scale, became the focus for Soviet military and economic activities. This form of regional co-operation in itself produced an opening of the hitherto air-tight Soviet system. Four sets of pressures that might be cited as system openers today have to do with foreign aid, scale of industrialization, economic prosperity, and national self-confidence. As the more open system develops, we find the following characteristics:

1) *Foreign aid and military adventures, representing entanglements with domestic implications.* The long-term assistance program for the

Arab Republic of Egypt, exchanging missiles and engineering skills for cotton, will have an impact on the previous Soviet desire and need for self-sufficiency in cotton. Sugar from Cuba to East European countries has a long-term effect upon Soviet beet production.

2) *Successful development of large-scale mineral and industrial enterprises requiring foreign markets.* Now that petroleum is in considerable national surplus (e.g. second and third Emba fields), the need to sell to the outside world, not simply Eastern Europe, but also Maritime Europe, and recently to Japan, has involved the U.S.S.R. in a major distribution and sales program. Pipelines, ports, and tankers are becoming a major feature of the Soviet landscape. Negotiations over large-scale Japanese capital investment in developing Soviet Far Eastern petroleum and natural gas, and over immense American investment in developing Soviet liquified natural gas resources for export to the United States, are portents of the significance of mineral exports as a systems opener.

3) *Economic prosperity being enhanced by national specialization—* a lesson that has been learned by the Soviet Union. Soviet steel, when exchanged for German ships and East European grain, serves all concerned, and opens the Soviet system. So does Soviet lumber and oil when exchanged for Japanese capital or Italian auto-making know-how.

4) *Replacement of feelings of inferiority and military fear of the West by a spirit of national self-confidence—*changing previous needs which used the closed system as a protective device. Victory in the Second World War, elimination of the German threat, the dependence of Eastern European Communist parties on the Soviet Union, the decline of Western Imperialism, and the space-age achievements all contribute to the new spirit.

Granted that the Soviet search for security is a consistent, long-term goal, the fear of invasion coupled with the fear of the restoration of Capitalism is not what it was either in 1919-20 or during the Second World War. Acting with relative impunity, first in Hungary, Poland, and then Czechoslovakia, the U.S.S.R. has expressed both its long-term search for security (military and ideological, in terms of the one-party system) and its short-term economic development needs as related to Eastern Europe.

In our appraisal of the changing Soviet geographical scene we have touched upon several points. Outward expansion of the Soviet state to present borders poses serious threats to neighboring states. In the process of Czarist and Soviet territorial expansion, large non-Russian minorities were absorbed. To resolve the problems of Colonialism-Imperialism that attended this expansion, Marxist-Leninist theory created a federated state format that offered theoretical equality to all nationality groups. To insure control of the national territory in a practical sense, however, Communist leaders are carrying out large-scale Russification programs within these peripheral areas.

In the Soviet Union, agriculture, mining, and manufacturing are moving eastward—away from major sea lanes and optimum transport conditions for international trade. Emphasis in agriculture continues to be on dry farming under hazardous climatic conditions, rather than on more stable but far more expensive irrigation facilities. The result is that greater investment capital is available for manufacturing—an economic strategy that can prove sound only if the agricultural gamble succeeds.

Within the Soviet state, a degree of self-sufficiency has been achieved that is unique among today's modern states. This self-sufficiency is likely to be a major stumbling block to Soviet trade relations with other parts of the world—particularly those areas that have thrown off European imperial and colonial rule, which continue to depend heavily upon the export of raw materials in their foreign commerce.

In Eastern Europe, despite efforts of nationalist Communism to take up more independent economic and ideological positions, the strategic vulnerability of the region to Soviet pressures appears to preclude any possibility of its breaking away to become part of some genuinely neutral Central European buffer zone. The Soviet Empire has, with the exception of Yugoslavia, Austria, and Finland, expanded to its full continental European limits. Elsewhere in World Island, the contest for the Shatterbelts intensifies. Beyond these regions of direct strategic concern lies the zone of global conflict, wherein military and economic goals are secondary to ideological ones.

Current inland extension of the economic frontier is but a continuation of the historic Russian thrust from the forested lands around Muscovy into the drier, more marginal lands of the Eastern Ukraine and the Volga, and into the mountainous and desert reaches of Asia populated by Turkic and Mongol peoples. This thrust has always faced the challenge of serious natural and environmental liabilities. Marxism-Leninism was not unaware of nature's limitations, but nonetheless took the position that Soviet man could and should ignore the implications of environmental restrictions in extending agriculture and in creating industrial combines in areas of rigorous challenge to human use. Communist Party policies of seeking to achieve self-sufficiency, rejecting most forms of dependence upon foreign raw materials, especially food, have remained the consistent national aim. Complete utilization of domestic natural resources has had the further objective of opening up remote, backward areas populated by national minorities with the express purpose of giving to the latter a share in the nation's total productive capacity. Finally, to compensate for the liabilities of distance, Lenin formulated the policy of establishing the means of production close to the sources of raw materials, thus reducing transportation hauls. As a result of these processes, the U.S.S.R. was subdivided into small-scale economic regions, inefficient in factory output and in use of local raw materials. The inefficiency and impracticality of this policy prevented its meeting the original hopes and goal, and long-distance movement remains a problem feature of the Soviet landscape.

One might ask whether the United States, with an economy that has developed in stimulated response to regional specialization, does not show parallels to the Soviet experience. The differences, however, are more significant than the parallels. Development of the Gulf and West Coast regions have taken place within far more favorable physical settings and with better water- and land-borne access to the major population and economic core of the Northeast and Midwest. Moreover, national self-sufficiency has not served as the tail to wag the dog, as illustrated by the use and dependence upon such foreign materials as iron ore, copper, petroleum, sugar cane, meat, and raw steel. The United States has passed from the age of national self-sufficiency to the era of superabundance and global interdependence. Self-containment cannot satisfy an economy of superabundance, which must seek out foreign markets.

We must recognize that Soviet international policy goals differ from place to place because of the differences in their geopolitical values. Economic unrest, radicalism, and vestiges of Western imperialism are exploited by the Soviet Union wherever they occur, as a means of expanding Soviet influence. But over and above this, specific locales have uniquely important qualities from a Soviet standpoint. Achieving defensive depth for border ports, securing land gateways into the U.S.S.R., unifying minority nationalities, using global sea lanes for international trade—these are among the more important territorial considerations that have motivated recent Soviet foreign policy. Proper assessment of these values in each instance will better prepare us to cope with Soviet global designs.

7 MAINLAND CHINA

Locational Perspective

The geographic locational setting that a nation sees for itself in the world—its locational perspective—has much to do with how that nation shapes and conducts its foreign policy. Its view is cognitive in that it stems from locational "facts" as perceived by the elite and conveyed to the public. It is affective in that it becomes the embodiment of national folklore and myth that inspires the leadership to try to adapt the conduct of its international affairs in consonance with this perspective. A France that sees itself in the center of Europe (the Gaullist view) conducts its policies differently from a France that saw itself in the center of NATO. A United Kingdom that saw itself as the center of a world empire is a far cry from the United Kingdom that sees itself as the western edge of Europe. National locational perspectives, then, change through time. They also differ in the eye of the beholder. While Americans may view Australia as "the end of the world," Australians view themselves as focal to Offshore Asia, Southeast Asia, and South Asia.

The topic of this chapter is the role that locational perspective plays for China in its regional and global affairs.[1] The thesis to be developed is that China's locational perspective is a product of historic, national, and cultural postures of egocentrism. In one sense

[1] In addition to the works subsequently cited in this chapter, the reader may wish to make general reference to John K. Fairbank, "China's World Order," *Encounter* (December 1966), pp. 1-7; Benjamin I. Schwartz, "The Maoist Image of World Order," in *Image and Reality in World Politics,* John C. Farrell and Asa P. Smith, eds. (New York: Columbia Univ. Press, 1967), pp. 92-102; John C. Stoessinger, "China and America: The Burden of Past Misperceptions," *ibid.,* pp. 72-102.

this egocentrism leads to a perspective that places China as central in the world and therefore focal in world revolutionary affairs. In another sense, the egocentrism leads to a perspective that is aloof and isolated, and therefore quite capable of limiting its goal to regional rather than global primacy. These two positions are not mutually contradictory. They can be explained both in terms of the variation in spatial scale (the global versus the regional) and as an expression of the dialectic which in Maoist thought rationalizes these apparent contradictions as occurring at different times as well as in different places. The positions therefore become reconcilable and symmetrical.

Locational perspective provides an understanding of the geopolitical motives of Mainland China. It helps explain the relationships between China and the U.S.S.R. within the Eurasian Continental world and the rationale for the uniquely Chinese global strategic role that has evolved under the leadership of Mao Tse-tung and his would-be successor Lin Piao. This is a role in competition concommitantly with both the Maritime World and with the Soviet Union. In the case of the former, the competition is independent; in the case of the latter it is interdependent.

Perspectives Through Time

Fundamental to the discussion is the traditional Chinese view of their place as being the center of the world, a view that goes back to before the beginnings of the literate period some 3,000 years ago. While the centrality of the Chinese perspective did not change until most recent times, the scale did. Three perspectives can be seen to have developed over time: the *local*, the *regional*, and the *global*.[2]

The *local* or primitive sense of space originated during the preliterate period when the Chinese had no knowledge of Western or Southern Asia. China, the Central Kingdom, was the sown area. This civilized world was differentiated from the surrounding desert and mountain wastelands to the north and west by being agricultural. It owed nothing to surrounding cultures. China was more than a place, it was a cultural unity. At the outset of the literate period, the Central Kingdom sprang from the concept of a loose group of

[2] This discussion derives much of its direction from the historic perspective presented by C. P. Fitzgerald in *The Chinese View of their Place in the World* (London: Oxford University Press, 1964) and the space-time theories of Derwent Whittlesey in "The Horizon of Geography," *Annals of the Association of American Geographers*, 35, No. 1 (March 1945), pp. 1-36.

separate states (the Hsia Kingdom) located within Northern China. The South, from the Yangtze onwards, was then not yet part of this civilized world. It was to be absorbed into Chinese civilization between 1,000 and 200 B.C., to become part of China by conquest, as the southern forest dwellers—backward rice cultivators—were overrun and embraced as Chinese. What made the forest dwellers candidates for becoming part of China was their potential for agriculture. The nomads to the north and west belonged to a separate, non-Chinese world. The view that the Chinese held of the Central Kingdom as the center of the world was finite, based on a finite sense of space.

The *regional* sense of space evolved during classical times, beginning with the Han who were the first to unite China through a strongly centralized government. This was a period when the Chinese met other worlds—the Romans, the Persians, the Indians, the Byzantines, and the Arabs. The Roman Empire was recognized as a great civilization but was too remote to be regarded as a political competitor. Thus the discovery of another world created, in effect, a regional sense of space, the period being characterized by fitful international trade and by the diffusion of Buddhism from India into China after the end of the Han dynasty, essentially by land routes.

This period was also characterized by consolidation and unification. Chinese dynasties were interrupted by nomadic rules, but never did the barbarians transform Chinese civilization; instead the barbarians were absorbed culturally. The Chinese Empire successfully acculturated the people of the lands south of the Yangtze; indeed when the Tartars invaded the more populous North, it was the South that was able to retain the tradition of the Empire. By the end of the T'ang Dynasty in the early tenth century, all of what is today China had been absorbed save Yunan. For a time under the T'ang, Korea and the Tonkin Delta were conquered and colonized, but then they were left to be treated as non-Chinese, tributary kingdoms rather than provinces. Save for the brief Mongol interlude, both the Ming and Manchu dynasties continued the T'ang policy of a strong Chinese civil service and professional army—the props of a stable empire.

The regional sense of space took a further twist during the early modern period (sixteenth to twentieth century) when the Chinese first encountered the "barbarians" of post-discoveries Europe. Then, in the eighteenth and nineteenth centuries, they faced the issue of modernization, and in the early twentieth century had to stave off territorial encroachment by Russians, Japanese, and Europeans. In this period, the Chinese had come to recognize the world as polycentric, but the continued view of their being at the center of the most civilized portion thereof reinforced Chinese self-confidence during the period of intense European cultural and technological pressure. Indeed, this self-centeredness contributed tremendously to the spirit of over-confidence and naïveté with which the court and other traditional institutions sought to counteract and then to dislodge the Europeans.

The *global* sense of space began to be developed by the early twentieth-century modernists, for whom Westernization was a means to save China. Within this context, the view held by the Chinese was still one of regional emphasis, but now in interaction with the rest of the world. It remained for Chinese Communism, and especially Maoism, to reach out simultaneously to restore a China separate and aloof from the rest of the world and to forge a China with a global revolutionary mission. From the regional viewpoint, concern is with territorial integrity and regional hegemony. From the global viewpoint, concern is with establishing the central position for China in the world revolutionary camp. Unlike the global views of the United States and Soviet Union, which are, in a sense, infinite because of the successful mastering of outer space, the Chinese view of the globe is that of a finite world, or a more traditional, three-dimensional one in which the missile age and the conquest of outer space are still essentially goals rather than realities. Indeed, even the capacity to range widely and freely over the seas, a Western tradition only now being fully realized by the Russians, is still denied to the Chinese, thus further distinguishing their spatial view of the world as finite from the infinite view of their power-core competitors.

Perspectives in Space

In his essay on Chinese group values toward their national space,[3] Theodore Herman suggested that from the beginning of the nineteenth century Chinese nationalism held three basic values: 1) pride in its old, centralized culture, which included a prescription for world order; 2) strong defensiveness against inroads on Chinese areal control; and 3) demand for economic, political, and social improvements within China. Ginsburg suggests that China had a traditional view of herself in world order that placed different values on territories within and beyond her control, with controlling power tapering off concentrically from China proper to an Inner Asian zone, and

---

[3] Theodore Herman, "Group Values Towards the National Space: The Case of China," *Geographical Review* (April 1959), pp. 164-82.

then to two non-Chinese controlled zones, Outer Asia and the Outer World. The historic boundary embracing the first two zones included Korea, Formosa, North Borneo, Mainland Southeast Asia, Assam, the Trans-Himalaya Kingdoms, eastern Soviet Central Asia, Mongolia, Manchuria, Trans-Amur, East Siberia, and Sakhalin.[4]

From this starting point, we would like to explore the relationship between the way the Chinese perceive and value their environment and the national policy that results. The analysis will be at three scales—national, regional, and global.

National space continues to be clearly tied to the concept of culture. Culture and civilization are treated as co-terminus with concepts of territoriality. Where Chinese expand into areas historically non-Chinese or incapable of absorbing large masses of Chinese, they find it difficult to include these areas as national space. The offshore Chinese islands, with Hong Kong, Macao, and Taiwan, are to the Chinese unattained national space. Parts of Soviet Central Asia, the Soviet Far East, Korea, and Vietnam—areas controlled in the past by the Chinese, but never culturally Chinese—belong to the regional space over which hegemony, not national absorption, is the goal. Should rule of Taiwan be seized from the Kuomintang by the native Taiwanese, the Chinese Communists might be able to accept the view more easily that modern Chinese settlement of the island represents a period of suzereignity, not territorial control. A Taiwan ruled by Chinese Nationalists remains alienated space to the Chinese People's Republic.

Of course, the concept of national space is not static. Some non-Chinese culture areas continue to be absorbed or are candidates for absorption. But these are areas that were empty or only lightly populated by others, such as Manchuria, since the start of the twentieth century or Tibet during the last quarter of a century. The target area for absorption into the Chinese national space is what formerly was termed "Outer China" (i.e. Manchuria, Sinkiang, and Tibet). These regions have in recent years become an integral part of national space through large-scale Chinese settlement efforts and economic and military activities.

Regional space might best be described as those areas considered by the Chinese as vital to the integrity of the national space and the

---

[4] Norton Ginsburg, "On the Chinese Perception of a World Order," in Tang Tsou, ed., *China's Policies in Asia and America's Alternatives* (University of Chicago Press, 1968), pp. 73-91.

security of its periphery. These are the territories from which non-Chinese forces (Maritime or Russian) might undermine China's defenses; they also include lands from which Chinese (Nationalist or Bourgeois) forces operate as a threat to the Chinese revolution. Chiang's armies on Taiwan, bands of Chinese ex-Nationalist mercenaries in Burma, or anti-Communist bastions of Overseas Chinese were viewed as having the potential to undermine the Mainland regime.

Denial of bases to hostile parties in Outer Mongolia, Korea, Japan, Indo-China, Burma, northern India, and northern Pakistan is the regional security goal of Chinese Communist leadership. Whether this denial has to be achieved by hegemony or can be achieved by neutralization or treaty, is surely one of the major questions of our time. On the answer to this are pinned hopes for an enduring Sino-American detente.

The *global space* is that part of the world to which China considers itself focal for purposes of furthering world revolutionary Communism. This is a polycentric view, the Chinese distinguishing between their underdeveloped rural world and the developed urban world.[5]

Very early the Chinese rejected a satellite role in their relationship to the U.S.S.R., for in 1949 Liu Shao Chi (deposed in 1968) proclaimed the Chinese revolution to be the model for the underdeveloped world. The Chinese global view developed as a Maoist contradiction or dialectic. On the one hand, the Chinese saw themselves contained by the Maritime World operating from Asian bases and joined by the U.S.S.R. exercising pressure from the Sino-Soviet borderlands (threats both to national integrity and regional security); on the other hand Lin Piao articulated a view which saw China leading a counter-encircling, world-wide, revolutionary movement that would contain the Maritime World from rural bases in Asia, Africa, and Latin America.[6]

---

[5] Ginsburg, in presenting his current model for China in a world order, emphasizes the Sinocentric, Asia-oriented power system (i.e. the regional scale). On the global scale he speaks of the Outer World: the Developed (Capitalist), the Developed (Socialist), and the Underdeveloped. He suggests that the underdeveloped rural world provides a superb milieu from which to distract and threaten the West while China buys time for internal economic development. Ginsburg, *ibid.*, pp. 89-91.

[6] *New York Times,* September 4, 1965, p. 2. Excerpts from "Peking Declaration Urging 'People's War' to Destroy U.S.," an article by Marshall Lin Piao published in all major Chinese newspapers on Sept. 3 and made available in English by Hsinhua, the official Chinese press agency.

This rural world is the world which, according to Maoism, must achieve its liberation through revolution or "Peoples' Wars." Race and color were raised as issues when Lin Piao deplored Khrushchev's revisionism in adopting a "scornful or passive attitude towards the struggles of non-white peoples," and accused Khrushchev of inciting hatred and fear of the "yellow peril." In the wake of the acrimony of the most recent exchanges between China and the U.S.S.R., the concept of the encircled urban world is extended to include Russia.

Recent historic events support this threefold space theory. With respect to the national space, the Chinese Communists set to the task of achieving national territorial integrity immediately upon coming into power. In Central Asia, the East Turkestan Republic, established under Soviet protection in 1944, was reintegrated into Sinkiang in 1949. In 1950, the Chinese Communists pressured the Russians to turn over to them the Manchurian Railway and the Port Arthur (Lushun) Naval Base (the railway was actually transferred in 1952; withdrawal of Soviet forces from Port Arthur had to await the end of the Korean War in 1955). Concern over the return of the Offshore Islands was not solely tied to Sino-American relations. During the 1958 Quemoy crisis, Mao rejected the idea of a joint Sino-Soviet war fleet. He feared control of China's coast by the U.S.S.R., for no foreign hold or influence, even Russian, was acceptable. Thus Mao demanded Soviet support, but on his own terms. Failure of Mao's Offshore Islands policy (as well as failure of his economic and social policies) was a major reason for Mao's being replaced by Lin Shao Chi as chairman of the Republic. When Mao regained power, the issue of the Soviet attitude toward the Offshore Islands, as well as the limited nature of Soviet help in Korea, became a major bone of contention between Mao and Khrushchev and his successors.

China's concerns over regional space were expressed in several ways. In 1950, the Sino-Soviet treaty called for preventing Japan from repeating its aggression. Several years later, nuclear policy within the region became a concern, for this related to Chinese considerations of regional security and hegemony. In 1957 the Russians had agreed to supply aid to China in manufacturing nuclear weapons. Two years later, however, the U.S.S.R. proposed an atom-free zone in the Far East and the Pacific—a proposal that Mao chose to ignore. Then the U.S.S.R. repudiated the 1957 agreement with China and proceeded to develop the partial Nuclear Test Ban Treaty with the United States and Great Britain. This was denounced by China—a logical step in China's insistence on being able to develop its own means of regional hegemony without being subject to a United States–Soviet Union agreement.

The differences with the U.S.S.R. over what China considered its regional space also surfaced in the Indian question. In 1959 the Longju incident took place when the Chinese occupied a garrison post in the Northeast Frontier Agency. Khrushchev then spoke of the need for cooperation between the U.S.S.R. and India, as well as of Sino-Soviet bonds, in trying to mediate the dispute. This was followed by the brief war over Ladakh in 1962, when Khrushchev described the area as "uninhabited, with no particular significance." The Chinese thought otherwise. They regarded Ladakh not merely as being historically theirs; Ladakh was needed to provide a secure road from Sinkiang into Tibet. Ladakh, for the Chinese, was an issue of regional security and on a par with Soviet regional interests in Eastern Europe. Just before the fighting broke out, the U.S.S.R. had agreed to deliver and build MIGs for India, and when the fighting broke out the U.S.S.R. remained neutral. This, from a Chinese standpoint, was a betrayal of China's regional security needs by the "revisionist" camp.

Finally, the quarrel between the two former allies focused on Vietnam. In 1965 the Chinese began to express their fears that the Russians wanted to keep the situation in Vietnam under their control and to strike a bargain with "American imperialism" on the Vietnam issue. The following year, Marshall Chen Yi suggested that a new "Holy Alliance" was in the making, with the Russians attacking from the north and the Americans from the south. Here, then, in a regional space sense, is expressed the fear of containment and encirclement, a containment to be countered by shifting the scale to the world.

The *global space* perspective has been cast in rural versus urban (or developed versus underdeveloped) terms. For purposes of the Sino-Soviet controversy, the Chinese have classed the Russians as urban. They have criticized the U.S.S.R. for being overly cautious in assisting colonial and underdeveloped countries because of Russia's relations to the West. Thus, in 1958, Mainland China recognized the provisional government set up by the Algerian nationalists. Because the Russians did not wish to antagonize the French, they did not accord the Algerians recognition until 1960, and then only on a de facto basis.

The controversy, in broader terms, was tied to the issue of coexistence. Khrushchev visited the United States in 1959 and came out in favor of peaceful co-existence. He then visited Peking and spoke of ruling out war and of letting each country decide on how to embark on the socialist road. This the Chinese deplored as revisionism. They especially rejected the Soviet fear that a single spark anywhere in the world would result in global nuclear destruction. The Chinese held that peaceful co-existence could not be applied to the relations between oppressed and oppressor nations, countries, or classes and saw Soviet revisionism as a sell-out of the class struggle.

From these origins of the controversy, it is possible to understand the depth of the split that brought Lin Piao, in 1969, to use the term "socialist-imperialist" countries in describing the U.S.S.R. and its allies, reserving the term "socialist" countries for China and its supporters. The context of the world view differences are deep: the Chinese have taken the position that world revolution can be gained by the sweeping of socialism through the rural areas, the Russians retaining the traditional Marxist notion that world revolution is to be gained through the urban, industrialized proletariat. Within this framework, placing the Soviet Union in the urban camp is logical from the Chinese world-view.

Place and Area Impact

These spatial views may also be considered in terms of place and area impact. It is hypothesized that place, in the national sense, looms very large in Maoist thinking. Place has a function—to preserve a unique racial and national culture, with a rural, proletarian character. Place has a structure—development of a political, territorial hierarchy in which the administrative subdivisions play a subservient role to central authority, and in which the presence of national minorities is to be neutralized by the settlement of Chinese. Place has a territorial framework—the base area concept was developed by Mao as a rural revolutionary base from which cities could be surrounded and overwhelmed.[7] Such bases were isolated and protected by inaccessible mountains, thus affording them the opportunity to develop their strength. Place has boundaries—for China the national space is bounded by the Himalayas and the Yalu. In all probability, the Amur and the China Sea will suffice as boundaries to the north and the east.

[7] *Quotations from Chairman Mao Tse-Tung* (Peking: Foreign Language Press, 1966).

Area impact is a term applied in the regional and global senses. It is the external area upon which influences from the place radiate. Maoist thought alludes to the strategy of the struggle for external, non-Chinese areas as an expansion via a series of waves. The direction of the expansion appears to be concentric, if we use the analogy of the base area concept, with China, the rural base, in alliance with other rural bases, surrounding the urban areas of the world. The timing of the area impact is two-staged: Mao has spoken first of the democratic revolution, and second of the socialist revolution. The democratic, or national, revolution was one that the Chinese conducted in conjunction with bourgeois forces. The socialist revolution, or the dictatorship of the proletariat, came as the second stage for the Chinese, unlike the situation in the U.S.S.R., where the dictatorship of the proletariat was a one-stage effort. Thus it is that the Chinese view themselves as having a unique capacity to direct the revolution in the rural reaches of the world, first through supporting bourgeois national forces against colonialism, and then through supporting the social revolution. This is in keeping with the theory of contradictions, where contradictions, when staged or paired, become part of a dialectic process and come into equilibrium.

It is this theory of contradictions which leads to the conclusion that the Sino-Soviet conflict, as bitter and pervasive as it is, is one of competitive interaction and not of ultimate division. Certainly the Chinese revolution, when added to the Yugoslav national Communist experiment and the Castroite revolution, has made of Communism a polycentric movement. For nearly thirty years only one socialist country existed, and it was the duty of all Communist parties to preserve the revolution in that country. Now there are thirteen countries in the Communist camp. The issue is to preserve the revolution for all in a polycentric world where unity cannot be achieved through uniformity. No one would deny that polycentrism now exists; the question both for the Communist and the Maritime World is how this polycentrism can contribute to a balancing or ordering of forces within each geostrategic region and between them to help maintain global equilibrium.

Internal and External Problems

Revolutionary China has tackled a set of internal problems that are staggering in their complexity and magnitude. Diffusing the impress of central authority is complicated by distance, isolation, and regional traditions that have very deep roots. Integrating North and South China involves the blending of two different agricultural and cultural realms—the North, the land of wheat, single cropping, mineral resources, manufacturing, water shortages, land transportation, and continental orientation; the South, the land of rice, multiple cropping, irrigation, flooding, river transportation, and partly maritime orientation. Developing the frontier is a task that has particular challenge for the population of the North and the Northwest. Historically the South Chinese had as their frontier the lands of overseas immigration. With the close of this frontier, the territories that adjoin the Soviet Union and are populated by national minorities are the focus for current developments. Defusing of population pressure for a state whose population can only be guessed at, but which adds in the neighborhood of 15,000,000 people annually, cannot be handled by frontier settlement alone, or even mainly. Unlike so many other societies, urbanization has not been accepted as the solution to overpopulation. Indeed, perhaps to avoid the instability that plagues so many of the cities of the developing world, with their under- and unemployed populations, the Chinese have used state power to reduce urbanized pressures by sending hundreds of thousands of students and "intellectuals"—sources of potential urban instability—into the country. Finally, internal problems are being tackled within a Maoist governmental framework whose object it is to prevent an elite from emerging that will develop as a rigid and conservative force. The revolution is to be continual and self-purifying.

Externally, the problem of China's finding a role for itself centers on reconciling global and regional postures. The search for territorial integrity and consolidation is still unresolved, although the 1962 war with India and the border settlements with Burma, Pakistan and Nepal have stabilized most of the southern frontier. Unresolved are the border disputes with the U.S.S.R., the Offshore Chinese Islands, Hong Kong, Macao, and Taiwan. Fear of containment by the United States, operating to the east and to the south, and by the U.S.S.R. on the north continues to color much of China's foreign policy attitudes. Globally, the issue is to carve out a special role for China within the world revolutionary camp. In the long run, the likelihood is that polycentrism will mean dominance by the U.S.S.R. of the urban Communist nations and by China of the rural Communist states. Sino-Soviet relations will be a "love-hate" or "enmity-amity" type of association, in which the basically continental orientation of China will prevail over its maritime leanings, leading to a maintenance of the Eurasian Continental geostrategic realm in a state of dynamic tension. As external relationships develop and mature, we expect China to see its main competitor not as the United States or as any of the European countries, but rather as Japan. The competitive pairing, then, to be anticipated within the clash of the two geostrategic regions is that of the United States and the U.S.S.R., and of China and Japan, with Maritime Europe serving as a cooperator with the United States, and the United States with Japan in these respective competitions.

For China, the concept of place has boundedness and is tied up with cultural, racial, and national independence. Chinese aggression is not likely to be aimed at trying to absorb directly areas that are not "Chinese." With respect to China's impact area, extension of influence is likely to be attempted through wave-like or step-by-step expansion. The base-area concept explains the objectives of Korea, Vietnam, Thailand, Burma, and Taiwan as target areas—that is, as nearby rural areas from which to extend influence to other parts of the rural world (a rapidly developing, industrializing Taiwan is a phenomenon that tests the theory). In the process of projecting this influence, the two-stage theory of World Revolution provides the Chinese with ideological competition to the Soviet Union.

In viewing Chinese relations with the U.S.S.R., we can see the evolution of a major interdependent effort, beset by conflict over strategy, tactics, and ideology. The contradictions that characterize this "love-hate" relationship are likely to be rationalized by future Sino-Soviet leaderships as logical and inevitable, because of the polycentric nature of the Communist world. Mutual vulnerability in a strategic sense and common adherence to the Marxist revolution are likely to prevent any realignment that would see either of the two side with the Maritime World against the other. A strategy for the Maritime World that mistakes Communist polycentrism for lasting and unreconcilable division within the Continental Eurasian Realm will be even more disastrous than the strategy that mistook Soviet single-power domination of world Communism for unity.

SPHERES OF CONTACT
AND INFLUENCE

Today's Shatterbelts

We have discussed the characteristics and functions of Shatterbelts
in Chapter 3. The Shatterbelt is defined as a "large, strategically located region that is occupied by a number of conflicting states
and is caught between the conflicting interests of the Great Powers."
At present we recognize two such regions—the Middle East and
Southeast Asia. Each is a zone of contact between the Continental
Eurasian Realm and the Trade-Dependent Maritime World, easily
reached from them, and commanding transit lanes and significant
mineral wealth. Both regions, recently emerged from colonialism,
have been unable to attain the economic and political unity to which
many of their leaders aspire. Instead, internal divisions have become
accentuated by the East-West struggle, and the Shatterbelts have become areas of contention rather than neutral buffers.

This chapter presents brief surveys of the two regions. The primary purpose is to explain their geopolitical functions more fully.
However, a study of these Shatterbelts can shed light upon the conditions under which new Shatterbelt regions might emerge. For as
the Central European Shatterbelt has disappeared from the map,
so might the two present ones disappear, to be replaced by other regions caught up between new constellations of opposing Great Powers.

In the Middle East and Southeast Asia, we find the two regions
that 1) directly border through land and sea channels populous portions of the Eurasian Heartland Region (western China, Ukraine,
Caucasus). They are also easily accessible to the Maritime World
from an Inner Ring consisting, respectively, of Maritime Europe
and Offshore Asia, buttressed by the more distant United States; 2)

are physically dissected by land and water bodies so as to interrupt the unity of movement on land that other comparable parts of World Island possess; 3) are composed of a variety of political and cultural subdivisions and an unevenness of population distribution that is unique to the World Island scene. Compare the following statistics:

	Land Area (sq. mi.)	Population (in millions)	Population Density	Number of States	Cumulative No. of Bordering States	States Bordering Eurasian Heartland
Southeast Asia	1,375,000	255	190	10	33	2
Middle East	2,000,000	145	72	19	20	2

These reflect some of the qualities which help to explain the Shatterbelt status of the two regions.

The Middle East

Consideration of the Middle East as a distinct geographical region is a point of view that meets with general acceptance. Names[1] applied to this area may vary and boundaries[2] may change, but the concept of a Middle Eastern region is implicit in international affairs, and especially in political and military strategy.

[1] The terms *Near East, Nearer East, Levant, Hither East, Classical Deserts, Arab World, Cradleland of Civilization, Southwest Asia,* and *Most Ancient East* are among those which have been applied to parts or all of this region.

[2] a. The Middle East Supply Centre established by the British government in 1941 included the area from Tripolitania eastward through Iran and southward through the Sudan, Ethiopia, and the Somalilands. Cyprus and Malta were also within the Centre's framework, while Turkey, because of its neutral position, was omitted.

b. The United Nations Commission to Foster Economic Development in the Middle East includes the countries from Greece through Pakistan and south through Ethiopia.

c. The British geographer, W. B. Fisher, in his definitive study *The Middle East* (London: Methuen & Co., Ltd., 1950), includes the area that extends from Western Cyrenaica and Egypt through Turkey and through Iran.

d. The U.S. Department of State's Office of Near Eastern Affairs covers Egypt, the Sudan, the Arabian Peninsula, the Levant, and Iraq. In addition, there is an Office of Greek, Turkish, and Iranian Affairs. Both offices are included within the Bureau of Near Eastern Affairs.

In discussing a part of the world like the Middle East, it is easy to become involved in an analysis of some very specific and exciting item of crisis. Such an approach is tempting, but the path is strewn with pitfalls. First, it is likely to become hopelessly out of date. Second, each event can acquire full meaning only when it is related to the broad pattern of events that occur within and around the Middle East.

The most dramatic change that has taken place within the Middle East in its modern history has been its sudden conversion to the status of a Shatterbelt. First Turkish, and then British-French control of the region has been replaced by a variety of conflicting internal and external forces that threaten to divest it of whatever qualities of regional unity it might have possessed formerly.

If we were to measure the density of national tensions and stresses in terms of unit areas, the Middle East would lead all other regions. There is not a single Middle Eastern state that lives at complete ease with its neighbors, and almost every Middle Eastern state struggles with internal tensions that are the product of deep-rooted cultural clashes and geopolitical immaturity. Truly, the Middle Eastern geopolitical environment is a jungle. Territorial disputes rage, or are liable to flare up, between Turkey and Syria, Egypt and the Sudan, Israel and her neighbors, Saudi Arabia and Jordan, Saudi Arabia and the Federation of Arab Emirates, Saudi Arabia and Yemen, Iraq and Kuwait, Iraq and Iran, Iran and Bahrein, Afghanistan and Pakistan, and Yemen and South Yemen. Over-all political tension exists between Egypt and Iraq, Iraq and Iran, Turkey and Syria, Lebanon and Syria, and Israel and the Arab states, to name just a few. Military dictatorships rise and fall with rapidity, and iron-fisted monarchs cling to tenuous thrones. Everywhere the struggle is to consolidate states in the face of internal divisions and external pressures.

Overshadowing the entire region looms the pressure of the Soviet Union. The U.S.S.R. has unresolved claims against Turkish and Iranian border provinces. It is increasing its influence upon Iraq, directly through the Iraqi government and indirectly through Iraqi Arab Communists and Kurdish Nationalist elements. It has made strong inroads in Egypt and Yemen through general trade and specific naval base activities. Above all, it has evinced its ability to forestall counteractions to the spread of Nasserism or other anti-Western movements. This ability was demonstrated in events that started with the Suez crisis of 1956. It prevented any Western countermeasures to the overthrow of the monarchy in Iraq. It influences Israel's relations with its neighbors. It may affect Western ability to act against future coups in Iran.

Shatterbelts evolve from both internal fragmentation and external pressures. While the U.S.S.R. fashions one ring of pressure around the Middle East, the Maritime World, from the Mediterranean and from Africa south of the Sahara, forms a counter-ring of pressure. And the Indian subcontinent is not without some influence in the region. These pressures are cultural and economic, as well as political and strategic. Middle Eastern cultures, economies, and even races reflect the outside world. Western customs, dress, and speech, Western economic patterns, and Western-sustained Christianity and Judaism are present along with Indo-Iranian and African influences to help shape the Middle East. We can view Pan-Arab aspirations of modern Arab nationalism as being in basic revolt against the forces that have conspired to make the Middle East a Shatterbelt. But such a revolt can by no means hope to sweep the entire region by its own efforts, for it runs headlong into forces of internal fragmentation, as well as outside opposition.

In Chapter 3, the geographical region has been defined as a "community of physical, biotic, and societal features that depict, or are functionally associated with, man's occupance of an area." While the Middle East meets the standards of this definition, its regionality is not easy to perceive because of two factors: the strength of its geographical components or subregions, and the political divisions that have tended to fragmentize the entire cultural landscape.

The Middle East lacks a single core and therefore it may be described as a polynodal region, whose character is most clearly expressed on a subregional basis. Each of the nodes serves subregions organized through features that are functionally associated in groupings of different sizes or ranks. Attention must therefore be directed to diverse components, such as physiography, climate, agriculture, industry, religion, and strategic space, and to the area patterns these features form within the Middle East. When superimposed upon one another, such patterns constitute new subregions that are often more significant than the over-all region. If there is a broader uniformity to the region, it expresses itself most clearly in over-all location terms as a crossroads for the three continents, in its movement patterns, and in its environmental and cultural distinctiveness from neighboring regions.

The political consequences of the existence of geographical subregions within the Middle East challenge the significance of some of the regional generalizations that are so often bandied about—namely, that the region is the crossroads of the earth's greatest landmass; that land, sea, and air points of transition make the Middle East of importance to the West, the U.S.S.R., and the African-Asian world; that within the region is the single greatest storehouse of petroleum; and that the Middle East is the focal point for Islam and a potential bridge between the Muslims of Asia and Africa.

If we recognize the difficulties of trying to treat the Middle East as a monolithic region, our political approach finds firmer footing. We know that its various parts are experiencing differing rates of development, and these differences are rooted in the environment and in the people. This is a region of rainy mountains and lowland deserts, of dry interior plateaus and wet coastal fringes, of broad river valleys and isolated oases, of bare rock, sands, and gravels, and of alluvials. This is a region of nomadism and sedentary agriculture, of landlocked peoples and seafarers, of westernized contact zones and eastern cultures, of foreign trade and economic isolation. Whereas internal diversities such as these have not prevented other regions from unifying politically, Middle Eastern diversities are heightened by the fiercely competitive drives of modern nationalism and by the centrifugal pressures that outside interests bring to bear upon the region.

It is because internal differences are so marked, and because they are found in a region that is crushed between outside interests, that we have defined the Middle East as a Shatterbelt, divided into three zones. In the Northern Zone we find a great variety of metallic minerals, iron, coal, and petroleum. In the Median Zone we find the sandstones that have trapped oil in their slight foldings to create the storage places for the world's richest petroleum reserves. Potash, phosphates, and limestone are also widespread there. The Southern Zone's crystalline rock platform is mineral-poor, save where overlaid by sedimentary deposits, as along the Isthmus of Suez or northern Libya, or where broken up by highlands, as in the case of the iron ore-bearing East Egyptian highlands near Aswan. The significance of these structural zones is that they relate to the ability of the various countries to obtain foreign exchange and to broaden the base of local industry.

Differences of climate are of overwhelming importance because the Middle East is so dependent upon agriculture and grazing. Rainfall variations form striking patterns. In essence, these rainfall patterns and their attendant soils and vegetation influence the formation of three Middle Eastern agricultural zones: 1) winter and summer farming, 2) irrigation farming, and 3) grazing. The critical rainfall line is the 16-inch isohyet. Those areas with 16 inches or more rainfall annually can engage in year-round farming operations, with either dry cereal farming and tree or vine crops in summer, and grains, fruits, and vegetables in winter. Unless they practice irrigation, those areas with less than 16 inches of rainfall can carry on only winter crop cultivation, and summer grazing and olive culture. Below eight inches, only grazing is possible, although the four-inch isohyet is sometimes accepted as the absolute minimum for grass.

The 16-inch isohyet has political, as well as economic and social significance, for it is a potential key to stability and strength within Middle Eastern agrarian societies. This is the line that divides normal, year-round farming operations from part-time agriculture, grazing, or irrigation farming. In the majority of cases, these latter three types of activities, suffering from inadequacies of water and soil resources, are carried on within a framework of overcrowding, unrest, poverty, and tenancy. Fertile riverine soils and water for irrigation—the very attractions of the great oases—are, in a social sense, their greatest weakness. This is because oases are not easily enlarged. The major exception to this within the Middle East today is the Tigris-Euphrates Valley, which appears capable of absorbing considerably more people.

The accommodation of rural populace to its land and water resources is a valuable guide to economic and social structures in the Middle East. Those countries, the majority of whose farmers live in areas with over 16 inches of rainfall or in the Tigris-Euphrates Valley, do not suffer from agricultural overcrowding. This is in marked contrast to the countries of the southern Middle East and the Levant, east of the Jordan Rift Valley. It should be noted that climate is not the only cause of overcrowding. Lebanon and Yemen are also agriculturally overpopulated, not because of lack of rainfall, but because of lack of level land.

Middle Eastern industry reflects the region's mineral distribution, its agricultural and water base, and its capacity to import raw materials. Turkey, Egypt, and Israel are the major producing countries of the region. Turkey leads in total output of industrial electricity, steel, and woolens; Egypt leads in persons employed in manufacturing, cement, fertilizers, and cotton textiles. Israel, the most industrialized and urbanized of all, in a relative sense, has a highly varied output that ranges from food processing and textiles to industrial diamonds, tires, automobiles, fertilizers, steel, electronics, aircraft and military industry. The three countries lead in rate of manufacturing growth, manufacturing employment, mechanization of agriculture, and caloric intake.

Turkey has the broadest industrial base potential within the region, with its minerals, foodstuffs, and employable labor force. Israel, with its skilled labor force, outside capital, chemicals, and locational advantages, continues to forge well ahead of all other Middle Eastern states in breadth and pace of development. Egypt's industrial future is more dependent upon its agricultural base than is that of Israel or Turkey, and few of the promises of the Nasser era for industrial development, save for the Helwan steel industry, have been fulfilled.

Today's Middle Eastern industry is concentrated along the Mediterranean coast, emphasizing the significance of imported raw materials. Elsewhere, the only industry of note is Persian Gulf petroleum refining. While this pattern shows a division along east-west lines, there is reason to believe that the progress of interior Turkey and southern Israel, and developments in Iraq and possibly Syria, may some day extend industrialization to the north, and to the drier sections of the Levant-Persian Gulf. It is interesting to note how little relationship there is between the map of Middle Eastern petroleum and industrial activity. While petroleum production is about 30 per cent of the world's total, refining amounts to only 5 per cent, and domestic consumption to only one per cent. This points out the almost purely extractive nature of the Middle Eastern petroleum industry and its extraregional service function.

A final illustration of the diversity of the Middle East is its religions and peoples. (See Map 18.) It would be fallacious to equate the Middle East with the Arabic Islamic World, and to ignore sectarian differences within Islam, or the differing political roles that Islam plays within various states, would also be a mistake. Thus, Shiite Iran has little in common with Sunnitic Egypt, and Muslim Turkey is a secular state, while the influence of Islam is strong in the political affairs of Saudi Arabia.

All of these diversities help to explain why there is little likelihood that one power center within the Middle Eastern Shatterbelt will be able to unify and dominate the entire region. Iran, Turkey, and Israel together have as large a population as the entire Arab world combined. Historically, the Turkish and Iranian plateaus have housed power centers independent of the Arab world. Today, with

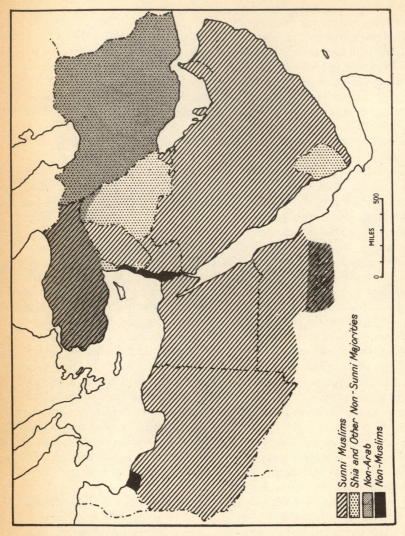

Sunni Muslims
Shia and Other Non-Sunni Majorities
Non-Arab
Non-Muslims

MILES
0   500

MAP 18. Religions and Peoples of the Middle East

Ankara and Teheran emerging as associated seats of power, there is practically no possibility that they will be merged with an Arab coalition dominated by Cairo or by Baghdad.

What stands as the crucial problem today is whether the Middle Eastern Shatterbelt will remain as it is; whether it will become divided into two hostile blocs, Arab and non-Arab, one or both supported by an outside Great Power; or whether three blocs can emerge. The latter might be most desirable, because an intermediate group of states could act as a buffer, in terms of both internal regional politics and Great Power rivalry. Moreover, a three-bloc Middle East would be in closer conformity with sub-regional geographical patterns. Before Egypt took over the mantle of Pan-Arab leadership, such a three-fold division might have evolved, if the British-backed Greater Syria scheme had been successful.

If the Middle East should become a two-bloc region, it would do so through Arab unity, which would stand distinct from, and in opposition to, the non-Arab parts of the region. In the event that Arab unity should emerge under the leadership of Cairo, then, under the most favorable circumstances, the neutrality of the Arab bloc would be colored by a violent anti-Western bias that might be partly balanced by an anti-Communist stance, should traditional Islamic points of view retain a powerful position in government (as is the current trend in Libya, the Sudan and Saudi Arabia). If Arab unity should emerge through a Communist take-over in Baghdad or Damascus, then a new Iron Curtain would be drawn between the Western-oriented and Communist worlds in the Middle East. A Communistic take-over of the Arab world through a process of internal subversion and infiltration has been prevented to date only by the efforts of Arab military leadership. Whether this military leadership, if backed to the wall, could or would invoke Western intervention against Communist pressures is doubtful. For the unremitting anti-imperialist sloganeering of Arab leadership during the past few years would make it most difficult to maintain the support of the masses under such turn about circumstances.

Federation continues to be sought as a means of unifying the Arab world. In 1971, the Federation of Arab Republics, consisting of Libya, Egypt, and Syria, was formed, with the Sudan waiting in the wings for entry. Libyan money, Egyptian mass population, and Syrian left-wing politics, converging on the common enemy, Israel, and backed by Soviet arms and military personnel are the props for the Federation. But this Federation would appear to have as little

possibility of surviving as did the still-born Egyptian-Syrian federation of 1958-61. Egypt has the most to fear and lose from the military
struggle with Israel and is also most susceptible to Soviet pressures,
which are likely to try to keep the lid on the conflict. Still, the present Federation may serve the purpose of dragging an unwilling
Egypt into another war with Israel, given the temper of the other
two partners. Also, it may serve to keep the current governments
enthroned longer than might ordinarily be the case, because of the
mutual assistance clauses of the agreement by which two of the
governments may act to keep a third from being overthrown. This,
ironically, may serve to keep Communist parties out of power, despite the overwhelming military presence of the U.S.S.R. and dependence of the Federation upon Soviet arms and men. If Sudan,
fresh from its anti-Communist purge, joins the Federation, its anti-
Communist nature will be strengthened.

While the split in the Arab world continues to be one between
so-called revolutionary regimes and the monarchies of essentially
desert reaches, the basic and long-term division will probably continue to polarize around Cairo and Baghdad. In this process, the
Levantine and Persian Gulf Arab states will remain the key pawns
in the power struggle. Their ability to retain a neutral footing within
this field of internal Arab struggle is already being sorely tried,
and there is likely to be little stability within the Arab world until
the fate of these intervening countries is resolved.

The divisions within the Arab world are reflected in various issues. To Nasser, Arab nationalism meant Arab internationalism—
that is, political unification of the entire Arab world under a centralized government. To Kassem, Arab nationalism was viewed through
the traditional nation-state framework, and to the Ba'th through
some form of Pan-Arab Federalism. To many, Arab nationalism
means vaguely defined social reforms. To Iraqi and Syrian Ba'thists
and Communists, social reform means thorough nationalization and
socialization, under a Communist framework. To the Saudi rulers,
social reform is hardly a tenet of Arab nationalism. To petroleum
"have-nots" of the Arab world, Arab nationalism means a sharing of
regional wealth. A limited amount of sharing has been grudgingly
carried on as a way of staving off revolutionary pressures in the cases
of Kuwait and Saudi Arabia. Only Libya, in its zeal to spread the
revolution, has enthusiastically shared its national wealth, and mainly
with military rather than economic assistance.

POLITICAL ALIGNMENTS

To relate rigidly political alignments in the Middle East to the various physical and human activity groupings already cited, is not possible, if only because the boundaries of those various sets of zones are not coextensive. Nevertheless, the construction of two broad political zones with flexible frontiers, and a third and intermediate one, has geopolitical validity and strategic tenability because these zones reflect three geographical sub-regions.

The Middle East has rarely been united. Instead, several fixed loci of power have been the bases of regional rivalries.[3] The contests between Babylonia and Assyria; Babylonia and Egypt; the Graeco-Romans and the Parthian-Sassanians; the desert empires of Petra, Palmyra, Nabataea and their neighbors; the Ummayads and the Abassids; the Crusaders and the Saracens; the Mongols and the Mamelukes; the French and the British—all had their roots in opposing power centers. The periods of political fragmentation represented by these various conflicts were far longer than those of unified regional control (as achieved by Babylonia, Alexander the Great, and Rome). Even during the Arab and Turkish eras (each of which lasted for four centuries), strong central government held only brief sway.

Time and technology have changed the significance of some of these loci of power. The desert way stations, for example, lack the land and manpower base necessary to regain for them their past imperial glories. Underpopulated Mesopotamia, open to invasion from the north, cannot, by itself, stand fast. Turkey and Persia were rival seats of empire during the sixteenth and seventeenth centuries because of their size and isolation. Today they are emerging as an allied power center, because of a common fear of Soviet pressure and with the help of improved transportation and communication. Certainly, if they should try to stand in isolation they would be more vulnerable to political and military infiltration.

[3] These areas are:

a. The Nile River Valley, one of the two most extensive areas of irrigated land in the Middle East.

b. Mesopotamia, the region's other great river valley.

c. The "Fertile Crescent" land area, which connects the Nile and Mesopotamia. Within the "Fertile Crescent" are the Levantine ports, the interior access ways, the Assyrian Piedmont, and the Syrian desert oases.

d. The Anatolean Plateau and rimming southern and eastern mountains.

e. The Iranian Plateau and rimming western mountains.

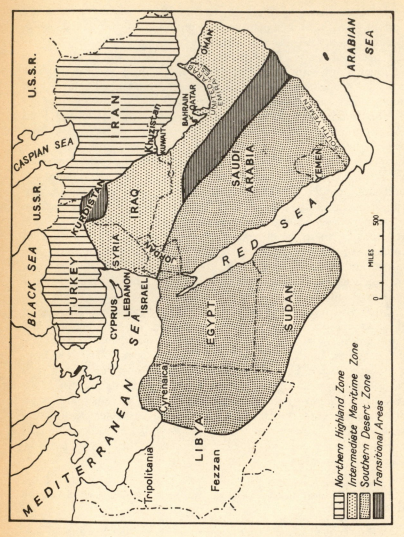

MAP 19. The Middle East in Three Geopolitical Zones

Northern Highland Zone
Intermediate Maritime Zone
Southern Desert Zone
Transitional Areas

The airplane, train, automobile, and ship have consolidated and regrouped the Middle East's loci of power within its geographic subregions. Today three significant zones stand out: 1) the Northern Plateaus, 2) the Nile and the Red Sea, and 3) the intervening "Intermediate Maritime Zone." The latter, though smaller and less populous than the other two, has coastal ports, interior accessways, and petroleum, as strategic sources of strength. (See Map 19.)

The Northern Highland Zone

The non-Arab northern highland countries of Turkey and Iran contain the single largest population grouping in the region (65 million persons); they have the broadest land bases, potentially the most stable agricultural economies, and the possibilities for wider industrialization thanks to fuel, mineral, and capital resources. Kurds and Azerbaijani are separatist elements within their countries. Their very existence, however, forces their governments to greater centralization efforts, such as the expansion of internal communications. Finally, Sunnitic Mohammedanism is weakest in this zone, and Orthodox Islam can, therefore, not be cited as a reason for political ties to the rest of the Middle East.

In general, the northern political zone corresponds with the northern structural and climatic zone. The one area of overlap is Khuzistan in southwestern Iran—west of the Central Zagros, which lies within the median structural and southern climatic zones. As a source of petroleum and a foothold overlooking Mesopotamia, southwestern Iran gives added strength to the northern political grouping.

The Southern Desert Zone: The Red Sea Bloc

The lands of the southern deserts and irrigated oases, extending from Libya through Arabia, are coming under the increasing threat of domination of Cairo. Nearly two-thirds of the zone's entire population of 50 million lives along the Nile Valley, and the Suez Canal is the most significant geopolitical asset of this part of the Middle East. The Canal is important for its economic potential, its strategic significance to the U.S.S.R. and to the West, and its possible role as an instrument of compromise in the Arab-Israeli conflict.

In recent years, Egypt's attentions have been focused northward, toward the Levant and the rest of the Arab world. But Egypt and some of its neighbors are only peripheral to much of the Middle

East. Their concern with areas and events taking place to their south and west may one day be as great as the concern that the northern states now have with the U.S.S.R. Egypt, especially, may have to involve itself more deeply in African affairs, and look southward to the sources of the Nile. In this respect, ambitious Egyptian rulers regard the Sudan as only the first and the immediate objective of the extension of Egypt's sphere of influence into Africa. In the future, the Central and East African Nile headwater areas may become the focus for Cairo's geopolitical ambitions. In the very long run, these may extend to the Muslim world of North and Black Africa, and to the entire continent.[4] In the recent past, Egypt's stake in events in the Sudan has been expressed in the negotiations to facilitate the Sudan's entry into the Federation of Arab Republics. President Sadat's support of General Numeiri during the abortive Communist coup against the latter was unequivocal.

Libya is transitional, for its westernmost sections are culturally and agriculturally parts of the Maghreb. This recently created state may yet find difficulty in retaining its unity, since it is composed of two different culture worlds—the nomadism of Cyrenaica and the North African coastal farming of Tripolitania. Overturn of the Libyan monarchy brought into power the Gadaffi regime, which has chosen to take a strong pro-Egyptian stand. It is questionable how lasting this will be in the face of alternative possibilities of orientation to the Maghreb. A force to maintain the bond is the pull of Egypt toward Libya and the Sudan, a significant factor that may well prove more lasting than the involvement of Egypt with Syria. The attraction of Libya's vast petroleum resources and Sudan's control of the Nile are major lures for Egypt. For the long run, the Egyptian orientation to Africa may come at the expense of its ties with the Arab world, and help to bring about an accommodation between Egypt and Israel.

Saudi Arabia, too, has dual characteristics. The bulk of its population lives along the moister Red Sea coast—or northern interior desert—part of the southern structural unit. Petroleum, however, the basis for the country's wealth, lies along the Persian Gulf coast of the median structural zone. This separation of population concentration from the major mineral resources may some day lead to greater political divisiveness in the Arabian Peninsula, although, conversely,

---

[4] For an insight into this problem, see Gamel Abdel Nasser, *Egypt's Liberation* (Washington, D.C.: Public Affairs Press, 1955).

the petroleum could conceivably buy for the Saudi Arabian government, the political and military power to strengthen its kingdom's unity, and to maintain a Persian Gulf orientation, free of Egyptian dominance. Whether this petroleum can one day stimulate the growth of a large industrial population along the Gulf is doubtful in view of the cultural pull of Mecca-Jidda and the feudal nature of the state. Indeed, the very element that might strengthen Saudi Arabia's orientation to the Persian Gulf—industrialization—contains within it the seeds of revolutionary nationalism and the pull to the Egyptian-controlled southern zone.

Withdrawal of Britain from the Persian Gulf removes the issue of "British imperialism" from Gulf affairs and creates an arena of direct confrontation among Saudi Arabia, Iraq, Iran, and the various emirates. Iraqi claims upon Kuwait, Iranian upon Bahrein, and Saudi upon the Trucial States (the Federation of Arab Emirates) will now have to be resolved without using Western powers as whipping boys. It is likely that the rivalries within the Persian Gulf area can be resolved through new, loose, federal arrangements that will recognize some of the historic claims of the larger Middle Eastern powers. But for many years to come, the Gulf area will be a locus of intraregional contention.

The Intermediate Maritime Zone

With both the northern and southern blocs exercising pressures against the intermediate areas, we must now ask ourselves whether an intermediate zone, oriented toward both the Eastern Mediterranean and the Persian Gulf, is politically viable. Political instability has characterized this area in the past, for it has the characteristics of an internal Shatterbelt.

But this intermediate zone does stand apart from its neighbors. It has a large measure of unity that stems from common and interdependent human and physical resources. We find forces for unity in the ports of the Eastern Mediterranean and their accessways (like the Tripoli-Homs Gap, the Col du Beidar, and the Valley of Jezreel) to the deserts that lead eastward; and in the petroleum of the Persian Gulf fields and their land bridges to the Mediterranean (the 1040-mile TAP-line to Saida, the 530-mile IPC pipeline to Tripoli, (Tarabulus) the 556-mile IPC pipeline to Banias, and the 160-mile Eilat to Ashkelon pipeline). These pipelines carry about 100 million tons (almost all crude), or about 20 per cent of all the Middle East's petroleum that is exported to Europe, North and West Africa, and North America. We find potential unity in the dependence of land-locked Jordan and interior Syria upon the ports of other Levantine states for effective outlets to the sea. We find a force for unity in the intraregional trade of the Levantine states that is higher than that of the Middle East as a whole. We find such a force in the fact that countries like Lebanon and Kuwait are too small to solve their economic problems in isolation. Lebanon needs the markets of neighboring states to modernize its agriculture, replacing grain with fruits and vegetables. Kuwait needs the markets of its neighbors to enable it to invest some of its surplus capital in modern factories that could give to the Kuwaiti populace a productive and purposeful economic role. We even find unity in the religious and ethnic diversities within this zone—for these diversities set apart the zone from the non-Arab Islamic North and the Arabic Islamic South. They make of it a cultural, ethnic, and religious mélange which may one day recognize that its survival rests upon some form of political unity.

Thus, while location has made the intermediate zone vulnerable to pressures from both sides, and while a bipolarized Middle East is neither inconceivable nor lacking in historic precedent, this unique area has within it a basis for political distinctiveness. A coalition of Levantine-Persian Gulf states, standing as a neutral between the northern and southern zones, could give greater stability to the region as a whole, and might serve to isolate petroleum as an issue in East-West politics. However, the emergence of such an intermediate zone requires, first, the creation of an Iraqi, Syrian, and Jordanian Federation, and second, peace between Israel and her neighbors. Neither eventuality is likely to occur within the next few years, and the intermediate zone should be considered as a long-range hope, not a short-range target.

To sum up, treatment of the Middle East as a threefold political-economic region, rather than as a unitary one, finds support within its geographic framework. The distinguishing elements within the northern political zone are: 1) proximity to the U.S.S.R., 2) mountainous terrain and minerals including petroleum, 3) non-Arabic peoples, and 4) a stable agricultural base. Those which distinguish the southern political zone are 1) The Suez Canal, 2) deserts, 3) Egypt's Nile as a center of population and local power, and 4) a subsistence agricultural base. To distinguish the intermediate political zone there are 1) Levantine ports and accessways, 2) petroleum, 3) smaller but heterogeneous population, and 4) historic and cultural associations with the Western world. This is not to suggest that a rigid ternary approach be adopted for the Middle East. This would be unrealistic owing to the overlapping zonal characteristics of some of the countries concerned. The threefold political approach, based as it is upon physical and human-use tiers, should therefore be accepted as a broad, flexible framework, constantly open to reevaluation. It should serve as a guide, not a dogma, to understanding the Middle East.

MARITIME WORLD FOOTHOLDS

The Shatterbelt status of the Middle East can be more easily maintained if some degree of internal stability is realized, as against the current patterns of sudden political squalls and upheavals. The West has tried to buy friendship within the intermediate zone through past alliances with Iraq and Lebanon. We failed. Perhaps a lesson from the past suggests that Jordan and Saudi Arabia be encouraged to take a similarly neutral position, rather than to try to maintain their shaky stance as Western allies.

Obviously there is no guarantee that avowedly neutral nations will not become neutral in favor of the Soviet Union. This is a chance that we take when we offer to extend economic aid, and even to sell arms to countries that announce their neutrality and indicate, by deeds, a willingness to accept accommodation and arbitration in international economic disputes. But the chance is worth taking, so long as we do not neglect our most pressing task—the safeguarding of allies who want and deserve our support.

Many reasons can be cited for not recommending Arab states as footholds for the Maritime World. The most telling one is that Arab nationalism is, on many issues, bound to be anti-Western. The legacy of European imperialism; the issues of Israel and Algeria; the Suez Campaign; the rivalry for Africa south of the Sahara; the 1967 war; the control of Nile headwaters by former European-influenced political areas; the distribution of petroleum profits—these are all part and parcel of Arab nationalism. We must recognize that accommodation on some of these issues will not be possible for many years to come.

It has become obvious that the West's most advantageous associations rest, not with the Arab world, but with Turkey, Iran, and Israel. Turkey furnishes a Black Sea base for overseeing the Ukraine and the Caucasus. The Turkish Straits can be used as a counterweight to the Suez Canal, should the Canal, upon reopening, fall under direct Soviet influence. Most important, the people of Turkey are ideologically oriented to the West—to them, westernization is a thoroughly acceptable ideal.

Iran overlooks the Caspian and the Muslim-inhabited portions of the U.S.S.R. Now the world's third leading oil producer, it can meet one-third of all Maritime Europe's Middle Eastern oil needs. Strategically, Iran dominates the Persian Gulf oil principalities and Iraq's Mesopotamian Valley.

Israel has the most skilled manpower pool in the Middle East, the most sophisticated industrial and military establishment and is a genuine democracy. Its location separates Egypt from the rest of the Arab world and provides a land route that is an alternative to the Suez Canal. It has the only Middle Eastern army capable of foiling Arab advances without necessarily precipitating a Great Power conflict over the region. In this context, lack of formal military alliances between Israel and the Western world may have some advantages, provided that all of the tangible elements of an alliance are enjoyed. Above all, these three countries know and fear the consequences of Soviet intervention in their affairs—something that, for the most part, Arab states have taken as a lesser evil than Western intervention.

Military and economic assistance alone is not enough. These countries need help and encouragement in the realm of social and political advancement. Turkey needs judicious counsel with respect to the restoration of political freedoms. It also should be included in as many Maritime European organizational activities as possible to strengthen its ties with the West. The Shah of Iran needs our continued encouragement in carrying through his land-reform program and deserves preferential oil-policy treatment. Israel needs assistance in its drive to westernize Jewish refugees from Arab lands, to resettle Soviet-Jewish refugees, and to solve its Arab minority problems. No "crash" economic assistance program to these countries will be meaningful unless we focus on all aspects of national-state development. This means bread, arms, *and* social aspirations. By strengthening these footholds in the Middle East, we will not reduce the possibility of obtaining an agreement with the U.S.S.R. on preserving the Shatterbelt characteristics of the Middle East. On the contrary, the stronger our allies become, the greater will be the opportunity to gain such an agreement.

International alliances are agreements between governments, not between peoples. Consequently, the form of government, the character of its leadership, and the role played in the governmental process by the majority of the inhabitants, are factors that have to be assessed in evaluating the effectiveness of alliances. The preference of the American people is for broadly-based, republican forms of government among its allies. In most parts of the underdeveloped world, such governments do not exist. We are, therefore, forced to deal with alternatives to democratic governments and should not close our eyes to the realities of these alternatives.

Iran is a good case in point. In Iran, the alternatives to the Monarchy are the landlords, the intellectual-student classes, and the military. At present, the Throne, backed by the military, is attempting to maintain political stability and to press economic progress and reform. If the Shah should fail, then presumably any of the three alternative groups could come to power. The landlord class represents no hope to Iran or to the West because this is the class which is essentially responsible for Iran's current plight. The intellectual-student class consists of both the Iranian National Front—a heterogeneous group that includes individuals with Neutralist and pro-Communist sentiments, and the Communists themselves. For the West to turn to the National Front and to assume that under its leadership Iran would remain an ally would be quite risky. The fact that Iranian hostility toward the U.S.S.R. is traditional is no guarantee against a sudden turn to neutrality or even to Communism. Moreover, it is unlikely that the very small, urbanized middle class of Iran would have a greater concern for the peasantry than either the Monarchy or the military.

Experience elsewhere suggests that the young officer class may offer hopes for carrying out land reform under a government less tainted with corruption than the present Iranian government. Military government goes against the grain of the United States political tradition. However, the realistic alternative in Iran is not representative government as we know it, but dictatorship in one of its several forms. Iran's best hope appears to lie in a dictatorship benevolent to its own people, genuinely concerned with land reform and industrialization, and interested in creating a grass-roots type of village democracy. Elsewhere in the world, military rule has proclaimed programs dedicated to such ends.

This leads to the consideration of military juntas as a ruling force. From Egypt, Libya, Algeria, the Sudan, Turkey, Greece, and Iraq to Pakistan, Burma, Thailand, Ghana, Uganda, South Vietnam, and South Korea, military groups control national politics with varying degrees of success. Where these groups, usually "The Generals," represent the aristocratic class or the entrenched interests, genuine reform is not possible. Where these groups consist of reform-minded elements with no stake in the economic status quo (usually the younger officers), they offer an opportunity for progress within a framework of political stability. Military rule, however, provides no guarantee of political stability, and countries like Syria, Iraq, and Thailand offer examples of military governments succeeding each other with monotonous regularity. Stability requires a government both firmly in control and dedicated to the welfare of its people.

A promising experiment with the military was tried in Burma. There, the armed forces were used as an educational device to wipe out illiteracy among the recruits, to train men to become modern farmers and technicians, and to use officers as area and departmental administrators. Such programs may become the base from which military rule can be most readily converted to civil controls through the build-up of an articulate farm-labor class and of a responsible civil service. That they have not been especially successful in Burma is due to other considerations, such as the zenophobic attitude toward all outside contacts and the capricious nationalization and socialization of commerce and industry, irrespective of the damage done by that policy in making it impossible to retain skilled manpower and capital investment.

Keeping in mind the fact that military governments can run the gamut from despotic, self-seeking totalitarianism to more enlightened, reform-directed, dictatorship, we can realistically weigh the power struggle in Iran. If the alternative to the Monarchy should become a choice between a pro-Western military reform group and one of the other groups previously described, the former would warrant our support.

Because petroleum is so significant in the Maritime World's relations with the Middle East, we shall consider some aspects of this topic. First there is the building of additional pipeline alternatives to the Suez Canal—the trans-Syrian pipelines, and the Suez-Alexandria pipeline under construction. Middle Eastern petroleum production, now about 30 per cent of the world's total, is on the rise. The best estimates are that the dependence of the Maritime World upon oil will continue to rise over the next decade, despite the possibilities of increased nuclear power, solar energy, and synthetic petroleum and gas. The source of these imports will be mainly the Middle East and the Maghreb. The United States, which now obtains only a small fraction of its petroleum needs through the Middle East imports, may, unless current American oil policies are changed, import

15 per cent of the oil that it uses from the Middle East. This is based upon projections that 30 per cent of American needs will have to be met by imports by 1980. Moreover, by that time, Maritime Europe and Japan may double their current Middle East oil use, such use accounting for three-fourths of their total petroleum imports. The bulk of the oil (70 per cent) is exported to Europe, (which obtains half of its crude from the Persian Gulf), and as has been noted, pipelines carry about 20 per cent of these exports. When Egypt and Syria are combined, the U.A.R. monopolize the accessways. No wonder, therefore, that Persian Gulf areas are so susceptible to Cairo's influence. Even separated, Egypt's and Syria's control over the oil transit ways is a serious threat to Western security.

Alternatives to these routes place us in a better position to support our allies and to deal with neutrals and with enemies. Of these alternative routes, one has been completed—the Eilat-Ashkelon pipeline. This has a current through-put capacity of 22 million tons, with construction under way to increase this to 45 million tons. Eventually the line is planned for a total of 66 million tons. With the Suez Canal closed, this pipeline reduces average shipping costs to Maritime Europe by about 40 per cent as compared with the Cape of Good Hope route. The other alternative, recently agreed upon by Turkey and Iran but yet to be built, is from Ahvaz in Southern Iran, connecting southern and central oil fields to Iskenderun in Turkey. Building the Israeli line has already freed Iranian oil from considerable dependence upon transit through Arab countries. Building the Iranian-Turkish line would provide complete independence of transit. The current step-up in exploring for alternative sources of petroleum with good water access to Europe, as in Latin America, Alaska, the North Sea, and the Maghreb, is bound to help counteract oil transit blackmail politics in the Middle East.

It should be stressed that reference in this discussion is to the transportation issue. Insofar as pricing is concerned, the oil exporting countries have legitimate demands in seeking to receive a higher return for their raw materials from the developed world. The success of the OPEC (Organization of Petroleum Exporting Countries) in 1971 in raising their share of profits to a range of 55 to 70 per cent, and in raising the posted price of petroleum, is a substantial step in narrowing the gap.

The combination of escalating prices and mounting production holds serious problems both for Middle East petroleum producers and for importers in developed and developing countries. To the

United States, Maritime Europe, and Japan the drain of petroleum imports upon trade balances is likely to become increasingly burdensome. For the Middle East producers, the temptation and pressures to deplete the resource base may cause production rate declines at the end of the 1980's. Moreover, they face the problem of how to absorb the oil revenues. By 1980, billions of dollars per annum will be accruing to them. Saudi Arabia alone may be earning 15 to 20 billion dollars, or $2000 per capita, and Kuwait and Libya could earn two to three times as much per capita. For such countries as Saudi Arabia, Kuwait, Libya, Bahrein, and the Federation of Arab Emirates, the narrowness of the population base and of the economic infrastructure creates tremendous obstacles to the use of these earnings for domestic and social development. The temptation to devote funds to external military adventures, now so pronounced in Libya, may become endemic. Alternately, the piling up of large-scale foreign reserves would seriously disturb the international money and investment market and aggravate tensions between Middle Eastern producers and the Maritime World. One possibility for expanding the rational investment of these resources within the region is a series of political arrangements which would link the economies of the more populous and broadly based agricultural and industrial countries to the oil producers. The trizonal subregionalization previously discussed may provide the framework for such arrangements.

The key to the Maritime World's position in the Middle East lies in the selective support of allies and in the general support of neutrals. Fortunately, population pressures within Turkey, Iran, and Israel are not such as to make the task of economic assistance hopeless. Moreover, the physical and human resource base in these countries is sufficiently broad to enable them to achieve economic stability.

What is crucial about the strategic location of the Middle East is its relationship to North Africa and Africa south of the Sahara, as Africa in turn impinges locationally on the Middle East. Petroleum and the Suez Canal are secondary elements. We can increase Iranian petroleum production and exploit alternative sources of petroleum in such parts of the world as Latin America, Alaska, Canada, Offshore Asia, and North Africa. We can continue to use the circum-African route and our position in the Turkish Straits as checks against Soviet manipulations in Suez. If the U.S.S.R. should obtain direct control of Persian Gulf petroleum and seek to deny it to or dump it upon the Maritime World, we can counter this most dangerous cold war weapon by rigid embargoes and far-reaching measures of cooperation in Maritime World oil production and distribution and by accelerating the development of alternate energy sources. But we cannot find substitute political and military positions for our Middle East footholds. Without such positions of strength and counterweights, the Middle East's Shatterbelt character cannot be maintained. With such positions, the Maritime World will not see itself swept out of the Middle East or find itself confronted with a hostile world power perched on the southern Mediterranean and West African coasts. It is for this reason, above all, that the Maritime World must seek positions of strength through Middle Eastern footholds. The only way to maintain these footholds is to base them upon mutual aspirations and interests—not on expediency, accident, and intrigue.

Southeast Asia

Southeast Asia is new to the regional map of the world. Prior to the Second World War, when only one sovereign state (Thailand) existed there, what is now Southeast Asia was a mixture of colonies with little sense of internal identification. So great was regional diversity that even the term "Southeast Asia" was not generally accepted.[5] In less than three decades, however, the picture had changed. Nine new states had emerged, and there was a groping by all of the region's components for some new role on the international scene.

In surveying the region we find that every single state is plagued with problems that touch upon the very existence of the state. Far more than with economics, these problems have to do with centralization of government, securing of borders, and basic foreign policy orientation.

Every one of the states, with the exception of Singapore, has had to contend with serious internal rebellions. Every one has a boundary dispute or a territorial problem on its hands. Six of the countries concerned—Thailand, Malaysia, Singapore, Brunei, Cambodia, (Khmer Republic) and South Vietnam—are allied with the Maritime World; Burma, Indonesia (neutral but pro-Western), and nominally Laos are neutral; and one, North Vietnam, is allied to the Eurasian Continental World. There are no strong blocs within the region. Even an attempt by Thailand and South Vietnam to achieve greater internal

[5] Ginsburg, ed., *op. cit.*, p. 290.

cooperation has to be made in association with a peripheral nation —the Philippines.

So rapidly must the focus of our attention shift from problem area to problem area that we quickly forget past preoccupations. Burma, Indonesia, and Malaysia have been eclipsed, as danger spots, by Laos, Cambodia, and Vietnam. All that we can say with confidence is that no part of Southeast Asia is an island of calm within the troubled seas.

The instability and unrest that is prevalent reflects the Shatterbelt nature of Southeast Asia, with the deep-rooted diversities that both attract outside interference and prevent internal cohesion.[6]

These diversities in Southeast Asia are the result of the cross-currents that have shattered the region into fragments in the past, the internal physical and cultural barriers that have frozen these fragments into separate political entities, and the external pressures that intensify these differences.

Southeast Asia has lain in the path of Indian, Chinese, European, American, Australian, and Japanese pressure. Indian influence was first felt through the spread of Hinduism and Buddhism into Burma, Thailand, Laos, and Cambodia nearly 2,000 years ago. Some of the great empires of the past, like those centered at Ankor, were cultural outliers of Indian civilization. Bali is a "relict" area of Hinduism. The Chinese, moving along the coast and down the river valleys of the interior, were the forefathers of the Annamese, Lao-Thai, and Thai. The cultural influence of the Chinese is strongest among the Annamese, and has been established in the Tonkin Delta for 2,000 years. Muslim merchants from India, in the fourteenth century, established trade centers in Malaya, throughout the Indies, and up to the southern Philippines. Their religious stamp has been indelibly etched upon insular Southeast Asia. Then came the recent colonialists: the British in Burma, Malaya, and Borneo; the Dutch in Indonesia; and the French in Indochina. They have left strong marks in the economic and political field and lesser ones in the religious field. Encouraged by the Europeans, Indians migrated as plantation workers to Burma and Malaya, as did Chinese to Malaya, Vietnam, and Indonesia.

European penetration of the region had an especially lasting effect upon urban patterns. The creation of new cities, or the conversion

[6] Jan Broek, "Diversity and Unity in Southeast Asia," *The Geographical Review,* XXXIV, No. 2 (1944), pp. 175-95.

of small, native settlements to modern Western cities was a product of the strong maritime orientation of European colonialism. Singapore, established in 1824, is the outstanding example. Others include Rangoon, which emerged as a large modern city in the mid 1800's in response to economic developments, especially the shift of plantation rice from the Arakan coast to the Irrawaddy delta. Saigon, captured by the French in 1859, was not a new settlement. However, it had only been in Vietnamese hands for the previous two centuries, prior to which it was an ancient Khmer settlement. It was only with the French entry that Saigon moved forward to become the large metropolis and center for the South that it now is. Even in Thailand, which was free from either British or French political control, the impact of British commercial interests was strong enough to cause a shift of focus from the interior to Bangkok, which became the capital of the country in 1782.

During the colonial era, the various countries had their main contacts with European or Asian states, not with one another. Since the end of the Second World War, there have been some regional attempts like the Mekong River Valley development, Maphilindo, a Pan-Thai Buddhist bloc (Thailand, Cambodia, Laos, Burma), and a Thai–South Vietnamese–Philippines economic association. All, save the first, have had little to show for the efforts that have been invested to date.

Actually, the separateness and isolation of national ecumenes, religions, cultures, and peoples; the differing national orientations to separate parts of the world—these are the diversities that have made it so difficult for Southeast Asia to find common economic, political, and military expressions.

Economic differences exist, partly because Southeast Asian states are so isolated from one another and partly because their products are similar and therefore competitive in the world export markets. The Malaysian or insular Southeast Asian portion is highly competitive in its plantation crops and minerals. And Mainland Southeast Asia, from Burma through Vietnam, with similar physical environments, subsistence agriculture, and export rice, has little basis for internal interchange.

One of the clearest indications of the fragmented nature of Southeast Asia is the restricted extent of its various national ecumenes, without even the hint of the development of a regional ecumene. (See Map 20.)

Only the Tonkin Delta, the northwest coast of Java, and Lower

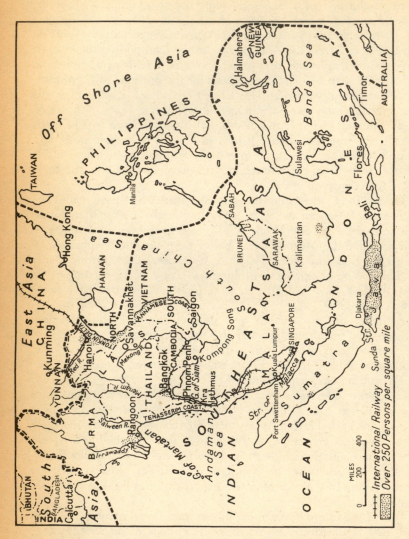

MAP 20. The Southeast Asian Shatterbelt

Burma (heavily settled in the past century) are moderately developed economic and population cores within their national frameworks. To envisage a regional ecumene, we should have to consider the Annamese coast, Northern Java, the lands bordering the Strait of Malacca, and the Gulf of Martaban as the best possible framework. The current gaps in both population and movement links and the extraregional orientation of each of these areas suggest that the emergence of such a framework will be a long time in coming. Absence of a regional core makes regional cooperation difficult and weakens the ties of peripheral areas to Southeast Asia.

Uneven distribution of population is characteristic of most of Southeast Asia. The physical framework of lowlands and mountain festoons, as well as the development of plantation crops and minerals for the outside world, has concentrated the population of this Shatterbelt on such river plains as the Red, Mekong, Menam, Salween, and Irrawaddy, and on such coastal lowlands as western Malaya and south-central Java. Where soils are periodically renewed, as are the river flood plains, or are unusually rich intrinsically, population densities attain great heights, and the areas tend to serve as political cores for national states. The Volcanic belts that extend across the southern island arc from Sumatra to Flores to the Banda Sea, and northward to Halmahera, the Celebes, and up through northern Luzon in the Philippines, provide the best soils and attract coastal populations. But in most parts of Southeast Asia the soils are poor, either because they are intensely leached lateritics or swamps along the coasts (New Guinea, Borneo, Sumatra, Malaysia) or because they are thin, acidic, and mountainous. The result is underpopulation throughout most of the region. Only 8.5 per cent of all of Southeast Asia is under cultivation. The central dry zone of Burma, the seat of ancient Burmese civilization, is now only sparsely settled. The same is true for the central valley of Thailand, and for the flood plain of the Mekong in Cambodia—once centers of great civilizations, but now empty. The populations of most of these valleys are today concentrated along the deltas, rather than along middle valley portions.

In over-all terms, the average population density of Southeast Asia (190 persons per square mile) is only one-third that of India or China, and one-sixth that of Japan. But the full story of maldistribution of population emerges when we consider that rural parts of Lower Thailand have densities of over 1,000 persons per square mile, while northwest of Bangkok and on the grassy plains of Cambodia the density is only 2 to 25 persons per square mile; or that the gross population density of Vietnam is three times that of such countries as Burma and Cambodia.

Absence of water control and fertilizers, overemphasis on paddy rice, especially where Chinese settled in the Red River Delta and Annam and where plantation agriculture created a need for labor and food for this labor in Java, shifting cultivation in the uplands, problems of land tenancy, soil erosion, the spread of deep-rooted grasses—these are all factors in the limited productivity of the lands of Southeast Asia.

Differences within and between states are sharpened by the absence of extensive transportation links. The only rail lines that exist to tie countries together are the two between China and North Vietnam, one between Cambodia and Thailand (the "Cambodian Gateway"), and one between Thailand and Malaysia. Road connections are poor everywhere outside the major cities. Shipping within the region is slow and spotty, the more modern services being oriented to Europe, South Asia, or the United States, and reflects external orientations. If the Kra Canal project to link the Andaman Sea and the Gulf of Siam and thus bypass the Strait of Malacca should ever materialize, it would probably enhance external trade even more than it would intraregional shipping (although the latter would be a factor that would strengthen internal bonds). A by-product of such a canal would be to press Burma and Thailand to joint economic action.

One of the basic weaknesses of Southeast Asia's states is that their revolutions have been carried out within the political frameworks laid down by European colonialism. The national boundaries that exist are mostly the heritage of empire building and accommodations between rivals. Despite boundary disputes within the region, the European-designed political boundaries are the basic lines that new states have accepted. With nationhood have come desires for self-sufficiency. Singapore, the trading entrepôt for the Indies and Malaysia, is losing ground in its share of the rubber and tin trade. In compensation, it has developed large-scale industrialized activities and seems to be following the Hong Kong model of development. Port Swettenham in Malaysia and Sumatran ports have been developed in response to national pressures to take business away from Singapore. Cambodia, rather than relying on the Mekong or the Thai Railway, has developed its first deepwater port at Kom Pong Son, (Sihanoukville) on the Gulf of Siam and has connected this port to Phnom Penh by a modern highway, the subject of so much military maneuvering during the Cambodian War. These are steps that intensify regional fragmentation, rather than interdependence. Moreover, many minorities entered the scene because of the need of plantations or mines for outside labor. Some of these minorities are so prominent, and antagonisms are so acute, that the drive of national majorities to centralize governmental functions has threatened to split countries like Malaysia and Indonesia. Major cities like Rangoon (half Indian) and Singapore (three-quarters Chinese) were dominated by national minorities. Resulting tensions in Burma have eventuated in the expropriation of property and business owned by Indians and the emigration of many of them. Similarly, Malay-Chinese friction precipitated the breakaway of Singapore from Malaysia.

A basic problem is that some national states are too large and contain too many minorities to warrant a strongly centralized state, or are too small and lacking in the earmarks of the modern national state to be able to function as such. Real national unity in Southeast Asia will have to come about through the help of diverse cultures and peoples, not in spite of them. In some cases, these can only mean federated units.

In this context, one must take special note of the Overseas Chinese. Other sizable minorities exist—the Shans of Burma; the Outer Islanders of Sumatra, the Celebes, and the Moluccas; the Javanese of Sumatra; the Malayans and Vietnamese in Thailand; the Indians in Malaya and Burma; the Annamese in Cambodia. But the 20 million Overseas Chinese—by their numbers, their economic vitality, their cultural and political ties to either Peiping or Taipei, and their failure to secure acceptance from the peoples among whom they have settled—pose a serious threat to national stabilities in Southeast Asia. Malaysia, with 40 per cent Chinese, and Thailand, with 20 per cent Chinese, have especially difficult problems to solve. But even Burma, which is 70 per cent Burman and has only 400,000 Chinese, finds problems in the fact that many of its Chinese are concentrated along the northeast border or the Tenasserim coast—both far removed from the Lower Burmese core.

Frequently the Overseas Chinese problem is regarded in the light of competition between Communist and Nationalist China for the allegiance of this community. But the problem has to be viewed in another light, as well. The Overseas Chinese must be assimilated within the mainstream of the respective national movements of the various countries, especially Malaysia, Vietnam, Thailand, and Indonesia, to avoid the possibility of forced repatriation. Economic restraints against the Chinese in Thailand and Indonesia are particularly strong. Moreover, the bloodbath that was provoked in the wake of the ill-fated Indonesian Communist uprising was at least partially racial in its character. Scores of thousands of Chinese were slaughtered by the Indonesians merely for being Chinese, rather than for association with the Indonesian Communist party. In Malaysia, the political tension between Chinese and Malays made it impossible for Singapore to remain part of the new state. When the Chinese-dominated Singapore government opted for independence, this was accepted by Malaysia with a sense of relief, because of the fear held by the Malays that Singapore would tip the population balance in favor of the Chinese. As it is, racial tensions are high in Malaysia, where Malay and Chinese populations are nearly balanced and where the Chinese are denied full political representation. It is ironic that Britain, which saw Chinese immigration during the nineteenth century as a means of developing Malaya, is now accused by Malay nationalists of being responsible for having undermined the Malay character of the state by its "Imperialist" policies.

It is difficult to view Southeast Asia national problems from a purely national vantage point, because in almost every instance complications arise from relations with neighboring states or with extraregional states.

For example, Burma, with a lower population density than that of its neighbors, a broad agricultural base, and some minerals, including oil, has hopes for substantial economic progress. Her problems are essentially political, not economic, since political unification has been Burma's biggest stumbling block. But relations with China and India are also factors in explaining some of Burma's problems. Statehood found Burma devoid of a strong civil service, because Indians had pre-empted so many of the jobs. And creation of a Kachin autonomous state on the Chinese side of the border, unchecked movement of former Chinese Nationalist troops in the north, and dispute over the boundary with Communist China all weakened the effectiveness of the central government in northern Burma, during the early years of independence. Settlement of the border dispute with China in 1960 brought a thaw in Burmese-Chinese relations, but most recently there has been a hardening of the lines between the two countries. The military regime that overthrew U Nu has retreated behind a veil of zenophobic neutralism, closing the system markedly in an attempt to sustain itself. In all likelihood, isolation will not provide the regime with the security that it desires, for with the isolation has come a slow-down in development. Outside Burma's borders, the leaders of the former civilian government that brought Burma to independence wait to restore some sort of socialistic parliamentary democracy to the scene.

Thailand appears uniquely capable of acting as a cohesive political entity. Bangkok is an excellent focus for rivers and coastal routes. It is a good trail and air hub. It is unchallenged as the country's primate city. The rural populace is almost exclusively Thai and the country has never been dominated by European imperialism. On the other hand, Thailand has its internal Chinese problem and has had recent frontier disputes with Laos, Cambodia, Burma, and Malaysia. The most depressed part of its country, the Nam Mun Basin, adjoins Laos and Cambodia, and is therefore exposed to subversive action. Finally, the Communist "Free Thai" movement is based in Chinese Yunnan, and will be capable of operating much more freely against Thailand if Laos should go Communist.

Indonesia's control over Sumatra is complicated by the orientation of much of that island to Singapore. While culturally Malaysia, Indonesia, and the Philippines are part of the Malaysian world, and voices for forging a Pan-Malayan Union are not completely mute, the extra-regional economic and military ties of both Malaysia and the Philippines dim any prospect of such a union.

Finally, has it not proven impossible for Laos to solve its problems without outside contact? Physically and culturally, Laos is closely related to Thailand. Indeed, Pan-Thai proposals have sometimes raised the prospects of a Buddhist bloc to include Thailand, Cambodia, Laos, and Burma. But the best route linking Laos with the outside has been via Savannakhet to South Vietnam—the product of the transport pattern that was forged during French rule. And today, the routes—land and air—from North Vietnam to North Laos and the Vietminh trails southward to South Vietnam are increasing its outside orientation and dependence in that direction.

Can any sort of regional economic or political pattern be foreseen that will give some hope for the harmonious development of Southeast Asia as a region? Do such ideas as the Buddhist bloc of the north and the Malayan bloc of the south offer realistic prospects for some sort of long-term economic and political balance for Southeast Asia? We doubt it, because of the strength of those elements that make of Southeast Asia the Shatterbelt that it is.

Two rings of external pressure surround Southeast Asia, Inner and Outer. The Inner Ring consists of India, Mainland China, Japan, and Australia. Its interests are economic, cultural, ideological, and strategic. The Outer Ring consists of the Soviet Union, Maritime Europe, and the United States—the Soviet Union operating in competition with Mainland China; the others in cooperation with Australia and Japan. Outer Ring interests are economic and global strategic.

National sovereignty and various forms or espousals of neutralism have not freed Southeast Asia of these encircling pressure rings. On the contrary, the struggle between East and West has made each Southeast Asian nation the scene of internal struggle, the more acute because it is now a "brother against brother" conflict rather than the former conflict between native nationalism and European or Japanese colonialism.

In assessing the external relations of Southeast Asia, we can observe four trends since the recent Western European withdrawal:

1) A weakening in international trade;

2) Greater Western interests in adjoining parts of Offshore Asia (Japan, Taiwan, the Philippines, and Australia);

3) Direct penetration of Communist China into the region via Chinese support of North Vietnam;

4) Closer involvement of Southeast Asia in Asian affairs.

Southeast Asian trade has not kept pace with the general increase of international trade. Its current proportionate share of world exports is only half of what it was in 1938. Both Maritime Europe and the United States have redirected much of their former commerce with this region to tropical Africa and tropical Latin America. In part, the weakened international trade position of Southeast Asia stems from local economic pressures against Western trading interests; in part it has been occasioned by desires to broaden and diversify national economies at the expense of specialized international trade commodities; in part by the ravages of war and revolution; and in part it is the result of less well-developed regions of the tropical world beginning to catch up with Southeast Asia. Certainly, the desire of independent Southeast Asia states to turn partly from industrial crops to food crops, and to divert some investment in plantations and mines to consumer industries, is to be understood within the context of national ambitions and goals. Its effect upon the international trade picture is cited, therefore, not as a criticism, but rather as the result of basic national forces.

With the political and military retreat of Europe from Southeast Asia, and with the shift of the arena of competition to the Northwest Pacific, the United States and its allies have put their major emphasis upon developments in Japan and the entire Offshore Asian line from the Aleutians to Australia. Western political and economic interests in Southeast Asia have, in this sense, been proportionately reduced.

The direct involvement of the Chinese People's Republic in North Vietnamese, Cambodian, and Laotian affairs was coupled with a resolution of the border dispute with Burma. Strengthened economic and military postures in eastern Tibet and Yunnan enhance Communist China's ability to intervene in Southeast Asia.

The location of the Shatterbelt foreshadows its greater involvement in Asian affairs, as surrounding regions seek ties with one another. Thus Southeast Asia can be expected to assume new importance as a focus for interaction between the U.S.S.R. and China, as a land link between China and India, and as a sea link between the northern and southern portions of Offshore Asia.

We have described Southeast Asia as a Shatterbelt, internally fragmented and externally pressured. The region is not an inert body, but a zone of contact. The maintenance of key Maritime World alliances within the region through SEATO helps to insure that the Communist world will not swallow up the entire region, thus radically affecting events in the western Pacific and Indian ocean areas. They also make it clear that the Maritime World has no intention of withdrawing to positions so rigid and crucial as to leave no alternative but nuclear war. They enable economic and political competition to serve as alternatives to military competition. Finally, they make it strategically possible for the West to encourage neutralism elsewhere within Southeast Asia. But the alliances that we have forged must be with willing partners, with governments that know how to use military and economic aid for the good of their peoples, not for the aggrandizement of the few. As for neutralism, what we refused to recognize as a sound principle for Laos and Cambodia in the past has now been turned against us. It is not likely that genuine neutrality can be maintained in Laos, in the light of what has occurred. We must now turn our attention to Indonesia and Burma—where popularly supported governments desire to be neutral and where our backing of such desires can have fruitful results; and Thai neutrality, a deep-rooted tradition for this country, may re-emerge as foreign policy, if events in adjoining areas should dictate such a discretionary attitude.

Southeast Asia is not strictly comparable with the Middle East from the following standpoints: (1) The region lacks near-monopolistic control over an export commodity such as the Middle East holds over petroleum. Rubber and tin, Southeast Asia's strategic exports, can be replaced by synthetics and by other raw materials, or can be extracted from other parts of the world. (2) Independent and competing Southeast Asian centers of power did not persist over such lengthy periods as did the Middle Eastern power cores. This was because of Southeast Asia's exposure to Indian, Chinese, and European land and sea movement. (3) The U.S.S.R. and the major Western allies do not meet directly in Southeast Asia, as they do in the Middle East. Rather, China and Offshore Asia represent the direct contacts with the Shatterbelt in the struggle between the Maritime and Communist worlds.

As a consequence, it is difficult to project key sites or states which should be sought as the Maritime World's Southeast Asian footholds. But the securing of Malaysia, because of its Western orientation, its raw material base, its central, narrow, seas-dominating location with respect to the rest of the region, and its record of victory against Communist guerilla warfare is of first-rank priority.

Burma, also, warrants our wholehearted acceptance of its neutrality, because of its prospects for economic development, its relative physical isolation from China, and its location astride the land and sea approaches to South Asia.

South Vietnam might have been an important foothold had it been possible for a democratic, pro-United States regime to emerge after the fall of Diem. When it was clear that this was not possible, and Buddhist opposition to the government became widespread, we would have been justified in supporting the establishment of a Buddhist government with an avowedly neutralist policy. But our foreign policy was too rigid to accept the concept of support of a neutral government. For a variety of reasons—pride, arrogance, involvement in support of a minority Catholic elite, misleading political appraisals, and blind acceptance of the untenable "falling domino" theory—America became entrapped in the quagmire of Vietnam. Withdrawal from South Vietnam has been achieved, and at this writing we can only hope that full military disengagement from the rest of Indo-China will follow. If one lesson has been learned by the United States from the Vietnam War, it is that we must not allow national pride to stand in the way of reason.

We have failed to distinguish between strategic and tactical considerations, as well as between moral and immoral ones. Strategically, South Vietnam is only important to the Maritime World as

one of several components of a Shatterbelt. The major concern of
the United States in Southeast Asia is the relation of the latter to
Offshore Asia and, more remotely, to the rest of the Maritime World.
To have dragged out a war designed to prop up a corrupt South
Vietnamese dictatorship in the name of freedom for the South Vietnamese and security for the Maritime World has had three incredibly
disastrous effects: 1) to ravage and despoil a land and its people
who were presumably being "protected" by us from outside aggression—a case of the policeman killing the victim while protecting
him from an assailant; 2) to alienate the very peoples and countries
for whose strategic well-being the war was presumably launched—
e.g., Japan and Australia in Offshore Asia, many of our NATO
allies and Sweden in Maritime Europe—a case of throwing out the
baby with the bathwater; and 3) to embitter the American people,
undermining national unity and the will to interact positively and
purposefully with the rest of the world, in "the national interest"—a
case of destroying the patient's will to live.

Resumption of intensive bombings during the final agonies of the
Vietnamese peace negotiations caused three major reactions: American
outrage at the bombing; general fears that chances for détente among
the U.S., China, and the U.S.S.R. would be impaired; and violent
opposition by many of our allies to this policy. U.S. leadership publicly
ignored this impact on our allies. What is the *Realpolitik* of an American policy that alienates Sweden, France, Britain, Japan, or Australia in
the name of preserving the security of the Maritime World? What is
the *Realpolitik* of a policy that is so obsessed with gaining a standoff in
a battle that it risks losing the greater struggle—the struggle for freedom, security, the worth of the individual and humanity itself?

A distinction must be drawn between battles and wars. We can
lose the battle for South Vietnam without losing the struggle for
Southeast Asia. The same can be said for our position in Thailand—
a position that should be maintained as long as it is ideologically and
militarily feasible to maintain it, and as long as the Thais wish to
remain identified with the West in the East-West struggle. But loss
of Thailand and South Vietnam would not make retention of Offshore Asia strategically impossible. Nor would this loss make it impossible for the United States to maintain the Shatterbelt status of
Southeast Asia through footholds in Malaysia and Burma.

A neutral Burma is not to be equated with the military type of
foothold that is represented by countries that belong to the Western Alliance. Burma is, however, a foothold for Maritime World

security in that it contributes to the maintenance of the Shatterbelt status of Southeast Asia and to the security of South Asia. Genuine neutrals, such as Burma, can remain neutrals because of direct Western military positions in Southeast and South Asia. Burmese recognition of this factor, as well as Western recognition of the significant contribution of Burmese neutrality to the warding-off of Communist pressures, can inject greater realism into the West's relations with Burma.

Over the last decade, both proponents and opponents of SEATO have raised serious doubts about the efficacy and utility of the organization, owing to its failure to take action in the Laotian crisis. We must recognize that SEATO today cannot play the same role that was envisaged for it during its formulative years of 1953-54. Then, under the shadow of the Geneva Conference on Indo-China, SEATO was organized to counter existing or feared Communist uprisings in Malaysia, the Philippines, Burma, and non-Communist Indochina. It was, in fact, a hastily put together "fire fighting" brigade. Since then, conditions have stabilized throughout most of Southeast Asia, save in Laos, Cambodia, and Vietnam. Those states that are not members of SEATO have raised strong objections to being included within its joint defense-planning framework, and it is probably futile, as well as presumptuous, for SEATO to try to continue to regard itself as responsible for the security of non-members.

Thus, first the organization's responsibilities should be focused directly upon its members. Second, non-members of SEATO that have bilateral treaties with Western nations, such as Malaysia, but that do not wish to join SEATO, cannot and need not be forced to do so. Coordination of military activities in such cases can be achieved on an informal basis. Third, and perhaps most important, SEATO's treaty area warrants redefinition.

As defined, the treaty area includes the general area of the Southwest Pacific, but excludes the Pacific areas north of the Philippines, (latitude 21° 30".) A joint defense organization without the entirety of Offshore Asia, especially Japan and Australia, ignores the realities of Western Pacific security problems. Indian representatives who have criticized SEATO as "a Southeast Asian Alliance without Southeast Asia" have a telling point. Equally telling is that France and Pakistan, and to a lesser extent, Britain, Australia, and New Zealand are so disenchanted with the Indo-Chinese policies of the United States that their membership in the alliance has lost all or much of its meaning.

What SEATO needs, as a long-range goal, is to be merged

within a broader Maritime Asian Treaty Organization—("MATO"?). Such an alliance of Offshore Asia and selected portions of Southeast Asia would constitute a more realistic approach to the Maritime World's defense needs. NATO and MATO could well become the twin cornerstones of the Trade-Dependent Maritime Region.

Southeast Asia will never be completely realigned with the West. Nor dare we let it fall in its entirety to the Communist world. What we must do is encourage a combination of alliances and neutrality within part of the region and recognize Chinese and Soviet interests elsewhere. Hard and fast lines need not, and should not, be drawn. Southeast Asia is likely to remain a zone of contention for decades to come—in the military, economic, and political fields. The alternative to its present Shatterbelt status is broad regional bufferdom or a sharp, three-way split that will be produced from Communist, Maritime World, and Indian interests. Such a split may well take place with the military and economic maturing of China, India, and Offshore Asia. Or most of the region may be able to adopt political neutrality, as mutually defined and guaranteed by the contending great powers. For the present, however, the threat of Chinese or local Communist pressures, with or without Soviet help, makes any guarantees of neutrality meaningless. The Maritime World has two possible courses—to side with its allies where Western orientation is domestically acceptable and strategically tenable, and to encourage neutralism elsewhere. Such a policy will help to maintian the plasticity of the Southeast Asian Shatterbelt.

In this context, the Chinese break with the U.S.S.R. has increased the difficulty of preserving the Shatterbelt status. Admittedly, China's military position has been severely damaged by such a break. But its ability to sponsor far greater subversion efforts in Southeast Asia has not been curtailed. As a gesture to its people and the Communist world as a whole, Communist China might take considerable risks to bring Southeast Asia within its sphere of influence. In so doing, China could assume that the threat of direct Western retaliation would be nullified by the threat of Soviet counter-retaliation. For the U.S.S.R. would not be likely to countenance Western undermining of China that might topple a Communist regime, regardless of the gulf between the two Communist power centers.

Therefore, if the Shatterbelt can be maintained in its present form, the region will best be able to serve as a safety valve that provides both East and West with room to maneuver and to compete without touching off a world explosion.

Rounding Out the Maritime World

If the geopolitical alignment of this earth should take the rigid north-south orientation suggested by the pan-regionalists, the attendant economic competition and political strife might well touch off the great war that must be prevented at all costs. Pan-America, Euro-Africa, and Pan-Asia are neither desirable nor feasible as geostrategic units.

Thus, we have not placed the South American geopolitical region in any more special association with Anglo-America than with the other portions of the Trade-Dependent Maritime World. Some proponents of Western Hemispheric unity claim that physical connection of the two continents and common colonization experiences provide strong enough bonds for joint economic, political, and cultural activities. Events have proved this assumption invalid. Pan-America cannot stand alone, strategically or economically.

On the other hand, do the east-west axes of geopolitical alignment, along which NATO has been formed (as well as the Warsaw Pact) satisfy all of our strategic needs? Certainly the supply of raw materials—minerals, fibers, foodstuffs—that are drawn from South America and Africa are essential to the economies of the North Atlantic powers. In fact, then, North Atlantic unity cannot provide strategic self-containment. This can be achieved only by a crisscrossing of lines of orientation within the Atlantic and Pacific basins. Anglo-America and the Caribbean, and South America south of the Amazon, are likely to forge stronger bonds with each other, but not in isolation of the rest of the Trade-Dependent Maritime World. Already the Western Hemispheric units have close ties within this oceanic realm through the links between Canada and the United

Kingdom, the Caribbean islands and the United Kingdom, the United States and Maritime Europe, the United States and Japan, Brazil and Japan, Argentina and Maritime Europe, and the United States and Australia.

South America

It is frequently convenient to divide the Western Hemisphere along the cultural divide of the Rio Grande, separating Anglo-America from Latin America. Another divide is framed by the physical environment—the double line of the Central American-North Andean-Guiana Highland ranges and the Amazon. This is the divide along which we have drawn our geopolitical boundary. South America is a triangle, fronting the ocean, with two physical features of great magnitude that have profoundly influenced the political map. These are the Andes and the Amazon. The Andes, with their adjoining forests and deserts, separate western from eastern South America. The Panama Canal has strengthened this condition of separatism because it has made it easier for western South America to communicate with the Caribbean and the North Atlantic than overland with South American neighbors.

Amazonas acts as an effective barrier between South and Middle America, and reinforces the Andean division between east and west. Only in a very limited sense does the Amazon provide some measure of unity to both east and west coast South American states like Colombia, Ecuador, Peru, and Brazil, in that its resources are a force of attraction to all of these abutters. The centripetal force of such unifying elements as river navigation and petroleum prospects is far less significant, however, than the centrifugal effect of the rain forest barrier. Forces that have tended to fragmentize South America geopolitically, other than the Andes and Amazonas, are varied. There are the linguistic, cultural, and racial differences that can be traced to a variety of factors—sailing directions, local resources, and intra-European rivalry (the Partition of Tordesillas, 1493). Then there were the historic administrative organizations of viceroyalties (Peru, New Granada, Charcas) which formed powerful quasi-independent political units. To these may be added the separate river communication systems that lead to the open sea and thence to differing overseas contact points. Finally, there is the dependence on similar commodities by several countries with attendant absence of internal trade and competition for foreign markets.

It is noteworthy that, save between Argentina and Chile, the crests of the Andes do not serve as national boundaries. Here in the south, where they form a single range, they are sufficiently high, narrow, and unpopulated to warrant a barrier boundary function. To the north, with three distinct ranges separated by high valleys, and in the center, with two ranges and one high valley, they form a wide but habitable zone. There the Andes serve as zones of unity, not of separatism. The rain-forested areas on the eastern slopes of the mountains serve as the barriers.

An important facet of the geopolitical structure of South America is its population distribution. On the western side of the continent the populace has historically been highland-oriented. The Spanish settled in the mountains for the minerals. They found the Indians already there, and this coincidence of minerals and labor supply kept the European population in the highlands. Some attempts were made to bring Indians down to the coast to help develop ports. Most of these efforts ended in disaster. Oasis agriculture in the Peruvian desert is a modern attempt to develop the coast, but the population involved is limited. Until Chile is reached, then, the major centers of western South American population—the capital cities and business nodes—are in the highlands, in the Bogota Basin, Quito, the Peruvian Highland, and the Bolivian Plateau. This is an example that is carried over through much of Central America and Mexico, and indicates how higher altitudes cancel out the effects of latitude in tropical and subtropical areas. Proximity of the highlands to the coast and improvement of transportation and communications do, however, pose considerable potential for seaward orientation, and thus for urbanization. There exists, therefore, a basis for a radical shift in population structure from rural to urban industrial, but at considerable cost in terms of the movement factor. The population of eastern South America is, in contrast, coast-oriented. This is because of the attraction power of the fertile, droughty to well-watered, coastal plains that stretch from northeastern Brazil to Bahia Blanca in Argentina, and the low East Brazilian Highlands. The major population intrusion into the interior, along the Parana estuary, is a strong reflection of the economic orientation of that area to ocean ports and international trade.

While most of South America's population lives in western, coastal-rimming mountains or on the eastern coastal plain, the interior is a hollow core because of rain forest, dry grassland, or Patagonian desert.

The weight of population and resources is on the eastern side.

Brazil, Uruguay, Paraguay, and Argentina, for example, have over 125 million people, while the lands from Colombia to Chile have only 50 million. There is no unified regional ecumene as yet, but the link-up of Brazil's Rio-São Paulo core with the Pampas via southern Brazil's "pioneering fringe" may be anticipated. Sea ties with Chile and land links with the Gran Chaco into Bolivia suggest a further extension of this South American regional ecumene. With it should come greater geopolitical unity.

Trade-orientation of South America reflects two features. First, South America as a whole is not nearly so heavily oriented to the United States as is Middle America. In all, about 30 per cent of South American foreign trade is with the United States. Second, the west coast countries are more closely linked to the United States (40 per cent of their total trade is with the United States) than are the east coast countries (20 per cent of their total trade is with the United States). Europe is a more important trading partner with the east coast countries than is the United States. Intracontinental trade is very limited (only about 10 per cent), both because of the physical barriers to trade and because of the competitive nature of many of the national economies.

It is ironic that a region that has known national independence for so long as has Latin America is still plagued by geopolitical immaturity. While the national territorial cores are well defined, there are still boundary or territorial issues between Venezuela and Guayana; Ecuador and Peru; Argentina and Chile (only minor points); Guayana and French Guiana and Surinam; Brazil and French Guiana; and Argentina and Uruguay (the last two, inactive). Always ready to be reopened as a territorial issue is Bolivia's lack of an outlet to the sea as a result of Chilean war territorial gains in 1883 and 1929.

The separation of various racial and ethnic groups on both a national and a regional level has contributed to this immaturity. Examples are the Negro coastal enclaves of eastern Venezuela, northeast Brazil, and Colombia's Pacific; and the Indians of the Andes, the Eastern Andes Piedmont, Amazonas, and the Upper Orinoco. Laws perpetuating or protecting latifundia helped to keep these populations *in situ*.

The limited number of areas favorably endowed physically creates oases of prosperity in otherwise impoverished tropical and semitropical areas that suffer from soil poverty, droughts or floodings, distance from the sea, and mountain barriers to efficient land communication. The population which did move into favorable agricultural areas (e.g. the highland basins) developed surpluses that encouraged the development of commerce and industry. As these prosperous population nodes industrialized, they attracted the rural impoverished. The result is the dominant city, attracting hundreds of thousands of landless who cannot be housed or employed because population has outstripped the economic base. Provincial centers, overshadowed by the dominant city and, indeed, generally by-passed by highly centralized national governmental structures, tend to wither. The South American experience bears out Montesquieu's comment that concentration leads to depopulation by depriving local centers of the vigor of being themselves capitals.

Finally, contributory to geopolitical immaturity has been stop-and-go national economic development and international political attention. Sporadic Latin American development efforts all too often have been related to crisis politics (e.g. droughts in Brazil) or election politics (public works in Venezuela). This is a phenomenon widely recognized. It should also be acknowledged that the same stop-and-go process obtains with respect to international political attention. The United States, especially, has failed to apply an even, steady flow of political attention and economic aid to Latin America, but rather has wavered in its efforts, reacting to crises with programs that rarely outlast the presidential administration that launched them.

One might postulate that the strength of economic orientation, reinforced by the Andes barrier, the subsistence economy, and the basic Indian stock of its population makes of western South America a separate geopolitical entity from eastern South America. A counter to this thesis, however, is the political and economic dominance of the east, as well as the cultural bonds that bind all of South America. A geographical view of trends in population distributions and relationships helps to put the discussion of prospects for geopolitical unity in clearer focus. Four trends may be discerned: 1) the South American population, coastal in the east and highland in the west (but facing the coast), is increasing far faster than the population of the limited interior, where, under modern technological conditions, small numbers of people can produce the needed foodstuffs and minerals for economic growth. Paradoxically, people are fleeing the interior for the big cities at a time when the interior's resources are being developed at a rapid and significant rate. As spectacular as are developments in the Orinoco, Amazonas, and Brasilia, their population-absorption capacity is minimal. 2) Growing at a very rapid rate (more than 3 per cent per annum), South America's population is rapidly urbanizing and concentrating in the few major metropolitan areas that are either on the coast or, through modern highway and coastal connections, lead to the sea. In most countries, the largest metropolitan areas already contain 10 to 25 per cent of the population. Urban political stability, even more than rural development and reform, appears the key to South America's present and future politics. 3) With a generally weaker agricultural base, but a relatively stronger mineral base, western South America is capable of broadening its basis for exchange with eastern South America. In this exchange, sea and air routes offer alternatives to the barrier effects of mountains and tropical rain forest, although key highways (Brazil's Trans-Amazonian Highway Project) and pipelines are also beginning to serve as links. 4) While South America's interior is not destined to face as heavy a settlement wave as interior North America faced, South Americans cannot, nevertheless, turn their backs upon the interior with its rich, surplus resources. Opening up the interior, parallel with developing the coastal manufacturing and commercial economy that is needed to support the great majority of the population, is the challenge. In this process, major urban centers, grouped at or near the coast, can intercommunicate with each other across national boundaries and serve as the major force for continental unity. These are some of the reasons for optimism in projecting greater geopolitical cohesiveness for South America, oriented around the primacy of the east coast ecumene. Such unity is likely to be enhanced by extrahemispheric links, provided that these links are sought as complements to, and not substitutes for, bonds with Anglo-America and the Caribbean.

A Western Hemispheric view, as such, has merit in terms of place, common historic heritage, and psychological drive. It has, however, little geopolitical validity, for the Western Hemisphere is neither geographically, culturally, economically, nor strategically a unit. The issue, however, is not a North Atlantic Alliance versus an Alliance for Progress, nor for that matter, a Maritime Pacific Concord versus a Maritime Atlantic Concord. The issue is not *either/or:* it is *both*. Japan and Brazil, Spain and Argentina, Canada and Jamaica— and yes, the United States and Cuba. These are parts of one Trade-Dependent Maritime World—a world which holds out to its occupants the prospects of economic well-being, political understanding, and strategic security if they can but grasp its offerings. The unity of Latin America is likely to be forged through interdependence with all parts of the Maritime World, not with any single sector thereof.

Africa South of the Sahara

Is it overstating the obvious to say that "Africa is *not* South America?" Perhaps. But the temptation to link the fates of these two southern continents is constantly before those who look to such superficial similarities as southern latitudes, tropical climates, triangular shapes, modern export economies that are superimposed on the subsistence base, low population densities (30 to 35 persons per square mile), and thin networks of transportation lines that act as feeders to the open seas, rather than as continental interconnectors.

In fact, Africa is quite different from South America. In these differences lies the answer to the more limited possibilities for geopolitical unity in Africa south of the Sahara. Size, physical structure, and inaccessibility are elements that influence Africa's geopolitical fragmentation. Black Africa is one and one-fifth as large as South America, and has four times as many states as the latter. Its population is one and one-fifth times greater. This population is more scattered than South America's, partly because of the uniform spread of arable land throughout the tropical African highlands, and partly because of the restricted extent of Africa's coasts. No single coastal area in Black Africa possesses the population concentrations of the Brazilian coast and the deeply-embayed Pampas. Consequently, Black Africa lacks an incipient regional ecumene which would be capable of achieving geopolitical dominance over the entire continent. No single country or group of countries overshadows all others in population or resources. For example, Nigeria, the most populous state, contains only 24 per cent of Black Africa's population, while Brazil has 50 per cent of all of the population of South America south of the Amazon. Finally, Africa is essentially non-White, with Europeans constituting only two per cent of the populace. About two-thirds of the total South American population claims to be White, and Mestizos are another 25 per cent of the total. Thus South America is dominated by peoples of European descent—a most important aspect of its potential for geostrategic unity with the rest of the Maritime World.

While Mackinder first described Africa south of the Sahara as a "Southern Heartland," and later suggested a possible link with South America as a South Atlantic Basin unit, we are more inclined to expect that Africa will remain a geopolitically fragmented portion of the Trade-Dependent Maritime World. Two long-term alternatives can be posed. 1) Given the disappearance of the Middle East as a Shatterbelt and the shifting of the Maritime World-Soviet contest to the

Maghreb, Africa would become a Shatterbelt.   2) Given the expulsion of White settlement from Rhodesia and the Republic of South Africa and a resolution of the "Asian Problem," the Shatterbelt character of the continent could be increased through the introduction of Indian influence along the eastern side.

Africa is a large continent, but like South America, much of it is not suited to mass settlement. Lack of rainfall, disease, bush, and isolation are responsible for Africa's empty spaces. Most of Africa consists of high plateau that has experienced successive uplifts. This includes the Abyssinian Plateau, parts of the Sahara and West Africa, and the Great Central Plateau. Emerged coastal plains, smooth and narrow, occupy a much smaller proportion of the land area than do the coastal plains of other continents, and afford few good natural harbors. Where these plains are present, they are frequently too dry, and therefore are lightly populated, or quite narrow, being blocked off from the interior by highlands. Some coastal areas were depopulated by slaving activities. Lack of large, coastal-centered populations (save in South Africa, Cameroun, the mouths of the Niger, the Zanzibar coast, and eastern Malagasy), has limited Africa's ability to create large, urbanized manufacturing centers. So has the inaccessibility of the plateau interior of the continent, which hampers land and waterway penetration.

With much of the African population living in scattered fashion on the interior highlands, and this highland being a barrier to internal movement as well as to accessibility to the sea, the creation of a significant regional ecumene has not been possible. While modern railroads and ports have been built, their purpose has been to carry minerals and commercial crops to the sea and to export them, not to link interior areas. True, such a railroad as the one from Zambia and the Katanga through Rhodesia to Lourenço Marques had geopolitical significance, in that it enabled the Katanga to break away from the Lower Congo and Matadi. It thus acted as a counterforce to the centralizing aims of Congo nationalism. But the very fact that this railroad, as well as one from the Katanga to the Atlantic via Angola, was built for economic purposes and regardless of its possible effects upon Congo unity, proves the point that has been made—namely, that transportation lines frequently have no relevance to current national boundaries or hopes of regional unity. Another example of railway building, the Tanzan Railroad, was started in 1970 with the aid of loans from the Chinese People's Republic. It will be 1,116 miles in length from Dar es Salaam to its junction with the Zambian Railway system. While freeing Zambia of dependence on the Rhodesian railways for export of its copper, the Tanzan line may put Zambia into potential tension with Tanzania as the latter achieves control over the Zambian exitways.

The West's primary interest in Africa's resources has been in terms of their contribution to the raw material base of the Maritime World's defense structure. This interest is not confined to the need for war materials. It is grounded also in the broader raw material and financial support needs of the economies of many Maritime European countries. The orientation of African trade is essentially to the North Atlantic Basin. Seventy per cent of all of its exports are with Maritime Europe and another 10 per cent are with Anglo-America. The most important trading partners, by far, are France and the United Kingdom. They account for about half of all of Africa's international trade. Intra-African trade is relatively insignificant, amounting to only 11 per cent of total exports. As in the case of South America, this trade is small because exports are mainly primary products that cannot be absorbed by the domestic markets of the continent.

Among the minerals coming from Africa south of the Sahara are uranium, copper, gold, manganese, iron, tin, antimony, chromite, magnesite, lead, vanadium, cobalt, industrial diamonds, columbium, beryllium, and mica. Some of these minerals (like diamonds, gold, cobalt, manganese, and chromite) account for a large share of the total Maritime World supply. Others, like copper and iron ore, are high on the list of Africa's exports in terms of value. Indeed, copper ranks second in value only to oil seeds among the continent's exports.

Among the foods and fibers that are being exported, mainly to Europe, are oil seeds (palm, peanut, and sesame), cocoa, coffee, cotton, wool, wines, fruits and nuts, hides, tobacco, cereals, timber sisal, and tea. These have been listed in descending order of value.

Large-scale development of some minerals, especially bauxite and iron ore, hinges upon power, transportation, and politics. One almost untapped African resource is hydroelectric power. It holds great promise for the future, because it can provide the substitute for fossil fuels in many parts of Africa that do not possess them. Recent or planned hydroelectric developments in Uganda, Kenya, Ethiopia, Rhodesia, Zambia, Angola, Togo, Guinea, Ghana, Nigeria, Ivory Coast, and Cameroun reflect a speed-up in the tapping of this resource.

Single crop or mineral economies take advantage of specialized sets of environmental and market conditions, but they leave a people subject to forces beyond their control. To diversify the raw material base, without abandoning the advantages of the specialized materials that are the bases of Africa's modern export economy, is the basic problem from the African viewpoint. In the search for diversification, agriculture appears to be the key. The foodstuffs and fibers that Europe imports from Africa can be expanded. But more cereals, meat, fish (from both the ocean and ponds), vegetables, and dairy products must be produced to check the appalling effects of malnutrition. If the food supply cannot be significantly increased, then overpopulation is likely to become a major African ailment.

From the native African standpoint, the question of whether sufficient attention has been paid to development of small-holders's food crops is of primary importance. Seventy per cent of all Africans depend on the land for their subsistence. This is essentially a primitive agriculture, whose productivity is limited by present techniques, soil infertility and erosion, and inadequacy of transportation. The continued development of mining can employ only a relatively small percentage of the working force. Local manufacturing lacks capital, and labor must be trained. But even if an efficient labor force should be established to enable domestic manufacturers to compete with imports, there is little reason to assume that manufacturing would relieve the poverty of the majority of Africans. Most manufacturing is likely to emphasize the light products that can be readily absorbed within expanding domestic consumer markets, and consumer markets within a subsistence economy are apt to grow slowly.

It is not a question of *either* agriculture *or* mining and industry. It is rather a question of balance of emphasis in the sense of both timing and capital investment. Certainly farming can be improved only as the national funds derived from mining and manufacturing are plowed into agricutural development. And certainly the stimulation of transportation and power projects by mining industries will benefit agriculture as well. But it would be unwise to overemphasize one sector at the expense of the other, and to permit the living-standard gap between the subsistence farmer and city worker to become too great in the forthcoming years of African economic advancement. What Maritime Europe and the United States do with respect to this problem, directly or indirectly, will have much bearing upon whether Africans will continue to feel themselves victims of "exploitation."

Unquenchable desires for political self-expression have reshaped Africa's political map. This process will affect many native and European-imposed features of the cultural landscape. Perhaps the most fundamental question, in the political-geographic sense, is whether the area frameworks for Africa's emerging national states can be based upon existing lines, or whether new boundaries will have to be forged. Many of the present boundaries of Africa hark back to the Berlin Congress of 1885 or to decisions of European states that have been made since that period. These boundaries reflect, to a high degree, the location of European coastal footholds and the building of railroad lines into the interior.

As new national states evolve in Africa, their frameworks are heavily influenced by the European-derived image of the national state and its prerequisites (such as defensive depth, chunkiness, access to the sea, centrality of ecumene, land contiguity, unity of peoples). But complicating this image are existing colonial boundaries, tribal distinctions, and distribution of European and other non-Black groupings. The Nigerian Federation almost foundered for lack of effective centralized authority, because its political framework sought to embrace all that was British Nigeria and the Northern British Cameroons. Ghana seems to have found that its area is simply too small for it to be able to lead the West African national revolution. It was not possible to maintain a new national state composed of Guinea, Ghana, and the Mali Republic. And the Central African Federation did not have sufficient national state earmarks, proving merely a temporary device to serve as a source of, and corridor for, minerals that must be shipped to the sea.

A second basic issue that must be faced is the competition between Islam and Christianity for influence in Africa. Completely dominant in North Africa and the Sahara, Islam is also embraced by the majority of the population of Gambia, Cameroun, Northern Nigeria, and the Tanzanian coast. In former French West and Equatorial Africa, it has been adopted by about one-third of the population, and by one-fifth the population of Liberia. What makes the spread of Islam so politically significant today is its use by Arab nationalists as a broad anti-Western movement.

The relative weakness of Christianity in most of Africa's urbanized areas (as opposed to its strength in the villages) presents a danger to continued Western influence on the continent. Most political movements are born in the cities, and most revolutions are ignited there. In all likelihood, urbanized Africa will shape African nationalism, and it is in these urban areas that Christianity is particularly weak.

The third and most basic issue concerns the manner in which the European and Black African worlds are to work out their final accommodation. In multiracial Africa, the proportion of Whites to total population varies from 20 per cent in the Republic of South Africa, to 8 per cent in Rhodesia. Here the accommodation must be social and political, as well as economic. In those parts of Africa where the European is in the insignificant minority, the problem is no longer political—it is only economic. Investments and trade must take the path of common economic interests between two sets of political equals. It is in southern Africa and between southern Africa and the rest of the region, that the major racial issue has yet to be resolved. Partition in South Africa may yet be an answer to what appears to be an unresolvable conflict, but the partition cannot be based upon an apartheid policy that is built upon racial discrimination and exploitation on the one hand, and a series of small, scattered, economically non-viable "Bantustans" on the other. It is to be hoped that the lesson of Algeria will not be lost on White South Africa, granted that the former case is not analogous, because the French in Algeria did not possess the form and power of independent statehood. Because African leadership throughout most of the continent still is essentially pro-Western, we need not be unduly pessimistic about the prospects. But Africans will only think in Maritime World terms if they meet with rapid, rather than grudging, political accommodation, and with full-scale economic support that takes into account local desires to become secondary and finishing producers.

Today, Africa south of the Sahara is perhaps the most fragmented of the world's geopolitical regions. With nine states per 100 million population, Africa has the highest density of states to population, and with five states per million square miles, it ranks second in density to Maritime Europe only. Fragmentation of the region is attributable to some of the characteristics already suggested: 1) physical barriers to movement, 2) economic isolation and economic competition, 3) ethnic, linguistic, and other cultural differences, and 4) the legacy of European political controls. These characteristics have helped to create the bewildering mélange of national states, 25 per cent of the world's total, many of whose viability is in serious doubt and whose roles on the international political scene often widely depart from norms struck by older national states.

How many African states are viable, considering their limited populations, narrow economic bases, and absence of national accord? One can contend that viability is related to one element and one element alone—the strength of the *state idea* which is the *raison d'être* of the state. As states are formed, their state ideas must become powerful enough to overcome internal loyalties to regions or tribal areas, and must become distinct from the state ideas of nearby states to maintain unique national identities. Negative state ideas (e.g. independence *from* a colonial power or independence *against* the threat of neighboring state) are not in contradiction to positive state ideas, but may become part of them (e.g. Canada's independent stance vis-à-vis the United States). But once the state idea is internally accepted and internationally respected, then it may be argued that viability is assured.

Even if this line of thinking appears reasonable, the question still remains as to whether the state idea can flourish on both an internal and external plane, irrespective of the quality of geopolitical environments. For a state is the political structure which is established by a nation on its land to enable that nation to perform certain functions and to realize unique objectives which can be summed up by the phrase "national interests." The state cannot exist unless man wills it, but the state need not exist just because man wills it.

It is questionable whether the present political pattern of Africa south of the Sahara suggests that people have struck enough of a balance with their lands so that the structures that they have willed can be characterized as viable national states. It may be that the plethora of national units in relationship to both population and area are no more than a transitional period. It could be a portent of a "shaking out" process that, through federation and annexation, larger consolidated regions will emerge.

Rather than attempt to discuss the question of viability for a specific state, the discussion will center around the elements that contribute to national viability. These spatially-defined elements are long-term indicators or earmarks of the viable state, earmarks upon which national political structures must be built if stability and viability are to be attained. In listing these elements, individual African states can be measured against the standards:

1) One group (ethnic, racial, religious) should have a clear numerical preponderance over the largest minority, be at least equal on the cultural-technical plane with any of the smaller groups and have direct and rapid access to the center of the minority group if the latter possesses a specific area of concentration (e.g. the problem of Muslims and Biafrans in Nigeria).

2) The largest urban center should have indisputable primacy over the next center—a primacy reflected in size, manufacturing plant and occupance by majority group (e.g. the problem of the Federal District in Lagos, Nigeria, surrounded by the Yoruba majority).

3) The country should have only one ecumene, or, if there are two or more ecumenes, one should be clearly dominated by the other and they should be peopled by persons of like cultures and objectives (e.g. the problem of the Congo (Kinsaha) and the Katanga).

4) There should be a limited number of nearest neighbors. If not, then the ecumenes of these nearest neighbors should be more distant from the borders of the state concerned than the ecumene of the state itself (e. g., the problem of the Congo (Kinsaha) with ten adjoining states, and neighboring Lake Victoria and Zambian core areas).

5) Economic specialization requires direct access to the sea. If such is lacking, some form of federation or subservience is likely to result. Of today's 141 states, 29 are landlocked, fourteen of them in Africa (Mali, Central African Republic, Chad, Niger, Upper Volta, Malawi, Zambia, Rhodesia, Botswana, Lesotho, Swaziland, Uganda, Burundi, Rwanda). Of these, how many can hope to emerge as full-fledged national entities? In this connection we think of the problems faced by Rhodesia, Zambia, Botswana, Lesotho, and Swaziland.

The spatial elements cited are a departure from traditional indices used in appraising a state's viability potential—e.g. homogeneity of population, chunkiness of shape, centrality of ecumene and capital to borders, barrier nature of borders, contiguity of territory, minimal size of population, effective national territory for population and economic growth, balanced economy providing minimal food subsistence, and diverse economic base for foreign exchange. While not discounting these traditional indices, we have added a few less traditional, more easily weighed and, perhaps, more critical indices of viability potential. Application of these indices to individual national scenes in Africa south of the Sahara highlights the problems of political fragmentation and underscores the problems of political and even regional unity with which such organizations as the Organization of African Unity, OCAM (Common Afro-Malagasy Organization), or attempts to federate in East or West Africa must contend.

Maritime Europe can scarcely be accused of ignoring Africa's capital investment needs. On the contrary, the activities by state and privately chartered British, French, Belgian, German, and Common Market institutions are far more significant than United States investments and grants in Africa. In all likelihood the future will bring increased joint European economic activities. Decades late in coming, a partnership towards Africa is emerging within Maritime Europe. This, coupled with the European "presence" in the OCAM states, the Commonwealth, and the band of White settlement in South Africa and

Rhodesia, should continue to keep Africa within the Maritime Trade-Dependent region.

These forces will not necessarily inspire geopolitical unity. They may, on the contrary, reinforce the divisions between some African states—and South Africa and Rhodesia—and therefore with Maritime Europe. The greater the degree of economic cooperation between Maritime Europe and Africa, the more likely it is that Europe's trade with other parts of the world will experience a relative decline. But this is a far cry from saying that a Euro-African unity can or should emerge. It simply says that Europe has held the responsibility for bringing Africa to the threshold of political independence, and that Europe should continue to hold the prime responsibility for integrating independent Africa economically into the Trade-Dependent Maritime World. Logic favors such a course. On the other hand, failure of Europe to find an accommodation with Black Africa over economic and racial issues is still to be feared. In such an event, all of Africa south of the Sahara could become a Shatterbelt, within which the maintenance of footholds in the mineralized Highland South, and in West Africa, would become the minimal strategic requirements of the Maritime World.

Offshore Asia

Offshore Asia is a geopolitical region within the Maritime World that includes Japan, South Korea, Taiwan, the Philippines, Australian New Guinea, Australia, and New Zealand. Japan, the world's third largest single industrial power, is its core. Further integration of the region under Japan's leadership will develop Offshore Asia as the world's fifth major power region. This region stands in contrast to the East Asian mainland and South Asia. Caught among the three is the Southeast Asian Shatterbelt. Perspectives of Asia vary with the point of departure. For America, Offshore Asia is the nearest sector, followed by Southeast Asia, East Asia, and South Asia. All of these regions are approached via the Pacific. On the other hand, the Middle East and Siberia are generally approached by Americans from the Atlantic.

The traditional British view, on the other hand, is of Pacific Asia as "the other, or farther side of Asia." Long before the modern terms of Southeast and East Asia came into common use (and these are of recent origin), *Further India* and the *Far* (or *Farther*) *East* were used. To the Englishman whose empire-nourished eyes were focused on India, the lands farther east were peripheral. Whatever light was cast in the direction of the farther side of Asia was beamed and refracted through India. When the United Kingdom divested itself of its South Asian Empire in the wake of World War Two, many of its concerns with the lands farther east suddenly became relict concerns. The calm, almost impersonal reaction to recent events in both Offshore and Southeast Asia that is widespread among Englishmen today should not be surprising, since these areas were always considerably more remote than was India, and because the India base for their support is no more.

An Australian view of East and Southeast Asia, quite differently, is that of the "near North." To the Australian, whose shores were touched by the Second World War, and who can think back a century ago to a period when, had open immigration from Asia been permitted, the cultural map of Australia could have been fundamentally different than it is today, the "Near North" is a strategic and economic reality. Western geographers frequently describe Australia-New Zealand as remote and isolated, the "end of the line." But for Australians the view to and from the Eurasian littoral and insular lands is quite different. Djakarta is only 1600 miles from the nearest Australian Territory; Saigon, 2300; Canton, 2700; Tokyo, 3300; and Peiping, 3700 miles.

To the Japanese and the Chinese, Southeast Asia was the land of the Southern Seas or Far Eastern Tropics—a land that is not only close by, but because of its economic resources, a land of "exploitability."

The view, then, that is offered of Offshore Asia as a distinct geopolitical region is admittedly an American view. It is suggested, however, that this view has some basis in Australian and Japanese attitudes as well.

Nicholas Spykman suggested that the Western Pacific consisted of three broad zones: 1) the Asian Mainland (with Japan occupying a position similar to that of the United Kingdom to the European Mainland); 2) Australia and New Zealand—the Southern Continent; 3) the Asian Mediterranean—from Taiwan to Northern Australia, including the Southeast Asian Islands and most of the peninsula. This forms a large triangle, with Singapore controlling the Strait of Malacca, Cape York the Torres Strait, and Taiwan the Formosa Strait. This geopolitical view, derived from Anglo-American seapower interests, saw in the Asian Mediterranean a valuable buffer zone between the Asian Mainland and Australia.

The viewpoint of this volume differs. It presents a geopolitical view of Monsoonal Asia, the East Asian and South Asian subcontinents as two separate geopolitical regions and Offshore Asia as the third. Off-shore Asia, obviously, is a different realm from Southeast Asia in its insular character, its greater degree of orientation to the West, its land limitation which has accelerated its pace of industrialization, and its greater ability to defend itself because of the protective screen of water.

What presents Offshore Asia with the opportunity for geopolitical unity is not only its geographical position in the western Pacific and the pressures of Maritime World security needs. Economics and ide-ology are equally important factors. The economies of the Offshore Asian states are sufficiently complementary to provide harmony of interests. The states concerned are in a strong position to help and be helped by one another, and they do not have the overwhelming popu-lation problems that threaten to strangle the development efforts of much of the mainland. Offshore Asian peoples, because of their his-torical associations, are not the victims of the irrational anti-Western, anti-colonial spirit that characterizes other Asian countries.

Present trade within the region is less than may be anticipated. In this respect, we might point out that Australia and Japan, although partly temperate climate countries with strong manufacturing com-plexes, are not competitive. Their economic and population bases differ. Australia and New Zealand (not a heavy manufacturer) have wool, meat, dairy products, iron ore, lead, and zinc to export. They purchase fabrics, apparel, machinery, and other metal products. Semi-tropical northern Queensland and adjoining territories can become a source of rice and plantation crop supply. Even Australian wheat has begun to find a market in Japan, where wheat consumption is already one-fourth of rice consumption.

Intraregional trade does not dominate the foreign trade of Offshore Asia, nor is it likely to do. However, such trade is on the rise. About 20 per cent of Japan's foreign commerce is with other Offshore Asian countries. Taiwan's major trading partner is Japan and over 30 per cent of the foreign commerce of the Philippines is with Japan. Australia, with over 15 per cent of its trade with Offshore Asia, is in-creasing its regional economic ties. Already it sends Japan one-fourth of its exports. One-third of South Korea's trade is with Japan. We can foresee, in the very near future, an intraregional trade that will be at least as important as the region's extraregional contacts with Anglo-America, Southeast Asia, and Maritime Europe. Greater economic interdependence and closer political ties will not only strengthen Off-shore Asia as a geopolitical region; it will also enable it to expand its influence in Southeast Asia, thus strengthening the over-all position of the Maritime World in this Shatterbelt. The lead taken by Japan and Australia in developing intraregional links, as well as ties with Southeast Asia, is a bold and significant element in forging Maritime World unity. To amplify the picture of interchange within Offshore Asia and Southeastern Asia, we should note such exportable commodities as Japan's fabrics, textiles, chemicals, electronic and steel products; Taiwan's sugar, rice, textiles, and electronic goods; South Korea's textiles; the Philippines' copra, abaca, iron, chrome, manganese, and copper; Thailand's and Malaysia's tin and rubber; Indonesia's petroleum; and rice from several areas. The trading of these commodities can help to expand domestic markets, which will in turn spur their increased production. Over one-third of the trade of Japan and Taiwan, and 15 per cent of Australia's, is with Southeast Asia. We can anticipate the time when Southeast Asia will become the number one trading partner of Offshore Asia.

Placing the Philippines within Offshore Asia and not the Southeast Asian Shatterbelts, may warrant explanation at this point. While many of the geopolitical features of Southeast Asia also characterize the Philippines, this latter island-state has a uniqueness that justifies its being treated as part of the Offshore Asian geopolitical unit. True, the Philippines have in common with much of Southeast Asia such elements as monsoonal climate, rice and export crop emphasis, soil infertility, shifting agriculture, high percentage of idle farm land, Malaysian race, and wide gaps between present and optimum land-use standards. Because of these elements, the Philippines serve as a bridge to Southeast Asia.

But the orientation of the archipelago to other Pacific lands is stronger than to the Shatterbelt. In terms of sheer distance, Taiwan is its closest neighbor. Japan and Australia are nearer and more accessible than Burma and Java. The Westernized outlook of the people, stemming from half a century's contact with the United States, finds counterpart attitudes in Japan and Australia, not in Southeast Asia. Neither Buddhist nor Muslim, but Christian, their political institutions are modelled along the lines of those of the United States. Half of all foreign trade is with the United States, and most of the remainder (44 per cent of all exports) is with Japan. Finally, the islands' major military ties are not with Southeast Asia, but with the United States. These ties, fixed through common war, are firm and mutually desired. In the light of the above, the inclusion of the Philippines within Offshore Asia, appears geopolitically warranted.

The status quo that prevailed in Asia prior to the emergence of the

Chinese People's Republic as a major power requires that the boundary between Offshore Asia and East Asia be reconsidered. Specifically, we need to disengage ourselves from areas that are relicts of the past. One such area is the Quemoy and Matsu island groupings, overlooking the ports of Amoy (Xiamen) and Fuchou. It may well be that negotiations attending the China-United States détente included an agreement to maintain the territorial status quo for an indefinite period. But rather than risk a Communist Chinese takeover of the islands—an act that the United States would clearly no longer oppose militarily—we would be well advised to take the initiative and formally accept the Mainland Chinese claim. This would add a territorial dimension to the detente that has included various forms of mutual recognition: President Nixon's trip to China, the exchange of visits by athletes and scientists, the establishment of diplomatic missions, and the sale of United States wheat. Such an American initiative need not compromise the status of Taiwan. On the contrary, it would more clearly differentiate between those areas that we consider to be under Mainland Chinese sovereignty and those, like Taiwan, which we consider part of Off-shore Asia. The same initiative ought to be exercised by Britain and Portugal with reference to Hong Kong and Macao. Holding on until the Chinese decide to seize these areas merely delays the inevitable (and risks the chaos of an unforeseen rather than planned take-over), and deprives the Maritime World of an opportunity to demonstrate to the Chinese People's Republic recognition of its legitimate territorial interests.

The basic goal of the Maritime World should be to integrate Taiwan into the Offshore Asian framework. Such integration should be pursued through an independent Taiwan, rather than through a two-China policy. The island is militarily defensible under all conditions save those of nuclear warfare, and the emergence of a genuine form of Taiwanese nationalism, free of Mainland Chinese ambitions, is probably the best assurance of its safety.

It is true that United States policy toward Taiwan has not been consistent. In 1943 the United States played a leading role at the Teheran Conference in the decision to return Formosa to China when victory had been achieved in the Pacific. During the Communist drive to win the Mainland, United States policy was essentially hands-off, and there were no plans to protect the defeated Chiang on his Formosan bastion. This decision came about only after the invasion of Korea by the North Koreans and the subsequent involvement of the Chinese. Prior to the inva[...] cluded preparations for global war o[...] made for limited war, including the d[...] Since the Korean War, Taiwan has be[...] defense perimeter. In the light of the 197[...] munist China detente, the temptation in Wa[...] return gradually to the thinking of the Teheran [...] wan is an integral part of China. Such a formula wo[...] strategic changes that have occurred in the Western Pa[...] past twenty years, as well as the genuine aspirations of T[...] nationalism. Taiwan is not only a military asset for the Mar[...] World; its remarkable economic development through ties to the r[...] of Offshore Asia and the Maritime World is a dramatic demonstra- tion of the fruits of international trade and aid, and of the United States lead therein. If the United States should abandon its support of the Kuomintang and support the emergence of a democratic Tai- wanese popular government, Taiwan can take its place as a signifi- cant component of Offshore Asia.

What is needed today for Off-Shore Asia (South Korea, Japan, Tai- wan, the Philippines, Australia, and New Zealand) is not a SEATO, but rather a MATO (Maritime Asian Treaty Organization). This would bring selected portions of Southeast Asia into direct alliance with Offshore Asia and other Maritime World powers. Granted that political conditions have not permitted the establishment of such an organization *de jure*, it is becoming one *de facto*. Perhaps the frame- work for MATO may derive from the Asian and Pacific Council (ASPAC). This economic association has as its core all of the Off- shore Asian states, as well as South Vietnam, Thailand and Malaysia. NATO and MATO may well emerge as the twin cornerstones of the Trade-Dependent Maritime Region.

When the efforts of Offshore Asia are strategically coupled with those of Thailand, Malaysia, and Singapore, unified control of the links between the Indian Ocean and the Pacific are assured. More- over, Japan's ties to the rest of the bloc are strengthened. As impor- tant as considerations of military strategy, are those of economics. If economic contacts can be maintained between Offshore Asia on the one hand and the rice-bowl countries of Southeast Asia and the min- eral and food products of the Indonesian Islands on the other, greater economic stability is assured.

ere enclave, like Hong
n Australia and the is-
tion of western New
st the eastern half of
ern New Guinea as a
as a unit federated with
support of proposals to
ions and eventually un-
lonesia has absorbed the
drawn between Offshore
afford to see the extension
ea. Independence is forth-
n New Guinea. This does
the area, but points to a
the Melanesian New Guin-
ean pop...

South Asia

China, India, and Southeast Asia are often treated as one great physical and cultural world—Monsoonal Asia. Geopolitically, however, they are quite distinct. This is not to say that a geostrategic merger is an impossibility. In this context, the Sino-Soviet split might have the adverse effect of directing China toward such a geostrategic framework. Absence of Soviet restraints on Chinese regional ambitions, or the Chinese desire to take over the mantle of militant Communism from the U.S.S.R., could result in a direct attempt by the Chinese to unify the Monsoonal world. Were China to absorb Offshore Asia and the Southeast Asian Shatterbelt, South Asia would be hard pressed to remain outside the new framework. It is far more likely, however, that South Asia will retain its separate geopolitical identity, perhaps some day extending its influence across the Indian Ocean to create a new geostrategic region embracing East Africa and parts of Southeast Asia.

So long as South Asia remains politically divided, geopolitical unity remains a goal, not a reality. It is not necessary to erase national lines to forge a geopolitical region. However, economic and military cooperation, as well as a common approach to world problems, is a prerequisite for such a unity.

Separation from the rest of Asia, and cultural and human similarities, enhance South Asia's prospects for geopolitical distinctiveness. The Indian subcontinent stands aloof from its neighbors, behind a rimming barrier of desert, mountain, and monsoonal forest. Its best connections to the outside are via the Indian Ocean. Both the western and eastern littorals of this basin have absorbed considerable numbers of South Asians in the past century.

Within South Asia, the population follows such river valleys as the Brahmaputra, Ganges, and Indus, and the east and west coasts, to form an almost continuous ring around the Deccan, or South Indian plateau. Although population on the plateau is dense, it is far less so than that of the valleys and coastal plains, which also contain the bulk of the region's industry and transportation. This population core crosses national boundary lines in both Bengal and Punjab to further intertwine the fates of Pakistan, Bangladesh, and India.

What gives to South Asia geopolitical distinctiveness, apart from physical and cultural qualities, is its inward economic orientation. Though surrounded by water, the region is not a maritime one. Trade with other nations for industrial raw materials and consumer goods is of secondary concern. The major problem is agriculture. South Asia's 650 million people are mostly farmers. Regardless of the success of efforts to industrialize and urbanize, it is clear that most South Asians will continue to be agriculturists, and in all probability their major efforts will go toward feeding themselves—not toward feeding the big cities.

Considerable political significance is attached to the relative performance of India and China in the resolution of economic problems. China's industrial strides, stemming from a richer mineral base, earlier Japanese efforts, forced industrialization, and Soviet assistance, have been much more dramatic than those of India. But it is to the agricultural competition that we must look to judge the relative prospects of these two powers.

In any comparison with Chinese agriculture, Indian agricultural performance lags behind. Yields per acre are less, and there is relatively little application of fertilizer (India's animal manure has less organic value because of the poor fodder that is available, and human waste is not used). Farming methods are more backward, irrigation is less developed, and religious practices still maintain a high surplus cattle population. Still, Indian food staple production is beginning to compare favorably with China's on a per capita basis. Specifically, paddy rice production is 70 per cent of China's, wheat is two-thirds, and raw sugar is 125 per cent. India's population is 64 per cent of China's.

India's prospects are more encouraging than China's in the sense that she can achieve a relatively greater increase in agricultural productivity through her own efforts, with the set of resources available to her. Most of the country's farm areas have a longer growing season than has China. Because the temperatures are higher, there is less pressure on fuels and fibers for domestic use. About one-third of India's total land area is under some form of cultivation (520,000 square miles), and over one-fifth of this is under irrigation. Indian planners have hopes of eventually doubling their irrigated land, as have their Pakistani counterparts. Even if this target is not actually reached, there is little doubt that food production can be substantially increased. The elements that are required for such an increase —electricity, fertilizers, better seeds, livestock control, reforestation, and land reform—are all within the production capacity of the Indian peoples. Moreover, industrial and commercial crops, like jute, cotton, sugar cane, tea, tobacco, and peanuts, are well advanced, and serve both an export and manufacturing function. The "green revolution" is within the grasp of South Asia, as early successes in rice cultivation have already demonstrated.

With better land transportation facilities than those possessed by China, and a more realistic approach in its planning through emphasis upon agriculture, India has good prospects of improving its lot as a self-contained farm nation—that is provided that a strong national drive towards that end can be mounted and maintained.

The greatest obstacle at present in South Asia is overpopulation. Bangladesh, especially, exemplifies the inability of a national state to grapple with the problems of development, given the overpopulation factor. Food production is not increasing at a significantly faster rate than the rise in population; while a faster rise in production may be anticipated, the massive problems of storage and distribution will still remain. Moreover, industrialization is not likely to reach enough of the population to effect a decrease in the rate of growth. Without far greater outside assistance to control this population growth as well as a massive, internally directed program, South Asia is likely to fall behind in its development progress.

The Indian subcontinent is politically divided. Behind the boundaries, each country is working out its destiny in the manner that it sees fit. New patterns of population distribution, of movement, and of internal administrative boundaries are emerging within the countries concerned. None of the four major states can devote their full efforts to social and economic development, as long as political boundaries serve as economic barriers and foci for military buildups. Moreover, the entanglement of India and Pakistan in external regional alliances (with the U.S.S.R., the United States, and China) may serve short-term interests, but is likely to complicate the process of internal regional accommodation. With resolution of the Bangladesh problem, only Kashmir remains a major territorial issue (although India has some administrative territorial problems including that of the Nagas and in Pakistan, Pathan and Baluchi claims continue to simmer). Without political resolution, barriers to regional development, like cross-national use of waterways and hydroelectric power, rationalizing rail transportation and crop production, exchange of technological skills, and integrating the region's trans-Himalayan borderlands, will continue to persist. Whether the breakup of East and West Pakistan represents the final configuration of states for South Asia, or whether the configuration is a stage in a still-evolving pattern, is a matter of speculation. But irrespective of the ultimate configuration, South Asia will have to find a way of integrating its national political activities within a broader common geopolitical framework.

Greater geopolitical unity on the Indian subcontinent is the best means of preserving its current independence and of preventing the absorption of the region within a possible Monsoonal Asian geostrategic realm that would in all likelihood be dominated by China. Given the rapidity with which the external relations of South Asia have switched, it may seem difficult to grasp the pattern of these relations. Following independence, Pakistan was coaxed into the Western camp in 1954, as India opted for neutrality. Hindsight permits one to suggest that the Dulles policy of brooking no neutrals was in error, and that the United States would have been better served to have developed close ties with a neutral India, rather than a military alliance with a state of such limited possibility for viability as Pakistan.

In response to the United States alliance, the U.S.S.R. reacted by redoubling contacts with Afghanistan and India and by backing India on Kashmir. Then came the Sino-Soviet split, prompted in part by differences of opinion over strategy toward India. China, after warring upon India in 1962, did an about-face in its relations to Pakistan, settling its border differences in northern Kashmir in 1962 and increasing its economic and military ties. By 1971, when the Bangladesh rebellion broke out in East Pakistan, it was China that supported Pakistan openly, the U.S.S.R. that backed India, and the United States that found itself in the middle, satisfying neither its formal ally, Pakistan, nor India.

The unhappy experiences of the United States in South Asia in the past two decades, demonstrate that military involvement with either Pakistan or India is not warranted, either from the standpoint of United States security or from the long-term needs of these two South Asian states. If China and India choose to take sides over Pakistan, an understandable action given China's tactical stakes in events in South Asia, this is no reason for the United States and the Maritime World to follow suit. The bitterness between Pakistan and India over partition, the Kashmir War, the War of 1965, and Bangladesh rebellion of 1971, are issues that will ultimately have to be resolved by the peoples concerned. Whether Pakistan retains its present form and whether Bangladesh remains as it is, eventually emerges as a Greater Bengal, or is ultimately absorbed by India—the Maritime World can only look on with compassion, giving aid to suffering humanity where possible, but not fueling the flames with arms to either side or seeing in the agonies of South Asia an element of opportunism for pursuing Cold War politics. South Asia is an independent geopolitical region. The direction of its orientation has little impact upon the over-all relations of the major powers, and United States foreign policy that understands this, will be better able to deal rationally and humanely with the region.

From the Western point of view, Australia has already replaced South Asia as the strategic guardian of the southern waters that unite the Trade-Dependent Maritime World. It is in the maintenance of a strong, more populous, more industrialized Australia—oriented to the rest of Offshore Asia, as well as to Anglo-America and Maritime Europe—that our primary concern lies, not in the retention of the Indian Ocean as a "Maritime World Lake."

CONCLUSION

The divided world is a geopolitical reality. To ignore the political consequences of the earth's physical and cultural environmental distinctions would be to ignore fact. No form of international government is likely to be able to fulfill all of the needs of various national states and regional associations, from their specialized points of view. For the present, the world is divisible into two major geostrategic regions and their geopolitical components. But change is an essential feature of geopolitical life. As certain of the underdeveloped areas mature economically and politically they may well shift their external allegiances.

There is a growing tendency on the part of some American policymakers to divide the world into three neat frameworks—East, West, and Neutral—and to project neutrality as a desirable goal for emergent states, regardless of what they are and where they are. This attitude is a reaction to the "era of containment," when we tried to maintain a blanket of American influence over all parts of the globe in the vain hope of confining Soviet influence. In the past, we attempted to extend our influence over too broad a sphere. Today, we are in danger of going to the other extreme and of disengaging ourselves from too many areas. It is fallacious to assume that the underdeveloped world will remain neutral if allowed to grow strong economically. Once a state attains a truly independent posture, there is no guarantee that it will want to continue to remain neutral or that it will be capable of fighting off subversion. From the Maritime point of view, therefore, not all parts of the politically emergent world should be encouraged to seek an independently neutral course. Such a policy should be reserved for those areas that do not directly affect our security. Where our global security is involved, strong alliances remain our only possible course.

Within the framework of our system of alliances, we must be prepared to maintain bases throughout the world. Bases manned by soldiers of the Maritime alliance are more than simply offensive-defensive weapons against the U.S.S.R. or China. They are props for friendly governments, and a "presence" that helps to forestall Communist subversion. These bases should not represent an "American" presence, however; they should be the reflection of the concern of the entire Trade-Dependent Maritime geostrategic region for the security of key areas. As such, outside of the NATO framework, bases should be manned jointly by the Atlantic powers in concert with host forces.

In isolation of others, the United States cannot remain the world's leading power. In association with others, we can retain our position. We constitute the core of the Trade-Dependent Maritime World, and hold the main responsibility for its economic development and strategic security. Maritime Europe has evolved as a second core. Such a realm, including Europeans, Asians, Latin Americans, and Africans, provides a strategic, economic, and cultural framework for interdependent action. Unity within this framework will avoid the partition of the earth along strictly economic or racial lines.

The Soviet Union has welded together a powerful geostrategic union within this divided world, and China has become the region's second core. We have not been able to confine Soviet influence to the historic Heartland. Now we must adapt our own policies, not only to the primacy of Soviet interests in Eastern Europe and to its stakes in East Asia, but also to its ambitions in the Middle East; and to China's ambitions in Southeast Asia. We must also be on guard lest our efforts to exploit the Sino-Soviet ideological gulf boomerang. Complete orientation of Mainland China toward Monsoonal Asia could have, as its long-term result, the creation of a geostrategic region within this part of the world.

The polycentric nature of both geostrategic regions, the Maritime World with two cores and an emerging third, and the Eurasian Continental World with two cores, are better guarantees of global equilibrium than a two-power world.

A better understanding of the geographical setting provides us with the basis for a contemporary geopolitical view of the divided world. While change is inevitable, we have tried to present a framework that anticipates the geographic dynamism of our times.

BIBLIOGRAPHY

Ackerman, Edward A., *Geography as a Fundamental Research Discipline*, Chicago: Department of Geography Research, No. 53, 1958.

Ancel, J., *Manuel Géographique de Politique Européene*, Paris: Armand Colin, 2nd ed., 1937.

Aristotle, *Politics*, trans. B. Jowett, New York: The Modern Library, 1943.

Balchin, W. G. V., *Air Transport and Geography*, London: The Royal Geographical Society, 1947.

Banse, Ewald, *Germany Prepares for War*, trans. Alan Harris, New York: Harcourt, Brace, 1941.

Baransky, N., *Economic Geography of the U.S.S.R.*, trans. S. Belsky, Moscow: Foreign Language Publishing House, 1956.

Bertalanffy, Ludwig von, *General Systems Theory*, New York: George Braziller, 1968.

Boggs, S. Whittemore, *International Boundaries*, New York: Columbia University Press, 1940.

Boulding, Kenneth, *The Impact of Social Sciences*, New Brunswick: Rutgers University Press, 1966.

Bowman, Isaiah, *The New World*, Yonkers-on-Hudson: World Book, 1922.

————, "The Pioneer Fringe," *Foreign Affairs*, 6, No. 1 (October 1927).

Broek, Jan, "Diversity and Unity in Southeast Asia," *The Geographical Review*, XXXIV, No. 2 (April 1944).

————, "The Problem of 'Natural' Frontiers," *Frontiers of the Future*, University of California, 1940.

————, "National Character in the Perspective of Cultural Geography," *Annals of the American Association of Political and Social Science*, 370 (March 1967).

Cantori, Louis J. and Spiegel, Steven L., *The International Politics of Regions: A Comparative Approach*, Englewood Cliffs: Prentice Hall, 1970.

Carr, E. H., *Nationalism and After,* London: Macmillan & Co., Ltd., 1945.

————, *The Twenty Years' Crisis, 1919-1939,* London: Macmillan & Co., Ltd., 1946.

Cassirer, Ernst, *The Myth of the State,* New Haven: Yale University Press, 1946.

Cohen, Saul B. and Rosenthal, Lewis D., "A Geographical Model for Political Systems Analysis," *The Geographical Review,* LXI, No. 1 (January 1971).

Colby, Charles C., ed., *Geographic Aspects of International Relations,* Chicago: University of Chicago Press, 1938.

Cole, D. H., *Imperial Military Geography,* London: Sifton Praed, 12th ed., 1956.

Cole, J. P., and German, F. C., *A Geography of the U.S.S.R.,* London: Butterworths, 1961.

Cressey, George, *Asia's Lands and Peoples,* New York: McGraw-Hill, revised, 1951.

————, *The Basis of Soviet Strength,* New York: McGraw-Hill, 1945.

————, *How Strong Is Russia?* Syracuse: Syracuse University Press, 1954.

Dahl, Robert, *Modern Political Analysis,* Englewood Cliffs: Prentice Hall, 1963.

de Rivera, Joseph, *The Psychological Dimensions of Foreign Policy,* Columbus: Charles Merrill, 1968.

de Salles, Raoul de Roussy, *The Making of Tomorrow,* New York: Reynal & Hitchcock, 1942.

de Seversky, Alexander P., *Air Power, Key to Survival,* New York: Simon & Schuster, 1950.

————, *America: Too Young to Die,* New York: McGraw-Hill, 1961.

Deutsch, Karl, *Nationalism and Social Communication,* Cambridge: M.I.T. Press, 1966.

————, *Political Community at the International Level,* Garden City: Doubleday, 1954.

Dobby, E. G. H., *Southeast Asia,* New York: Wiley, 1950.

Dorpalen, A., *The World of General Haushofer,* New York: Farrar & Rinehart, 1942.

East, W. G., *An Historical Geography of Europe,* London: Methuen, 4th ed., 1962.

————, and Moodie, A. E., eds., *The Changing World,* Yonkers-on-Hudson: World Book, 1956.

————, and Spate, O. H. K., eds., *The Changing Map of Asia,* London: Methuen, 1950.

Easton, David, *A Systems Analysis of Political Life,* New York: Wiley, 1965.

Emeny, Brooks, *The Strategy of Raw Materials,* New York: Macmillan, 1934.

Fairgrieve, James, *Geography and World Power,* London: University of London Press, 1915.

Falls, C., "Geography and War Strategy," *Geographical Journal,* CXII, Nos. 1-3 (July-September 1948).

Farrell, John C. and Smith, Asa P., eds., *Image and Reality in World Politics,* New York: Columbia University Press, 1967.

Fawcett, C. B., *Frontiers: A Study in Political Geography,* Oxford: Clarendon Press, 1918.

———, *A Political Geography of the British Empire,* London: Hazell, Watson and Viney, 1933.

Finley, M. I., ed., *The Greek Historians,* New York: Viking, 1959.

Fisher, W. B., *The Middle East,* London: Methuen, 4th ed., 1961.

Frankel, S. Herbert, *The Concept of Colonization,* Oxford: The Clarendon Press, 1949.

Freeman, T. W., *A Hundred Years of Geography,* Chicago: Aldine, 1961.

Gentilli, J., "Australia—Indian or Pacific?", *The Australian Quarterly* (March 1949).

Gilfillan, S., "European Political Boundaries," *Political Science Quarterly,* XXXIX, No. 3 (September 1924).

Ginsburg, Norton S., "On the Chinese Perception of World Order," in *China's Policies in Asia and Africa,* ed. by Tang Tsou, Chicago: University of Chicago, 1968.

———, ed., *The Pattern of Asia,* Englewood Cliffs: Prentice Hall, 1958.

Goblet, Y. M., *Political Geography and the World Map,* London: Philip and Son, 1956.

Gottman, Jean, *La Politique des États et Leur Géographie,* Paris: Armand Colin, 1952.

———, *A Geography of Europe,* New York: Holt, 1954.

———, "Geography and International Relations," *World Politics,* III, No. 2 (January 1951).

———, "Political Partitioning of Our World" *World Politics,* IV, No. 4 (July 1952).

Guyot, Arnold, *The Earth and Man,* New York: Scribner, 1889.

Gyorgy, Andrew, *Geopolitics,* Berkeley and Los Angeles: University of California Press, 1944.

Haas, E. B., "The Balance of Power: Prescription, Concept or Propaganda," *World Politics,* V, No. 4 (July 1953).

Halle, Louis J., *Men and Nations,* Princeton: Princeton University Press, 1965.

Harris, Chauncey, *Cities of the Soviet Union,* A.A.G. Monograph Series No. 5, Chicago: Rand McNally, 1970.

———, "Ethnic Groups in the Soviet Union," *The Geographical Review* XLV, No. 3 (July 1955).

Harris, Norman, *Intervention and Colonization in Africa,* Boston: Houghton, Mifflin, 1914.

Hart, J. F., "Changing Distribution of the American Negro," *Annals of the Association of American Geographers,* L, No. 3 (September 1960).

Hartshorne, Richard, "The Functional Approach in Political Geography," *Annals of the Association of American Geographers,* XL, No. 2 (June 1950).

————, *The Nature of Geography,* Lancaster, Pa.: The Association of American Geographers, 1939.

————, *Perspective on the Nature of Geography,* Chicago: Rand McNally, 1959.

————, "Political Geography," in James & Jones (q.v.).

————, "Political Geography in the Modern World," *Journal of Conflict Resolution,* IV, No. 1 (March 1960).

————, *Suggestions on the Terminology of Political Boundaries,* Leipzig, 1936.

————, "The Role of the State in Economic Growth," in *The State and Economic Growth,* edited by H. Aitken, New York: Social Science Research Council, 1959.

Haushofer, Karl, *Grenzen, in Ihrer Geographischen und Politischen Bedeutung,* Berlin: Wowinckel, 1927.

Herman, Theodore, "Group Values Towards the National Space," *The Geographical Review,* XLIX, No. 2 (April 1959).

Herz, John, *Political Realism and Political Idealism,* Chicago: University of Chicago Press, 1951.

————, "Rise and Demise of the Territorial State," *World Politics,* IX, No. 4 (July 1957).

Holdich, Thomas H., *Political Frontiers and Boundary Making,* London: Macmillan, 1916.

Jackson, W. A. Douglas, *Russo-Chinese Borderlands,* Princeton: Van Nostrand, 1962.

————, and Samuels, M., eds., *Politics and Geographic Relationships: Toward a New Focus,* Englewood Cliffs: Prentice Hall, 2nd ed., 1971.

James, P. and Faissol, S., "The Problem of Brazil's Capital City," *The Geographical Review,* XLVI, No. 3 (July 1956).

James, Preston, and Jones, Clarence, eds., *American Geography—Inventory and Prospect,* Association of American Geographers, Syracuse University Press, 1954.

Jones, S. B., *Australia and New Zealand and the Security of the Pacific,* New Haven: Yale Institute of International Studies, 1944.

————, *Boundary Making, a Handbook for Statesmen, Treaty Editors and Boundary Commissioners,* Washington: Carnegie Endowment for International Peace, 1945.

————, "Global Strategic Views," *The Geographical Review,* XLIV, No. 2 (June 1954).

————, "The Power Inventory and National Strategy," *World Politics,* VI, No. 4 (July 1954).

————, "A Unified Field Theory of Political Geography," *Annals of the Association of American Geographers,* XLIV, No. 2 (June 1954).

————, "Views of the Political World," *The Geographical Review,* XLV, No. 3 (July 1955).

Jorré, Georges, *The Soviet Union,* translated & revised by E. D. Laborde, London: Longmans, 1960.

Kant, Immanuel, "The Principle of Progress," *Eternal Peace and Other Essays,* 3, World Peace Foundation, 1914.

Kasperson, Roger E. and Minghi, Julian V., *The Structure of Political Geography,* Chicago: Aldine, 1969.

Kennan, George, *Russia and the West under Lenin and Stalin,* Boston: Little, Brown, 1960.

Kimble, George, *Geography in the Middle Ages,* London: Methuen, 1938.

Kjellén, R., *Der Staat als Lebensform,* Leipzig: Hirzel, 1917.

Kropotkin, Pierre, *Orographie de la Siberie,* Institut Geographique de Bruxelles, Publication 9, 1904.

Lamb, Alastair, *The China-Indian Border,* London: Chatham House, 1964.

Leach, E. R., *Political Systems of Highland Burma,* Boston: Beacon Press, 1968.

Leiss, Amelia C., ed., *European Peace Treaties after World War II,* Boston: World Peace Foundation, 1954.

Lerner, Daniel and Gorden, Morton, *Euratlantica: Changing Perspectives of the European Elites,* Cambridge: M.I.T. Press, 1969.

Linden, Carl A., *Khrushchev and the Soviet Leadership: 1957-1964,* Baltimore: Johns Hopkins Press, 1966.

Luethy, Herbert, *France Against Herself,* New York: Praeger, 1955.

Lyde, Lionel W., *The Continent of Europe,* London: Macmillan & Co., Ltd., 1926.

Mackinder, Halford J., *Britain and the British Seas,* Oxford: Clarendon Press, 2nd ed., 1907.

————, *Democratic Ideals and Reality,* New York: Holt, 1919; reissued W. W. Norton, 1962.

————, "The Geographical Pivot of History," *Geographical Journal,* XXIII, No. 4 (April 1904).

————, "The Round World and the Winning of the Peace," *Foreign Affairs,* XXI, No. 4 (July 1943).

Mahan, Alfred T., *The Problem of Asia and its Effect upon International Policies,* Boston: Little, Brown, 1900.

Malin, James, "Mobility and History," *Agricultural History,* 17 (October 1943).

————, "Space and History," Part 2, *Agricultural History,* 18 (July 1944).

Mao Tse-tung, *Quotations from Chairman Mao,* Peking: Foreign Language Press, 1966.

Markham, S. E., *Climate and the Energy of Nations,* New York: Oxford University Press, 1947.

Maull, O., *Das Wesen der Geopolitik,* Berlin: Wowinckel, 1936.

The Middle East—A Political and Economic Survey, London: Royal Institute of International Affairs, 1950.

Moodie, A. E., *Geography Behind Politics,* London: Hutchinson's University Library, 1947.

Morrison, John, "Russia and the Warm Waters," *U. S. Naval Institute Proceedings,* 78 (November 1952).

Nasser, Gamel Abdel, *Egypts Liberation,* Washington: Public Affairs Press, 1955.

Newbegin, Marion, *The Mediterranean Lands,* New York: Knopf, 1924.

Nicholson, Norman, *The Boundaries of Canada, Its Provinces and Territories,* Ottawa: Department of Mines and Technical Surveys, 1954.

Ormsby, H., "The Definition of Metteleuropa and its Relation to the Conception of Deutschland in the Writings of Modern German Geographers," *Scottish Geographical Magazine,* 51, No. 6 (November 1935).

Parkins, Almon E., *The South,* New York: Wiley, 1938.

Pounds, N. J. G., ed., *Geographical Essays on Eastern Europe,* Bloomington: Indiana University Press, 1961.

Ratzel, Friedrich, *Politische Geographie,* Munich, Berlin, 1897.

Renner, George T., *Human Geography in the Air Age,* New York: Macmillan, 1942.

Russett, Bruce, *International Regions and the International System,* Chicago: Rand McNally, 1967.

Saucerman, S., *International Transfers of Territory in Europe,* Washington: U.S.G.P.O., 1937.

Schnitzer, E. W., *German Geopolitics Revised: A Survey of Geopolitical Writings in Germany Today,* The Rand Corporation, 1954.

The Science of Geography, The Ad Hoc Committee on Geography, Washington: National Academy of Science—National Research Council, 1277, 1965.

Semple, E., "The Barrier Boundary of the Mediterranean Basin and its Northern reaches as Factors in History," *Annals of the Association of American Geographers,* V, No. 1 (March 1915).

————, and Jones, C., *American History and Its Geographic Conditions,* Boston: Houghton, Mifflin, 1933.

Seton-Watson, H., *Neither War Nor Peace,* New York: Praeger, 1960.

Shabad, T., *Geography of the U.S.S.R.,* New York: Columbia University Press, 1951.

Siegfried, A., *Suez and Panama,* translated by H. H. and Doris Hemming, London: Jonathan Cape, 1940.

The Sino-Soviet Dispute, Kessing's Research Report 3, New York: Charles Scribner's, 1969.

Slessor, John, *Strategy for the West,* New York: Morrow, 1954.

———, *The Great Deterrent,* New York: Praeger, 1957.

Sprout, Harold & Margaret, *The Ecological Perspective on Human Affairs,* Princeton: Princeton University Press, 1965.

———, "Geography and International Politics in Revolutionary Change," *The Journal of Conflict Resolution,* IV, No. 1.

———, "Man—Milieu Relationship Hypothesis in the Context of International Politics," Center of International Studies, Princeton University, 1956.

Spykman, Nicholas, *America's Strategy in World Politics,* New York: Harcourt, Brace, 1942.

———, *The Geography of the Peace,* New York: Harcourt, Brace, 1944.

Stamp, L. Dudley, *Applied Geography,* London: Penguin Books, 1960.

Strabo, *The Geography of Strabo,* trans. H. C. Hamilton & W. Falconer, I, London: Bohn, 1854-57.

Taylor, Griffith, *Geography in the Twentieth Century,* London: Methuen, 1951.

Teggart, F., "Geography as an Aid to Statecraft," *The Geographical Review,* VII (October-November 1919).

Thomson, J. Oliver, *History of Ancient Geography,* Cambridge University Press, 1948.

Ullman, Edward, *American Commodity Flow,* Seattle: University of Washington Press, 1957.

U. S. Army War College, *Power Analysis of the Nation-State,* Discussion Topic 2-B, Carlisle Barracks, Pa., 1960.

van Loon, Hendrik, *Van Loon's Geography,* New York: Garden City Publishing Company, 1940.

Wanklyn, H. G., *The Eastern Marchlands of Europe,* London: Philip, 1941.

Weigert, H., *Generals and Geographers,* London: Oxford University Press, 1942.

Weigert, Hans *et al., Principles of Political Geography,* New York: Appleton-Century-Crofts, 1957.

Whittlesey, Derwent S., *The Earth and the State,* New York: Holt, 1944.

———, *German Strategy of World Concept,* New York: Farrar & Rinehart, 1942.

———, "The Horizon of Geography," *Annals of the Association of American Geographers,* XXXV, No. 1 (March 1945).

———, "The Impress of Effective Central Authority upon the Landscape," *Annals of the Association of American Geographers,* XXV, No. 2 (June 1935).

———, "The Regional Concept and the Regional Method," in James & Jones (q.v.).

Wolfe, Bertram, *Khrushchev and Stalin's Ghost,* New York: Praeger, 1957.

Wright, Quincy, ed., *The World Community,* Chicago: University of Chicago Press, 1948.

INDEX

Persons

Ad Hoc Committee on Geography, NAS-NRC, 18
Acheson, Dean, 76
Aristotle, 29-30
Banse, Ewald, 78
Bourghiba, Habib, 23
Bowman, Isaiah, 224
Chen Yi, 244
Cohen, Saul, and Lewis Rosenthal, 17-18
Cressey, George, 96-97
de Gaulle, Charles, 155, 184
de Seversky, Alexander, 52-54, 100
Easton, David, 18
Fairgrieve, James, 31, 42, 44, 74, 85-86
Gambetta, Leon, 183
Ginsburg, Norton, 240-41
Gottmann, Jean, 19, 156, 161
Guyot, Arnold, 38-40, 95
Harris, Chauncy, 218-19
Hartshorne, Richard, 5, 7, 15
Haushofer, Albrecht, 48
Haushofer, Karl, 44-45, 47-48
Hecateus, 34
Herman, Theodore, 240
Herodotus, 36
Hitler, Adolph, 48, 78
Jones, Stephen, 6, 21, 53-54
Kant, Immanuel, 37

Kasperson, Roger, 16
Kennan, George, 71
Khrushchev, Nikita, 213, 215, 217, 243-45
Kjellén, Rudolph, 44
Kropotkin, Pierre, 210
Leach, E. R., 18
Lenin, Nicolai, 233, 236
Lin Piao, 238, 242-43, 245
Liu Shao Chi, 242
Luethy, Herbert, 195
Lyde, Lionel, 156
Mackinder, Halford, 19, 27-29, 41-42, 44-45, 47, 55, 58, 60, 71, 74, 77-78, 150, 223, 294
Mahan, Alfred T., 48-49, 95-96
Malin, James, 96, 99-100
Mao Tse-tung, 238
McCune, Shannon, 76
Mela, 35
Minghi, Julian, 18
Nasser, Gamel, 253, 260
Parkins, Almon, 198
Parmenides, 34
Pliny the Elder, 36
Polybius, 34
Ptolemy, 35
Ratzel, Friedrich, 39-40, 44-45, 99, 134
Renner, George, 52-53

323

Places

Subject Matter

Geography and Politics in a World Divided

SAUL B. COHEN   Second Edition

Arguing that the order of relations among states and larger regions is inherent in the ecology of the global political system, Professor Cohen first discusses the earth's geopolitical foundations and the nature of political geography. He then focuses on the major world power cores in terms of their geopolitical environments, maintaining that without these "impact areas" or spheres of influence there would be either a monolithic world system or utter chaos.

Defining political geography as "the spatial consequences of political process," Professor Cohen outlines in Part One six approaches to studying it, making concrete applications of each, and traces the history of geopolitical thought. On this basis, he formulates a framework for dynamic geopolitical equilibrium.

Part Two treats the changing geopolitical environments of the major power cores: Anglo-America, Maritime Europe, the U.S.S.R., and Mainland China. In the United States this involves shifts in world affairs from a maritime orientation in colonial times, to a continental one for nearly one hundred years after the Spanish-American War, then to a continental-maritime stance, and finally to our present maritime-continental position, dating from the interwar period. Regional changes in population, agriculture and industry, and suburbanization, are other features of America's changing geopolitical landscape. For the U.S.S.R., implications of opening the political system are treated; for Maritime Europe, the unfolding integrative processes; and for China, her changing world views.

Part Three considers the Middle East and Southeast Asian Shatterbelts, and the African, South American, and Offshore Asian portions of the Maritime World, focusing on zones of contact and influence from the perspective of Western interests.

About the author

Saul B. Cohen is Professor of Geography and Director, Graduate School of Geography, Clark University. Past Executive Secretary and former Councilor of the Association of American Geographers, Professor Cohen is a Consultant to the United States Office of Education and to the National Science Foundation, as well as Councilor of the American Geographical Society. He is the author of four books and some fifty articles, and geographical editor of the "Oxford World Atlas" (1973).

Oxford University Press   New York

cover design by Egon Lauterberg   **ISBN 0-19-501695-5**